Gregg Shorthand
Functional Method

Shorthand written
by Jerome P. Edelman

New York / St. Louis / Dallas / San Francisco
Auckland / Bogotá / Düsseldorf / Johannesburg / London
Madrid / Mexico / Montreal / New Delhi / Panama / Paris
São Paulo / Singapore / Sydney / Tokyo / Toronto

Library of Congress Cataloging in Publication Data

Leslie, Louis A., date.
Gregg shorthand, functional method, series 90.

Includes indexes.
1. Shorthand–Gregg. I. Zoubek, Charles E., date. joint author. II. Title.
Z56.L632173 653'.427 77-856
ISBN 0-07-037731-6

Gregg Shorthand,
Functional Method, Series 90

4 5 6 7 8 9 0 DODO 7 8 6 5 4 3 2

Preface

Gregg Shorthand, the universal system

Gregg Shorthand was first published in 1888 and has been learned and used successfully by millions of writers throughout the entire world. Gregg Shorthand was written in English but has been successfully adapted to numerous other languages, including French, Spanish, and Portuguese. To most people the terms *shorthand* and *Gregg* are synonymous. Gregg Shorthand is truly the universal system of shorthand. It is used by more shorthand writers than any other system in the world.

Gregg Shorthand is used by stenographers and administrative secretaries as a vocational tool that enables them to obtain and hold interesting and rewarding positions. It is used by business and professional people who are relieved of the burden of writing longhand in making notes, preparing important papers, and drafting reports.

The success of any system of shorthand rests on the merits of its alphabet. The Gregg alphabet is the most logical, consistent, and efficient shorthand alphabet devised in more than 2,000 years of shorthand history. The fact that this alphabet, virtually without change, has been the basis of Gregg Shorthand for more than 90 years is a tribute to the genius of its inventor, John Robert Gregg.

Functional Method

The Functional Method of teaching Gregg Shorthand has for many years been used with great success by thousands of teachers of the system. The Functional Method type of presentation, fundamentally a language-art type of teaching, allows much scope for the ingenuity of the individual teacher within the framework of language-art teaching. It is distinguished, in general, by the provision of a printed key to the shorthand plates, and by the absence of verbalization of rules or principles.

Series 90

Objectives *Gregg Shorthand, Functional Method, Series 90,* is published in the ninetieth anniversary year of the invention of the Gregg system. This revision involves a small number of system changes which have been deemed desirable to make learning and writing Gregg Shorthand even easier and more consistent. A major change has been made in the order of presentation of the theory principles. This change was made to provide better, more logical business letters even in the very early lessons in the text. Teachers will find the system changes to be logical and the teaching and learning suggestions helpful. The major objectives of *Gregg Shorthand, Functional Method, Series 90,* are:

1 To teach the students to read and write Gregg Shorthand rapidly and accurately in the shortest time possible.

2 To provide the students with transcription readiness by building their vocabulary and developing their ability to spell and punctuate accurately.

Organization

Gregg Shorthand, Functional Method, Series 90, is divided into three parts—Principles, Reinforcement, and Shorthand and Transcription Skill Building. These parts are subdivided into 10 chapters and 70 lessons. The last new theory is presented in Lesson 47. The theory is presented in 40 lessons. Eight of the first 48 lessons are devoted to review.

Format

Gregg Shorthand, Functional Method, Series 90, is published in the same two-column format which proved popular in the last edition of Gregg Shorthand. This format makes it possible to present the shorthand practice material in columns that are approximately the width of the columns of the students' shorthand notebooks. The short lines make reading easier because the eye does not have to travel very far from the end of one line of shorthand to the beginning of the next. The format also makes it possible to highlight the words from the Reading and Writing Practice that are identified for spelling attention. The words are placed in the margins near the corresponding shorthand outline.

Building transcription skills

Gregg Shorthand, Functional Method, Series 90, continues to place great stress on the nonshorthand elements of transcription, which are taught concurrently with shorthand. It retains all the helpful transcription exercises of the former edition. These include:

Business Vocabulary Builders Beginning with Lesson 7, each lesson contains a Business Vocabulary Builder consisting of several business words or expressions for which meanings are provided. The words and expressions are selected from the Reading and Writing Practice. The Business Vocabulary Builders help to overcome a major student handicap—a limited vocabulary.

Spelling—Marginal Reminders Words singled out from the Reading and Writing

Practice for special spelling attention appear in the margins of the shorthand. Usually each word appears on the same line as its shorthand outline. These words appear in a second color in the shorthand so that they are easy to see.

In *Gregg Shorthand, Functional Method, Series 90,* spelling is introduced in Chapter 4.

Spelling—Families An effective device for improving spelling is the study of words in related groups, or spelling families. In the Series 90 edition, the students study six spelling families, beginning with Lesson 45.

Similar-Words Drills These drills teach the student the difference in meaning between similar words that stenographers often confuse—*it's, its; addition, edition; there, their, they're,* etc.

Punctuation Beginning with Lesson 31, nine frequent usages of the comma are introduced. Only one comma usage is introduced in any given lesson. The commas are encircled and appear in the shorthand; the reason for the use of the comma is shown above the circle.

Common Prefixes An understanding of the meaning of common English prefixes is an effective device for developing the students' understanding of words. In *Gregg Shorthand, Functional Method, Series 90,* the students study five common English prefixes, beginning in Lesson 56.

Grammar Checkup In a number of lessons, drills are provided on rules of grammar that students often apply incorrectly.

Transcription Quiz Beginning with Lesson 57, each lesson contains a Transcription Quiz consisting of a letter in which the students have to supply internal punctuation. This quiz provides them with a daily test of how well they have mastered the punctuation rules presented in earlier lessons.

Reading and writing practice

In *Gregg Shorthand, Functional Method, Series 90,* there are 53,423 words of shorthand practice material in the Reading and Writing Practice exercises. Most of the material is new.

A brief-form letter is included in *every* lesson of Part 1 (except the review lessons), beginning with Lesson 5.

Other features

Shorthand spelling helps When a new letter in the shorthand alphabet or a theory principle is presented, the shorthand spelling is given.

Chapter openings Each chapter is introduced by a well-illustrated spread that not only paints for the students a picture of the life and duties of a secretary but also encourages them in their efforts to acquire the necessary skills.

Student helps To be sure that the students get the greatest benefit from each phase of their shorthand study, they are given step-by-step suggestions on how to handle each phase when it is first introduced.

Reading scoreboards At various points in the text, students are given an opportunity to determine their reading speed by means of a scoreboard. The scoreboard enables the students to calculate the number of words a minute they are reading. By comparing their reading speed from scoreboard to scoreboard, they see some indication of their shorthand reading growth.

Recall charts In the last lesson of each chapter in Part 1 a recall chart is provided. This chart contains illustrations of theory principles taught in the chapter. It also contains many illustrations of theory principles the students have studied up to that chapter.

Checklists To keep the students constantly reminded of the importance of good practice procedures, occasional checklists are provided. These checklists deal with writing shorthand, reading shorthand, homework, proportion, etc.

Appendix The Appendix contains a number of additional teaching aids. These include:

1 A brief-form chart giving all brief forms in Gregg Shorthand, Series 90, in the order of their presentation.

2 A list of common geographical expressions.

3 A chart showing Gregg outlines for common metric expressions.

4 A list of word beginnings and endings.

Computer control

All of the connected matter in *Gregg Shorthand, Functional Method, Series 90,* has been checked by a carefully written computer program to ensure adequate, proper, and sequential coverage of the theory principles and brief forms. The computer program helped the authors of the book to ensure that the points were properly covered in the lessons in which they were presented as well as in the two lessons following their initial presentation.

• • •

Gregg Shorthand, Functional Method, Series 90, is published with pride and with the confidence that it will help teachers of Gregg Shorthand do an even more effective job of training rapid and accurate shorthand writers and transcribers.

The Publishers

Contents

Your Shorthand Practice Program

The speed with which you learn to read and write Gregg Shorthand will depend largely on two factors—the *time* you devote to practice and the *way* in which you practice. If you practice efficiently, you will be able to complete each lesson in the shortest possible time and derive the greatest possible benefit.

Here are some suggestions which will help you to get the maximum benefit from the time you invest in shorthand practice.

Before you begin, select a quiet place in which to practice. Do not try to practice while listening to music or watching television. Then follow the steps below.

Reading word lists

In each lesson there are a number of word lists that illustrate the principles introduced in the lesson. As part of your out-of-class practice, read these word lists in this way:

1 *With the type key available,* spell—aloud if possible—the shorthand characters in each outline in the list, thus: *"see, s-e; fee, f-e."* Reading aloud will help to impress the shorthand outlines firmly on your mind. Read all the shorthand words in the list in this way—with the type key exposed—until you feel you can read the shorthand outlines without referring to the key.

2 *Cover the type key* with a piece of paper and read aloud from the shorthand, thus: *"s-e, see; f-e, fee."*

3 If the spelling of a shorthand outline does not immediately give you the meaning, refer to the key and determine the meaning of any outline you cannot read. Do *not* spend more than a few seconds trying to decipher an outline.

4 After you have read all the words in the list, read them again if time permits.

Note: In reading brief forms for common words and phrases, which first occur in Lesson 3, do not spell the shorthand outlines.

Study the word lists by placing a slip of paper over the type key and reading the shorthand words aloud.

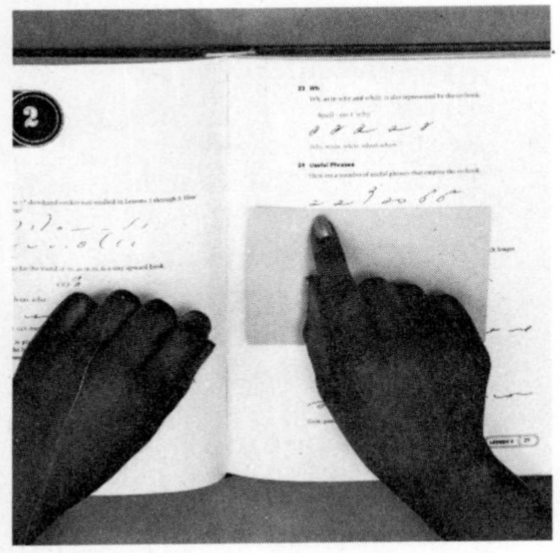

Read the Reading Practice, referring to the key whenever you cannot read an outline. Anchor your left index finger on the place in the shorthand; the right index finger, on the place in the key.

Reading sentences, letters, and articles

Each lesson contains a Reading Practice (Lessons 1-20) or a Reading and Writing Practice (Lessons 21-70) in which sentences, letters, or articles are written in shorthand. Your practice on this material will help you develop your shorthand vocabulary. The first thing you should do is *read* the material in this way:

1. Place your left index finger under the shorthand outline you are about to read.
2. Place your right index finger on the type key to that shorthand outline. The key is in the back of the text.
3. Read the shorthand, aloud if possible, until you come to a shorthand outline that you cannot read. Spell the shorthand strokes in the outline. If the spelling does not *immediately* give you the meaning, anchor your finger on the outline and turn to the key in the back, where your right index finger is resting near the point at which you are reading.
4. Determine the meaning of the outline you cannot read and place your right index finger on it.
5. Return to the shorthand from which you are reading—your left index finger has kept your place for you—and continue reading in this manner until you have completed the material.
6. If time permits, read the material a second time.

By following this procedure, you will lose no time finding your place in the shorthand and in the key when you cannot read an outline.

Remember, during the early stages your shorthand reading may not be very rapid. That is only natural, as you are, in a sense, learning a new language. If you do each day's lesson faithfully, however, you will find your reading rate increasing almost daily.

When copying, read a convenient group of words aloud and then write that group in your notebook. Keep your place in the shorthand with your left index finger.

Writing the Reading and Writing Practice

Before you do any writing of shorthand, you should give careful consideration to the tools of your trade—your notebook and your writing instrument.

Your notebook The best notebook for shorthand writing is one that measures 6 x 9 inches and has a vertical rule down the center of each page. It should have a spiral binding so that the pages lie flat at all times. The paper should, of course, take ink well.

Your writing instrument A pen is a satisfactory instrument for writing Gregg Shorthand. *A pencil is not recommended.* Because writing with a pen requires little pressure, you can write for long periods of time without becoming fatigued. A pencil, however, requires considerable pressure. In addition, the pencil point quickly becomes blunt. The blunter it gets, the more effort you have to expend to write with it. Penwritten notes remain legible almost indefinitely; pencil notes become blurred and hard to read. In addition, penwritten notes are also easier to read under artificial light.

Having selected your writing tools, follow these steps in writing the Reading and Writing Practice:

1 Read the material you are going to copy. *Always* read the Reading and Writing Practice before copying it.

2 Place a card in the proper place in the key so that if you must refer to the key for an outline you cannot read, you will be able to do so with a minimal loss of time.

3 When you are ready to start writing, read a convenient group of words from the printed shorthand; then write the group, reading aloud as you write. Keep your place in the shorthand with your left index finger if you are right-handed or with your right index finger if you are left-handed.

In the early stages your writing may not be very rapid, nor will your notes be as well written as those in the book. With regular practice, however, your notes will rapidly improve.

Good luck with your study of Gregg Shorthand.

PART

Principles

CHAPTER

Why Study Shorthand?

"Why should I study to perfect my shorthand skills?" "Is shorthand really necessary in today's business?" "In the world of automation, is manual shorthand skill still needed?" These are some of the questions students ask today as they prepare for careers. The answers are very clear:

Today there are more shorthand writers than ever before, and the number grows continually. Even so, the demand for secretaries in business exceeds the supply. The ability to take shorthand is a vital skill in the fast-paced world of business, a world in which recording data quickly and accurately is a necessity. So much of all business is transacted on written communications—letters, memorandums, reports, minutes—that the secretary who can take shorthand is in great demand.

Knowing shorthand is important not only when someone wants to dictate a letter or a report, but also when the phone rings and you must take a long, involved message. And what a help it is, when composing your own letters, to be able to jot down all your thoughts before they escape.

When you begin looking for your first job, you will find that the ability to take shorthand will increase your chances of getting just the position you want. The ability to use shorthand will also increase the size

of your paycheck. Whether your job is as a beginning worker or is on an advanced level, in almost every case, business pays more to the secretary who can take shorthand than to the one who cannot.

The dividends continue to pay off. After you have been on a job for a while, you will discover that your shorthand ability will very likely put you in line for a promotion. Good, above-average stenographic skill combined with language ability and a desire to work will put you at the top of the list when there is a chance for a promotion.

You are now starting to learn the basics of Gregg Shorthand. Take time to learn shorthand well. Spend some out-of-class time every day studying the current lesson. You will find that your ability to read and write shorthand will grow rapidly. Follow your teacher's instructions, and you will soon have a marketable skill which you can put to work in a business office.

Shorthand is a valuable skill that can open many doors for you. The time you spend in learning shorthand is well invested.

GREGG SHORTHAND IS EASY TO LEARN

As you leaf through the pages of this book and see the hooks and circles and straight lines in the shorthand outlines, you may wonder whether you can learn shorthand. Be assured that you can, just as millions of others have learned it. If you can write longhand—and of course you can!—you can learn to write Gregg Shorthand. The strokes you will write in Gregg Shorthand are the same strokes that you are accustomed to writing in longhand.

Actually, you will find Gregg Shorthand easier to learn than longhand. Skeptical? Well, the following illustration should convince you of the truth of that statement. In longhand there are many ways to write *f*. Here are six of them:

What is more, in many words the sound of *f* is expressed by combinations of other letters in the alphabet—for example, *ph*, as in *phase*; *gh*, as in *rough*.

In Gregg Shorthand there is one way—and only one way—to express the sound of *f*, as you will learn later in this lesson.

With Gregg Shorthand you can attain almost any speed goal you set for yourself. All it takes is regular, intelligent practice.

Principles

GROUP A

1 **S-Z**

The first shorthand stroke you will learn is *s*, one of the most frequently used letters in the English language. The shorthand *s* is a tiny downward curve that resembles the longhand comma.

Because in English *s* often has the sound of *z*, as in *saves*, the same tiny downward curve is used to express *z*.

S-Z

2 A

The second stroke you will learn is the shorthand *a*, which is simply the longhand *a* with the final connecting stroke omitted.

A

3 Silent Letters Omitted

In the English language many words contain letters that are not pronounced. In Gregg Shorthand these silent letters are not written.

For example, the word *say* would be written *s-a;* the *y* would not be written because it is not pronounced. The word *face* would be written *f-a-s;* the *e* would not be written because it is not pronounced, and the *c* would be represented by *s* because it is pronounced *s*.

In the following words, what letters would not be written because they are not pronounced?

right	*same*	*day*	*steam*
main	*save*	*snow*	*aid*

4 S-A Word

With the strokes for *s* and *a*, you can form the shorthand outline for a very useful word.

say, s-a

5 F, V

The shorthand stroke for *f* is a downward curve the same shape as *s*, but it is somewhat larger—about half the height of the space between the lines of your shorthand notebook.

The shorthand stroke for *v* is also a downward curve the same shape as *s* and *f*, but it is very large—almost the full height of the space between the lines of your shorthand notebook.

▶ Notice the difference in the sizes of *s, f, v*.

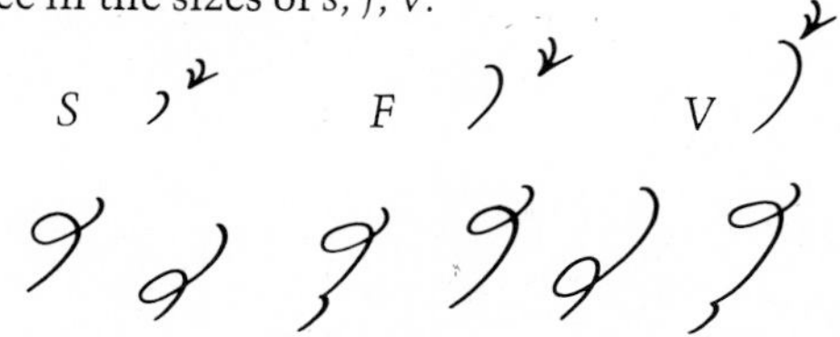

Safe, face, safes, save, vase, saves.

▶ Notice: ■ 1 The *c* in *face* is represented by the *s* because it has the *s* sound.

■ 2 The final *s* in *saves* has the *z* sound, which is represented by the *s* stroke.

6 E

The shorthand stroke for *e* is a tiny circle. It is simply the longhand *e* with the two connecting strokes omitted.

E

▶ Notice the difference in the sizes of *a* and *e*.

A E

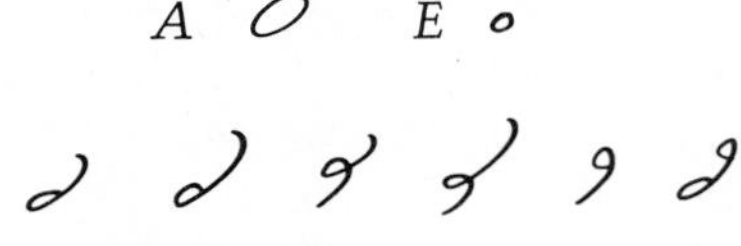

See, fee, sees, fees, ease, easy.

▶ Notice that the *y* in *easy* is pronounced *e*; therefore, it is represented by the *e* circle.

Suggestion At this point take a few moments to read the procedures outlined for practicing word lists on page 10.

GROUP B

7 N, M

The shorthand stroke for *n* is a very short forward straight line.
The shorthand stroke for *m* is a longer forward straight line.

N *M*

N

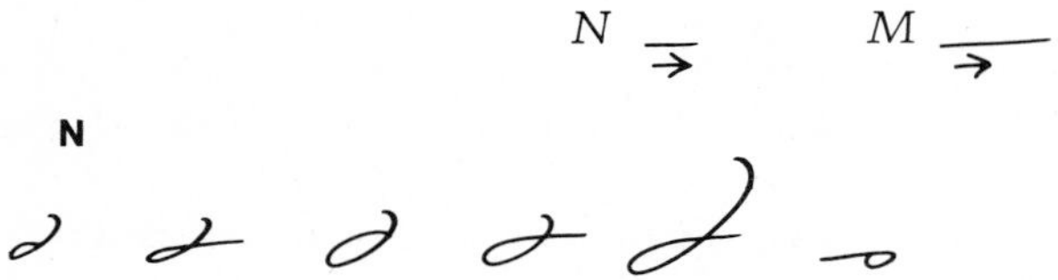

See, seen, say, sane, vain, knee.

▶ Notice that the *k* in *knee* is not written because it is not pronounced.

M

May, main, me, mean, name.
Aim, same, seem, fame.

8 T, D

The shorthand stroke for *t* is a short upward straight line.
The shorthand stroke for *d* is a longer upward straight line.

T D

T

Eat, neat, meet, seat, east, stay, team.

D

Day, date, need, aid, made, feed.

9 Punctuation and Capitalization

period — *paragraph* — *parentheses*

question mark — *dash* — *hyphen*

The regular longhand forms are used for all other punctuation marks.

Capitalization is indicated by two upward dashes placed underneath the word to be capitalized.

Fay — *Dave* — *May*

Reading Practice

With the help of an occasional word written in longhand, you can already read complete sentences.

Read the following sentences, spelling each shorthand outline aloud as you read it thus: *F-a, Fay; m-a-d, made; t-e, tea.* If you cannot read a shorthand outline after you have spelled it, refer to the key which follows the Reading Practice.

GROUP A

1 for on 4

2 a 3 the 5

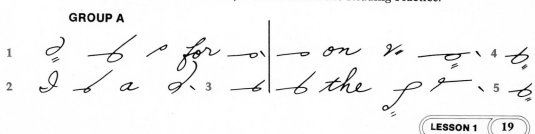

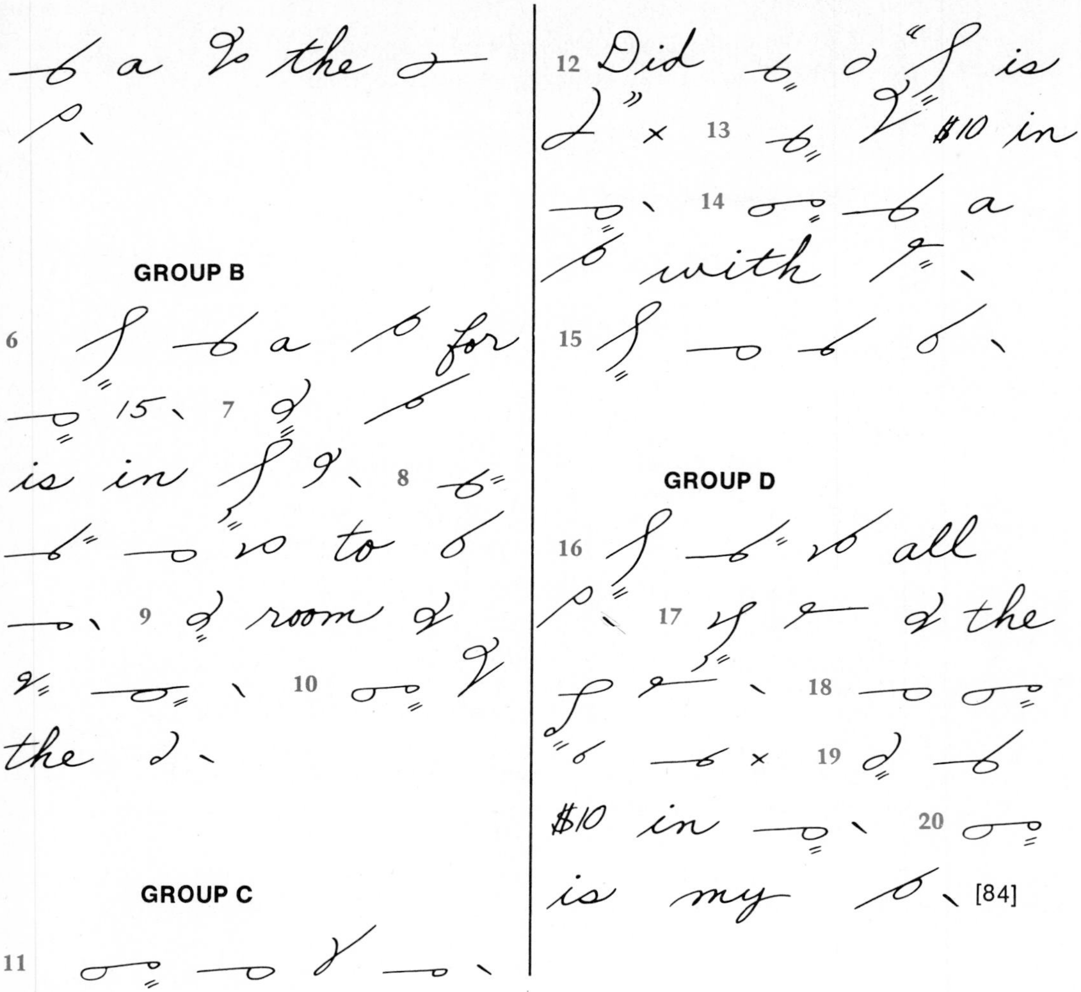

GROUP B

GROUP C

GROUP D

[84]

GROUP A *1. Fay made tea for me. 2. I need a vase. 3. Meet me on East Main. 4. Nate made the Navy team. 5. Nate made a safety the same day.*
GROUP B *6. Dave made a date for May 15. 7. Fay's deed is in Dave's safe. 8. Nate Meade may stay to aid me. 9. Fay's room faced East Main. 10. Amy saved the fee.*
GROUP C *11. Amy may feed me. 12. Did Nate say, "Dave is vain"? 13. Nate saved $10 in May. 14. Amy made a date with Dean. 15. Dave may need aid.*
GROUP D *16. Dave Meade stayed all day. 17. Steve's team faced the Navy team. 18. May Amy eat meat? 19. Fay made $10 in May. 20. Amy is my date.*

Principles

10 Alphabet Review

In Lesson 1 you studied the following nine shorthand strokes. How rapidly can you read them?

11 O, R, L

The shorthand stroke for *o* is a small deep hook.
The shorthand stroke for *r* is a short forward curve.
The shorthand stroke for *l* is a longer forward curve about three times as long as *r*.

▶ Note how these strokes are derived from their longhand forms.

O R L

O

No, snow, tow, so, phone.
Note, own, tone, dome, stone.

▶ Notice that in *own, tone, dome,* and *stone* the *o* is placed on its side. By placing *o* on its side before *n* or *m* in these and similar words, we obtain smoother joinings than we would if we wrote the *o* upright.

R

Ray, rate, raid, trade, ear, dear, near.
Or, store, more, fair, radio, free.

L

Lay, late, lead, ail, mail, deal.
Real, feel, leaves, low, flow.

▶ Notice that *f-r,* as in *free,* and *f-l,* as in *flow,* are written with one sweep of the pen, with no stop between the *f* and the *r* or *l.*

free   *flow*

12 H, -ing

The letter *h* is simply a dot placed above the vowel. With few exceptions, *h* occurs at the beginning of a word.

Ing, which almost always occurs at the end of a word, is also expressed by a dot.

He, hair, hole, heating, heeding, hearing.

13 Long Ī

The shorthand stroke for the long sound of *i,* as in *high,* is a large broken circle.

I

High, tire, right, light, line, my.
Style, side, fine, rely, mile.

14 Omission of Minor Vowels

Some words contain vowels that are slurred or not pronounced at all in ordinary speech. For example, the word *even* is really pronounced *e-vn;* the word *meter* is pronounced *met-r.* These vowels may be omitted if they do not contribute to speed or readability.

Even, meter, reader, motor, later, dealer.

Reading Practice

With the aid of a few words written in longhand, you can now read the following sentences. Remember to spell each shorthand word aloud as you read it. Refer to the key when you cannot read a word.

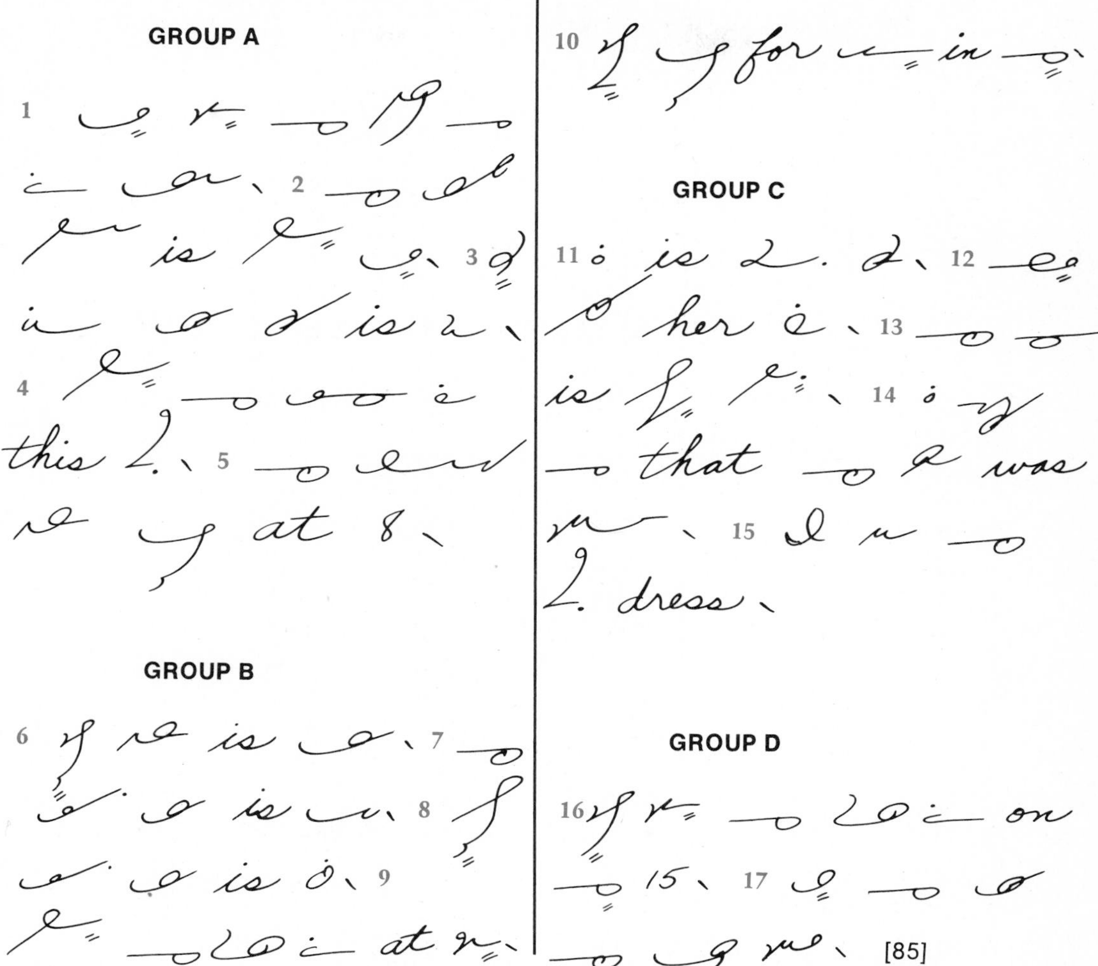

GROUP A 1. *Lee Stone may drive me home later.* 2. *My radio dealer is Dale Lee.* 3. *Fay's whole right side is sore.* 4. *Dale may remain here this evening.* 5. *My railroad train leaves at eight.* GROUP B 6. *Steve's train is late.* 7. *My reading rate is low.* 8. *Dave's reading rate is high.* 9. *Dale may fly home at Easter.* 10. *Steven leaves for Rome in May.* GROUP C 11. *He is feeling fine.* 12. *Mary dyed her hair.* 13. *My name is David Dearing.* 14. *He notified me that my tire was stolen.* 15. *I tore my evening dress.* GROUP D 16. *Steve Stone may fly home on May 15.* 17. *Ray may write my life story.*

Principles

15 Alphabet Review

Here are the strokes you studied in Lessons 1 and 2. How fast can you read them?

16 Brief Forms

The English language contains many words that are used over and over again. As an aid to rapid shorthand writing, special abbreviations, called *brief forms,* are provided for some of these words. For example, we write *m* for *am, v* for *have.*

You are already familiar with the process of abbreviation in longhand—you write *Mr.* for *Mister, Dr.* for *Doctor.*

Because these brief forms occur so frequently, you will be wise to learn them well!

I, Mr., have, are-our-hour, will-well, a-an, am, it-at, in-not.*

**In* is also used as a word beginning in such words as:

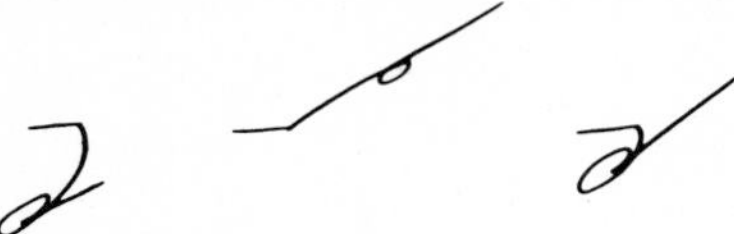

Invite, indeed, inside.

Did you notice that some shorthand outlines have two or more meanings? You will have no difficulty selecting the correct meaning of a brief form when it appears in the sentence. The sense of the sentence will give you the answer.

17 Phrasing

By using brief forms for common words, we are able to save writing time. Another device that helps save writing time is called *phrasing,* or the writing of two or more shorthand outlines together. Here are a number of useful phrases built with the brief forms you have just studied.

I have, I have not, I will, I am, he will, he will not, are not, in our.

18 Left S-Z

In Lesson 1 you learned one stroke for *s* and *z*. Another stroke is also used for *s* and *z* in order to provide an easy joining in any combination of strokes—a backward comma, which is also written downward. For convenience, it is called the *left s.*

At this point you need not try to decide which *s* stroke to use in any given word; this will become clear to you as your study of shorthand progresses.

S-Z

Lease, sales, seems, needs, raised, readers, days, most, names.

19 P, B

The shorthand stroke for *p* is a downward curve the same shape as the left *s* except that it is larger—approximately half the height of the space between the lines in your shorthand notebook.

The shorthand stroke for *b* is also a downward curve the same shape as the left *s* and *p* except that it is much larger—almost the full height of the space between the lines in your shorthand notebook.

▶ Notice the difference in the sizes of the left *s*, *p*, and *b*.

S P B

P

Pay, spare, hope, opens, pipe, pain, post, please, price.

B

Bay, base, boat, beat, bright, brief, blame, neighbor, label.

▶ Notice that the combinations *p-r*, as in *price*; *p-l*, as in *please*; *b-r*, as in *brief*; and *b-l*, as in *blame*, are written with one sweep of the pen without a pause between the *p* or *b* and the *r* or *l*.

price   *please*   *brief*   *blame*

● Reading Practice

You can already read sentences written entirely in shorthand.

Suggestion Before you start your work on this Reading Practice, read the practice procedures for reading shorthand on page 10.

GROUP A

1

2

3

4

5

[60]

GROUP B

6

7

8

9

10

[57]

GROUP C

11

12

13

14

15

[48]

GROUP D

16

17

18

19

20

21

[60]

GROUP E

22

23

24

25

26

[33]

Principles

20 Alphabet Review

Here is a review of the 17 shorthand strokes you studied in Lessons 1 through 3. How fast can you read them?

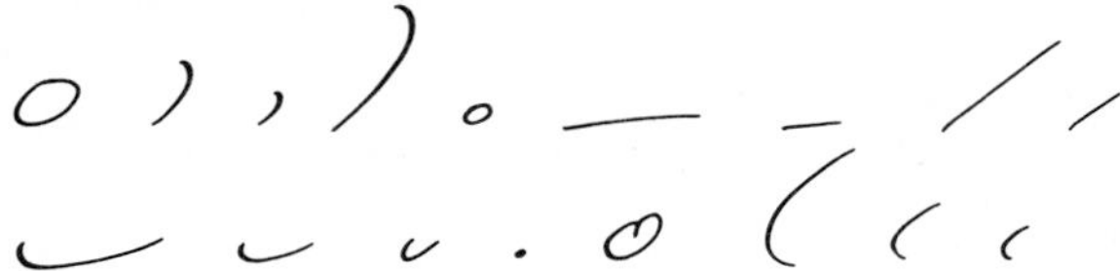

21 OO

The shorthand stroke for the sound of *oo,* as in *to,* is a tiny upward hook.

Spell: t-oo, to; h-oo, who

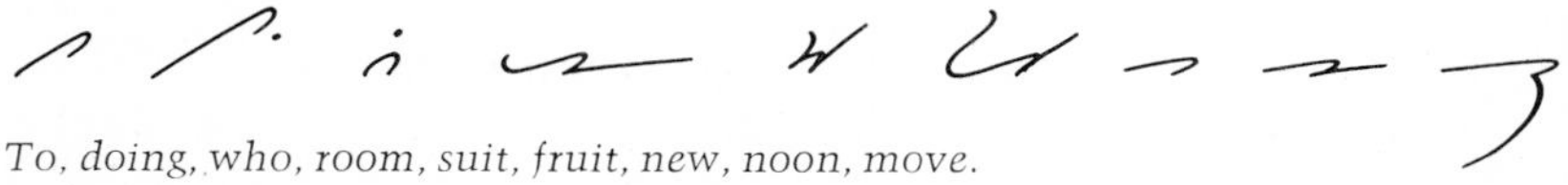

To, doing, who, room, suit, fruit, new, noon, move.

▶ Notice that the *oo* is placed on its side when it follows *n* or *m,* as in *new, noon, move.* By placing the hook on its side in these combinations rather than writing it upright, we obtain smooth joinings.

22 W, Sw

At the beginning of words *w,* as in *we,* is represented by the *oo* hook; *sw,* as in *sweet,* by *s-oo.*

Spell: oo-e, we; s-oo-e-t, sweet

We, way, wait, weighed, waste, sweet, swear.

23 Wh

Wh, as in *why* and *while,* is also represented by the *oo* hook.

Spell: *oo-ī, why*

Why, white, while, wheel, wheat.

24 Useful Phrases

Here are a number of useful phrases that employ the *oo* hook.

We are, we will, we have, we may, I do, I do not.

25 K, G

The shorthand stroke for *k* is a short forward curve.
The shorthand stroke for the hard sound of *g,* as in *game,* is a much longer forward curve. It is called *gay.*

▶ Notice the difference in the size and shape of *oo, k,* and *gay.*

K

Spell: *t-a-k, take*

Take, make, cake, like, keep, care, week, clean, increase.

G

Spell: *gay-a-n, gain*

Gain, game, gave, great, grade, going, legal.

▶ Notice that *k-r*, as in *increase*, and *gay-l*, as in *legal*, are written with a smooth, wave-like motion.

increase *legal*

But *k-l*, as in *clean*, and *gay-r*, as in *green*, are written with a hump between the *k* and the *l* and the *gay* and the *r*.

clean *green*

● Reading Practice

The following sentences contain many illustrations of the new shorthand strokes you studied in Lesson 4. They also review the shorthand strokes, brief forms, and phrases you studied in Lessons 1 through 3.

Read these sentences aloud, spelling each shorthand outline that you cannot immediately read.

GROUP A

1

2

3

4

5

[43]

GROUP B

6

7

8

9

10

[41]

GROUP C

11

12

13 14

15

[48]

GROUP D

16

17

18

19

20

[51]

GROUP E

21

22

23

24

25

[47]

GROUP F

26

27

28

29

[29]

Principles

26 Alphabet Review

Here are all the shorthand letters you studied in Lessons 1 through 4. See how rapidly you can read them.

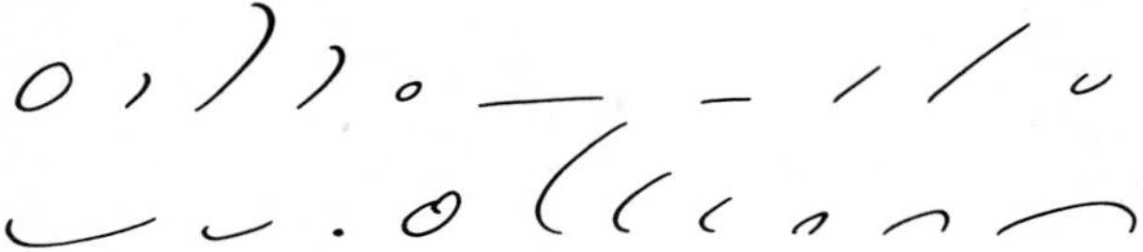

27 A, Ä

The large circle that represents the long sound of *a,* as in *main,* also represents the vowel sounds heard in *as* and *park.*

A

Spell: a-s, as

As, has, had, last, plan, happy, man, fact.

Ä

Spell: p-a-r-k, park

Park, mark, car, start, arm, far, farm.

28 E, I, Obscure Vowel

The tiny circle that represents the sound of $\bar{e}$, as in *heat,* also represents the vowel sounds heard in *best, him,* and the obscure vowel sound heard in *her, hurt.*

E

Spell: *b-e-s-t, best*

Best, help, letter, red, set, settle, sell.

I

Spell: h-e-m, him

Him, bill, bid, visit, city, did, give.

Obscure Vowel

Spell: *h-e-r, her*

Her, hurry, first, serve, earn, answer, hurt, learn.

29 Th

Two tiny curves, written upward, are provided for the sounds of *th*. These curves are called *ith*.

Over Ith *Under Ith*

Spell: *ith-e-s, these; ith-o, though*

Over Ith

These, thick, thicker, then, bath, teeth, smooth.

Under Ith

Though, those, three, throw, earth, both, health, clothing.

30 Brief Forms

Here is another group of brief forms for very frequently used business words. Learn them well.

Is-his, the, that, can, you-your, Mrs., of, with, but.

31 Phrases

Here are useful phrases formed with some of these brief forms.

In the, of the, with the, with you, you can.
Do you, you have, you are, I can, I cannot.

Reading Practice

Your progress has been so rapid that you can already read business letters written entirely in shorthand.

32 Brief-Form Letter

This letter contains one or more illustrations of all the brief forms in this lesson.

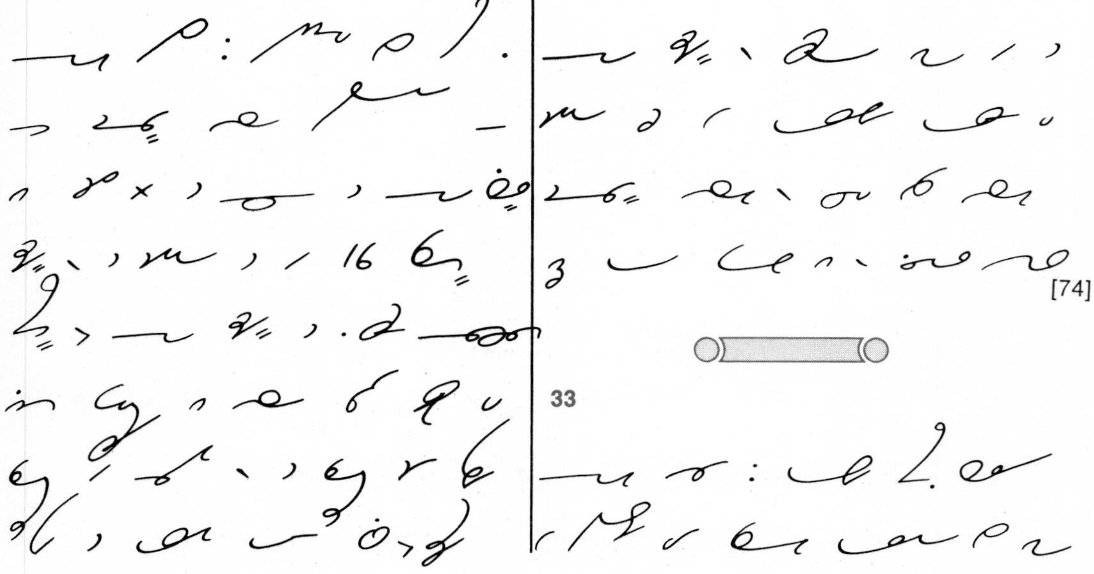

[74]

33

[73]

35

[68]

[74]

34

RECALL

Lesson 6 is a "breather." It contains no new strokes for you to learn. In this lesson you will find an Alphabet Review, a Recall Chart, and a Reading Practice employing the shorthand devices of Lessons 1 through 5.

36 Alphabet Review

Here are the shorthand strokes you studied thus far. Can you read them in 20 seconds or less?

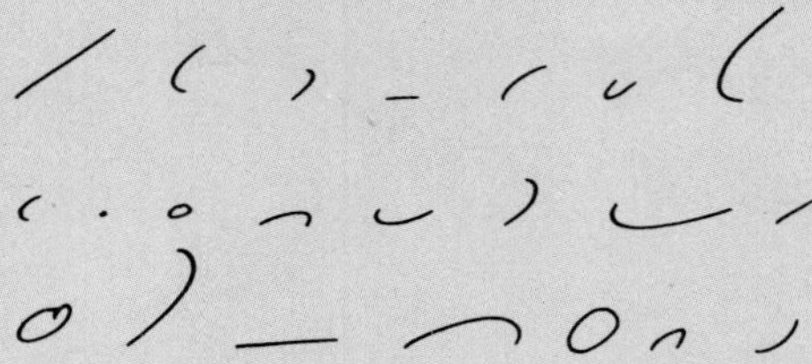

37 Recall Chart

The following chart reviews the shorthand devices you studied in Lessons 1 through 5. It is divided into three parts: words, brief forms, and phrases.

Spell each word aloud thus: *ith-r-o, throw.* You need not spell the brief forms and phrases.

There are 84 shorthand outlines in the chart. Can you read the entire chart in 10 minutes or less?

WORDS

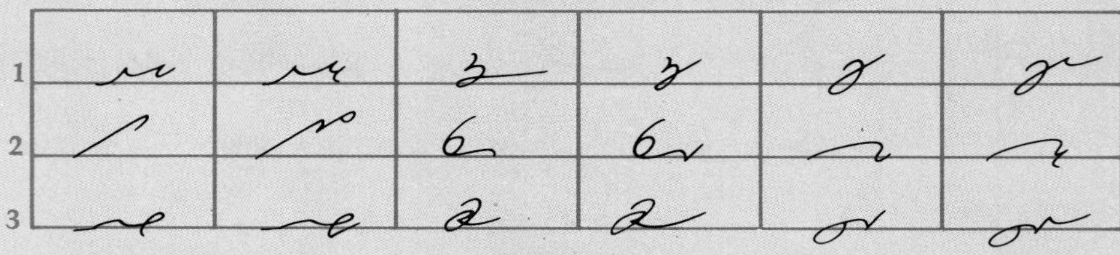

4

5

6

BRIEF FORMS

7

8

9

PHRASES

10

11

12

13

14

Reading Practice

38

[75]

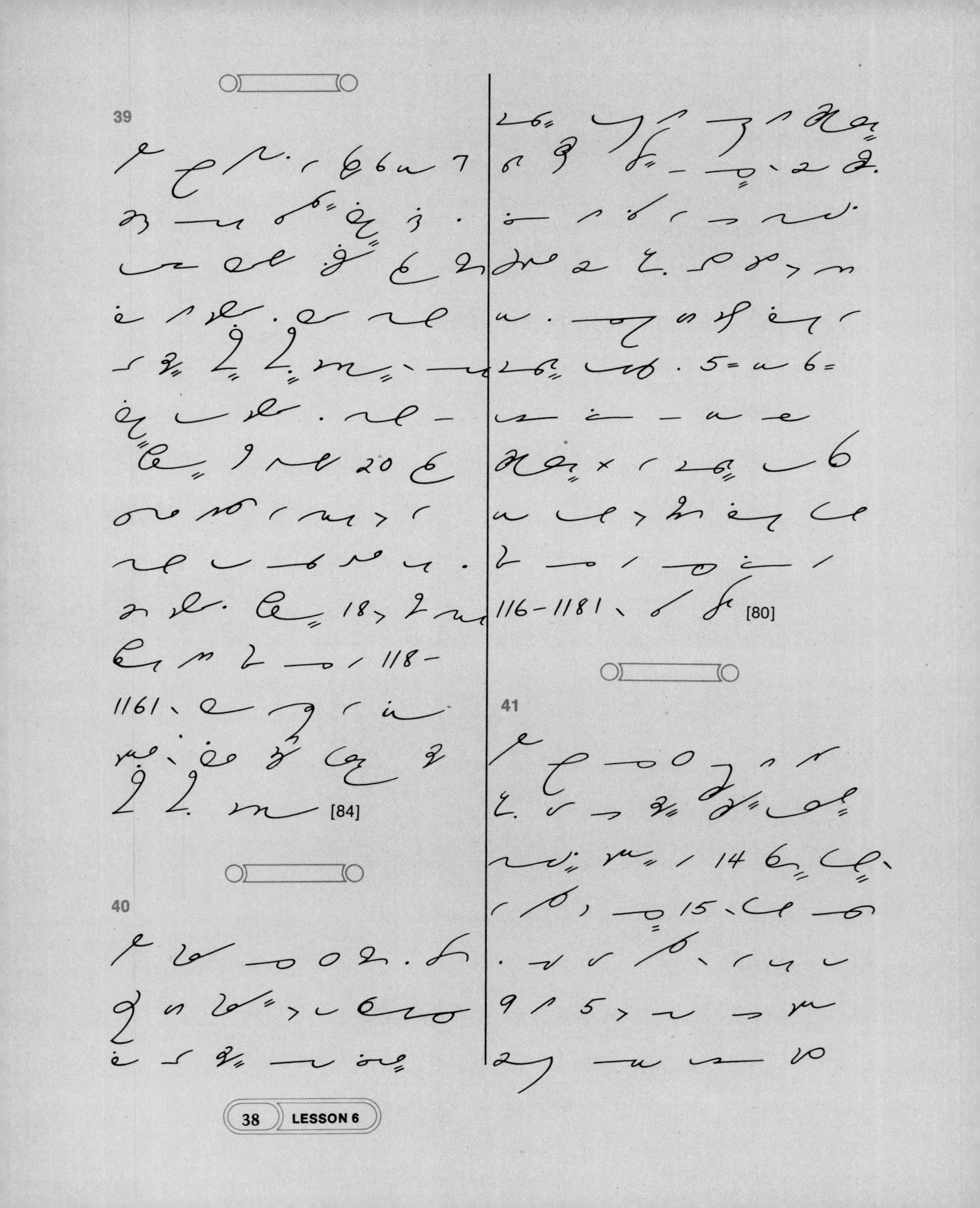

39

[84]

40

[80]

41

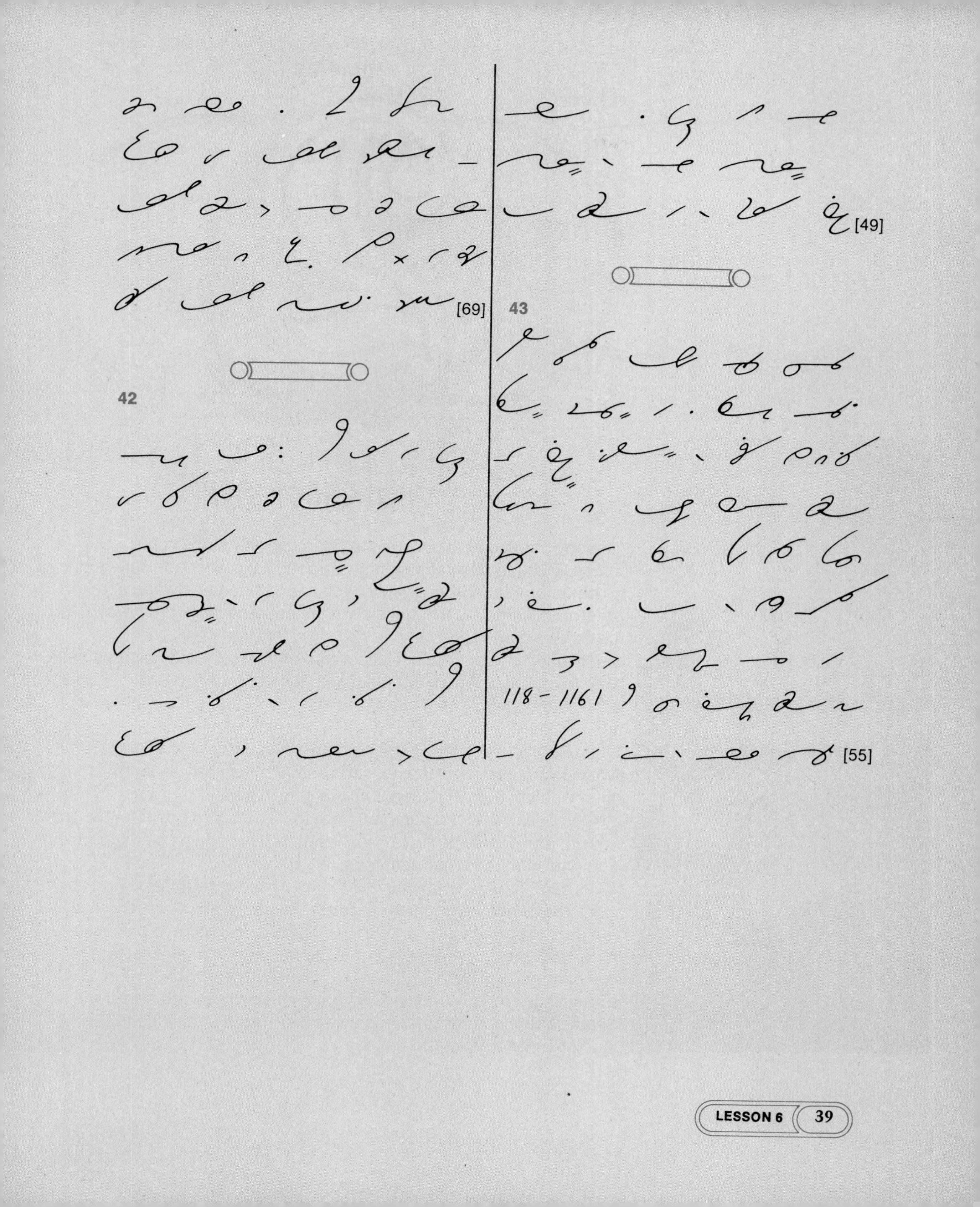

[69]

42

[49]

43

118-1161

[55]

CHAPTER

2 Shorthand A Vital Office Skill

Speedy communications are the heart of every modern business office. To keep business running smoothly, it is absolutely necessary to get information from one location to another quickly and accurately. Shorthand is the first step in the process of recording and transmitting information.

Let's take a peek at the activities in an office on an ordinary business day. We are listening to Mr. Johnson, the national product manager for a large distributor of electronic calculators, and his secretary, Ms. Rubin.

"Ms. Rubin, I have Mr. O'Brien on the phone from Los Angeles. Would you take down the revised specifications he has for the new line of calculators and then come into my office.

"Now, those specifications will have to be incorporated into the report, and copies of the revised report will have to be sent to all the regional managers immediately.

"Get a letter off special delivery to Mrs. Walters in Chicago and ask her to have her top engineer ready to revise the plans as soon as we get the specifications. After she has had a chance to discuss them with the engineer, ask her to let me know how extensive the changes will be.

"Ask Chuck to tell Lee Johnson that the final specs are in and will be ready for the national meeting next week. Make sure to send five copies by tomorrow afternoon.

"Get Albini and Pierce on the phone and tell them that they should be here the day before the meeting so that we can discuss the warehousing problems. I'll pick them up at the airport Monday afternoon.

"Call Mrs. Lopez in public relations and tell her that as soon as she gets the new specs, she can release the national campaign. Ask her if she needs any more pictures of the machine."

All this happened in less than three minutes. If the instructions given are not carried out correctly, many problems could arise. Since the flow of information may be like this all day in an office, these instructions must not be entrusted to memory. So many people and so many facts are involved, it would be too easy to confuse what Mr. Johnson just said. The information should be written. But in that short space of time, how can it all be recorded correctly? The answer is with shorthand!

With the fast pace of business today, everyone who works in an office would benefit from the ability to take shorthand. For a secretary, however, it is a must! Whether working for an accountant or a zoologist, a secretary has to be prepared to listen to, to record, and to act upon an enormous amount of information daily. What office skill could make this task easier than shorthand?

Principles

44 Sh, Ch, J

The shorthand stroke for *sh* (called *ish*) is a very short downward straight stroke.

The shorthand stroke for *ch* (called *chay*) is a longer downward straight stroke approximately half the height of the space between the lines in your shorthand notebook.

The shorthand stroke for the sound of *j*, as in *jail* and *age*, is a long downward straight stroke almost the full height of the space between the lines in your shorthand notebook.

▶ Note carefully the difference in the sizes of these strokes.

Ish / *Chay* / *J* /

Ish

Spell: ish-e, she

She, show, showed, shown, ship, share, shine, insure.

Chay

Spell: e-chay, each

Each, teach, attach, church, chair, check, cheap, speech.

J

Spell: a-j, age

Age, page, stage, large, charge, change, jail.

45 O, Aw

The small deep hook that represents the sound of *o*, as in *no*, also represents the vowel sounds heard in *hot* and *all*.

O

Spell: h-o-t, hot

Hot, lot, stock, top, drop, job, copy, college, sorry.

Aw

Spell: o-l, all

All, call, small, install, cause, bought, wall.

46 Common Business Letter Salutations and Closings

Dear Sir, Dear Madam, Yours truly, Sincerely yours, Yours very truly, Very truly yours.

▶ Note: While the expressions *Dear Sir, Dear Madam,* and *Yours truly* are considered too impersonal by experts in letter writing, they are still used by many dictators. Therefore, special abbreviations are provided for them.

Building Transcription Skills

47 BUSINESS VOCABULARY BUILDER

As a stenographer and secretary, you will constantly be working with words. Consequently, the larger the vocabulary you have at your command, the easier will be your task of taking dictation and transcribing.

To help you build your vocabulary at the same time that you are learning shorthand, a Business Vocabulary Builder is provided in Lesson 7 and in many other lessons that follow. The Business Vocabulary Builder consists of brief definitions of business words and expressions, selected from the Reading Practice, that should be part of your everyday vocabulary.

Be sure you understand the meaning of the words and expressions before you begin to work on the Reading Practice of the lesson.

Business Vocabulary Builder

vital Very important.

copier A machine for making printed copies.

obligate Bind; commit.

Reading Practice

48 Brief-Form Review Letter

This letter reviews the brief forms you studied in Lessons 3 and 5.

[104]

49

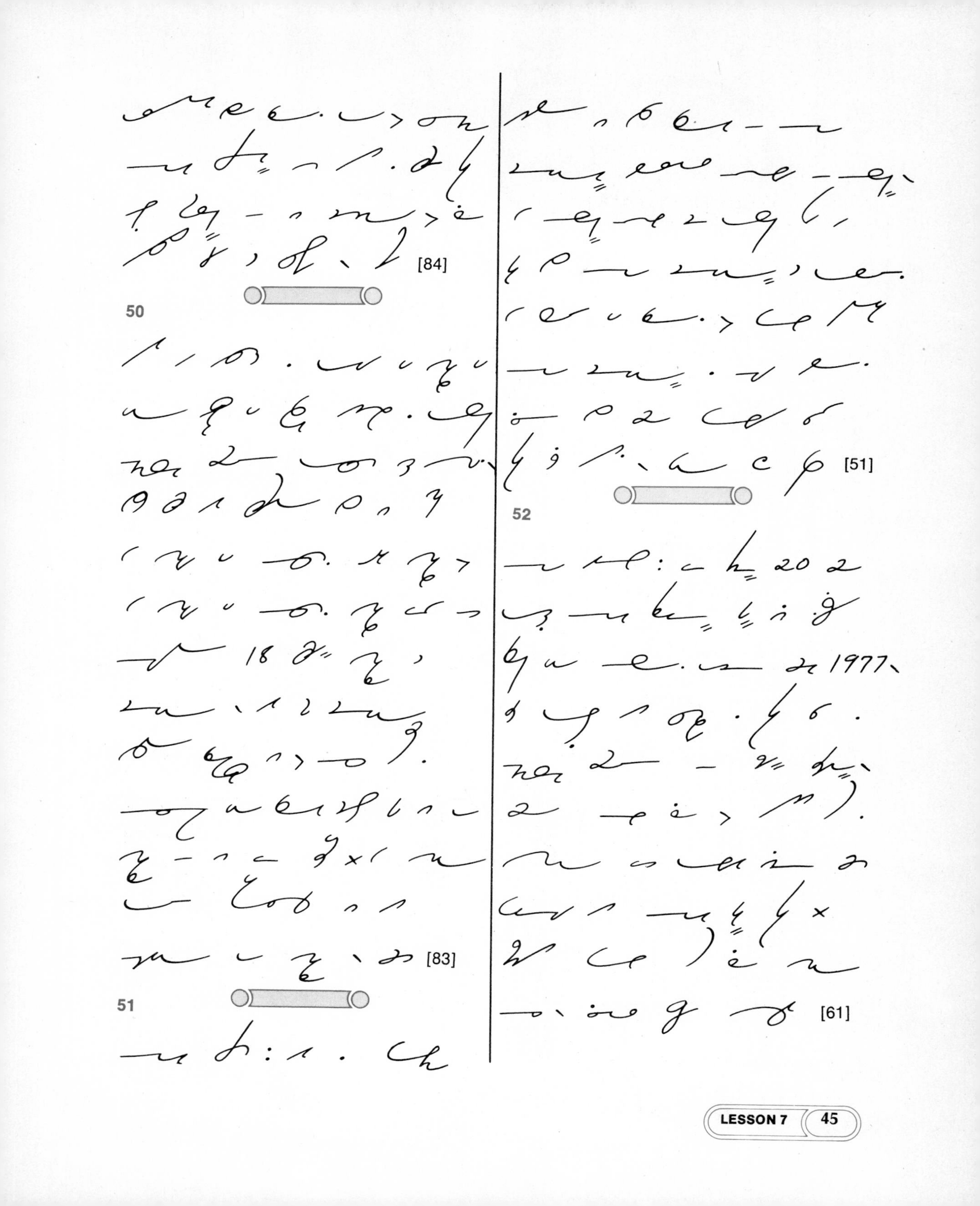

[84]

50

[83]

51

[51]

52

[61]

Principles

53 Brief Forms

Here is the third group of brief forms for frequently used words. Learn them well.

For, would, there (their), this, good, they, which, them, be-by.*

*Be is also used as a word beginning in words such as *begin* and *believe*.

Spell: be-gay-e-n, begin

Begin, belief, believe, because, beneath.

54 Word Ending -ly

The common word ending *-ly* is represented by the *e* circle.

Spell: n-e-r-lē, nearly

Nearly, only, early, fairly, properly, mostly, sincerely, highly, daily.

▶ Notice that the circle for *ly* in *daily* is added to the other side of the *d* after the *a* has been written.

55 Amounts and Quantities

In business you will frequently have to take dictation in which amounts and quantities are used. Here are some devices that will help you write them rapidly.

400; 4,000; 400,000; $4; $4,000; $400,000; 4 o'clock, $4.50, 4 percent.

▶ Notice that the *n* for *hundred* and the *ith* for *thousand* are placed underneath the figure.

Building Transcription Skills

56 **Business Vocabulary Builder**

brochure Booklet.

dry goods Textiles; ready-to-wear clothing.

cassettes Small plastic cartridges containing magnetic tape on reels.

packaging Wrapping.

● Reading Practice

57 Brief-Form Letter

The following letter contains one or more illustrations of the brief forms presented in this lesson.

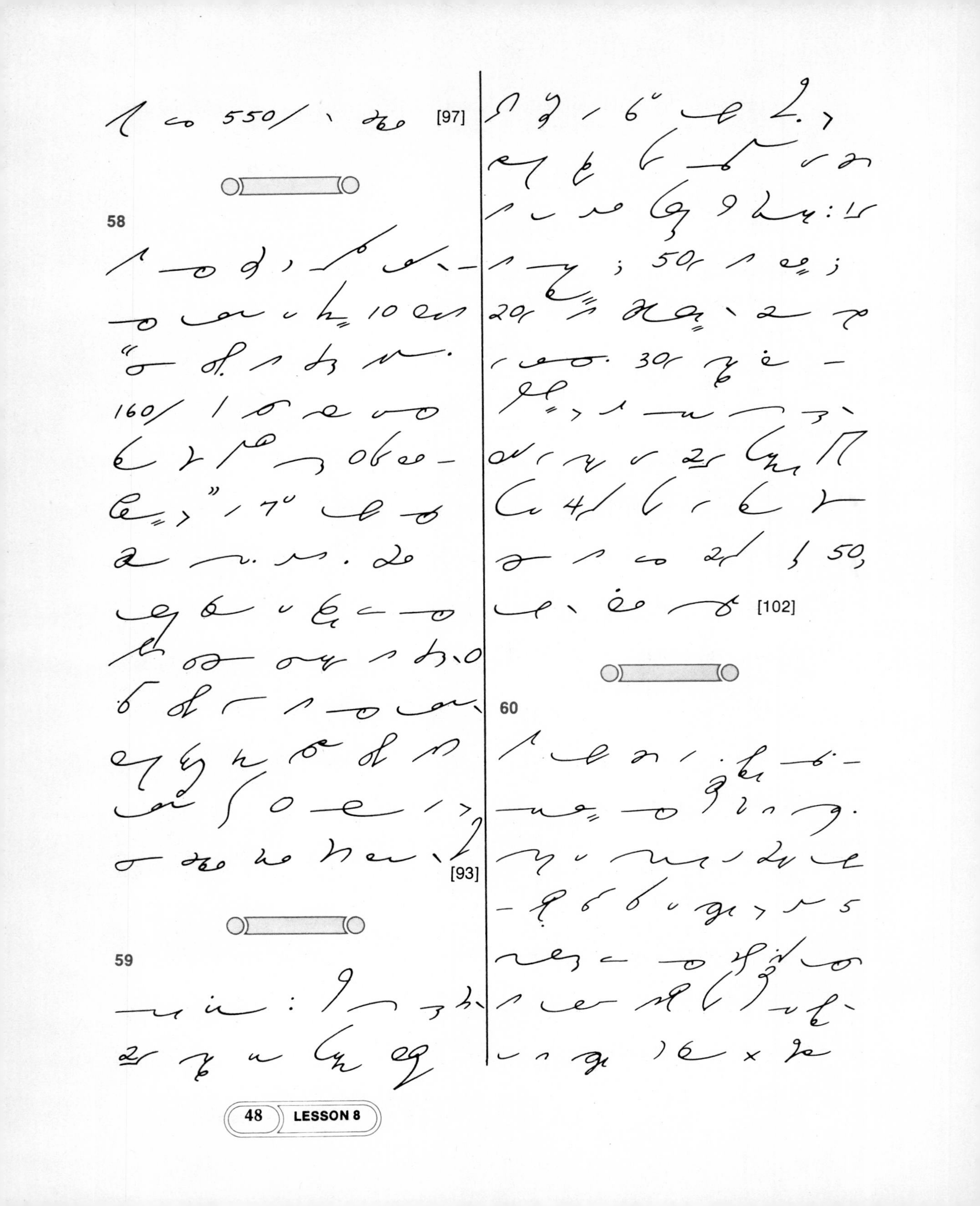

[97]

58

[93]

59

[102]

60

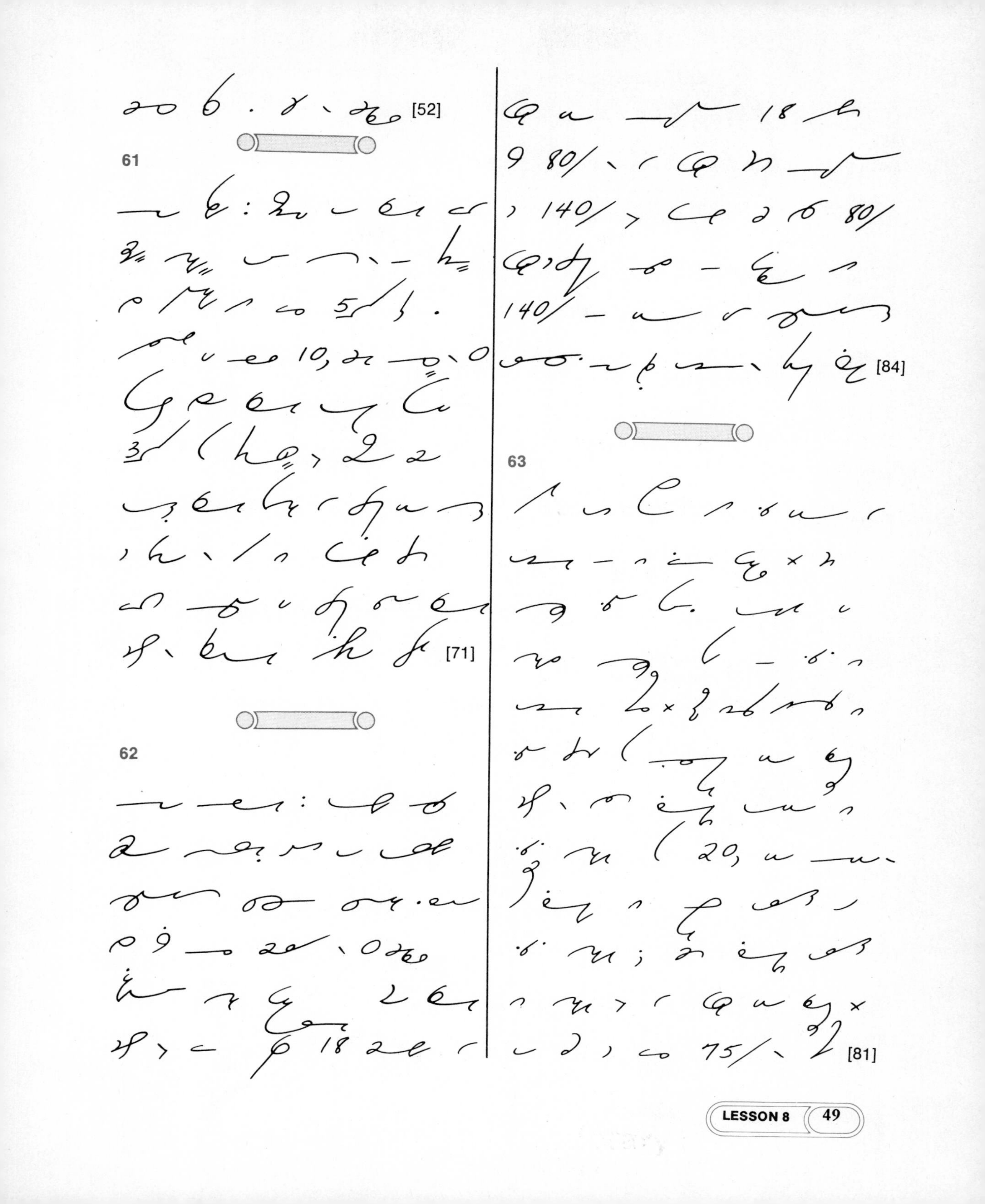

[52]

61

[71]

62

[84]

63

[81]

Principles

64 Word Ending -tion

The word ending *-tion* (also spelled *sion, cian,* or *shion*) is represented by *ish.*

Spell: s-e-k-shun, section

Section, operation, collection, vacation, occasion, nation, national, fashion, physician.

65 Word Endings -cient, -ciency

The word ending *-cient* (or *tient*) is represented by *ish-t; -ciency,* by *ish-s-e.*

Spell: e-f-e-shun-t, efficient; p-r-o-f-e-shun-s-e, proficiency

Efficient, patient, proficiency, efficiency.

66 T for To in Phrases

In phrases, *to* is represented by *t* when it is followed by a downstroke.

To be, to have, to plan, to fill, to place, to see, to say, to buy, to change.

Building Transcription Skills

67 Business Vocabulary Builder

authorize To give permission to.

staggering Alternating.

sectional Local; regional.

collection agency An organization that collects past-due accounts.

Reading Practice

68 Brief-Form Review Letter

The following letter reviews the brief forms in Lesson 8 as well as many of the brief forms in Lessons 3 and 5.

[100]

69

[93]

70

[107]

71

[93]

72

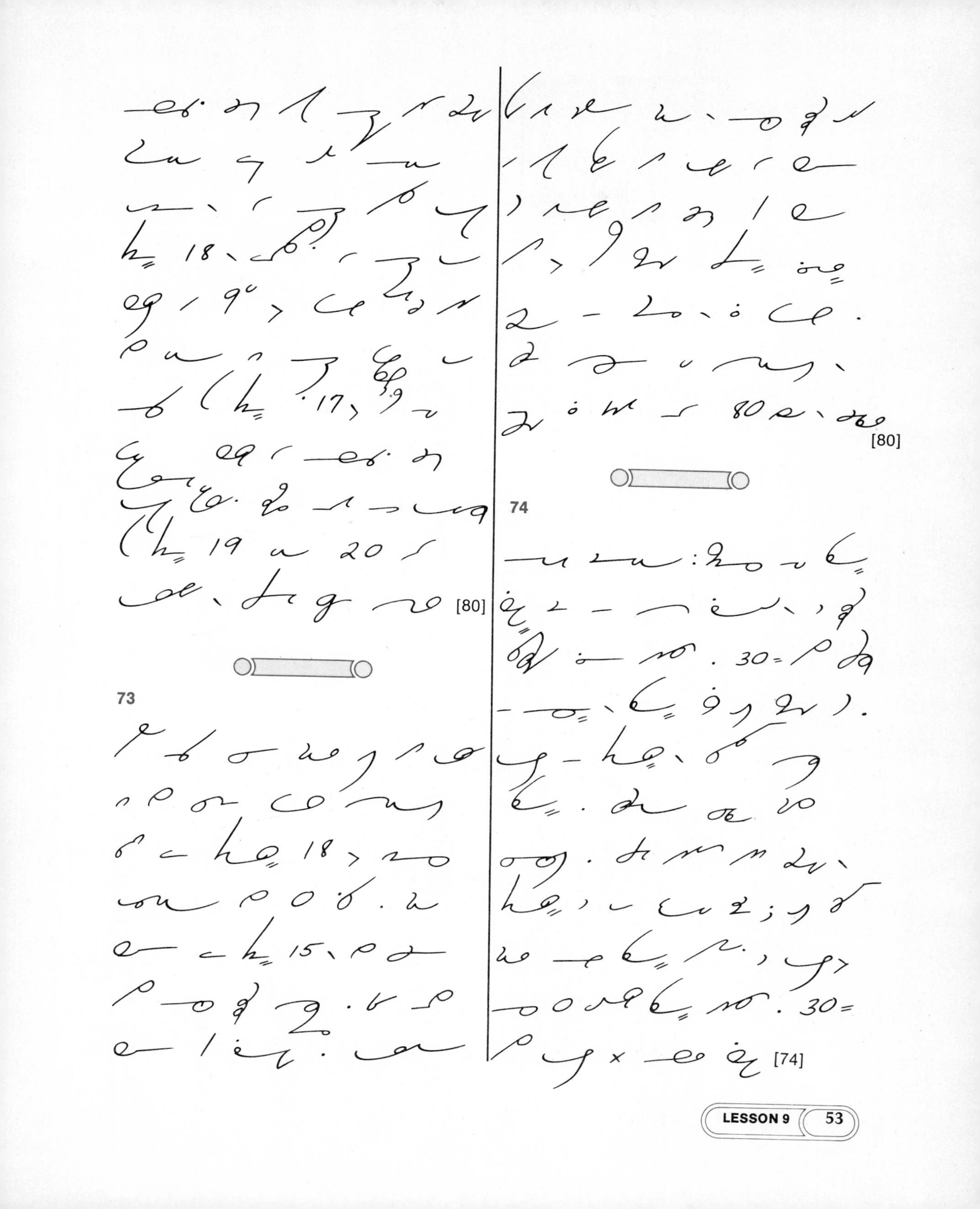

[80]

73

[80]

74

[74]

Principles

75 Nd

The shorthand strokes for *n-d* are joined without an angle to form the *nd* blend, as in *trained.*

Nd

Compare: *train* *trained*

Spell: *t-r-a-end, trained*

Signed, assigned, find, land, planned, kind, friend, spend, lined.

76 Nt

The stroke that represents *nd* also represents *nt,* as in *sent.*

Spell: *s-e-ent, sent; ent-oo, into*

Sent, print, rental, central, current, apparent, agent, into, entirely.

77 Ses

The sound of *ses,* as in *senses,* is represented by joining the two forms of *s.*

Compare: *sense* *senses*

face *faces*

Spell: s-e-n-sez, senses

Senses, services, offices, promises, processes, causes, losses, necessary.

78 Sis, Sus

The similar sounds of *sis,* as in *sister,* and *sus,* as in *versus,* are also represented by joining the two forms of *s.*

Spell: sez-t-r, sister; v-e-r-sez, versus

Sister, basis, assist, insist, analysis, versus.

Building Transcription Skills

79 Business Vocabulary Builder

processes *(noun)* Methods; procedures.

went astray Lost.

current Most recent.

Reading Practice

80 Brief-Form Review Letter

This letter reviews all the brief forms you studied in Lesson 8.

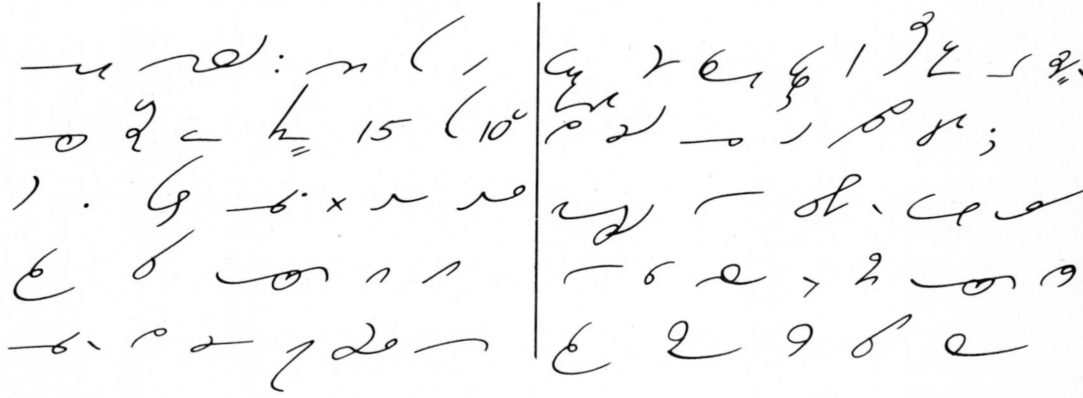

[73]

81

[98]

82

[64]

83

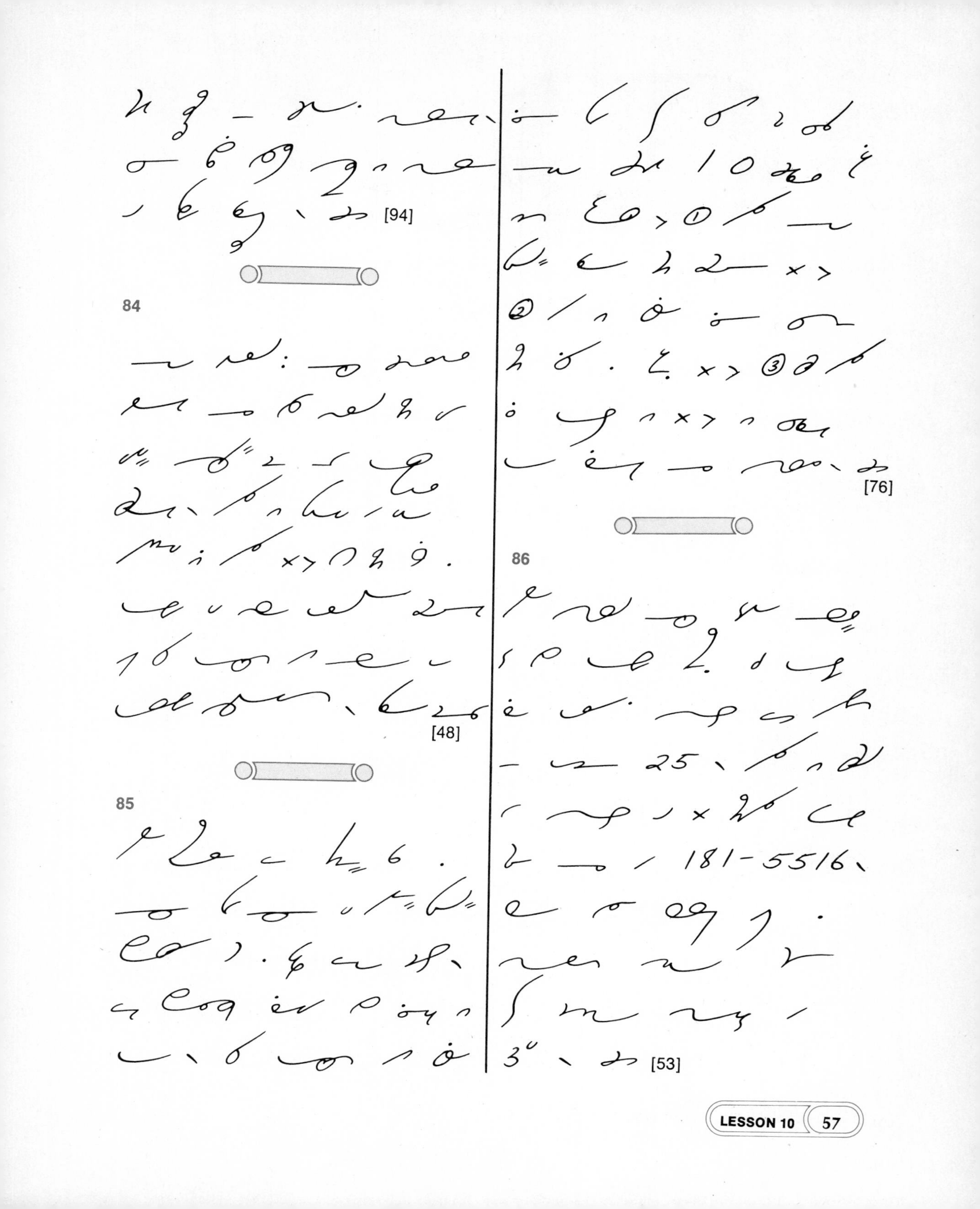

[94]

84

[48]

85

[76]

86

[53]

Principles

87 Brief Forms

And, when, from, should, could, send, after, street, were.

88 Rd

The combination *rd* is represented by writing *r* with an upward turn at the finish.

Compare: *answer* *answered*

Spell: *a-n-s-e-ärd, answered; h-e-ärd, heard*

Prepared, assured, ignored, heard, hard, harder, record, recorded, toward.

89 Ld

The combination *ld* is represented by writing the *l* with an upward turn at the finish.

Compare: *call* *called*

Spell: *k-o-eld, called; o-eld, old*

Called, held, child, failed, old, told, children, folded.

90 Been in Phrases

The word *been* is represented by *b* after *have, has, had.*

Had been, have been, I have been, I have not been, it has been, there has been, to have been, I should have been.

91 Able in Phrases

The word *able* is represented by *a* after *be* or *been.*

Have been able, I have been able, you have not been able, has been able, I should be able, you will be able, to be able.

Building Transcription Skills

92 Business Vocabulary Builder

plight Bad state or condition.

asset Advantage.

"on the drawing boards" In the planning stage.

ignored Neglected.

Reading Practice

93 Brief-Form Letter

The following letter contains one or more illustrations of every brief form in paragraph 87.

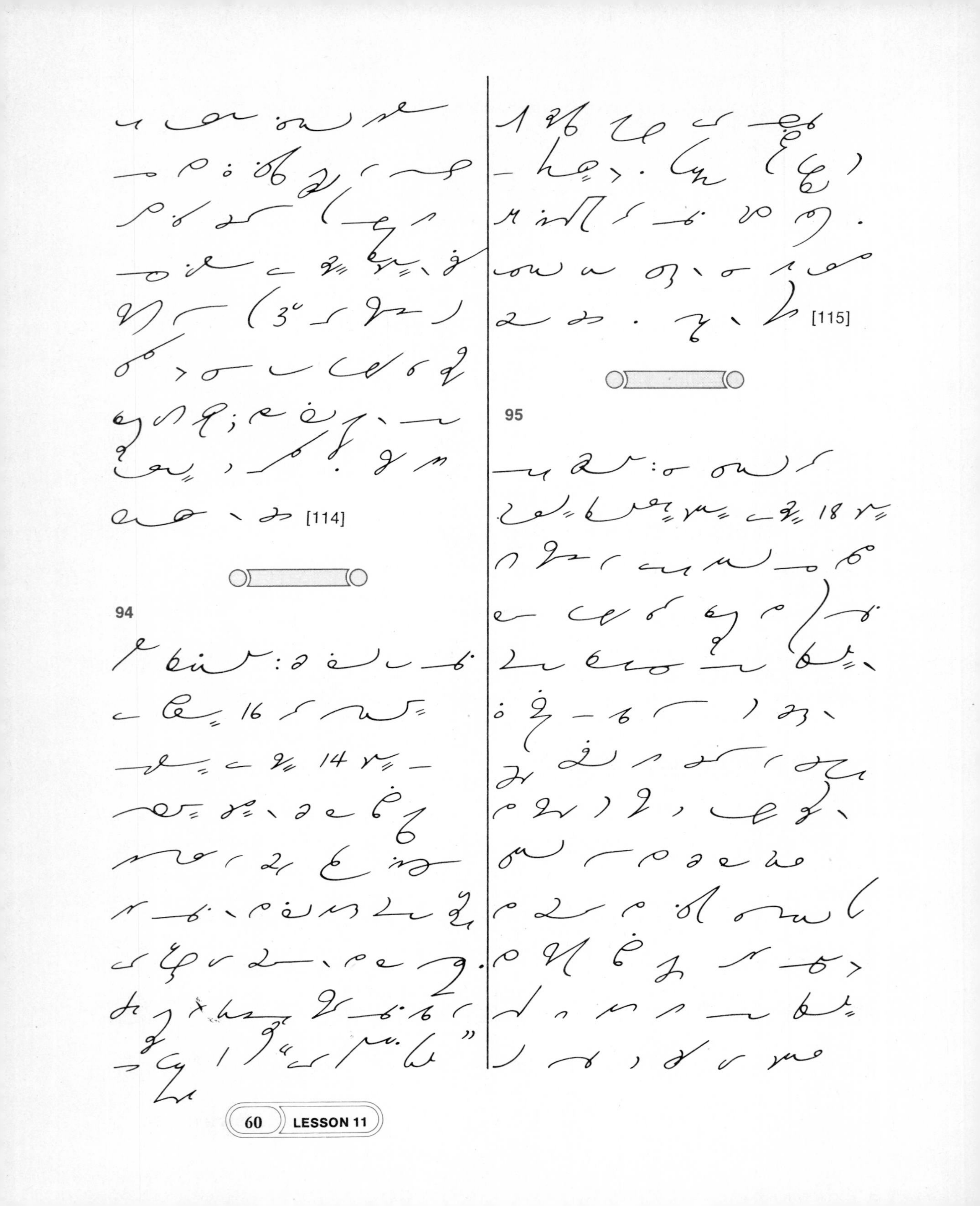

[114]

94

[115]

95

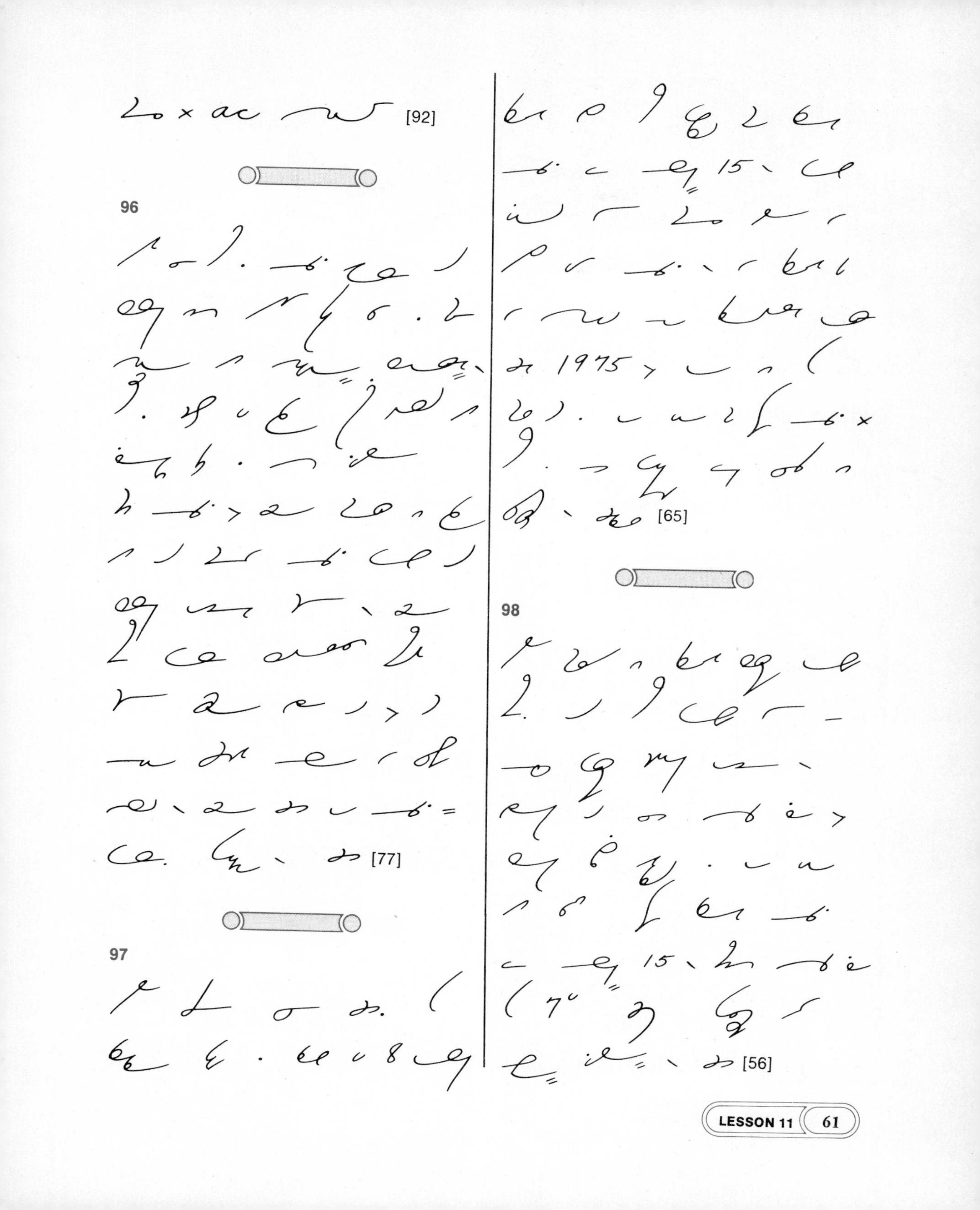

[92]

96

[77]

97

15

1975

[65]

98

15

7

[56]

RECALL

Lesson 12 is another "breather" for you; it presents no new shorthand devices for you to learn. It contains a helpful Recall Chart and several short letters that you should have no difficulty reading.

99 Recall Chart

The following chart contains all the brief forms presented in Chapter 2 and one or more illustrations of the shorthand principles you studied in Chapters 1 and 2.

Can you read the entire chart in 9 minutes or less?

BRIEF FORMS

1						
2						
3						

PHRASES AND AMOUNTS

4						
5						
6						
7						

WORDS

8						
9						

10						
11						
12						
13						
14						

Building Transcription Skills

100 Business Vocabulary Builder

fee A charge.

leaflet A single printed sheet of paper.

glowing Showing elation or great satisfaction.

Reading Practice

101

[113]

102

[82]

103

[89]

104

[69]

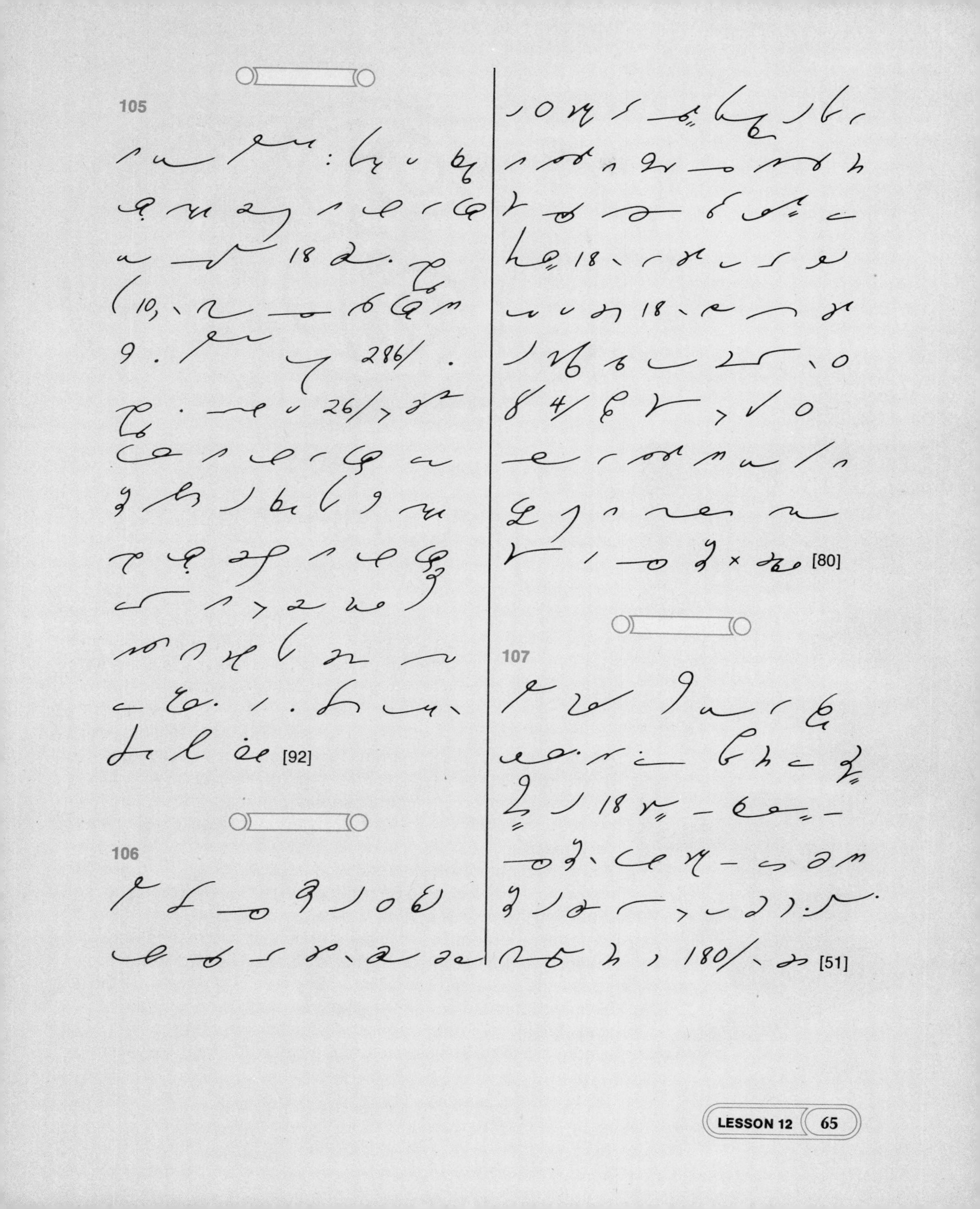

105

[92]

106

[80]

107

[51]

CHAPTER

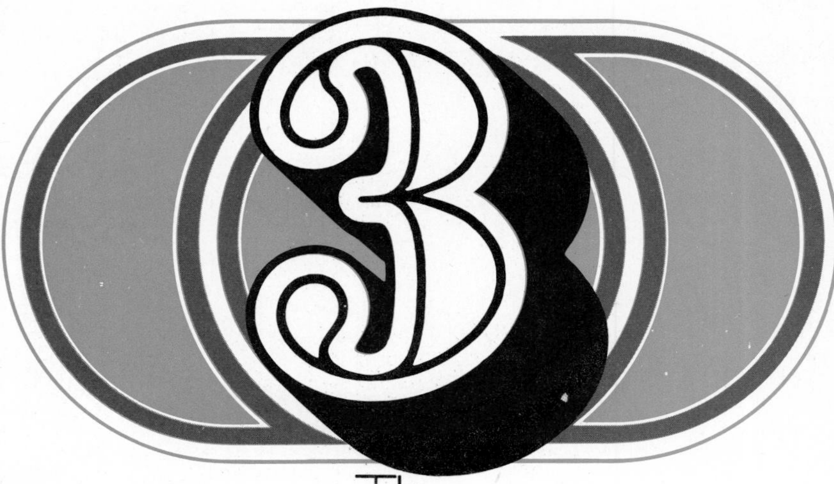

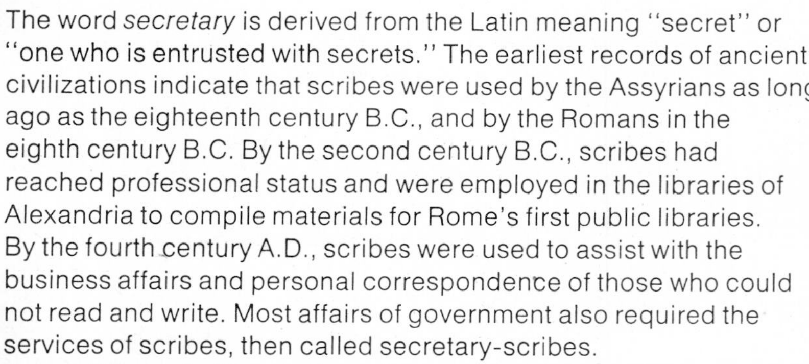

The Secretarial Profession
A Brief History

The Bettmann Archive

The word *secretary* is derived from the Latin meaning "secret" or "one who is entrusted with secrets." The earliest records of ancient civilizations indicate that scribes were used by the Assyrians as long ago as the eighteenth century B.C., and by the Romans in the eighth century B.C. By the second century B.C., scribes had reached professional status and were employed in the libraries of Alexandria to compile materials for Rome's first public libraries. By the fourth century A.D., scribes were used to assist with the business affairs and personal correspondence of those who could not read and write. Most affairs of government also required the services of scribes, then called secretary-scribes.

Toward the end of the nineteenth century, with the invention of the typewriter and the Gregg Shorthand system, many women became proficient in secretarial work and began to take over duties formerly performed by men. These "type-writers," as secretaries were then called, were trailblazers in business offices. They were eager to trade a life on the farm or in the factory for a very different life in a business office. Although their manner was quiet; their role, subservient; their dress, conservative; their pay, meager, the historical impact of these women was revolutionary. They were

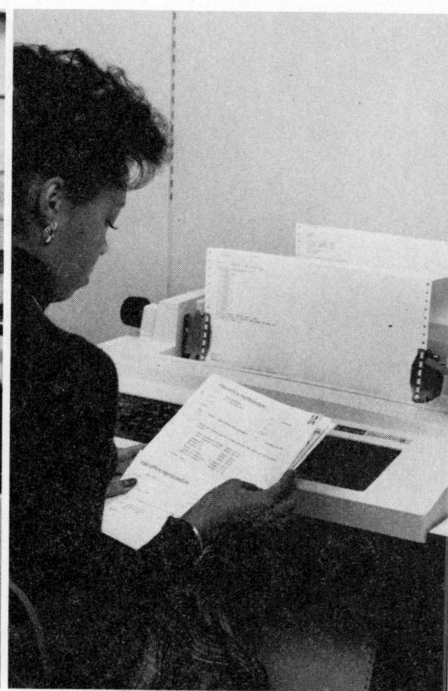

instrumental in changing the whole character of the business office. Today there are several million secretaries in the United States. Though the majority are women, many men are now choosing this as their profession. Secretaries' titles range from junior stenographer to administrative assistant; their work, from taking shorthand and transcribing verbatim notes on the typewriter to handling all administrative duties of a large modern business organization. Secretaries may work in many different kinds of places, from small, one-secretary offices to large communications centers in major cities. They may work for many executives or for only one. But their function is basically the same—keeping business running smoothly through the application of their secretarial skills and abilities.

The status of today's secretary ranks considerably higher than the status of a secretary 50 years ago. The secretary is really an executive aide who still does the traditional jobs of taking dictation, typing, filing, and handling calls and callers. But in many ways, today's secretary must know the job of the boss better than the boss does.

It has been said that behind every good executive there's a good secretary. Today there is a tremendous demand for good secretaries, and authoritative sources indicate that this demand will continue to grow. The secretary is an established and vital part of the structure of modern business.

Principles

108 Brief Forms

*Glad, work, yesterday, circular, order, soon, enclose, was, thank.**

*In phrases, the dot is omitted from *thank. Thanks* is written with a disjoined left *s* in the dot position.

Thank you, thank you for, thanks.

109 U, OO

The hook that represents the sound of *oo,* as in *to,* also represents the vowel sounds heard in *does* and *book.*

U

Spell: d-oo-s, does

Does, drug, product, enough, number, must, us, just, precious.

Notice: ■ 1 The hook in *enough, number,* and *must* is turned on its side;
■ 2 *oo-s* in *us, just, precious* join without an angle.

oo

Spell: b-oo-k, book

Book, put, pull, full, cook, push, took, foot, sugar.

Building Transcription Skills

110 Business Vocabulary Builder

promotion pieces Circulars or bulletins advertising a company's products.

sketches Rough drawings.

major Greater in importance.

Reading Practice

111 Brief-Form Letter

All the brief forms in this lesson, or their derivatives, are used in this letter.

[98]

112

[101]

113

[98]

114

[78]

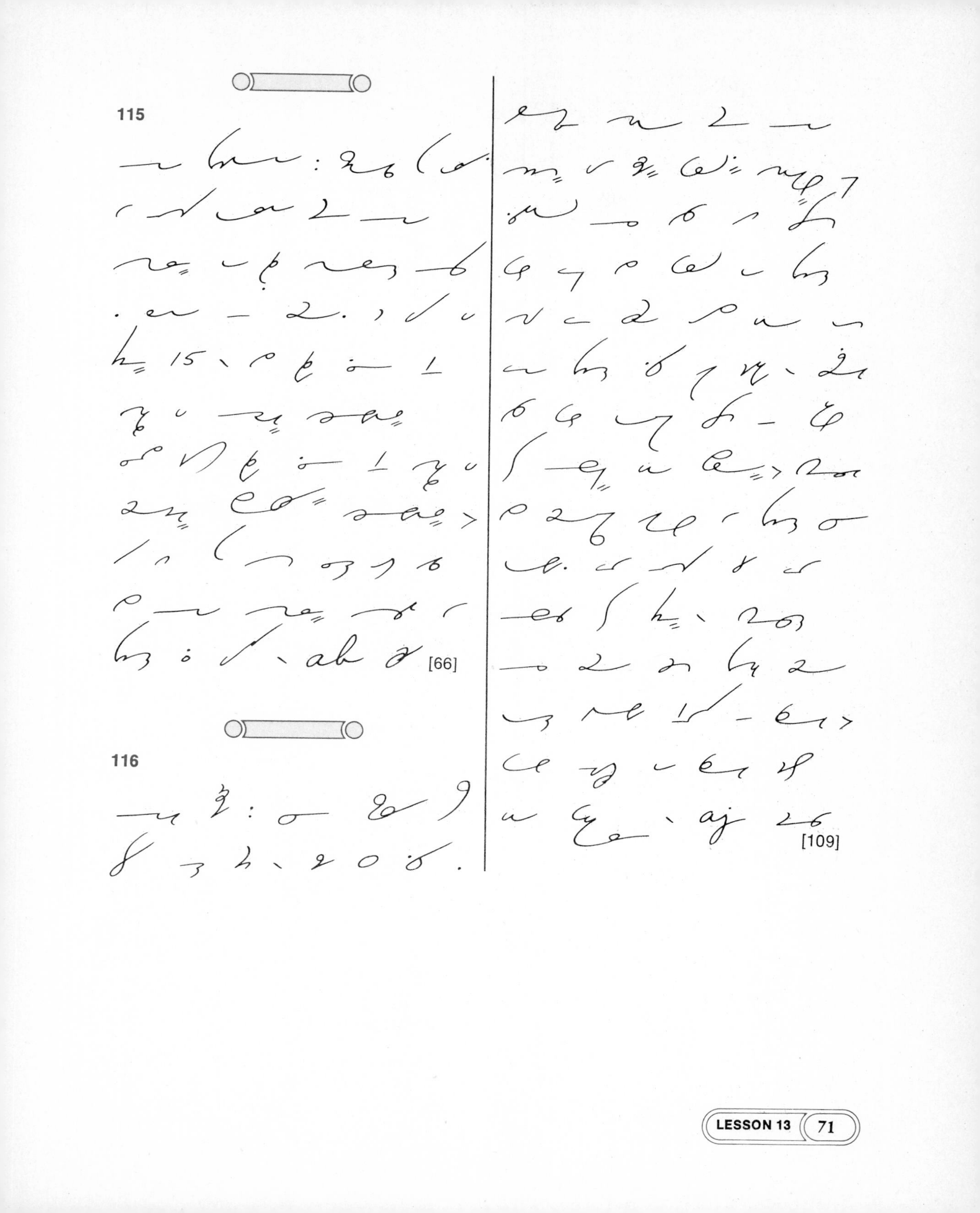

115

15

ab

[66]

116

[109]

Principles

117 W in the Body of a Word

When the sound of *w* occurs in the body of a word, as in *quick,* it is represented by a short dash underneath the vowel following the *w* sound. The dash is inserted after the rest of the outline has been written.

Spell: *k-oo-e-k, quick*

Quick, quit, quote, between, square, hardware, qualify, always, Broadway.

118 Ted

The combination *ted* is represented by joining *t* and *d* into one long upward stroke.

Ted

Compare: *heat* *heed* *heated*

Spell: *h-e-ted, heated*

Listed, drafted, acted, quoted, tested, accepted, rested, steady, today.

119 Ded

The long stroke that represents *ted* also represents *ded* and the similar sounds of *dit, det.*

Spell: gay-ī-ded, guided; det-a-l, detail

Ded

Guided, needed, added, graded, traded, deduct, deduction.

Det, Dit

Detail, debtor, credit, credited, audited,* edit, editor.*

*Notice that the *d* representing the past tense is joined to *det* with a jog.

Building Transcription Skills

120 Business Vocabulary Builder

drafted Made a rough copy of.

applicant One who applies for a job.

fine arts Music, literature, painting, etc.

Reading Practice

121 Brief-Form Review Letter

This letter reviews all the brief forms you studied in Lesson 13 as well as many from earlier lessons.

[78]

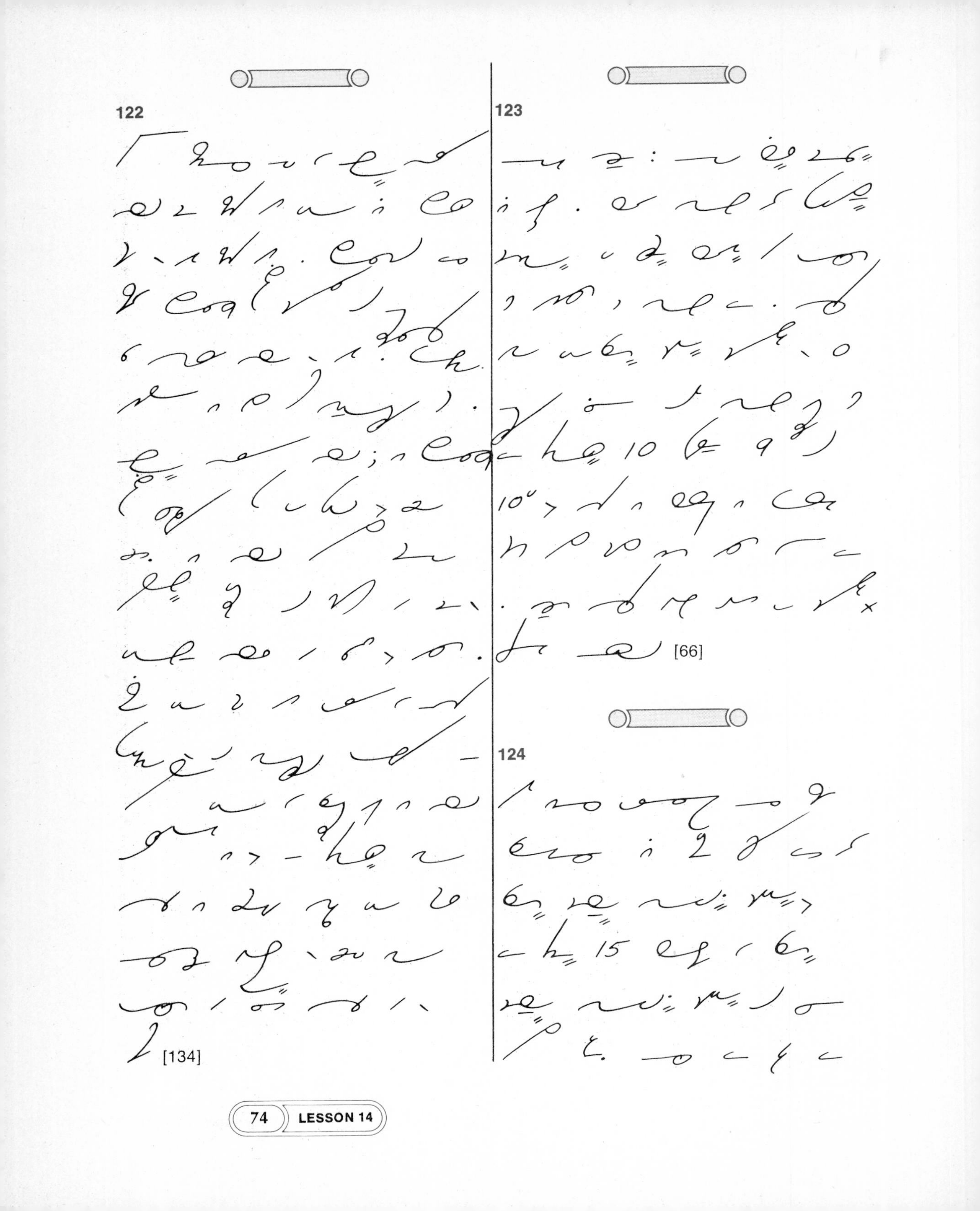

122

[134]

123

[66]

124

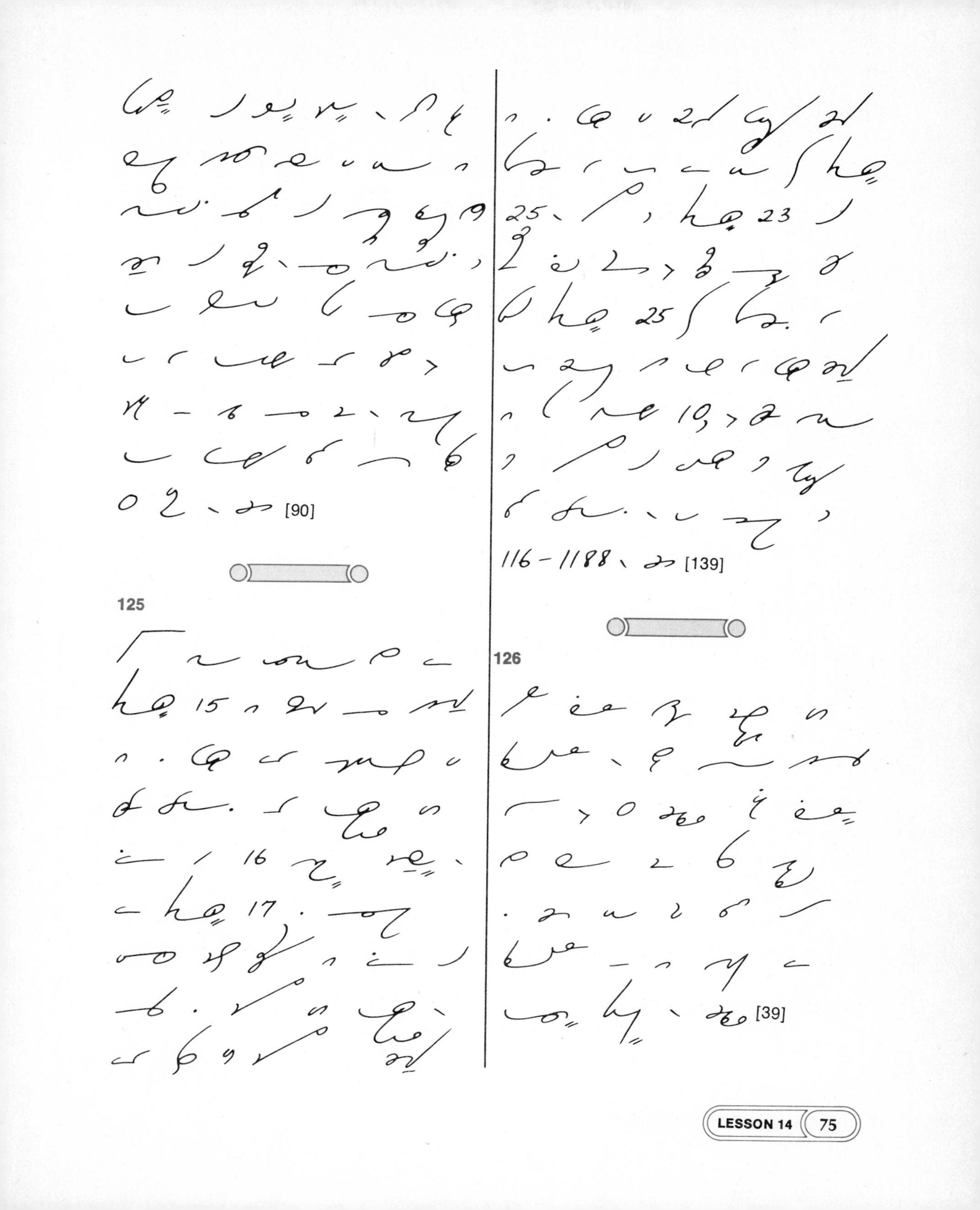

[90]

[139]

125

126

[39]

127

[86]

128

[42]

SHORTHAND READING CHECKLIST

When you read shorthand, do you—

- ■ 1 Read aloud so that you know that you are concentrating on each outline that you read?
- ■ 2 Spell each outline that you cannot immediately read?
- ■ 3 Reread each Reading Practice a second time?
- ■ 4 Occasionally reread the suggestions for reading shorthand given on pages 10 and 11?

Principles

129 Brief Forms

Value, than, one (won), what, about, thing-think, business, doctor, any.

130 Brief-Form Derivatives

Once, things-thinks, thinking, anything, businessman, businesses, values, doctors.

▶ Notice that a disjoined left *s* is used to express *things, thinks*; that the plural of *business* is formed by adding a left *s*.

131 Word Ending -ble

The word ending *-ble* is represented by *b*.

Spell: p-o-s-bul, possible

Possible, capable, reliable, available, favorable, sensible, table, trouble, troubled.

132 Word Beginning Re-

The word beginning *re-* is represented by *r*.

Spell: re-s-e-v, receive

Receive, replace, research, resigned, reception, repairs, reasonable, reappear, reopen.

Building Transcription Skills

133 Business Vocabulary Builder

queries Questions.

resigned Quit; gave up one's position.

patient *(adjective)* Bearing pains or trials without complaint.

Reading Practice

134 Brief-Form Letter

All the brief forms in Lesson 15, or derivatives of them, are used at least once in this letter.

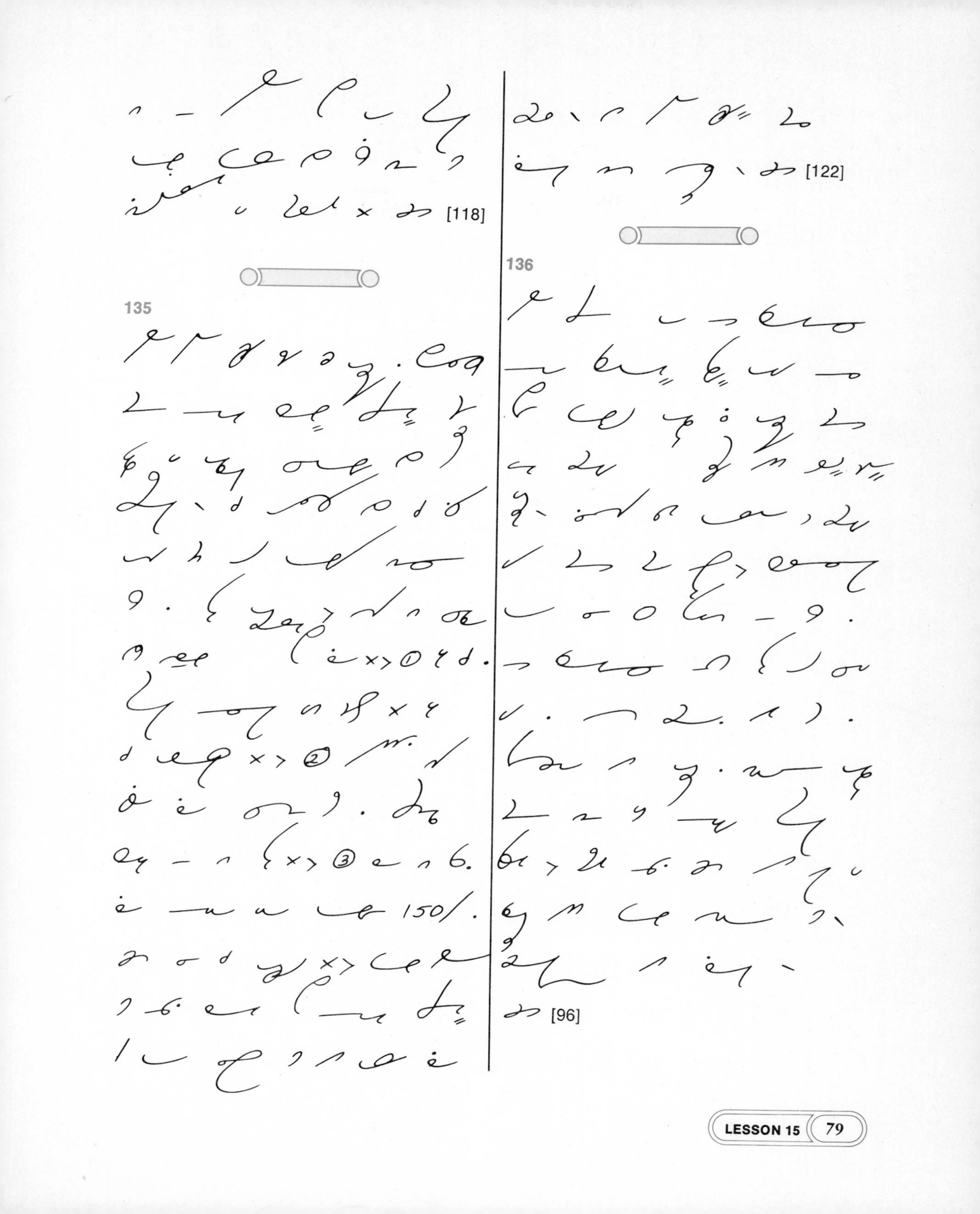

[118]

[122]

135

150/.

136

[96]

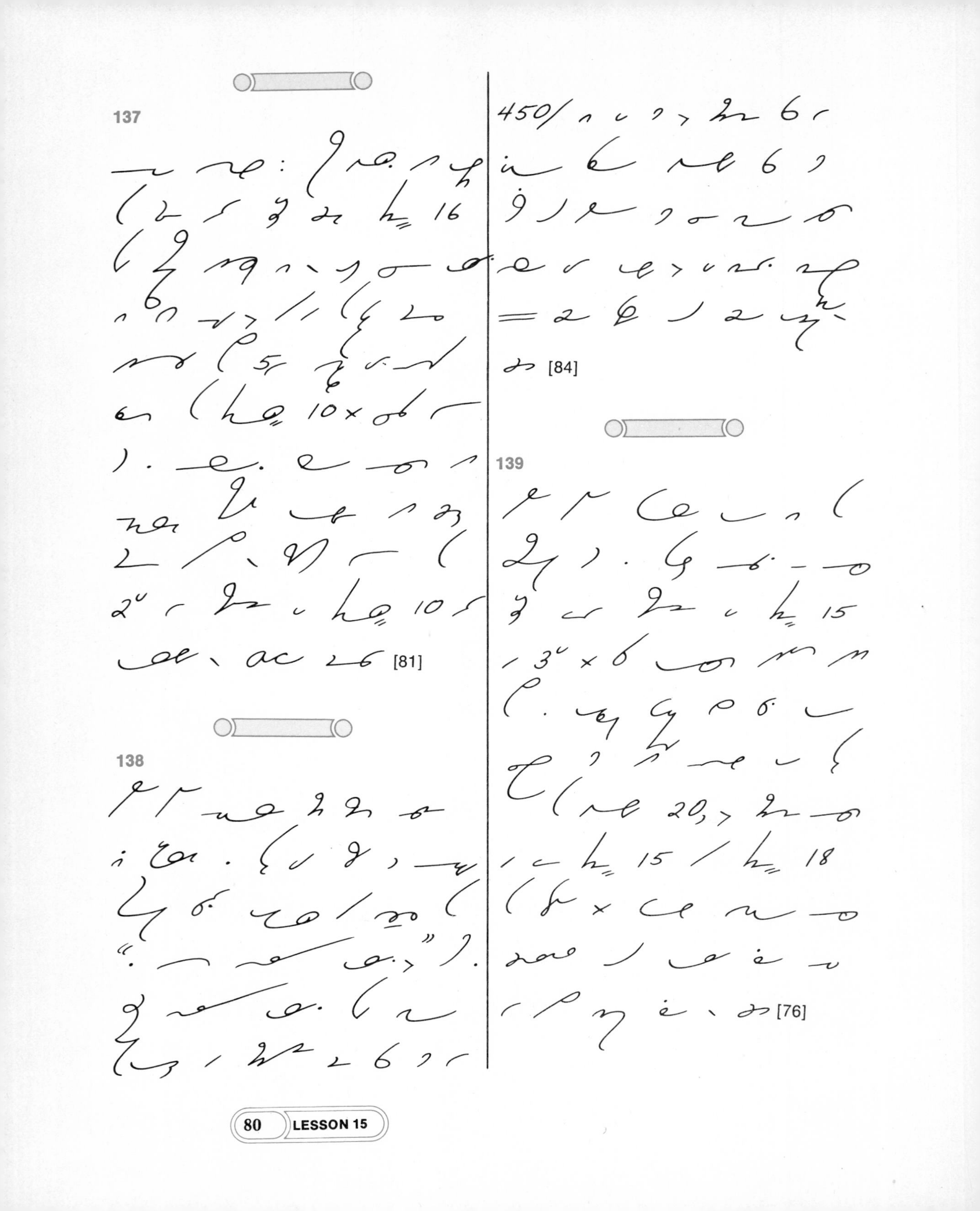

137

[81]

138

[84]

139

[76]

Principles

140 Oi

The sound of *oi,* as in *toy,* is represented by [shorthand outline].

Spell: t-oi, toy

Toy, boy, invoice, oil, soil, appoint, join, noise, royal.

141 Men

The sound of *men* is represented by joining *m* and *n* into one long forward stroke.

Men [shorthand outline]

Compare: knee [shorthand outline] me [shorthand outline] many [shorthand outline]

Spell: men-e, many

Men, many, mentioned, meant, mental, women.

142 Min, Mon, Man

The similar sounding combinations *min, mon, man* are also represented by the long forward stroke that represents *men.*

Spell: men-e-t, minute; men-r, manner

Minute, month, monthly, money, manner, manager.

143 Ye, Ya

Ye, as in *year,* is represented by the *e* circle; *ya,* as in *yard,* by the *a* circle.

Spell: e-r, year; a-ärd, yard

Year, yet, yes, yellow, yield, yielded; yard, yarn, Yale.

Building Transcription Skills

144 Business Vocabulary Builder

craftsmen Workers who practice a trade or handicraft.

net profit Amount remaining after the deduction of expenses.

sizable Fairly large; considerable.

decade Ten years.

Reading Practice

145 Brief-Form Review Letter

This letter reviews all the brief forms you studied in Lesson 15 as well as many from earlier lessons.

[105]

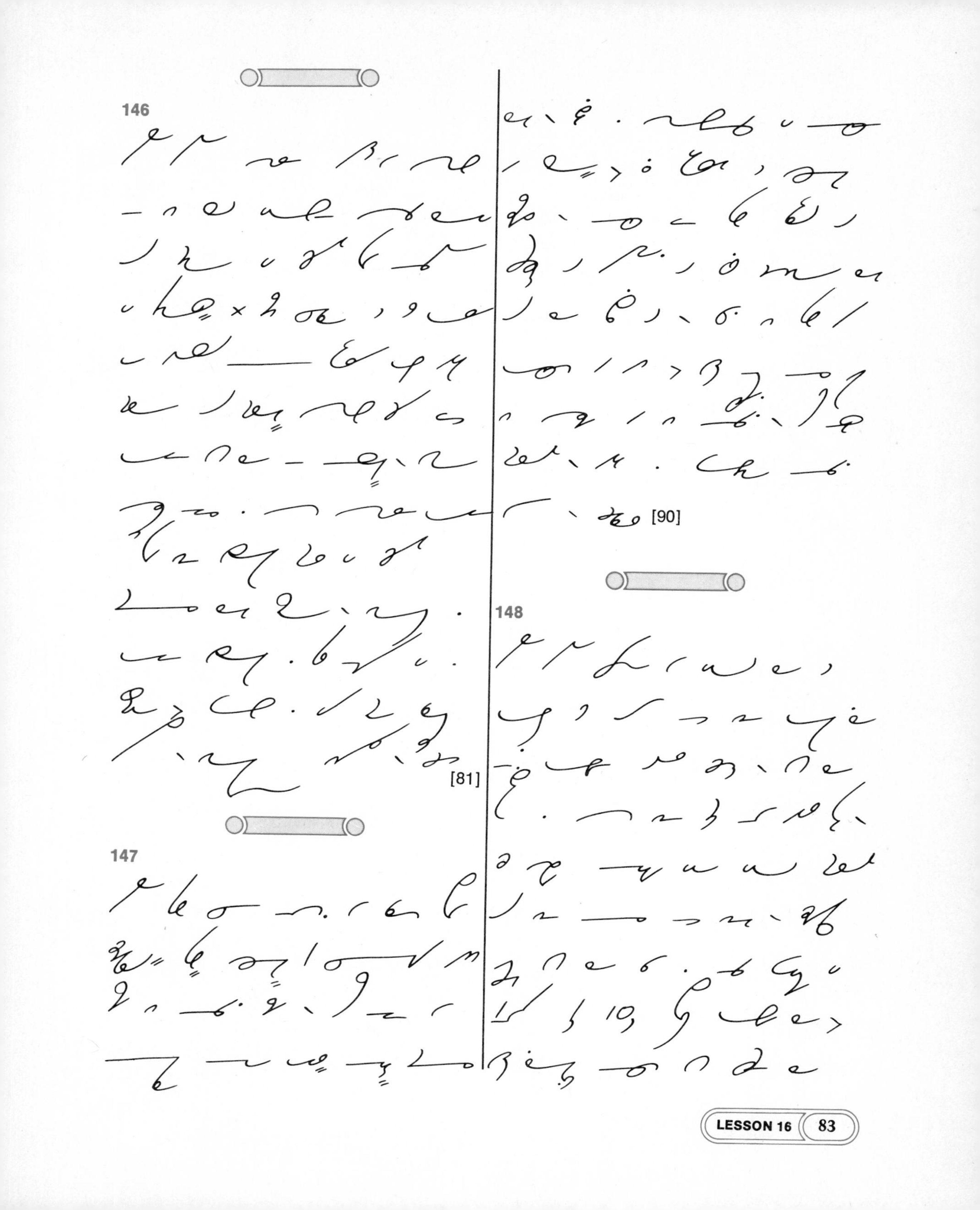

146

[81]

147

[90]

148

[104]

149

[47]

150

250

[65]

151

10

[54]

Principles

152 Brief Forms

When you have learned the following brief forms, you will have learned more than half the brief forms of Gregg Shorthand.

Gentlemen, morning, important-importance, where, company, manufacture, next, short.

153 Word Beginnings Per-, Pur-

The word beginnings *per-*, *pur-* are represented by *p-r*.

Spell: pur-s-n, person; pur-chay-a-s, purchase

Per-

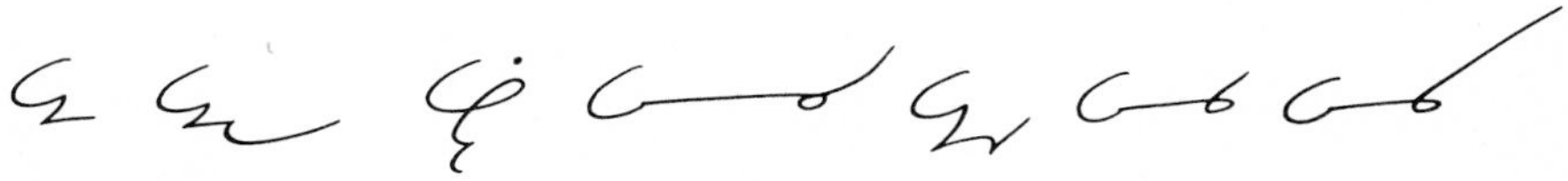

Person, personal, perhaps, permanent, perfect, permit, permitted.

Pur-

Purchase, purchased, purpose, purposes, purple, purses.

154 Word Beginnings De-, Di-

The word beginnings *de-*, *di-* are represented by *d*.

Spell: de-s-ī-d, decide; de-r-e-k-t, direct

De-

Decide, decision, depend, deposit, deliver, desirable, deserve.

Di-

Direct, directed, direction, diploma.

Building Transcription Skills

155 SIMILAR-WORDS DRILL The English language contains many groups of words that sound or look alike, but each member of the group may be spelled differently and have its own meaning.

Example: **sent** (dispatched); **scent** (a smell); **cent** (a coin).

In addition, there are many groups of words that sound or look *almost* alike.

Example: **area** (space); **aria** (a melody).

The stenographer or secretary who is not alert may, while transcribing, select the wrong member of the group, with the result that the transcript makes no sense.

In this lesson and in a number of others that follow, you will find a Similar-Words Drill that will call to your attention common groups of similar words on which a careless stenographer might stumble.

Study each definition carefully and read the illustrative examples in each similar-words exercise.

SIMILAR-WORDS DRILL personal, personnel

personal Individual; private; pertaining to the person or body.

Harry is a personal friend of mine.
Do you watch your personal appearance with care?

personnel The people who work for a firm; the staff.

Our personnel will take care of your needs.
Mr. Green is the personnel director of our firm.

156 Business Vocabulary Builder

purchasing agent A person responsible for purchasing goods or supplies for a company.

proceed To move ahead.

anticipated Expected.

Reading Practice

157 Brief-Form Letter

[153]

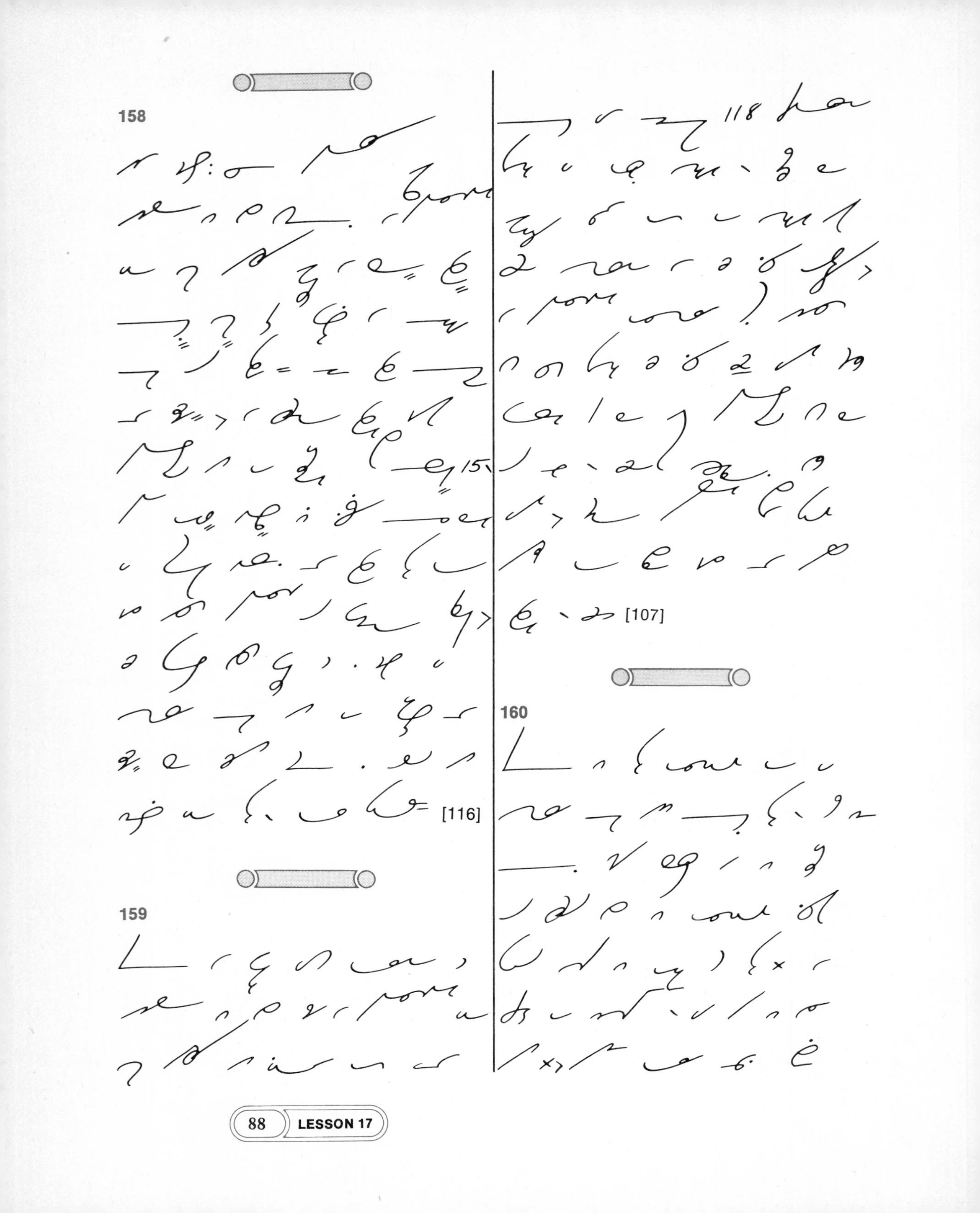

158

[116]

159

[107]

160

[102]

161

116

15

31

[70]

162

15

[74]

163

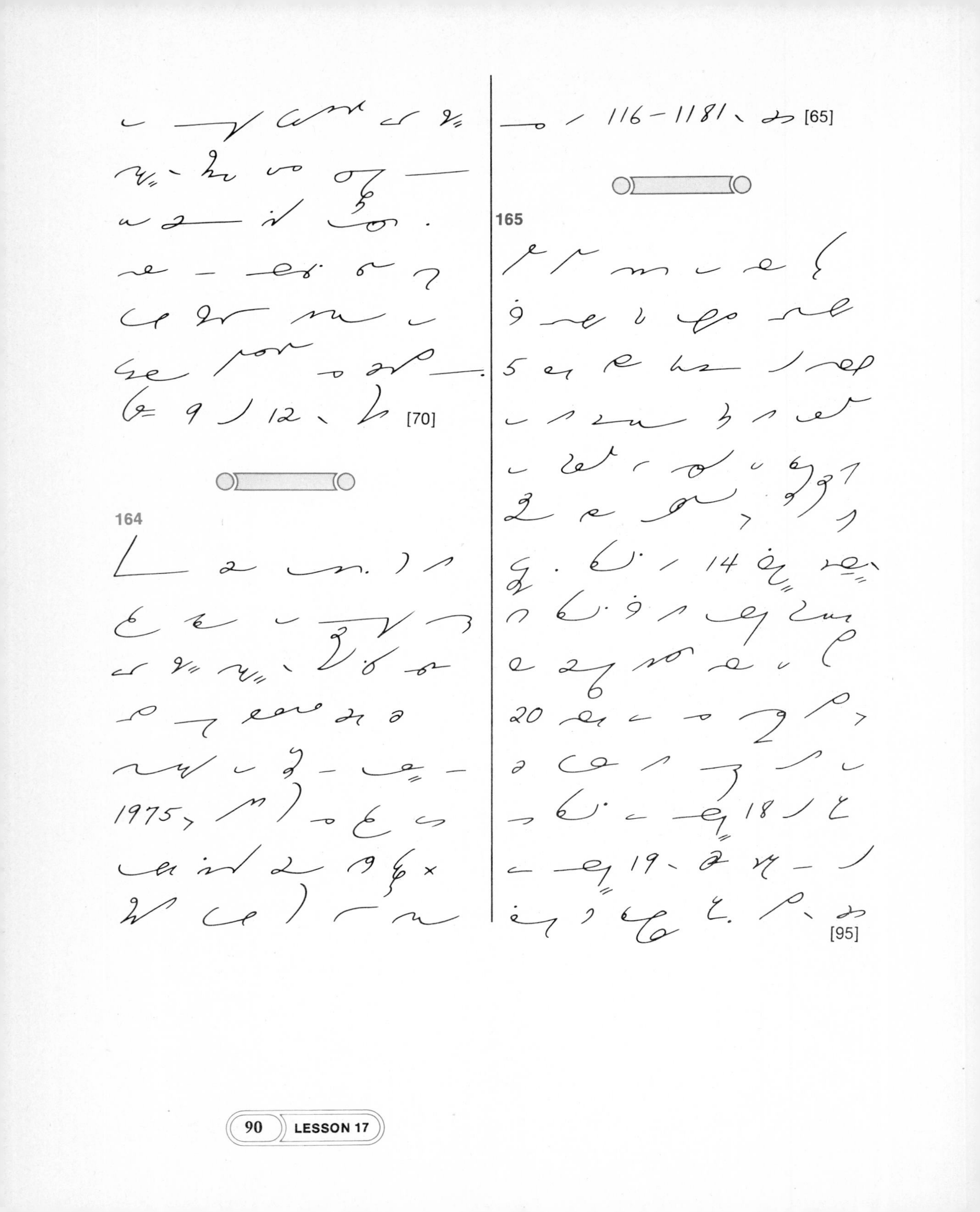

[70]

164

[65]

165

[95]

RECALL

Lesson 18 contains no new shorthand devices for you to learn. In this lesson you will find a Recall Chart and a Reading Practice that is interesting and informative.

166 Recall Chart

The following chart reviews all the brief forms of Chapter 3 as well as all the shorthand principles you studied in Chapters 1, 2, and 3. The chart contains 96 outlines. Can you read it in 9 minutes or less?

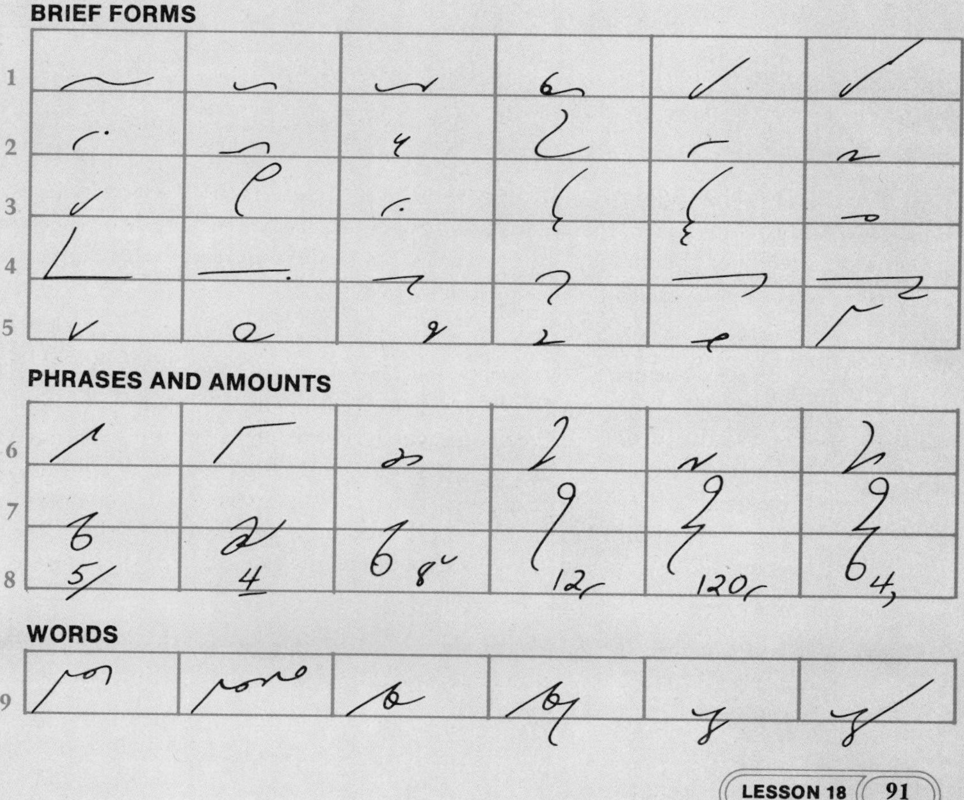

10						
11						
12						
13						
14						
15						
16						

Building Transcription Skills

167 Business Vocabulary Builder

adjacent Nearby; close to.
primary Of first importance.
routine Ordinary.

Reading Practice

Reading Scoreboard One of the factors in measuring shorthand growth is the rate at which you can read shorthand. Here is an opportunity for you to measure your reading speed on the *first reading* of the material in Lesson 18. The following table will help you determine how rapidly you can read shorthand.

Lesson 18 contains 576 words

If you read Lesson 18 in **22 minutes** your reading rate is **26 words a minute**
If you read Lesson 18 in **24 minutes** your reading rate is **24 words a minute**
If you read Lesson 18 in **28 minutes** your reading rate is **21 words a minute**
If you read Lesson 18 in **32 minutes** your reading rate is **18 words a minute**
If you read Lesson 18 in **36 minutes** your reading rate is **16 words a minute**
If you read Lesson 18 in **41 minutes** your reading rate is **14 words a minute**

If you can read Lesson 18 through the first time in less than 22 minutes, you are doing well indeed. If you take considerably longer than 41 minutes, here are some questions you should ask yourself:

- **1** Am I spelling each outline I cannot read immediately?
- **2** Am I spending too much time deciphering an outline that I cannot read even after spelling it?
- **3** Should I perhaps reread the directions for reading shorthand on page 11?

After you have determined your reading rate, make a record of it in some convenient place. You can then watch your reading rate grow as you time yourself on the Reading Scoreboards in later lessons.

168 Marketing

13 19

On occasion,

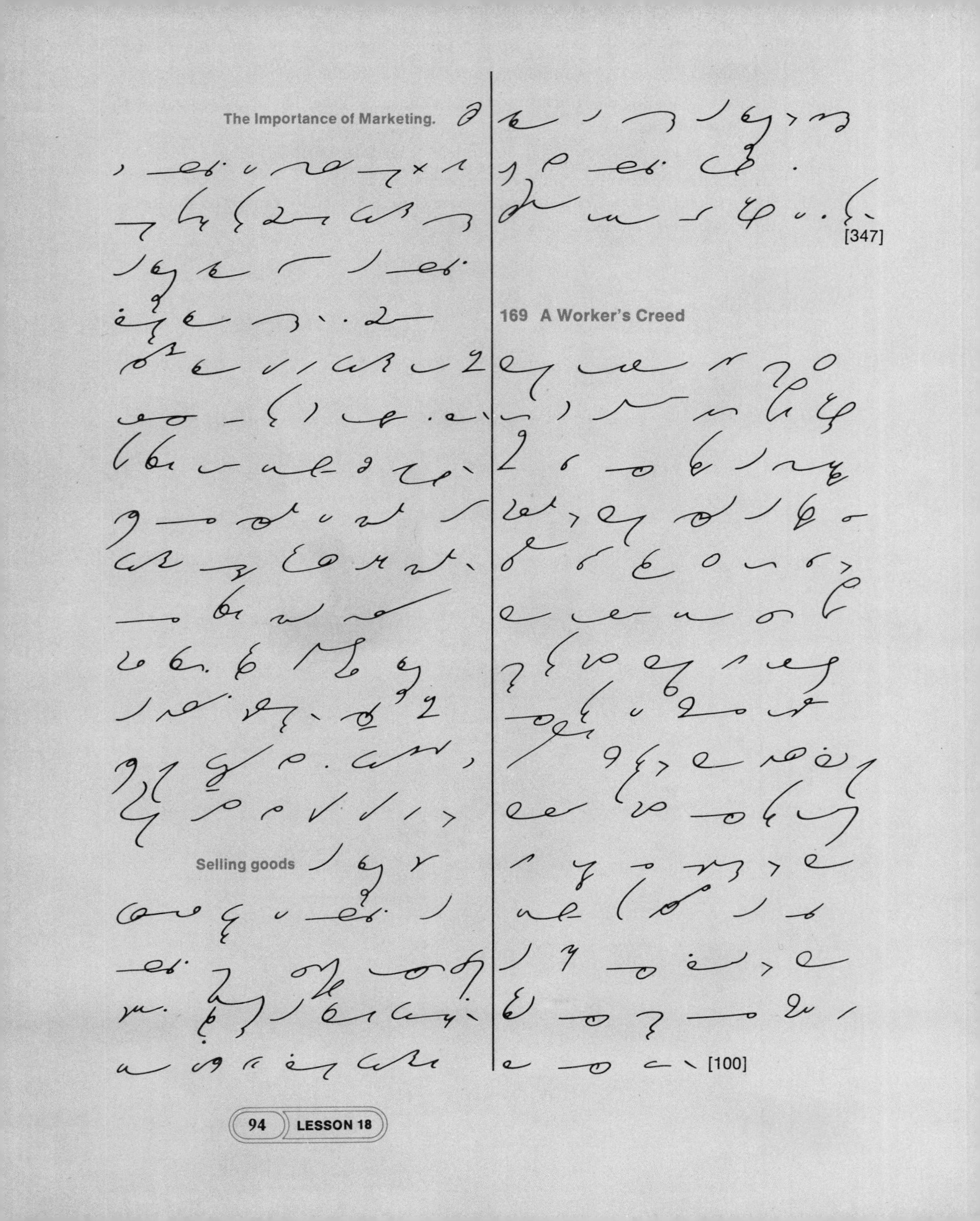

The Importance of Marketing.

Selling goods

[347]

169 A Worker's Creed

[100]

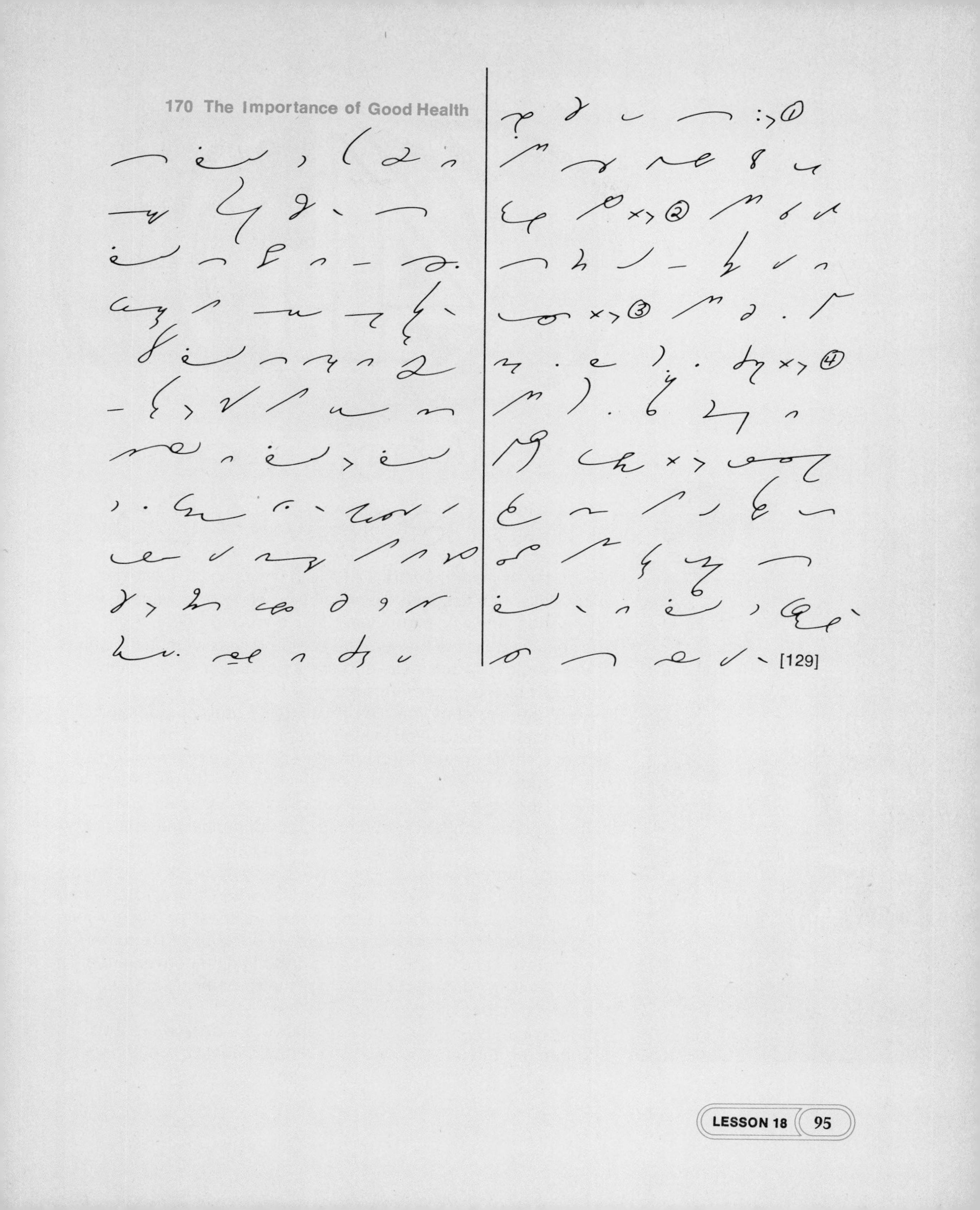

170 The Importance of Good Health

[129]

CHAPTER

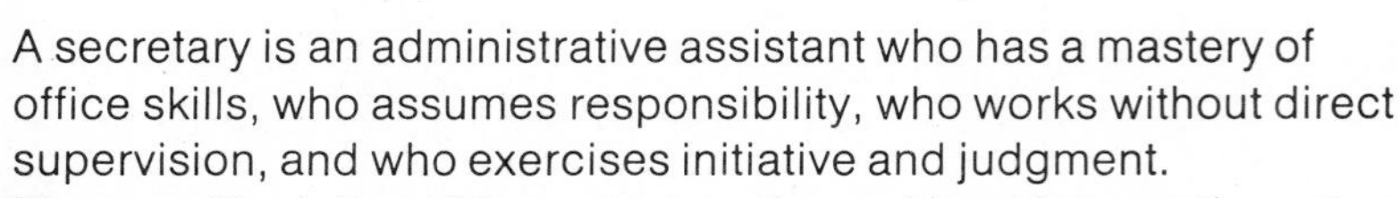

What Does the Secretary Do?

A secretary is an administrative assistant who has a mastery of office skills, who assumes responsibility, who works without direct supervision, and who exercises initiative and judgment.

The specific duties of the secretary depend largely upon the nature of the employer's business and the amount of responsibility delegated by the immediate superior.

Usually the secretary handles a variety of business details independently, in addition to stenographic duties. One important aspect of the secretary's job is to represent the employer to the public and to other business people. And it is the secretary who relieves the boss of routine duties, supervises clerical workers, handles correspondence, and records confidential material.

The secretary receives, sorts, and opens mail directed to the employer. Letters marked "Personal" may or may not be opened, depending upon the employer's instructions. The secretary, being the one most familiar with the employer's business practices, may answer much of the mail without supervision. Mail that requires the employer's personal attention is classified for convenience. The boss may either dictate replies or ask the secretary to answer the correspondence according to instructions.

In many instances, the secretary answers inquiries, obtains information, and refers calls to other departments or personnel without disturbing the employer. Many secretaries act as "buffers" by screening all visitors and callers before scheduling appointments. The secretary may take notes at meetings, office conferences, or large meetings. The secretary may also transcribe the reports of the meeting and handle the distribution of copies. In some offices, the secretary supervises other office personnel and assigns work to typists and other clerical workers.

The secretary must be thoroughly familiar with the filing system in order to retrieve information at a moment's notice. The secretary must be able to make travel arrangements and reservations for the employer's business trips and schedule luncheon or dinner dates with clients or customers. The secretary may also be required to take care of the employer's personal business files, business bank account, and business income tax records.

Other duties depend upon the secretary's specialization. A social secretary, for example, would be responsible for arranging social functions, sending invitations, keeping the employer informed of social activities, and answering personal correspondence. A legal secretary should know and be able to use legal terminology. A technical secretary employed by engineers, chemists, or biologists should understand scientific terms and be able to transcribe highly technical dictation.

Although a secretary's duties vary widely from position to position, the mark of every superior secretary is the ability to assume responsibility and do high-quality work without direct supervision.

Principles

171 Brief Forms

Here is another group of brief forms—only six this time.

Present, part, advertise, Ms., immediate, opportunity.

172 U

The sound of *u*, as in *use*, is represented by

Spell: u-s, use

Use, few, review, unit, united, unique, human.

173 Word Ending -ment

The word ending *-ment* is represented by *m*.

Spell: p-a-ment, payment

Payment, management, arrangement, appointment, shipment.
Advertisement, department, assignment, element.

▶ Notice that in *assignment*, *m* for *ment* is joined to the *n* with a jog.

174 Word Ending -tial (-cial)

The word ending *-tial* is represented by *ish*.

Spell: *e-n-e-shul, initial*

Initial, initialed, financial, social, special, especially.

Building Transcription Skills

175 SPELLING When you look at the letter on page 100, you get a favorable impression. The letter is nicely placed; the right-hand margin is even; the date, inside address, and closing are all in their proper places. When you read the letter casually, it makes good sense and apparently represents what the dictator said.

But that favorable impression vanishes when you read the letter carefully. In fact, the dictator will never sign it because it contains several misspelled words. No executive will knowingly sign a letter that contains a misspelled word!

If you are to succeed as a stenographer or secretary, your letters must not only be accurate transcripts of what your employer dictated but they must also be free of spelling errors. A stenographer or secretary who regularly submits letters for signature that contain spelling errors will not long be welcome in a business office.

To make sure that you will be able to spell correctly when you have completed your shorthand course, you will from this point on give special attention to spelling in each Reading Practice.

As you read the Reading Practice, you will occasionally find shorthand outlines printed in a second color. These outlines represent words that transcribers often misspell. When you encounter such an outline, finish reading the sentence in which it occurs; then glance at the margin, where you will find the word in type, properly syllabicated.

Spell the word aloud if possible, pausing slightly after each word division. (The word divisions indicated are those given in *Webster's New Collegiate Dictionary*.)

---

176 Business Vocabulary Builder

board of trustees A group of people who direct a company's work.

unique Unusual; one of a kind.

prospective Likely to become.

LUNN

LUNN INCORPORATED
245 PARK AVENUE
NEW YORK, NEW YORK 10035

CHARLOTTE
COLUMBUS
DENVER
DUBUQUE
ELGIN
FLINT
FT. WAYNE
FT. WORTH
HUNTINGTON
LEXINGTON
MADISON
MEMPHIS
NASHVILLE
NORFOLK
PORTLAND
ST. LOUIS
ST. PAUL
SANTA FE
SAVANNAH
SEATTLE
TEXARKANA
TUCSON
TULSA
WICHITA

September 22, 19--

Mr. John Case
2001 Huron Street
Seattle, Washington 98117

Dear Mr. Case:

It is a comfortible feeling to know that the heating system in your home does not have to depend on the elements. Snow and ice cannot leave you shiverring when you heat with gas. It travels under ground.

The dependability of gas is only one of its many virtues. A gas heating system costs less to instal and less to operate. It needs lots less serviceing, and it lasts longer. It has no odor and makes no filmy deposits that cause extra work.

No wonder more than 400,000 users of other feuls changed to gas last year.

Why not let us show you how easy it is to instal gas heat in your home.

Yours truely,

Thomas A. Frost
Sales Manager

TAF:re

Can you find all the errors in this letter?

Reading Practice

177 Brief-Form Letter

ap·pli·cants

di·rec·tor

as·sign·ment

de·sir·able

30

10

27

5 7

[152]

178

im·me·di·ate·ly

20 25

valu·able

through

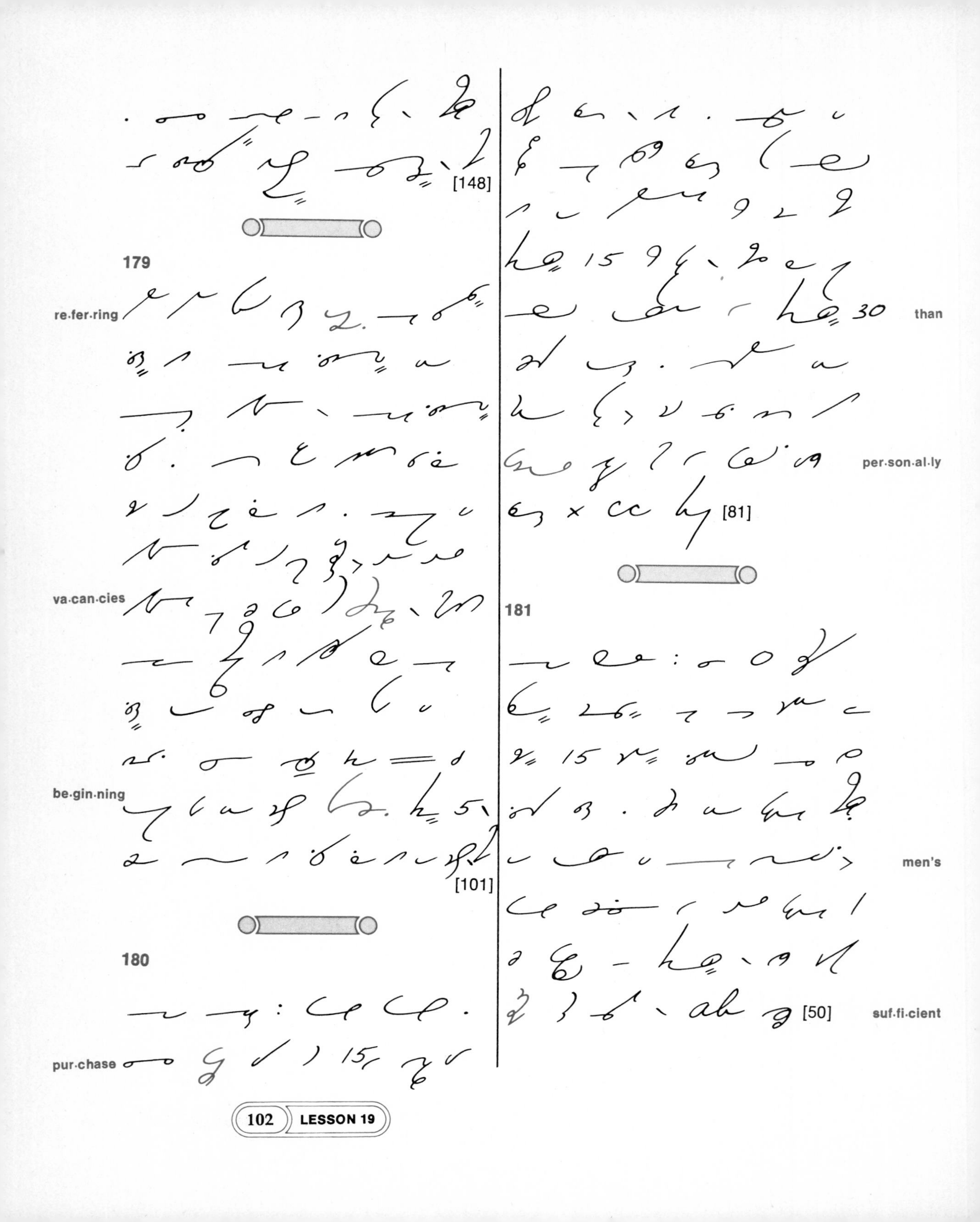

[148]

179

re·fer·ring

va·can·cies

be·gin·ning

[101]

180

pur·chase

than

per·son·al·ly

[81]

181

men's

suf·fi·cient

[50]

182

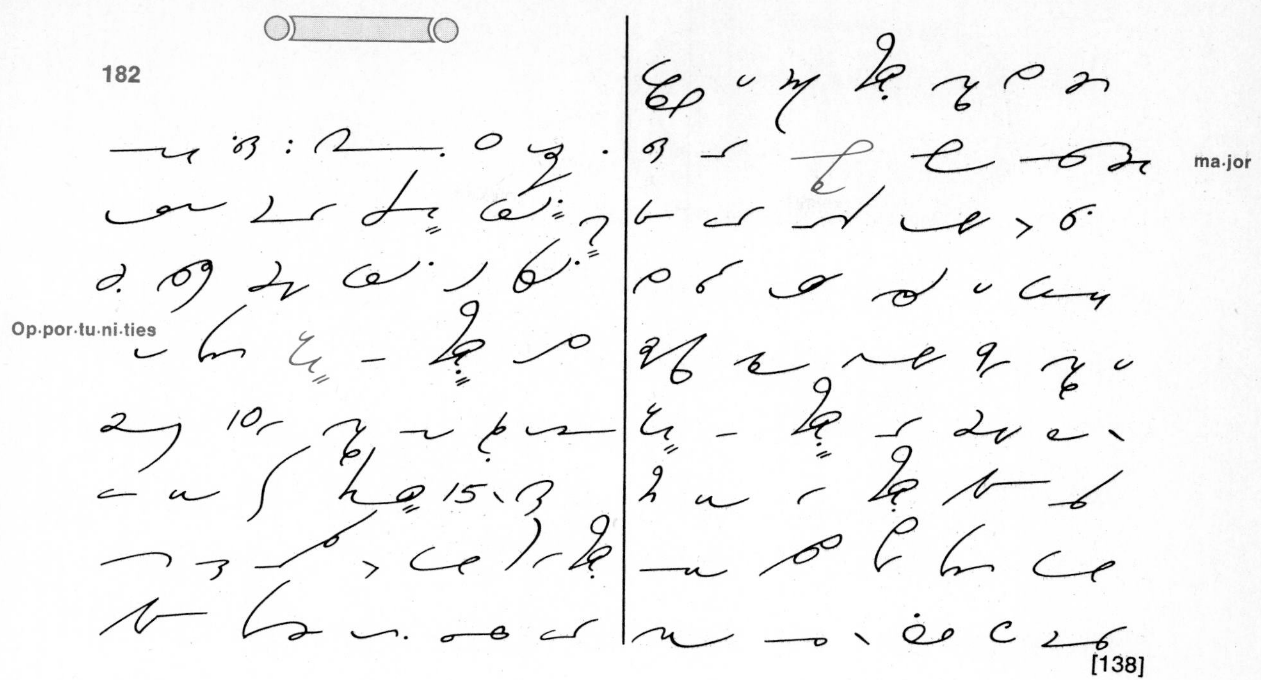

UP-AND-DOWN CHECKLIST *Do you always write the following strokes* upward?

■ 1 and   their (there)   ■ 2 it-at   would

Do you always write the following strokes downward?

■ 1 is-his   for   have   ■ 2 she   which

Principles

183 Ow

The sound of *ow*, as in *now*, is written [shorthand outline]

Spell: n-ow, now

[shorthand outlines]

Now, how, house, found, account, amount, announce, south.

184 Word Ending -ther

The word ending *-ther* is represented by *ith*.

Spell: oo-ther, other

[shorthand outlines]

Other, another, whether, mother, gathered, either, leather, bothered.

185 Word Beginning Con-

The word beginning *con-* is represented by *k*.

Spell: con-s-e-r-n, concern

[shorthand outlines]

Concern, concrete, considerable, control, consisted, contract, connect.

186 Word Beginning Com-

The word beginning *com-* is also represented by *k*.

Spell: com-p-l-e-t, complete

Complete, compare, computer, combine, complain, compliment, committee.

Building Transcription Skills

187 Business Vocabulary Builder

compliment *(verb)* To express a favorable comment.

comptrollers Persons who supervise the financial affairs of a business.

utilized Made use of.

comprehensive Covering completely or broadly.

Reading Practice

188 Brief-Form Review Letter

com·pli·ment

com·put·er

caught

comp·trol·lers

fi·nan·cial

[109]

189

re·ceived

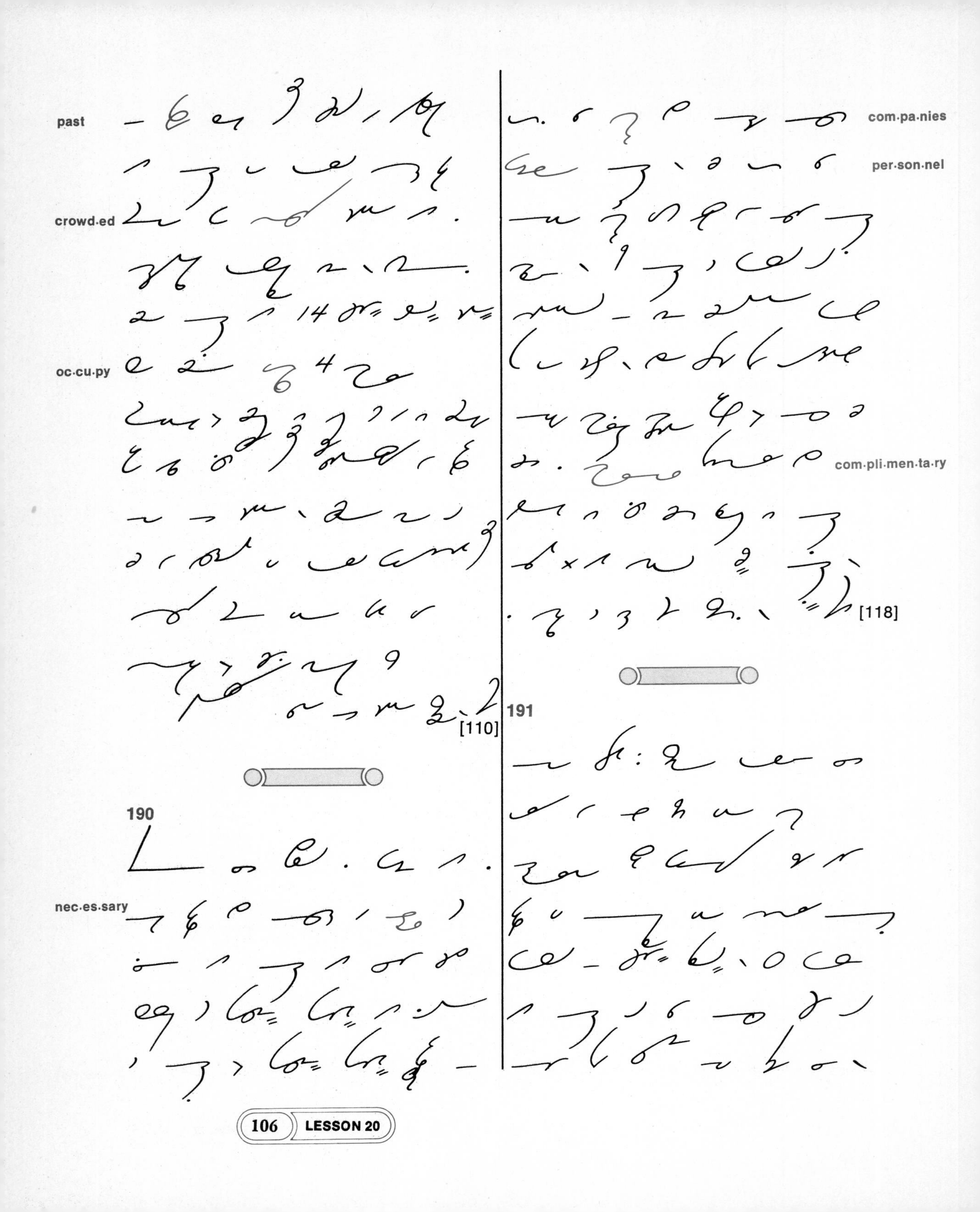

past

crowd·ed

oc·cu·py

[110]

190

nec·es·sary

com·pa·nies

per·son·nel

com·pli·men·ta·ry

[118]

191

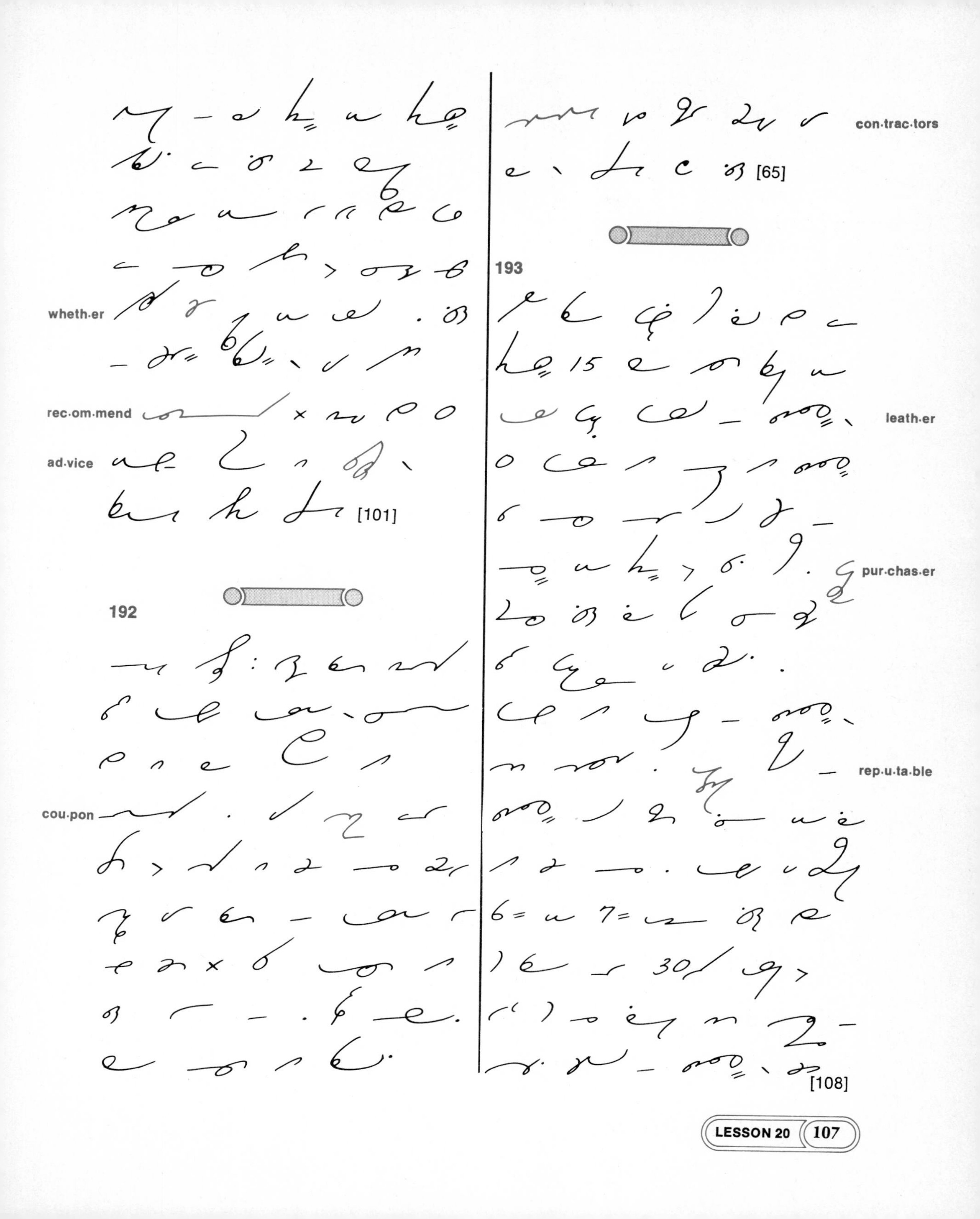

whether

recommend

advice

[101]

192

coupon

contractors

[65]

193

leather

purchaser

reputable

[108]

Principles

194 Brief Forms

Advantage, suggest, several, out, ever-every, very.

195 Ten

By rounding off the angle between *t-n*, we obtain the fluent *ten* blend.

Ten

Spell: a-ten-d, attend; k-o-ten, cotton

Attend, attention, written, tennis, remittance, stand.
Standard, assistance, bulletin, cotton, button, tonight.

196 Den

The stroke that represents *ten* also represents *d-n*.

Spell: e-v-den-t, evident

Evident, student, confident, president, deny, sudden, dentist, danger, dinner.

197 Tain

The stroke that represents *t-n, d-n* also represents *-tain.*

Spell: o-b-tain, obtain

Obtain, maintain, attain, obtainable, container, certain.

Building Transcription Skills

198 Business Vocabulary Builder

remittance Money sent to someone.

creditors Persons to whom money is owed.

browse To look over casually.

reproduced Made a copy of.

Reading and Writing Practice

199 Brief-Form Letter

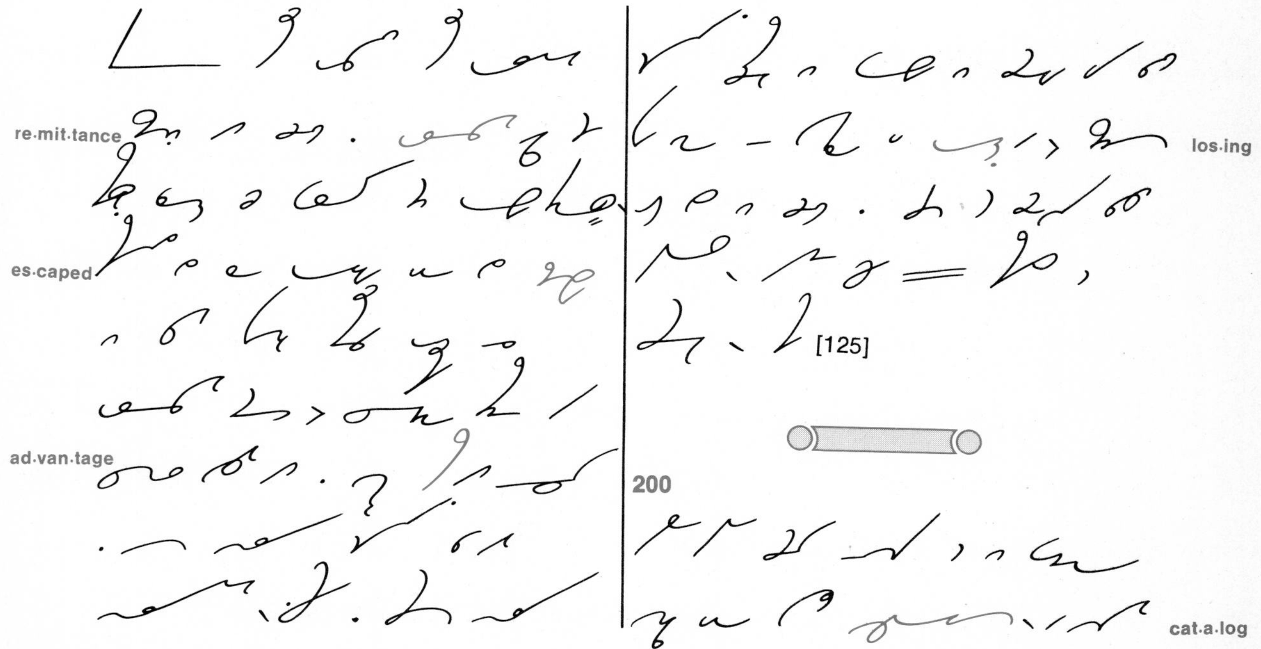

browse

women's

equipment

confident

[147]

201

copies

[130]

202

assistance

approval

assistant

salary

than

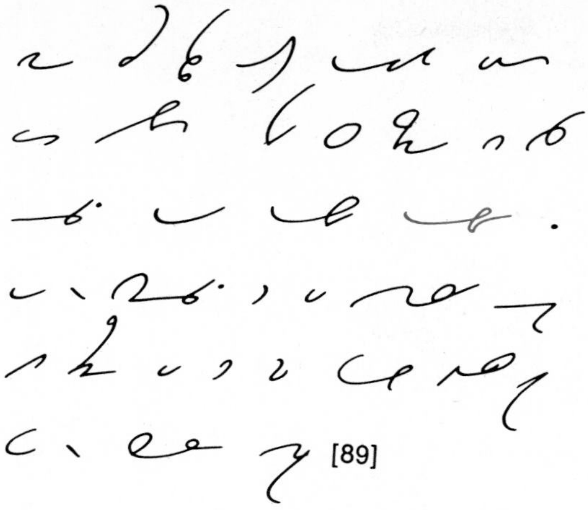

[89]

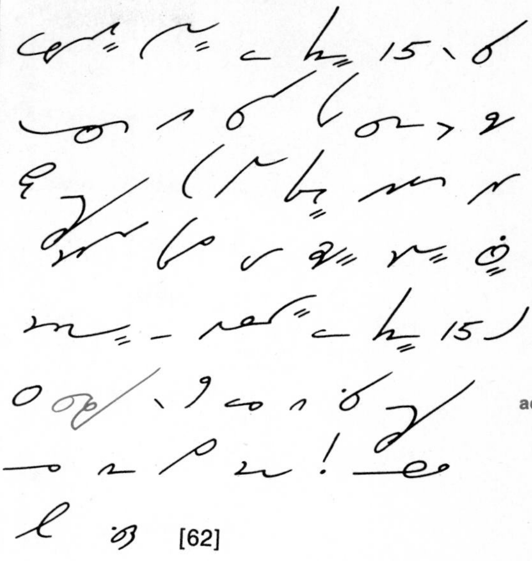

203

ac·cept·ed

[62]

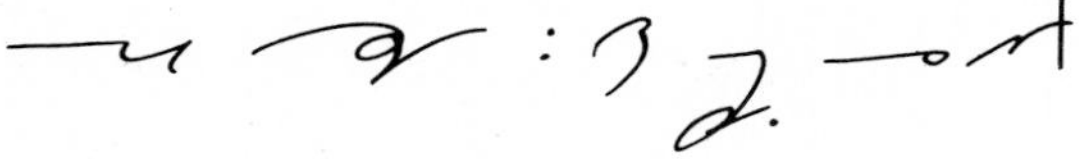

STUDY-HABIT CHECKLIST *No doubt as a conscientious student you do your home assignments faithfully. Do you, however, derive the greatest benefit from the time you devote to practice?*

- *You do* if you practice in a quiet place that enables you to concentrate.
- *You don't* if you practice with one eye on the television and the other on your practice work!
- *You do* if once you have started your assignment, you do not leave your desk or table until you have completed it.
- *You don't* if you interrupt your practice from time to time to call a friend or raid the refrigerator!

Principles

204 Tem

By rounding off the angle between *t-m*, we obtain the fluent *tem* blend.

Tem

Compare: ten *tem*

Spell: tem-p-l, temple

Temple, temporary, system, tomorrow, estimate, customer, automobile.

205 Dem

The stroke that represents *tem* also represents *d-m*.

Spell: dem-a-end, demand

Demand, demonstrate, demonstration, damage, domestic, seldom, medium.

206 Business Abbreviations

Here are additional salutations and closings frequently used in business.

Dear Mr., Dear Mrs., Dear Ms., Dear Miss, Yours sincerely, Cordially yours.

Principles

220 Brief Forms

After this group, you have only four more groups to learn.

Time, acknowledge, general, question, organize, over.*

*The outline for *over* is written above the following character. It is also used as a prefix form, as in:

Overdue, overcame, oversee, overdraw, overtake.

221 Def, Dif

By rounding off the angle between *d-f*, we obtain the fluent *def, dif* blend.

Def, Dif

Spell: def-n-e-t, definite

Definite, definitely, defeat, defend, different, differences.

222 Div, Dev

The stroke that represents *def, dif* also represents *div* and *dev*.

Spell: div-ī-d, divide

Divide, division, dividend, devised, develop, devote, devoted.

223 **Ea, Ia**

The sound of *ea,* as in *create* and *piano,* is represented by a large circle with a dot placed within it.

Spell: k-r-eah-t, create

Create, piano, created, appreciate, appropriate, brilliant, area.

Building Transcription Skills

224 **to** *(preposition)* In the direction of (*To* is also used as the sign of the infinitive.)

SIMILAR-WORDS DRILL
to, too, two

I would like to *talk* to *you about this matter.*

too Also; more than enough.

I, too, *am free on that day.*
Harry has too *many irons in the fire.*

two One plus one.

James bought two *new suits.*

The word in this group on which many stenographers stumble is *too.* They carelessly transcribe *to.* Don't make that mistake.

---

225 **media** (*plural of* medium) Channels of communication.

Business Vocabulary Builder

contemplate Consider.

associate *(noun)* Partner; colleague.

merge To combine into one.

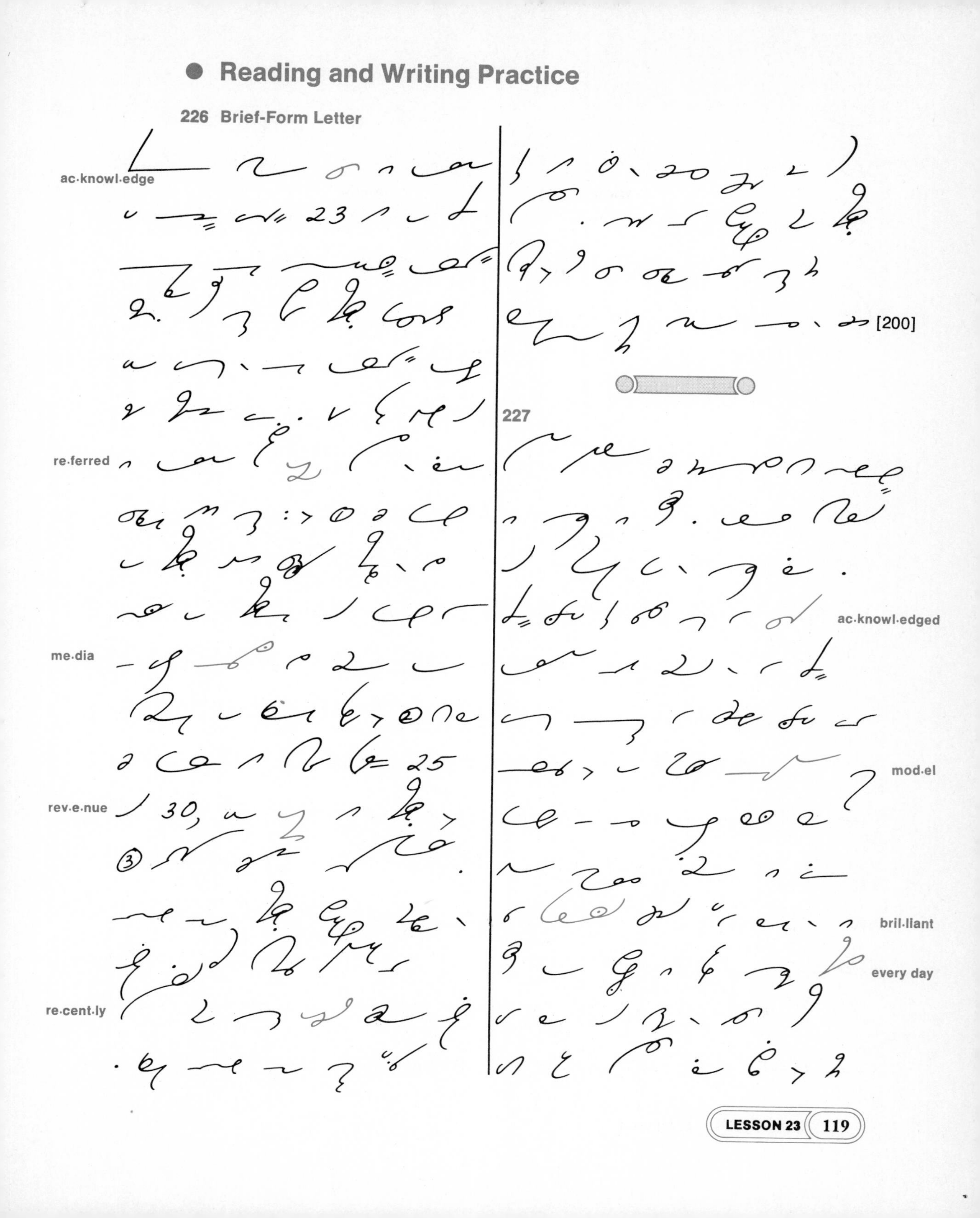

Reading and Writing Practice

226 Brief-Form Letter

ac·knowl·edge

re·ferred

me·dia

rev·e·nue

re·cent·ly

[200]

227

ac·knowl·edged

mod·el

bril·liant

every day

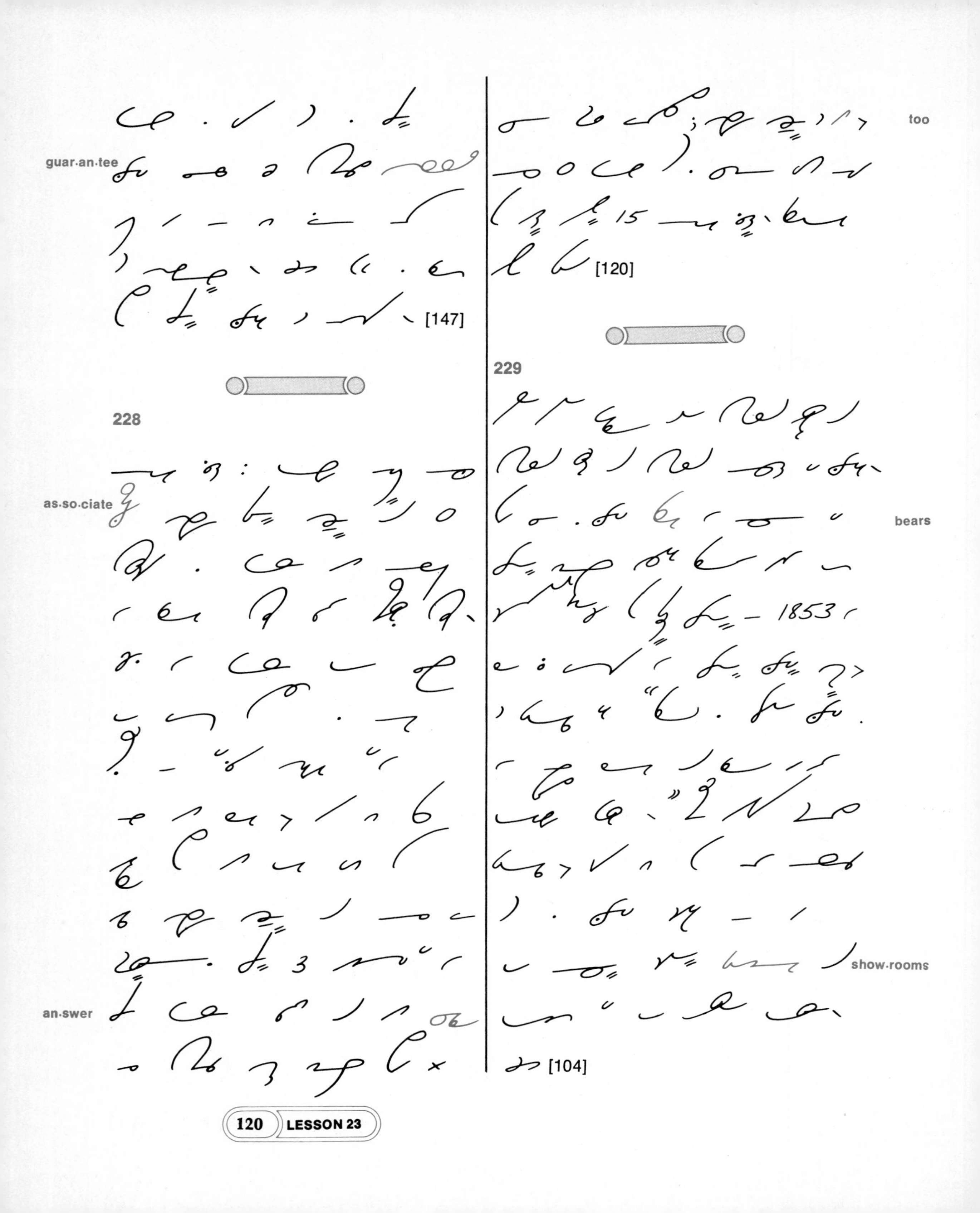

guar·an·tee

[147]

228

as·so·ci·ate

an·swer

too

[120]

229

bears

show·rooms

[104]

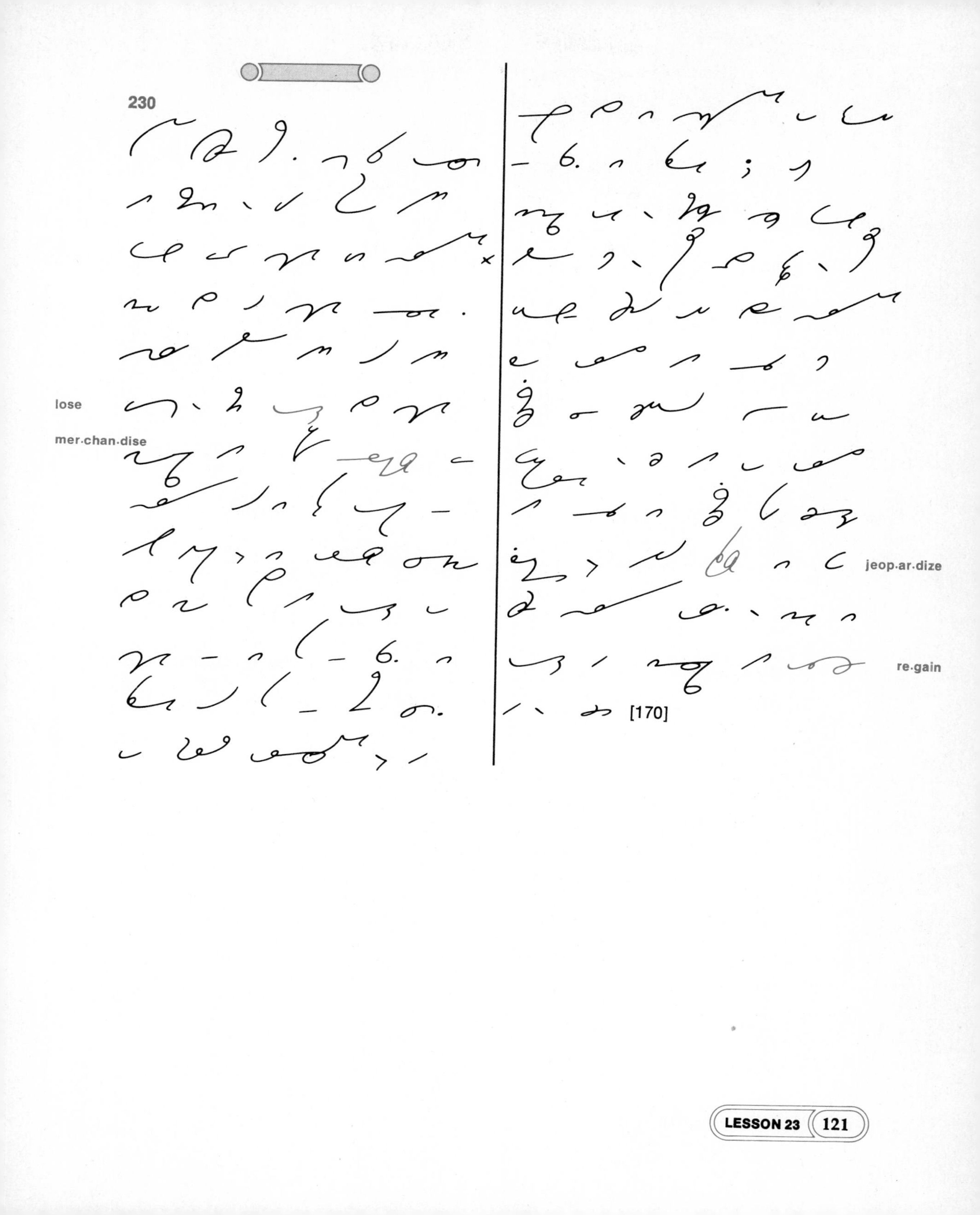

230

lose

mer·chan·dise

jeop·ar·dize

re·gain

[170]

RECALL

In Lesson 24 you will have no new shorthand devices to learn; you will have a little time to "digest" the devices that you studied in previous lessons.

231 Recall Chart

This chart contains all the brief forms in Chapter 4 and an illustration of many of the shorthand devices you studied in Chapters 1 through 4.

The chart contains 90 outlines. Can you read the entire chart in 7 minutes or less?

BRIEF FORMS

1

2

3

PHRASES

4

5

WORDS

6

7

8

9

10

11

12

13

14

15

Building Transcription Skills

232 Business Vocabulary Builder

commercials Advertisements broadcast on radio or television.

rejects Refuses to accept.

derive Receive.

sponsor One who pays the cost of a radio or television program in return for limited advertising time.

Reading and Writing Practice

233 Safe Driving

fas·ten

any·one

5. Do you always

ar·ea

de·fen·sive·ly

ap·proaches

[198]

com·mer·cials

lis·tens

ads

per·suade

234 Advertising

wheth·er

Who Pays for Advertising?

Truth in Advertising.

[404]

of·ten

praise

its

buys

spon·sor

bor·ing

CHAPTER

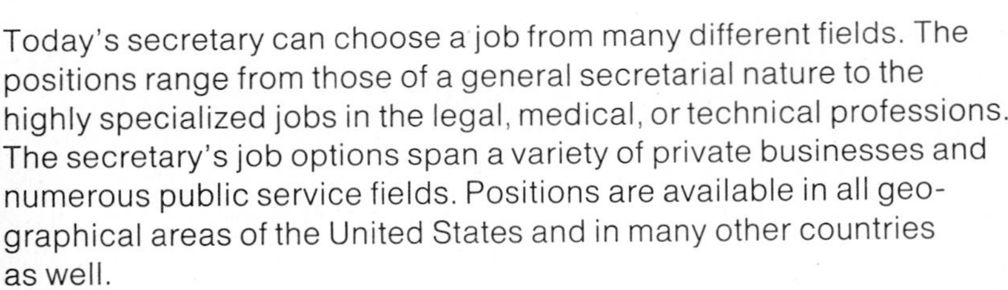

Secretarial Jobs
A Wide Range

Today's secretary can choose a job from many different fields. The positions range from those of a general secretarial nature to the highly specialized jobs in the legal, medical, or technical professions. The secretary's job options span a variety of private businesses and numerous public service fields. Positions are available in all geographical areas of the United States and in many other countries as well.

There are many fine opportunities for secretaries who are interested in developing their skills and increasing their knowledge in special areas. Let's take a look at just three of the many fascinating fields in which a secretary can become an active and indispensable participant.

Advertising and Public Relations

In the closely related fields of advertising and public relations, qualified secretaries are offered many challenging opportunities. In either field, the secretary must not only be able to work well under pressure but must also be able to communicate well with other people. The secretary must be people-oriented because employers in these fields deal constantly with clients, editors, account executives, freelance writers, artists, photographers, models, actors, and printers. The secretary must be able to work with details and be able to synchronize countless dates, facts,

figures, faces, names, and sources. In addition, the secretary must be able to both organize and follow through on many complicated, long-range campaigns and projects. Creativity is contagious, and the secretary in advertising and public relations has an enviable opportunity to cultivate special talents.

Government Service

The range of opportunities for the secretary in government is very wide. A civil service job may take the secretary to Washington, D.C. or to a number of other cities in the United States and other countries. The secretary may work for a senator, a representative, or a member of the President's staff. Or a position may be available with the Bureau of Indian Affairs, the Department of Housing and Urban Development, the Federal Bureau of Investigation, or with any number of other fascinating departments or agencies. The list is almost endless—and so is the challenge.

The Legal Field

The legal secretary may work for one attorney, for a large law firm, or for a corporation. The position may involve all types of legal work, or it may involve only one area, such as criminal, tax, or corporate law. The job may involve working for a judge whose court work is on the city, state, or national level. Regardless of the type of law office, the secretary must understand thoroughly the legal terminology and must be extremely accurate in all communication. The secretary may serve as receptionist, make appointments for clients, and notarize papers. Many times the job involves considerable responsibility in management of the business portion of the law practice. Of particular importance in every situation is the ability to keep close control of the employer's court calendar and the vital dates connected with each client's legal proceedings.

This is only a sampling of three of the many fields in which a secretary may work. Choose an area that matches your interests, and you are well on your way to an interesting, rewarding job in a secretarial field that fits you personally.

235 Brief Forms

*Difficult, envelope, progress, success, satisfy-satisfactory, state, request, wish, *under.*

*The outline for *under* is written above the following shorthand character. It is also used as a prefix form, as in:

Underneath, understudy, undertake, undergo, underground.

236 Cities and States

In your work as a stenographer and secretary, you will frequently have occasion to write geographical expressions. Here are a few important cities and states.

Cities

New York, Chicago, Boston, Philadelphia, Los Angeles, St. Louis.

States

Michigan, Illinois, Massachusetts, Pennsylvania, Missouri, California.

237 Useful Business Phrases

The following phrases are used so frequently in business that special forms have been provided for them. Study these phrases as you would study brief forms.

As soon as, as soon as possible, of course, to do, let us, I hope.

Building Transcription Skills

238 Business Vocabulary Builder

competitors Rivals.

reverse *(adjective)* Opposite.

invaluable Priceless.

Reading and Writing Practice

239 Brief-Form Letter

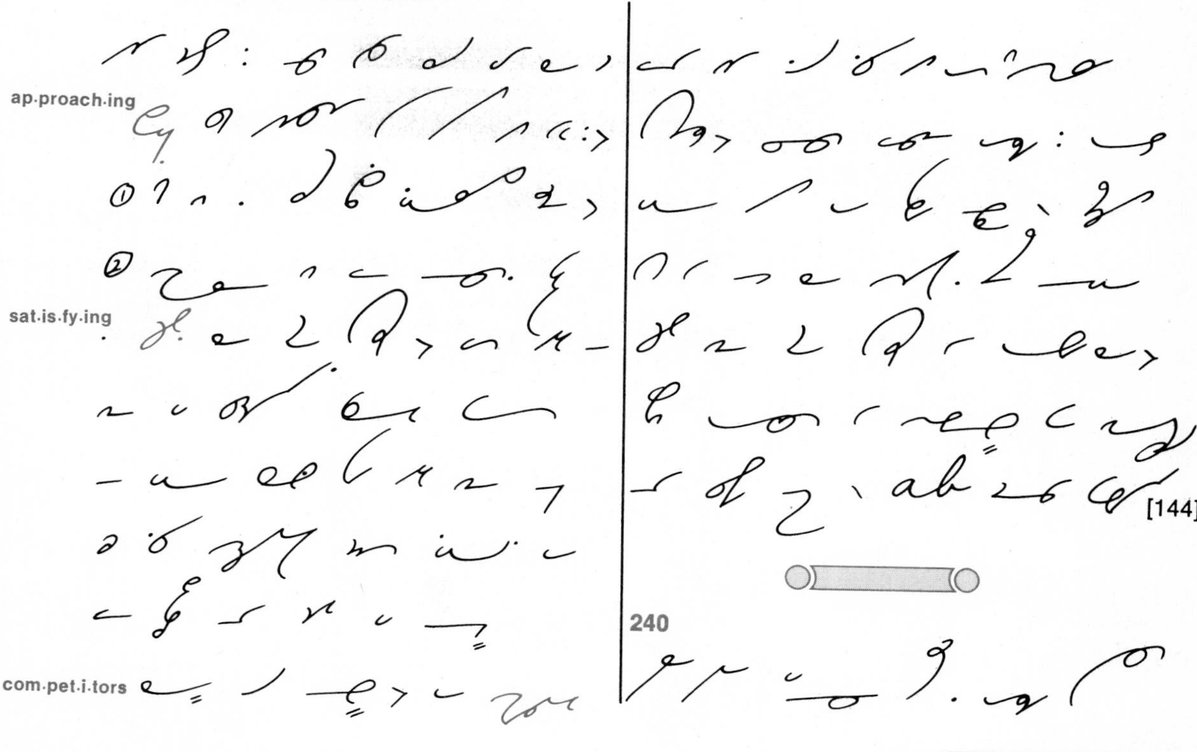

ad·van·tage

ap·pre·ci·ate

be·lieve

con·fi·dent

cus·tom·ers

im·me·di·ate·ly

co·op·er·a·tion

war·ran·ty

15

[173]

[153]

241

242

code

re·li·able

[138]

243

90 6 4

reg·is·tered

85

[118]

Principles

244 Long ī and a Following Vowel

Any vowel following long ī is represented by a small circle within a large circle.

Compare: signs [shorthand] *science* [shorthand]

Spell: s-īah-n-s, science

Trial, client, drier, prior, appliance, reliance, compliance.

245 Word Beginnings En-, Un-

The word beginnings *en-, un-* are represented by *n*.

En-

Spell: en-j-oi, enjoy

Enjoy, endeavor, encounter, engineering, encouragement, enroll, enrich.

Un-

Spell: un-p-a-d, unpaid

Unpaid, unpleasant, unless, unsatisfactory, unfair, unfilled, uncertain.

246 Useful Business Phrases

Here are additional frequently used phrases for which special forms have been provided. Study them as you would study brief forms.

More than, we hope, to us, let me, your order, you ordered.

Building Transcription Skills

247 Business Vocabulary Builder

office appliances Calculators, typewriters, duplicators, etc.

laymen Persons who are not expert in a particular field.

unbiased Fair.

precision Exactness.

Reading and Writing Practice

248 Brief-Form Review Letter

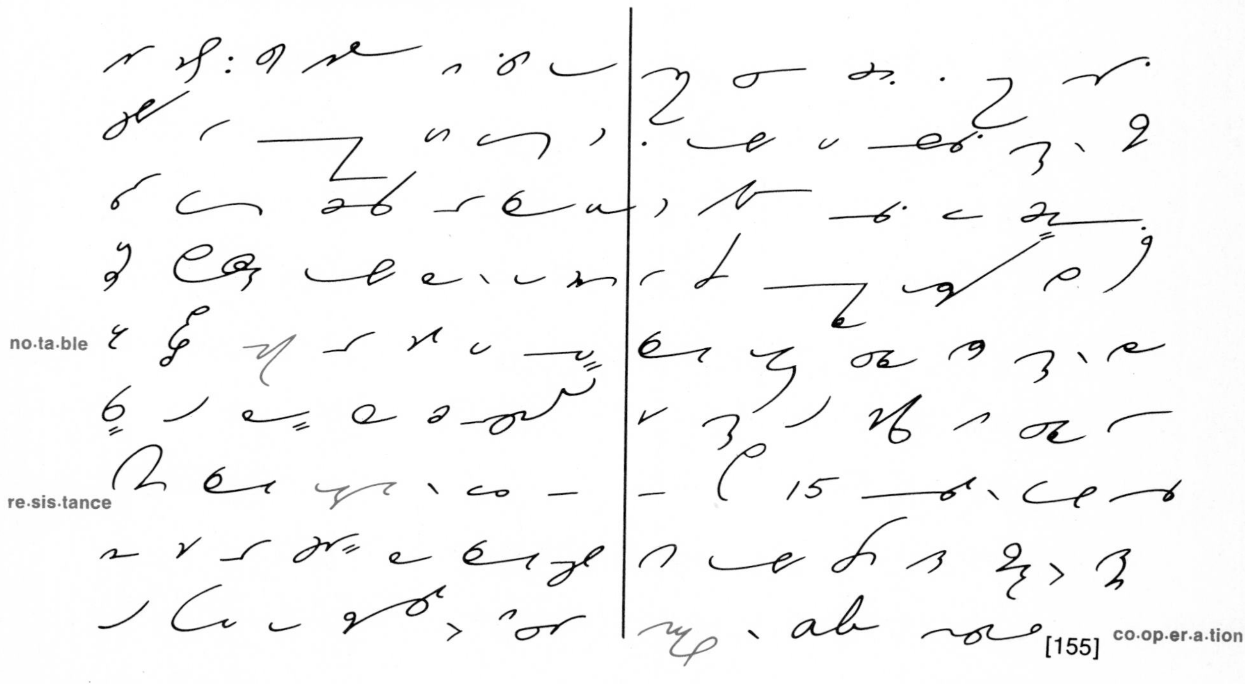

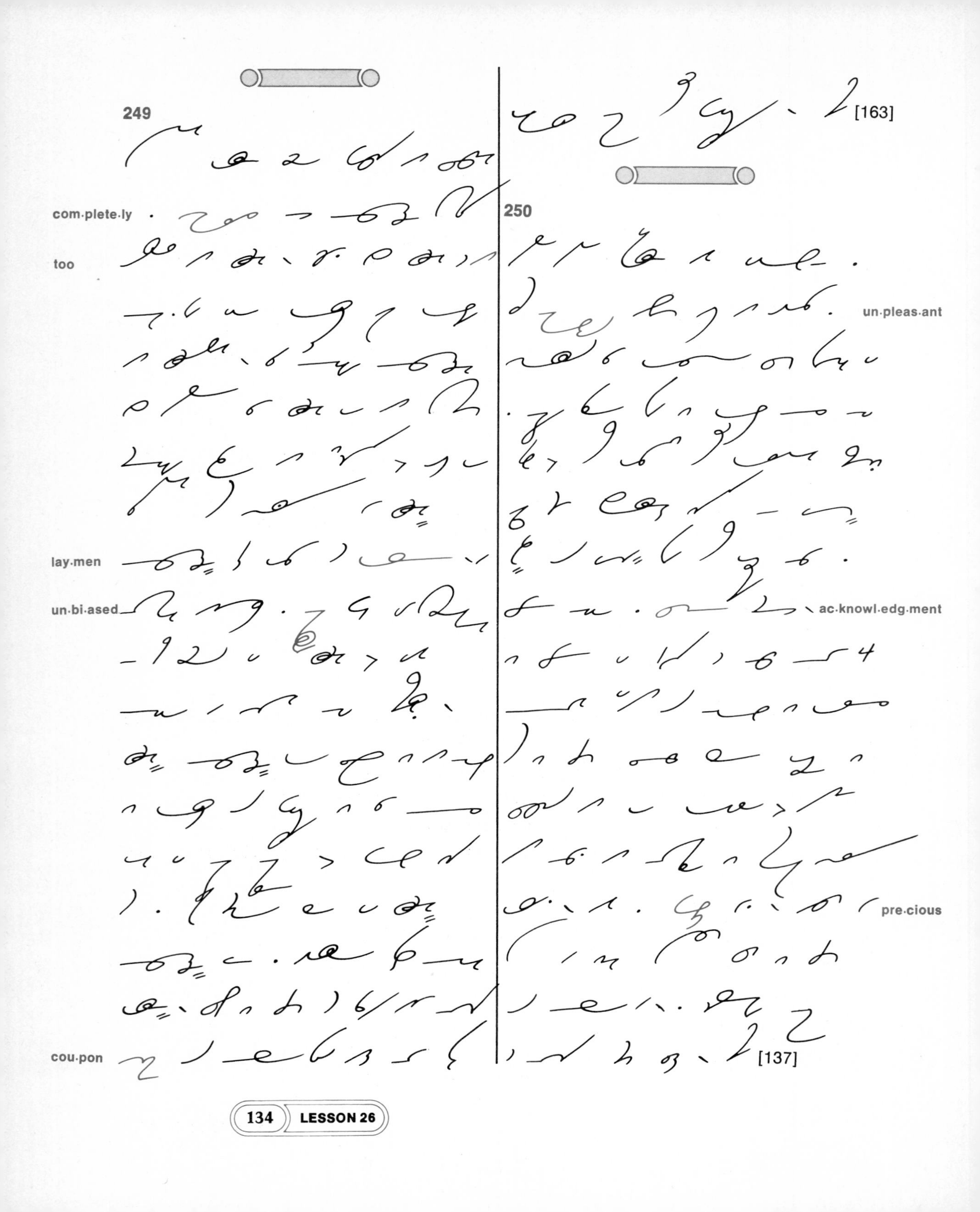

249

com·plete·ly

too

lay·men

un·bi·ased

cou·pon

[163]

250

un·pleas·ant

ac·knowl·edg·ment

pre·cious

[137]

251

en·gi·neer·ing

col·or

urge

proud

pre·ci·sion

view·ing

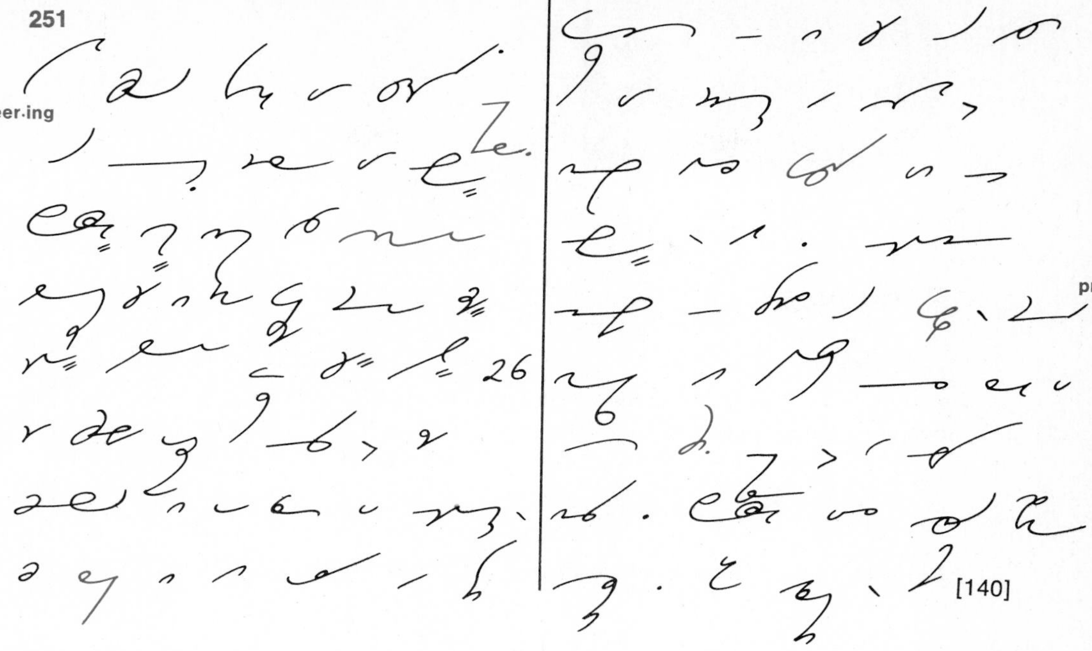

PROPORTION CHECKLIST *The writer who can read his shorthand notes fluently is the one who is careful of his proportions. In your shorthand writing, do you:*

- ■ 1 Make the large *a* circle huge; the small *e* circle tiny?
- ■ 2 Make the straight strokes very straight and the curves very deep?
- ■ 3 Make the *o* and *oo* hooks deep and narrow?
- ■ 4 Make short strokes, such as *t* and *n*, very short and long strokes, such as *ted* and *men*, very long?

Principles

252 Brief Forms

After you have learned the following group of nine brief forms, you will have only two more groups to go!

Particular, probable, regular, speak, idea, subject, regard, newspaper, opinion.

253 Ng

The sound of *ng*, as in *sing*, is written .

Compare: seen sing

Spell: s-e-ing, sing

Sing, sang, song, long, strong, bring, spring, single, young.

254 Ngk

The sound of *ngk*, as in *sink*, is written .

Compare: seem sink

Spell: s-e-ink, sink; oo-ink-l, uncle

Rank, frank, ink, bank, banquet, anxious, uncle, blank.

255 Omission of Vowel Preceding -tion

When *t, d, n,* or *m* is followed by *-ition, -ation,* the circle is omitted.

Edition, addition, condition, reputation, invitation, permission, donation, station, stationed.

Building Transcription Skills

256 Business Vocabulary Builder

enlightening Instructional.

medium A means of conveying information.

automation The state of being operated automatically.

Reading and Writing Practice

257 Brief-Form Letter

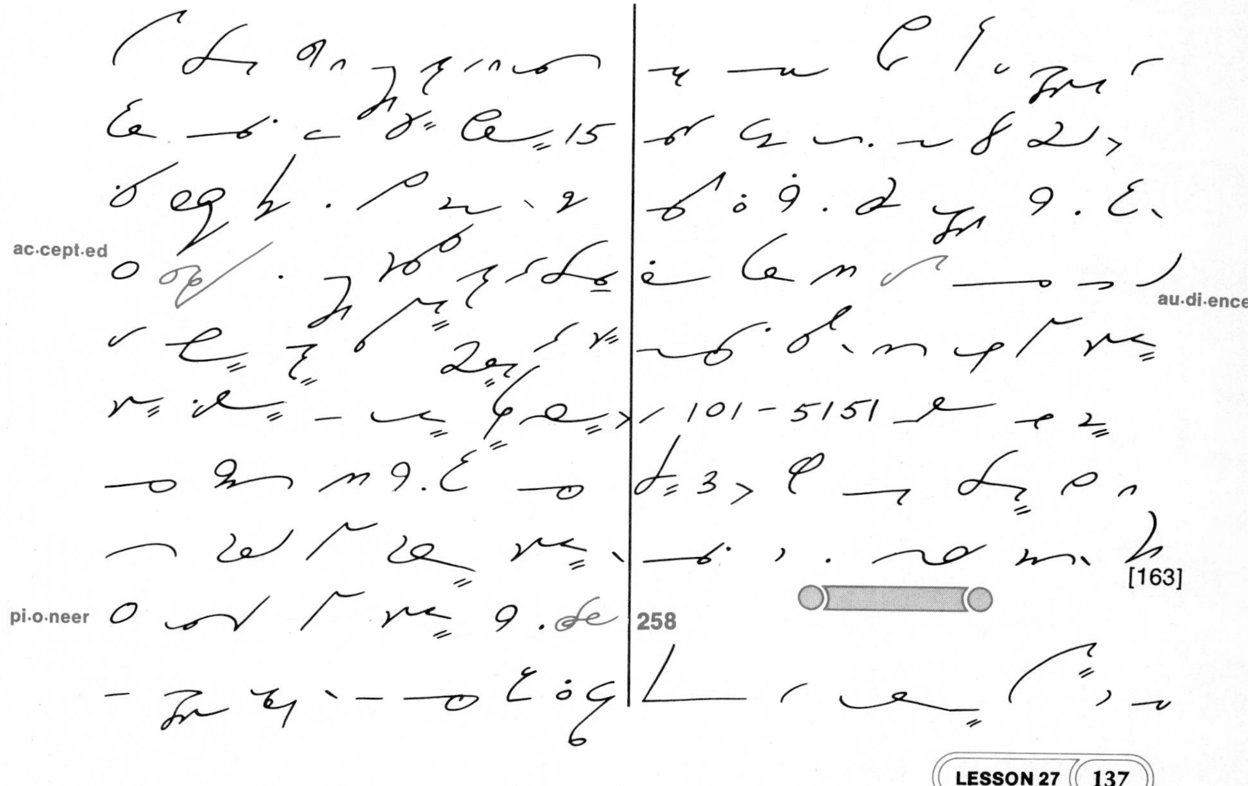

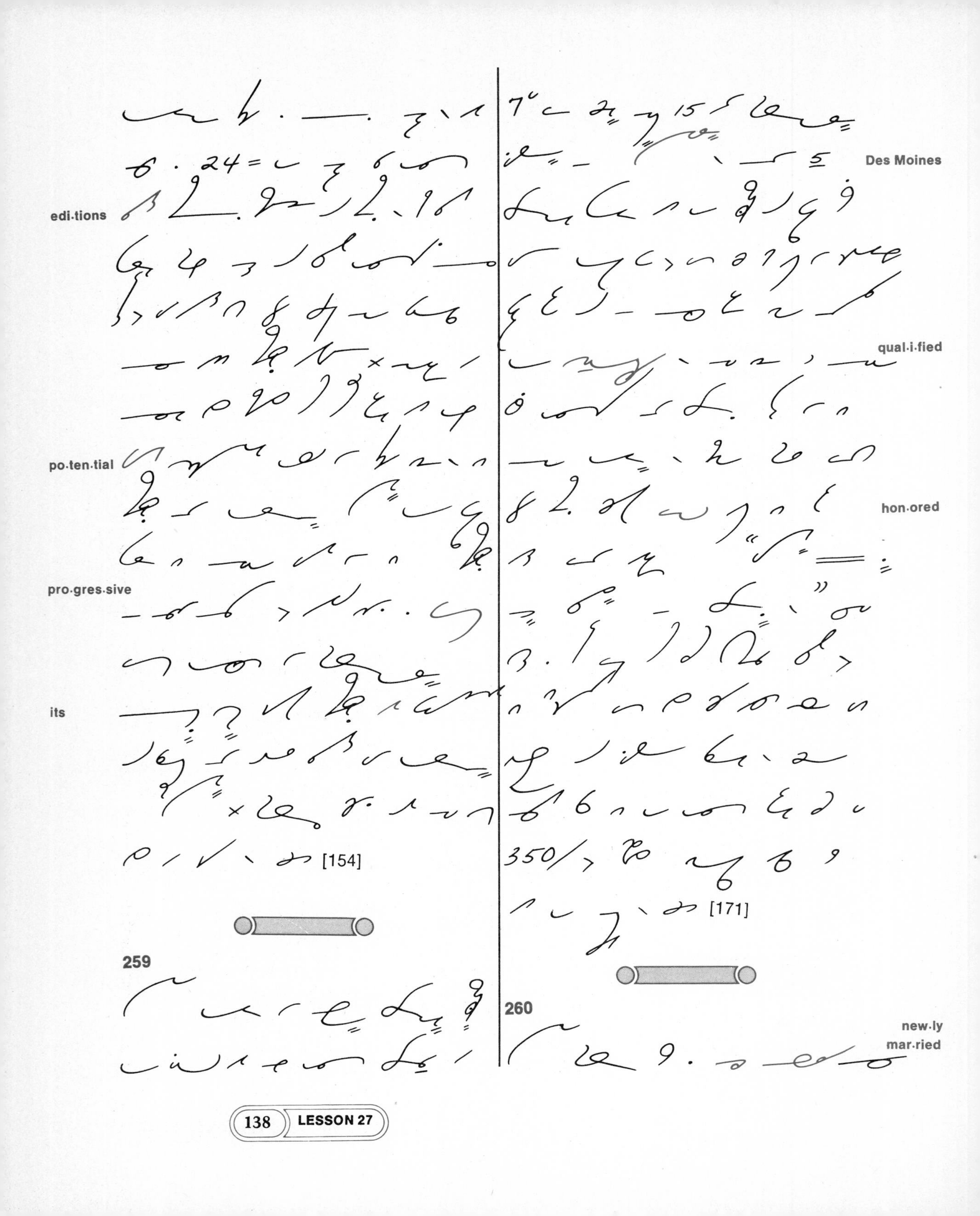

edi·tions

po·ten·tial

pro·gres·sive

its

[154]

259

Des Moines

qual·i·fied

hon·ored

[171]

260

new·ly mar·ried

pre·mi·um

ques·tion·naire

[130]

261

May·or

pre·vails

mi·nor

ma·jor

[111]

262

too

[72]

Principles

263 **Ah, Aw**

A dot is used for *a* in words beginning *ah* and *aw*.

Spell: a-h-e-d, ahead; a-oo-a, away

Ahead, away, await, awaited, awake, aware, award, awoke.

264 **X**

The letter x is usually represented by an *s* written with a slight backward slant.

Compare: miss — *mix*

fees — *fix*

Spell: m-e-x, mix

Box, tax, taxes, index, indexes, fix, fixes, relax, relaxes.

265 **Omission of Short U**

In the body of a word the sound of short *u*, as in *done*, is omitted:

Before N

Done, fun, run, begun, refund, luncheon.

Before M

Sum, summer, come, become, welcome, lumber.

Before a Straight Downstroke

Rush, such, touch, much, judge, budget, brushed.

Building Transcription Skills

266 Business Vocabulary Builder

peruse Examine; study.

budget The amount of money set aside for a particular purpose.

talents Abilities.

Reading and Writing Practice

267 Brief-Form Review Letter

your

han·dling

suf·fered

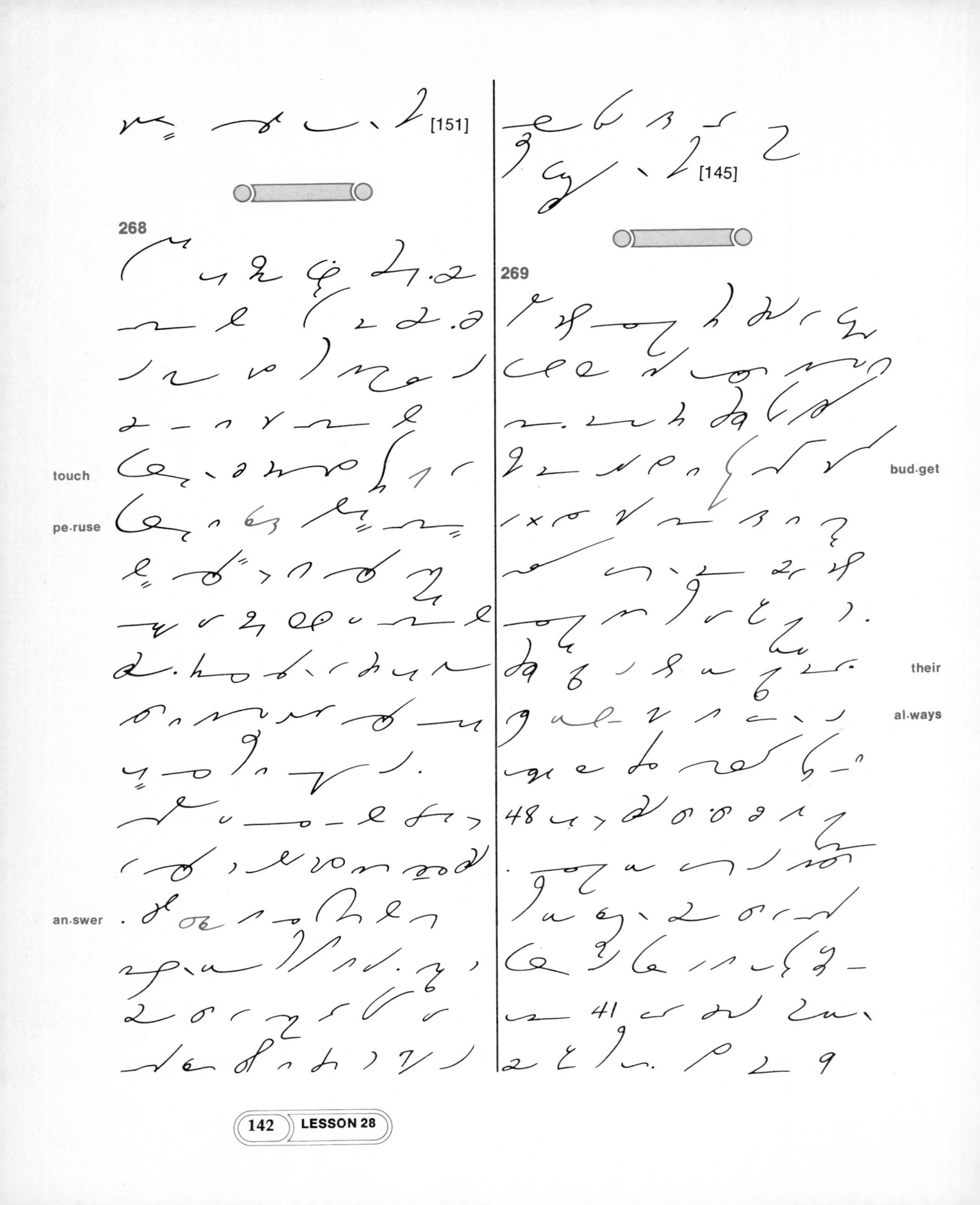

[151]

268

touch

pe·ruse

an·swer

[145]

269

bud·get

their

al·ways

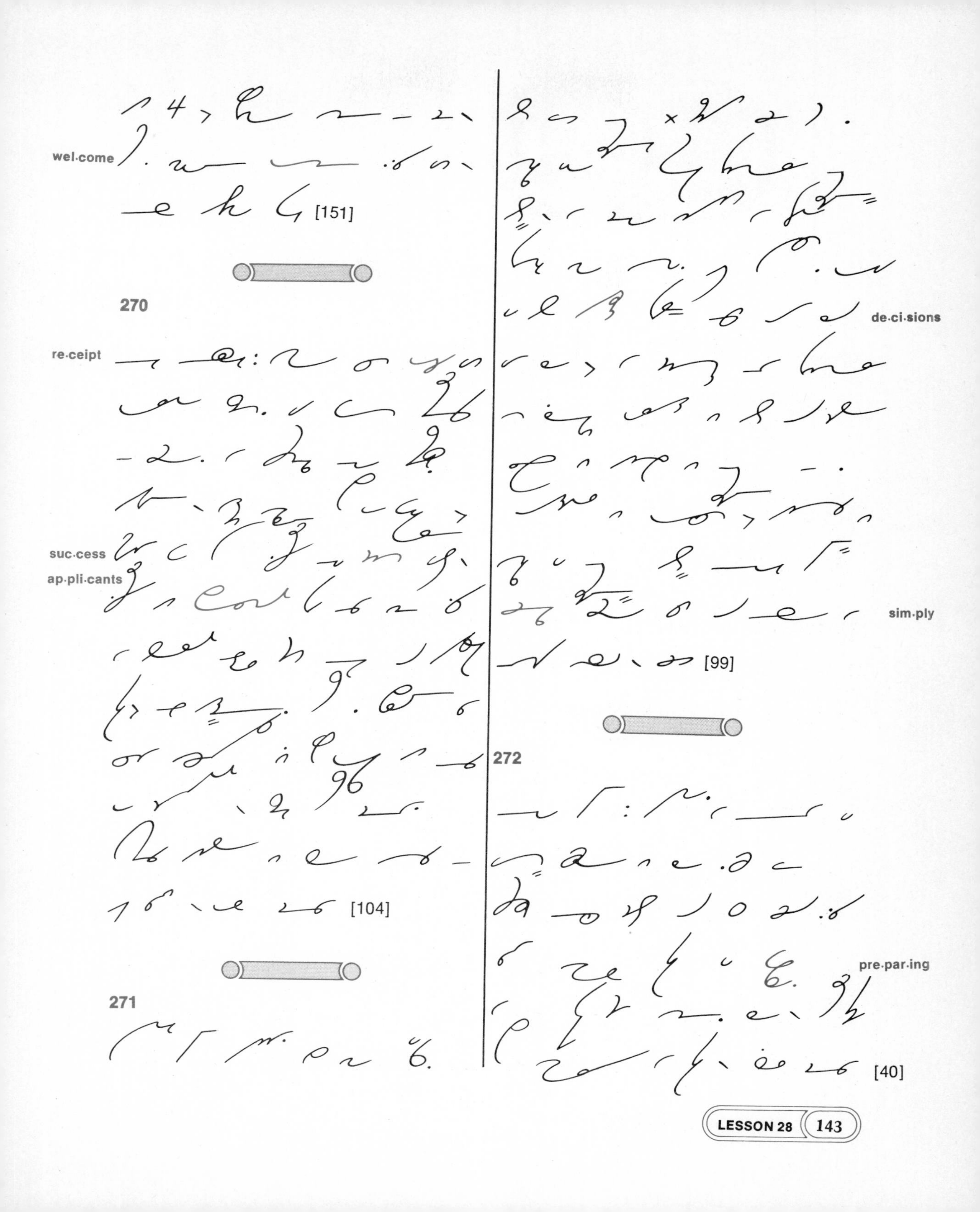

wel·come

[151]

270

re·ceipt

suc·cess

ap·pli·cants

[104]

271

de·ci·sions

sim·ply

[99]

272

pre·par·ing

[40]

Principles

273 Brief Forms

You have only one more group to learn after this one.

Responsible, worth, public, publish-publication, ordinary, experience, usual, world, recognize.

274 Word Beginning Ex-

The word beginning *ex-* is represented by *e-s.*

Spell: *ex-p-n-sez, expenses*

Expenses, expert, expectation, extremely, exactly, exceeded, extent, excuse.

275 Word Ending -ful

The word ending *-ful* is represented by *f.*

Spell: *k-a-r-ful, careful*

Careful, delightful, thoughtful, useful, successful, doubtful, helpful, helpfully, helpfulness.

276 Word Endings -cal, -cle

Word endings *-cal* and *-cle* (and the preceding vowel) are represented by a disjoined *k*.

Spell: t-e-k-n-ical, technical; a-r-t-ical, article

Technical, medical, logical, practical, economical, articles, physically.

Building Transcription Skills

277 SIMILAR-WORDS DRILL it's, its

it's Contraction for *it is.*

It's *his day to wash the dishes.*

its Possessive form of *it.*

Its *operating efficiency makes cooking on our stove a delight.*

---

278 Business Vocabulary Builder

maximum The most.

exceeded Went beyond.

franchises Rights granted to market a company's goods in a particular territory.

Reading and Writing Practice

279 Brief-Form Letter

it's

state's

men's

ex·pe·ri·enced

mon·ey's

its

[140]

280

per·son·nel

an·a·lyzes

their

cop·ies

[183]

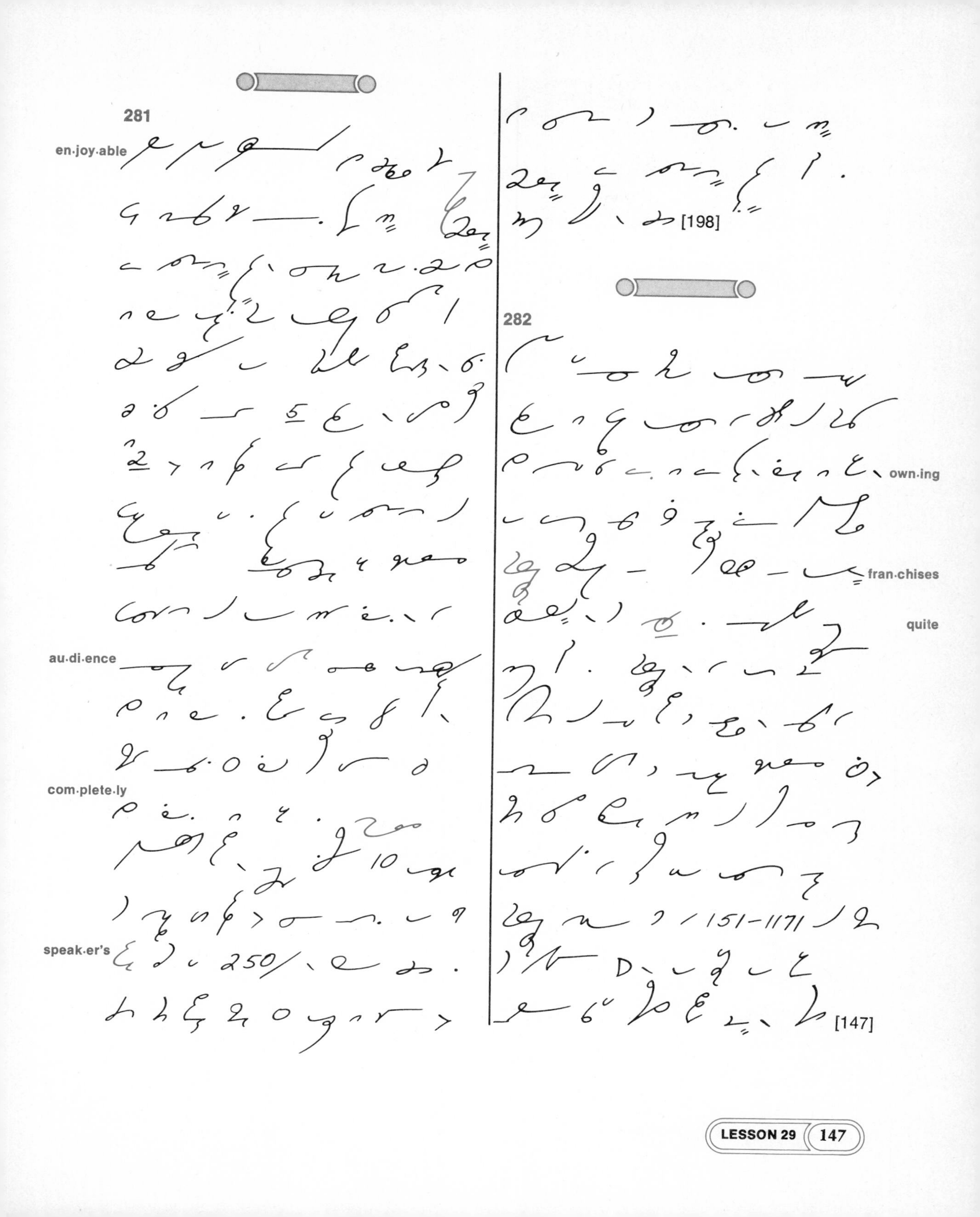

281

en·joy·able

au·di·ence

com·plete·ly

speak·er's

[198]

282

own·ing

fran·chises

quite

[147]

RECALL

After studying the new shorthand devices presented in Lessons 25 through 29, you have earned another "breather." Therefore, no new shorthand strokes or principles are presented in Lesson 30.

In this lesson you will find a Recall Chart and a Reading and Writing Practice.

283 Recall Chart

The following chart contains brief forms, phrasing principles, and word-building principles you studied in Chapter 5.

Can you read the entire chart in 6 minutes or less?

BRIEF FORMS AND DERIVATIVES

1						
2						
3						
4						
5						

PHRASES

6						
7						

WORDS

8

9

10

11

12

13

14

15

Building Transcription Skills

284 Business Vocabulary Builder

pastimes Things that amuse.

decipher To make out the meaning of.

facial Of or relating to the face.

Reading and Writing Practice

Reading Scoreboard If you have been studying each Reading and Writing Practice faithfully, your reading speed has no doubt increased since you last measured it in Lesson 18. Let us measure that increase on the first reading of the material in Lesson 30. The following table will help you:

Lesson 30 contains 902 words

If you read Lesson 30 in **25 minutes** your reading rate is **36 words a minute**
If you read Lesson 30 in **29 minutes** your reading rate is **31 words a minute**
If you read Lesson 30 in **32 minutes** your reading rate is **28 words a minute**
If you read Lesson 30 in **36 minutes** your reading rate is **25 words a minute**
If you read Lesson 30 in **39 minutes** your reading rate is **23 words a minute**
If you read Lesson 30 in **43 minutes** your reading rate is **21 words a minute**

If you can read Lesson 30 in 25 minutes or less, you are doing well. If you take considerably longer than 43 minutes, perhaps you should review your homework procedures. For example, are you:

- 1 Practicing in a quiet place at home?
- 2 Practicing without the radio or television set on?
- 3 Spelling aloud any words that you cannot read immediately?

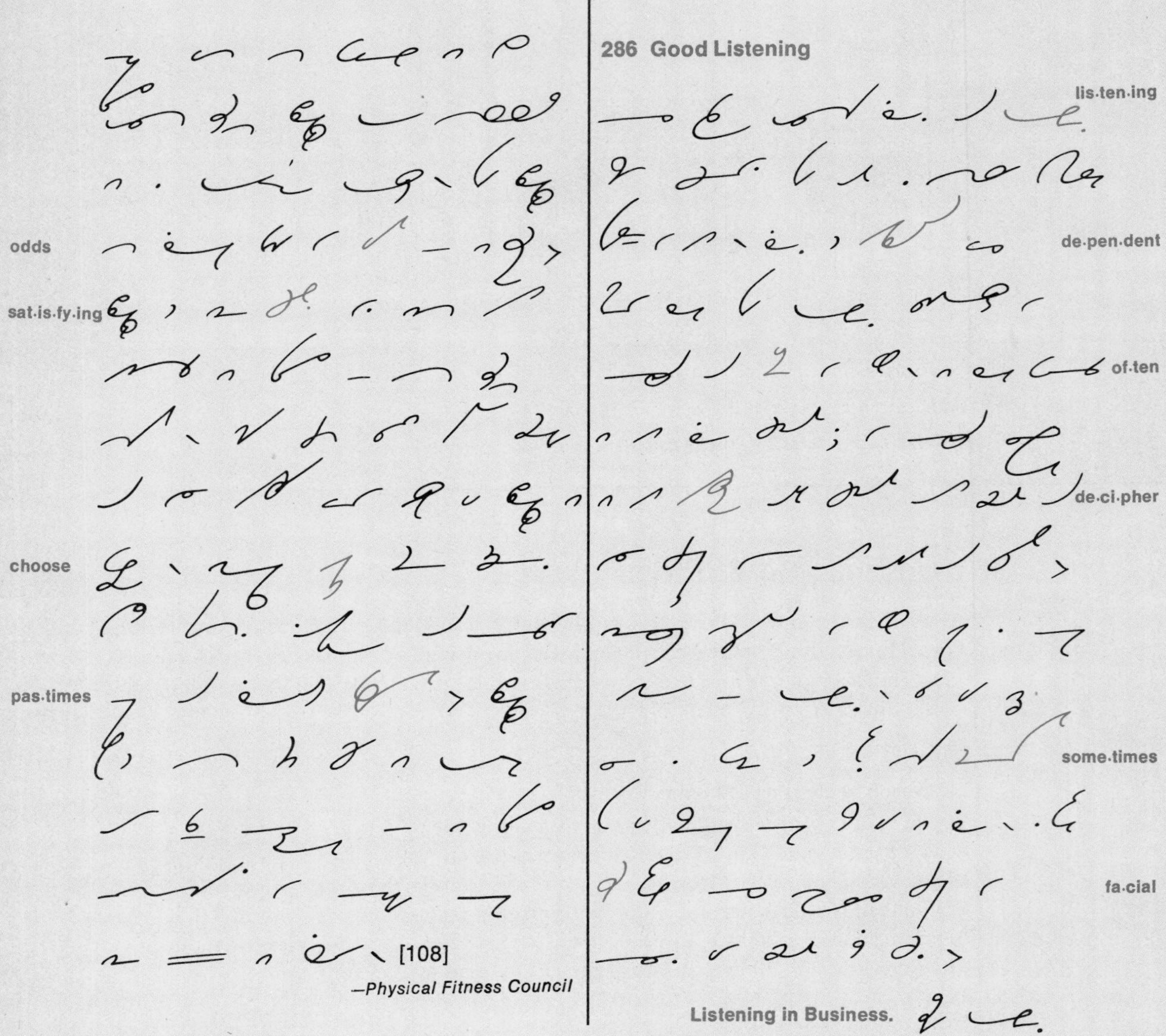

ar·eas

ex·pe·ri·enced

rec·og·nize

au·di·ence

Good Listening

rep·re·sen·ta·tive

re·spon·si·bly

duties

We All Listen a Lot.

than

sur·vey

stud·ies

Listening on the Job.

tan·gi·ble

crit·i·cism

[607]

287 Decisions, Decisions

some·times

vi·tal

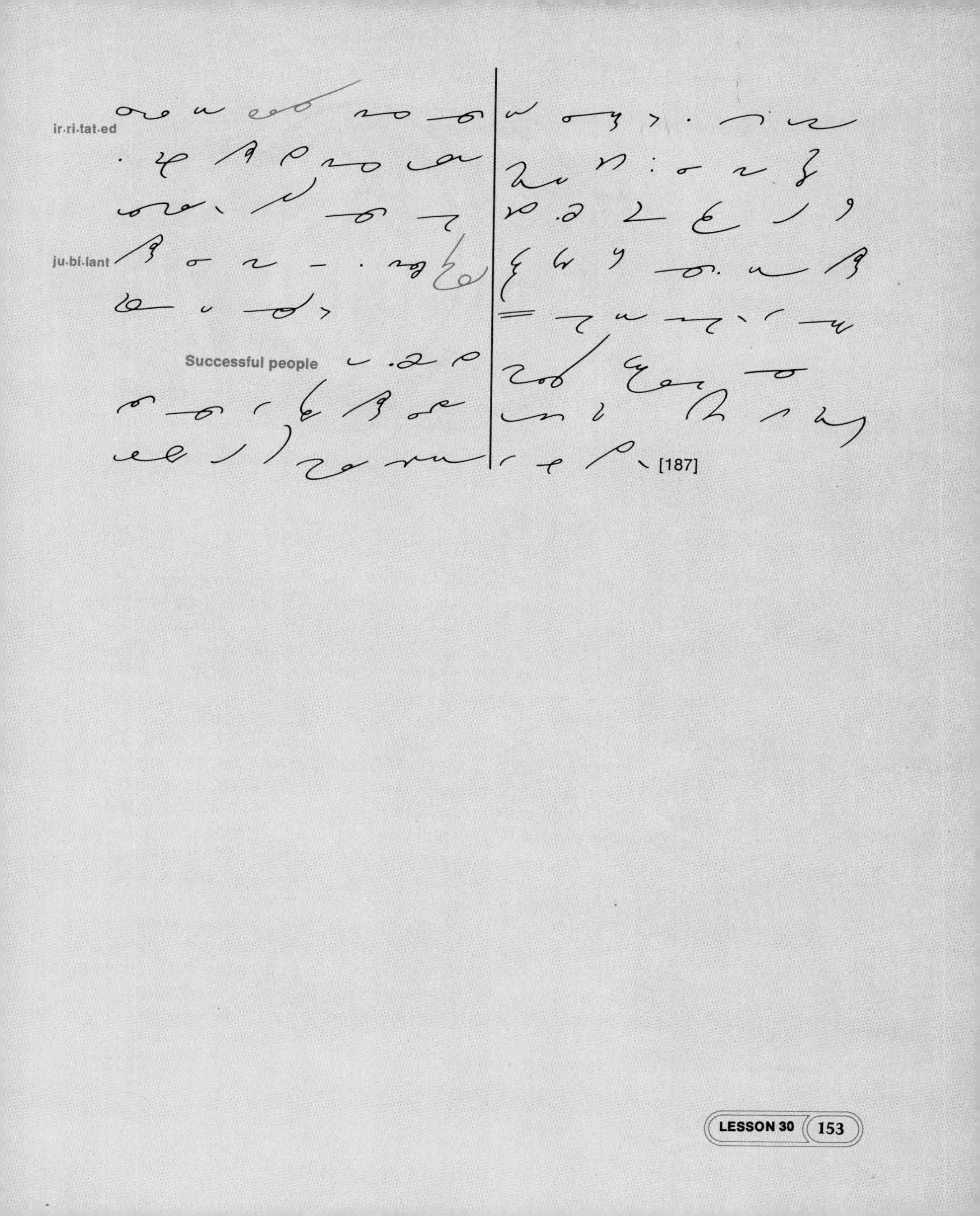

ir·ri·tat·ed

ju·bi·lant

Successful people

[187]

CHAPTER

6 The Secretary Communicates

Taking dictation, writing letters, answering the telephone, greeting visitors, interacting with co-workers or clients—all are part of the secretary's job and all depend on the ability to communicate.

In the office, *communications* refers to anything having to do with the written or spoken word. Therefore, most of what the secretary does in the office involves communicating.

Written communications are a vital part of any business. It is the secretary who is responsible for preparing most, if not all, of such communications. An effective business letter, for example, promotes goodwill and elicits the reader's favorable reaction toward both the writer and the organization represented. In all correspondence, the secretary is responsible for accuracy, appearance, and completeness. This means that no less than perfect grammar, spelling, punctuation, and typing will do. It also means that all facts and figures, including addresses and dates, must be accurate.

To produce superior correspondence, the secretary should have a thorough knowledge of English. Grammatical errors may not always be noticed during dictation, but they show up immediately on a typed page. The secretary must learn to correct such errors before they reach the printed page. There is little value in typing at top speed if the resulting work must be redone because of misspelled words.

Employers expect their secretaries to spell correctly words which are in general use and to learn to spell technical words that are part of the language of the particular business or profession. Punctuation, too, must be correct. If punctuation does not clarify the writing, the reader may misinterpret the ideas. Incorrect punctuation can easily lead to misunderstanding.

Other important ways of communicating are speaking and listening. The good secretary can handle visitors and telephone callers intelligently and courteously by speaking in a well-modulated voice, enunciating distinctly, choosing words that convey thoughts clearly, and expressing sincere interest.

Studies have shown that executives may spend one-half to two-thirds of their time listening to others. Secretaries must listen nearly as much. Misunderstandings are avoided and work production is increased when the secretary listens intelligently.

Writing, speaking, and listening are skills every secretary needs in order to fulfill one of the most important aspects of the secretarial job—communication.

Principles

288 Brief Forms

This is the last group of brief forms you will have to learn.

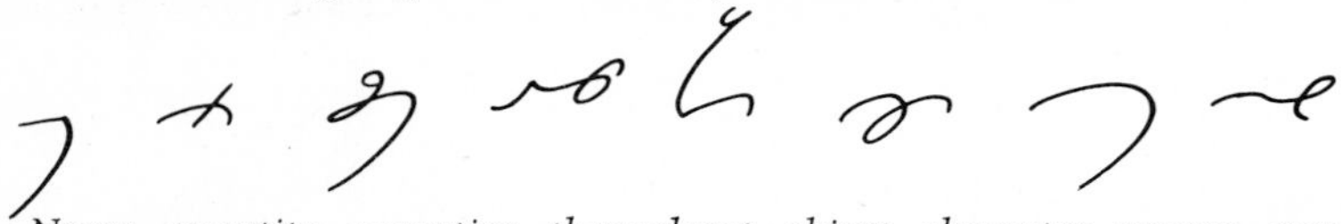

Never, quantity, executive, throughout, object, character, govern, correspond-correspondence.

289 Word Ending -ure

The word ending *-ure* is represented by *r*.

Spell: f-u-t-r, future

Future, picture, venture, failure, miniature, nature, natural.

290 Word Ending -ual

The word ending *-ual* is represented by *l*.

Spell: gay-r-a-d-l, gradual

Gradual, individual, actual, annual, equal, eventually.

Building Transcription Skills

291 PUNCTUATION PRACTICE Another skill you must possess if you are to be a successful stenographer or secretary is the ability to punctuate correctly. Some executives dictate punctuation, but most of them rely on their stenographers or secretaries to supply the proper punctuation when they transcribe.

To sharpen your punctuation skill, you will hereafter give special attention to punctuation in each Reading and Writing Practice. In the lessons ahead you will review nine of the most common uses of the comma. Each time one of these uses of the comma occurs in the Reading and Writing Practice, it will be encircled in the shorthand, thus forcefully calling it to your attention.

Practice Suggestions If you follow these suggestions in your homework practice hereafter, your ability to punctuate should improve noticeably.

■ 1 Read carefully the explanation of each comma usage (for example, the explanation of the parenthetical comma given below) to be sure that you understand it. You will encounter many illustrations of each comma usage in the Reading and Writing Practice exercises, so that eventually you will acquire the knack of applying it correctly.

■ 2 Continue to read and copy each Reading and Writing Practice as you have done before. However, add these two important steps:

■ a Each time you see an encircled comma in the Reading and Writing Practice, note the reason for its use, which is indicated directly above the encircled comma.

■ b As you copy the Reading and Writing Practice in your shorthand notebook, insert the commas in your shorthand notes, encircling them as in the textbook.

PUNCTUATION PRACTICE , parenthetical A word or a phrase that is used parenthetically (that is, one not necessary to the grammatical completeness of the sentence) should be set off by commas.

If the parenthetical expression occurs at the end of the sentence, only one comma is used.

There is, of course, *no charge for our services.*

Please let us know, Mr. Strong, *if we can help you.*

We actually print your picture on the card, Ms. Green.

Each time a parenthetical expression occurs in the Reading and Writing Practice, it will be indicated thus in the shorthand: par (,)

---

292 Business Vocabulary Builder

miniature A copy which has been reduced in size.

ventures Business matters involving risk.

exhausted Used up.

Reading and Writing Practice

293 Brief-Form Letter

gov·ern·ment

cor·re·spon·dence

sym·pa·thy

par

par

sta·tio·nery

par

par

crit·i·cal·ly

[178]

294

par

par

ap·ply·ing

amazed

par

1978

re·spon·si·ble

par

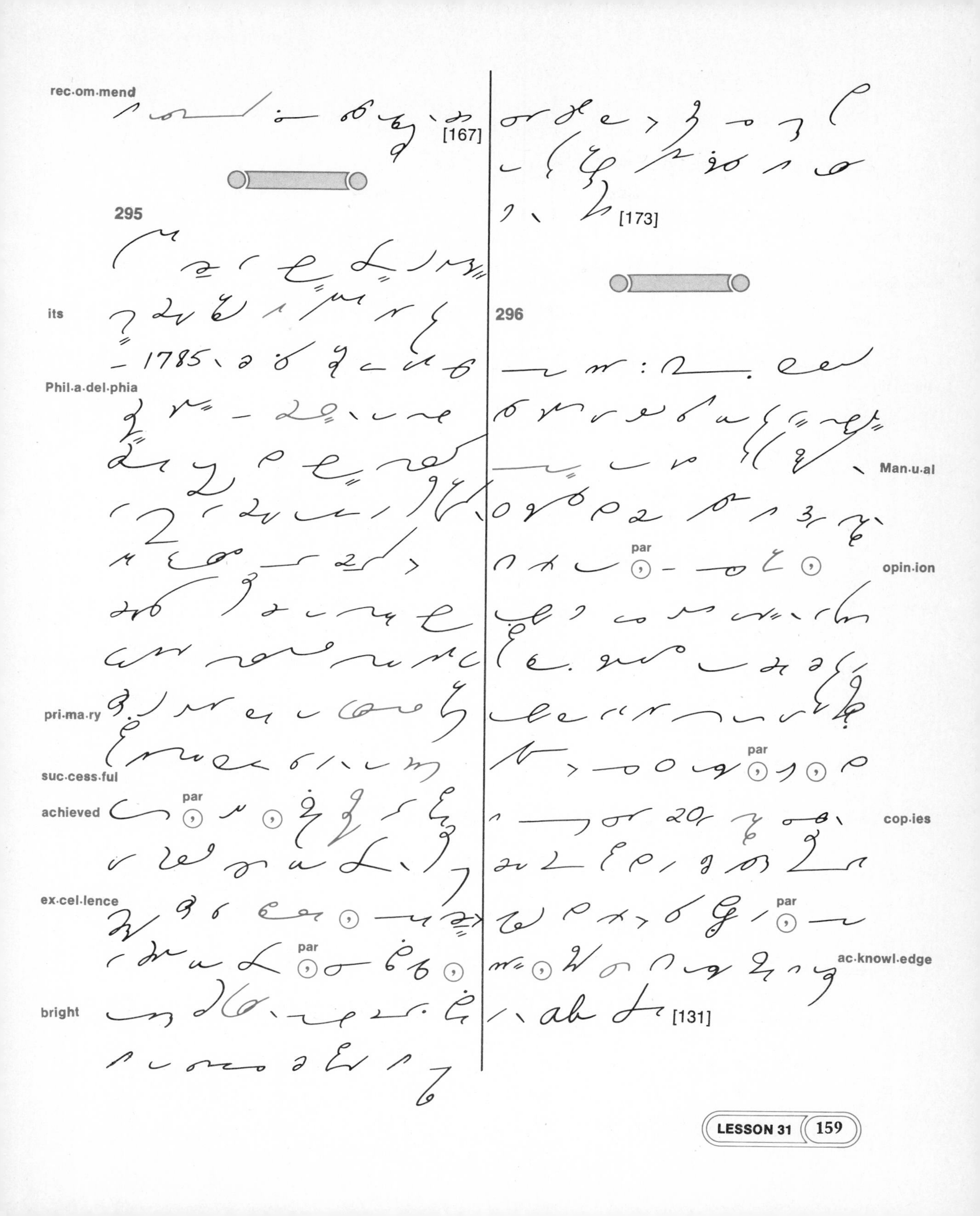

rec·om·mend

[167]

295

its

1785

Phil·a·del·phia

pri·ma·ry

suc·cess·ful

achieved

par

ex·cel·lence

par

bright

[173]

296

Man·u·al

par

opin·ion

par

cop·ies

par

ac·knowl·edge

[131]

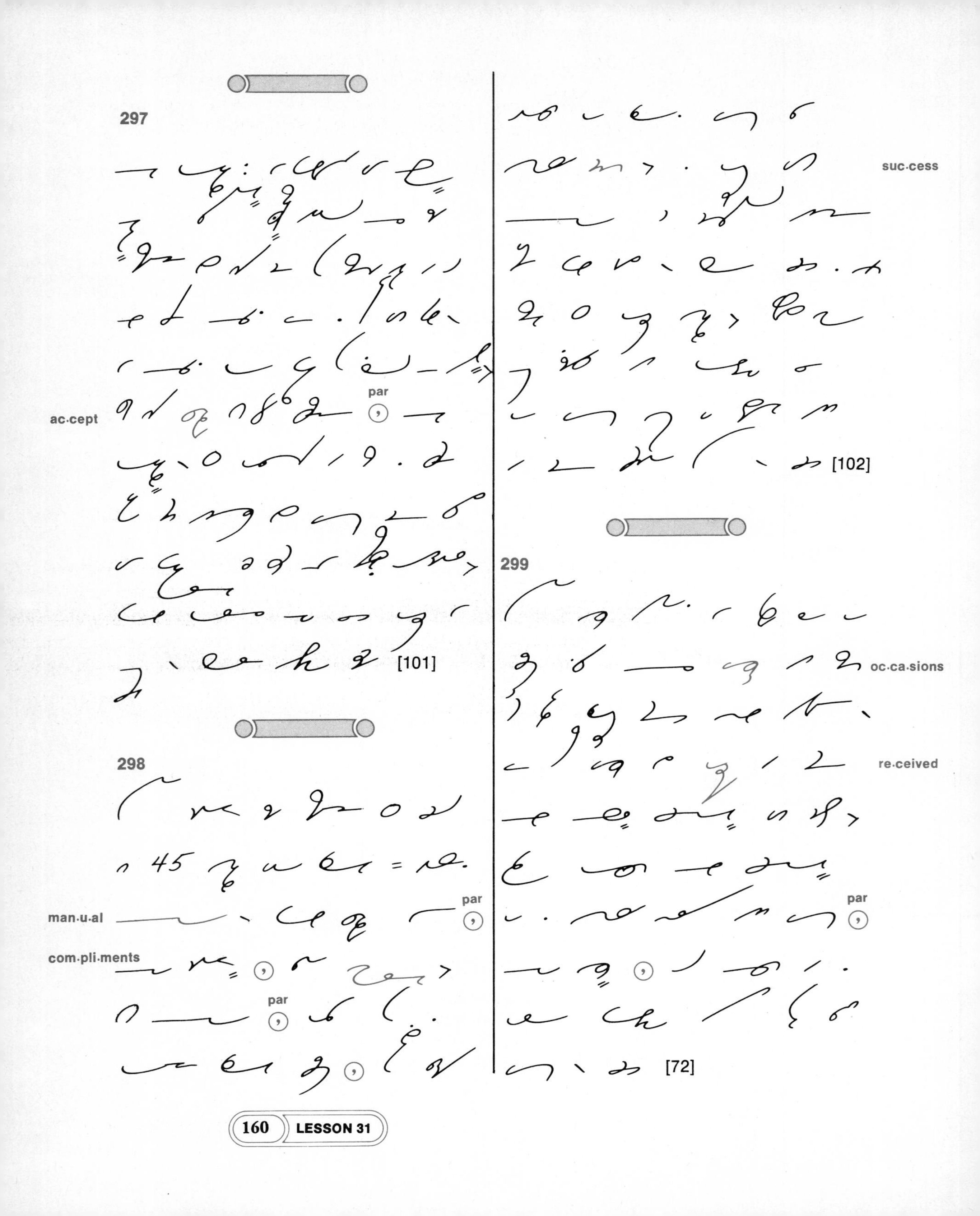

297

ac·cept

par

[101]

298

man·u·al

com·pli·ments

par

par

suc·cess

[102]

299

oc·ca·sions

re·ceived

par

[72]

Principles

300 Word Ending -Ily

The word ending *-ily* is represented by a narrow loop.

Compare: ready *readily*

Spell: r-e-d-ily, readily

Easily, steadily, speedily, temporarily, heartily, family, families.

Note the special joining of *s* used in *families*. This special joining enables us to form an outline that is easily read.

301 Word Beginning Al-

The word beginning *al-* is expressed by o.

Spell: all-m-o-s-t, almost

Almost, also, altogether, already, although, alter, alteration.

302 Word Beginnings Dis-, Des-

The word beginnings *dis-, des-* are represented by *d-s.*

Spell: dis-k-oo-s, discuss; dis-k-r-ī-b, describe

Dis-

Discuss, discussion, disturb, discover, discouragement, disposal, dismiss.

Des-

Decribe, described, description, destination, destroy, despite.

Building Transcription Skills

303 PUNCTUATION PRACTICE , apposition An expression in apposition (that is, a word or a phrase or a clause that identifies or explains other terms) should be set off by commas. When an expression in apposition occurs at the end of a sentence, only one comma is necessary.

My employer, Mr. Frank Smith, *is on a business trip.*

I will see him on Friday, June 15, *at 3 o'clock.*

His book, Principles of Accounting, *is out of stock.*

For more information call Mr. Brown, our production manager.

▶ Note: When the clarifying term is very closely connected with the principal noun so that the sense would not be complete without the added term, no commas are required.

My brother Fred *arrived yesterday.*

The word embarrassed *is often misspelled.*

Each time an expression in apposition occurs in the Reading and Writing Practice, it will be indicated thus in the shorthand: ap (,)

304 Business Vocabulary Builder

fumes Irritating smoke or gas.

sturdily Strongly; substantially.

apathy Lack of interest or concern; indifference.

endorsement Approval.

Reading and Writing Practice

305 Brief-Form Review Letter

or·ga·ni·za·tion ap (,) ap (,) pol·lu·tion (,)

de·stroy

al·ter

ap

cor·re·spon·dence

par

de·scrip·tive

[162]

sturdi·ly

than

ap

de·scribes

ad·van·tages

par

al·ready

[158]

306

ac·com·plish

ap

307

ap·a·thy

be·lieve

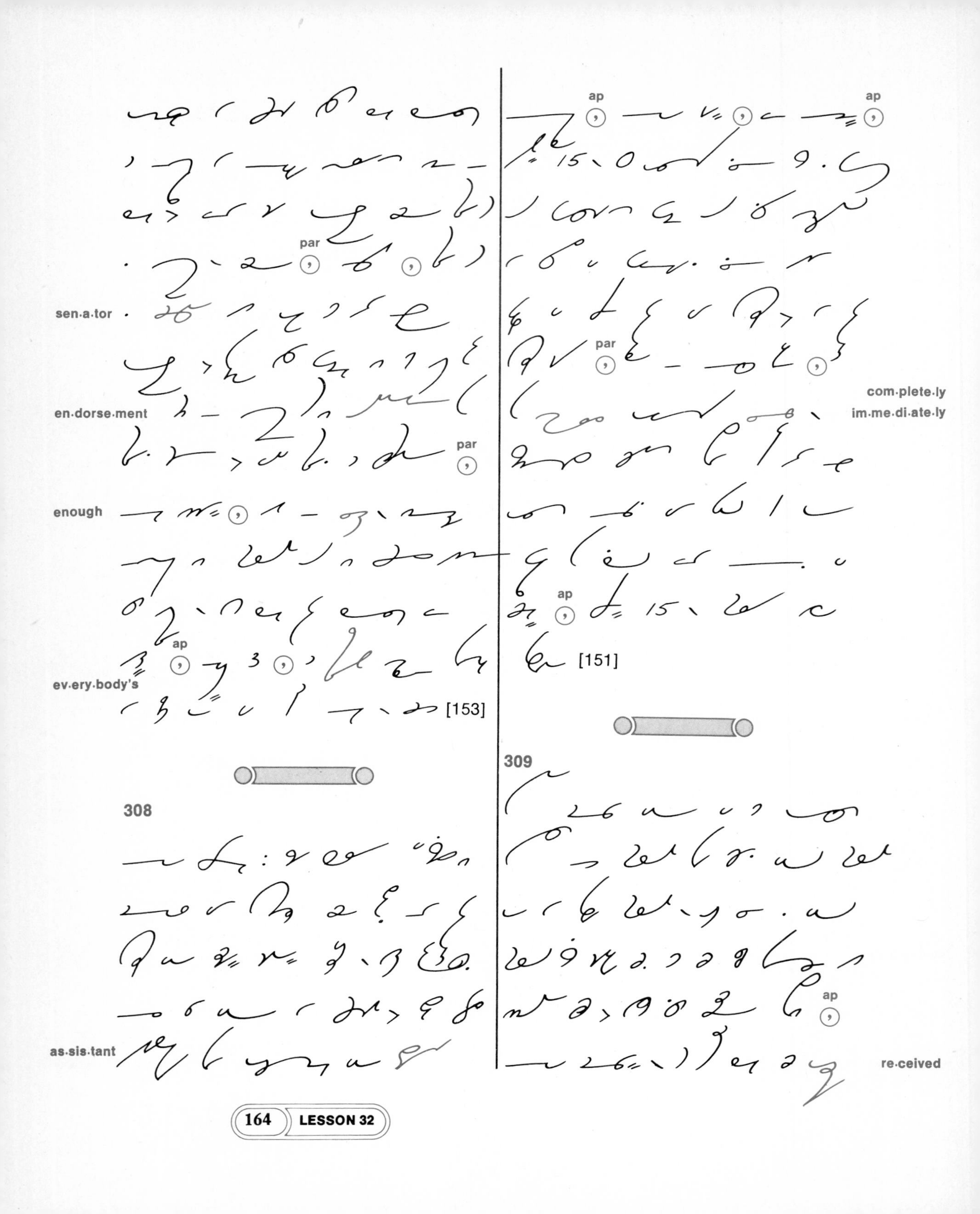

ap ap

sen·a·tor

par

com·plete·ly

en·dorse·ment

im·me·di·ate·ly

par

enough

ap

[151]

ap

ev·ery·body's

[153]

309

308

ap

as·sis·tant

re·ceived

[116]

310

ap

dis·turb·ing

ap

in·ject

ap

[87]

PERSONAL-USE CHECKLIST

Do you substitute shorthand for longhand wherever possible when you—

- 1 Take down your daily assignments?
- 2 Correspond with your friends who know shorthand?
- 3 Draft compositions and reports?
- 4 Make entries in your diary?
- 5 Make notes to yourself on things to do, people to see, appointments to keep, etc?

Principles

311 Word Beginnings For-, Fore-

The word beginnings *for-, fore-* are represented by *f.*

Spell: for-gay-e-v, forgive

Forgive, forget, form, inform, information, force, foreclose, forerunner, forever.

312 Word Beginning Fur-

The word beginning *fur-* is also represented by *f.*

Spell: fur-n-a-s, furnace

Furnace, further, furthermore, furnish, furnished, furniture, refurnish.

313 Ago in Phrases

In expressions of time, *ago* is represented by *gay.*

Weeks ago, years ago, days ago, several days ago, months ago, minutes ago.

Building Transcription Skills

314 PUNCTUATION PRACTICE , series When the last member of a series of three or more items is preceded by *and* or *or,* place a comma before the conjunction as well as between the other items.

For his birthday he received a tie, a shirt, and a wallet.

I need a person to take dictation, to answer the phone, and to greet callers.

I can see her on July 18, on July 19, or on July 30.

▶ Note: Some authorities prefer to omit the comma before the conjunction. In your shorthand textbooks, however, the comma will always be inserted before the conjunction.

Each time a series occurs in the Reading and Writing Practice, it will be indicated thus in the shorthand: ser (,)

---

315 Business Vocabulary Builder

suites *(of furniture)* Sets of matched furniture for a room.

refurnish To equip with new furniture.

canceled check A check which has been processed by a bank.

● Reading and Writing Practice

316 Brief-Form Review Letter

15 ser (,) (,) par (,) (,)

char·ac·ter

ef·fect

30 40, par (,) (,) [133]

suites

re·fur·nish

317

15 ser (,) (,)

show·room

cor·re·spon·dence

ser

re·spon·si·ble

par

fur·ther·more

ours

[166]

318

ap

ap

Fac·to·ry

can·celed

is·sues

ser

par

[119] re·ceipt

319

40 For·ty

ap

rec·og·nized

con·quered

ser

prac·ti·cal

par

com·pa·nies

[124]

320

[104]

321

[50]

322

[69]

cre·ate

suite

over·coat

Feb·ru·ary

re·cent·ly

Principles

323 Want in Phrases

In phrases, *want* is represented by the *nt* blend.

You want, if you want, we want, I wanted, do you want, he wants, he wanted.

324 Ort

The *r* is omitted in the combination *ort.*

Spell: re-p-o-t, report

Report, support, airport, export, sort, quarterly, mortal.

325 R Omitted in -ern, -erm

The *r* is omitted in the combinations *tern, term, thern, therm, dern.*

Spell: t-e-n, turn

Turn, return, eastern, term, determine, southern, thermometer, modern.

326 Md, Mt

By rounding off the angle between *m-d,* we obtain the fluent *md* blend. The same stroke also represents *mt.*

Md, Mt

Compare: *seem* *seemed*

Spell: *s-e-emd, seemed; emt-e, empty*

Framed, claimed, informed, termed, confirmed, named, welcomed, empty.

Building Transcription Skills

327 SIMILAR-WORDS DRILL addition, edition

addition Anything added.

This picture is a fine addition *to our collection.*

edition All the copies of a book published at one time.

We sold 50,000 copies of the second edition *of the book.*

328 Business Vocabulary Builder

undependable Unreliable.

quarterly Every three months.

confirmed Acknowledged.

Reading and Writing Practice

329 Brief-Form Review Letter

edi·tion

ap

par

var·ied

>un·de·pend·able

par

re·spon·si·ble

ad·di·tion

ap

ad·ver·tis·ing

[178]

330

par

fam·i·ly

year's

ap

ser

Jan·u·ary

mod·ern

Phil·a·del·phia

[196]

331

dif·fer·ence

ser

far·ther

ser

wor·ry

ser

eco·nom·i·cal

dis·tance

[135]

332

re·ceived

ap

passed

ac·cept

par

[110]

333

ex·pe·ri·enc·ing

ser

par

Mas·sa·chu·setts

[82]

Principles

334 Word Beginnings Inter-, Intr-, Enter-, Entr-

The similar sounding word beginnings *inter-, intr-, enter-, entr-* (and the word *enter*) are represented by a disjoined *n*. This disjoined word beginning, as well as other disjoined word beginnings that you will study in later lessons, is placed above the line of writing close to the remainder of the word.

Inter-

Spell: *inter-s-t, interest*

Interest, interested, international, interrupted, interfere, interfered, interval.

Intr-

Spell: *intro-d-oo-s, introduce*

Introduce, introduces, introduction, intricate, intrude.

Enter-, Entr-

Spell: *enter-ing, entering*

Entering, entered, enterprise, enterprises, entrance, entrances.

335 Word Ending -ings

The word ending *-ings* is represented by a disjoined left *s*.

Spell: o-p-n-ings, openings

Openings, evenings, hearings, meetings, dealings, lodgings, proceedings, earnings.

336 Omission of Words in Phrases

It is often possible to omit one or more unimportant words in a shorthand phrase to gain writing speed. In the phrase *one of the,* for example, the word *of* is omitted; we write *one the.* When transcribing, the stenographer will insert *of,* as the phrase would make no sense without that word.

One of the, one of these, one or two, some of them, men and women, in the world, up to date, in the future.

Building Transcription Skills

337 Business Vocabulary Builder

turnover The number of persons hired within a period to replace those leaving a work force.

perplexing Puzzling.

eligible Qualified.

limousine A large chauffeur-driven sedan.

Reading and Writing Practice

338 Brief-Form and Phrase Letter

This letter contains many brief forms and derivatives as well as several illustrations of the phrasing principle you studied in this lesson.

dis·turbed

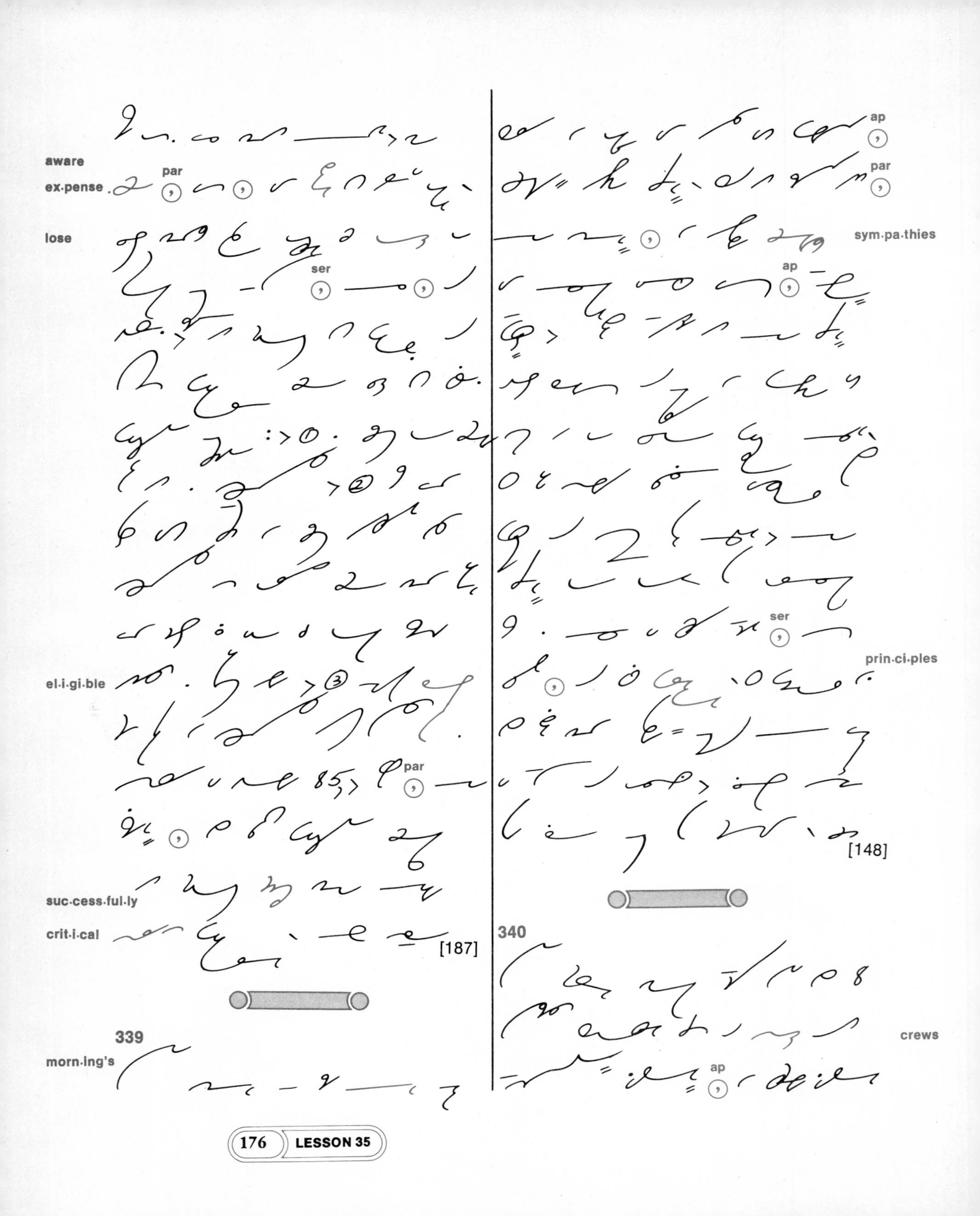

aware

ex·pense

lose

el·i·gi·ble

suc·cess·ful·ly

crit·i·cal

[187]

339

morn·ing's

sym·pa·thies

prin·ci·ples

[148]

340

crews

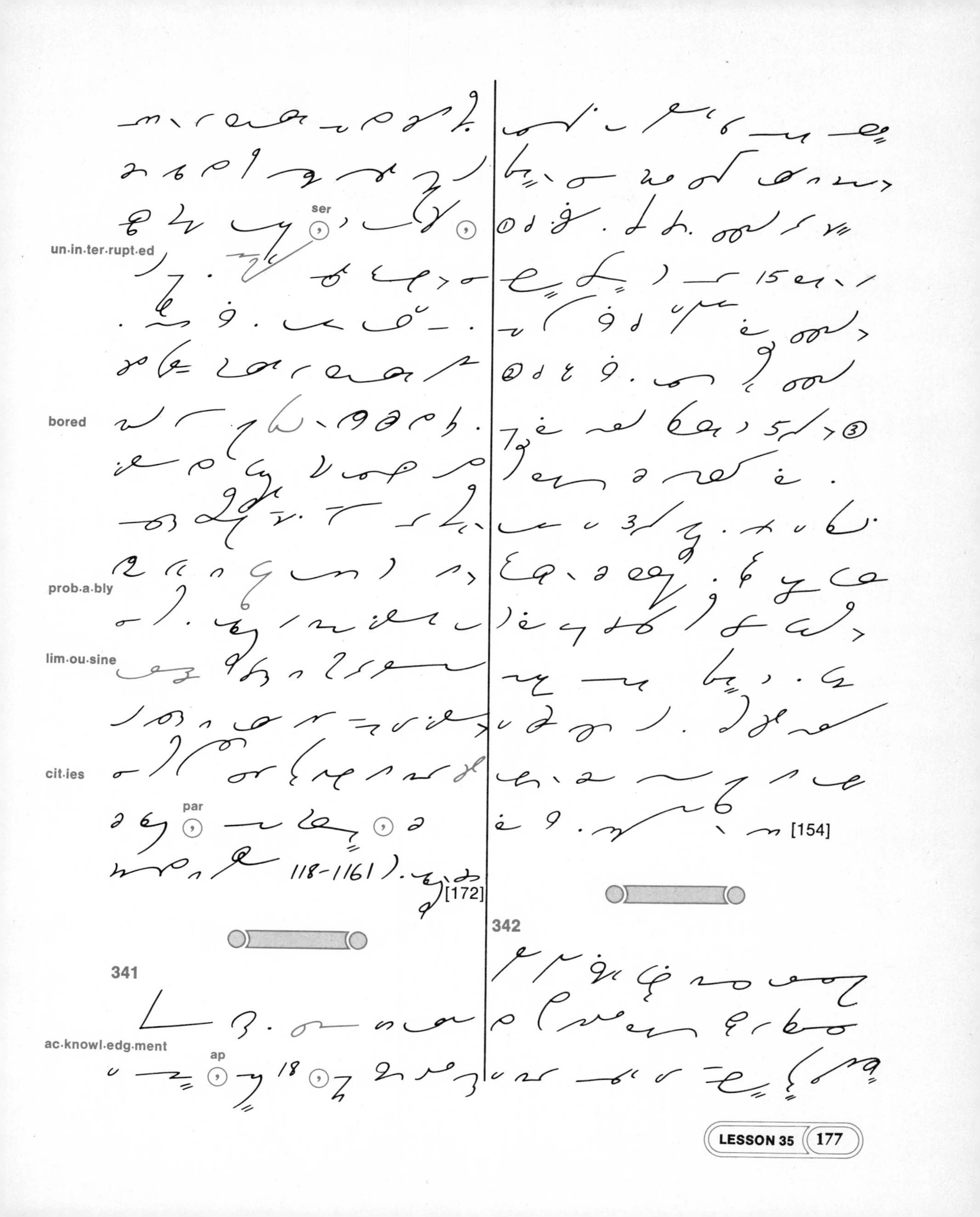

ser

un·in·ter·rupt·ed

bored

prob·a·bly

lim·ou·sine

cit·ies

par

118-1161 [172]

15 5 3 [154]

341

ac·knowl·edg·ment

ap

18

342

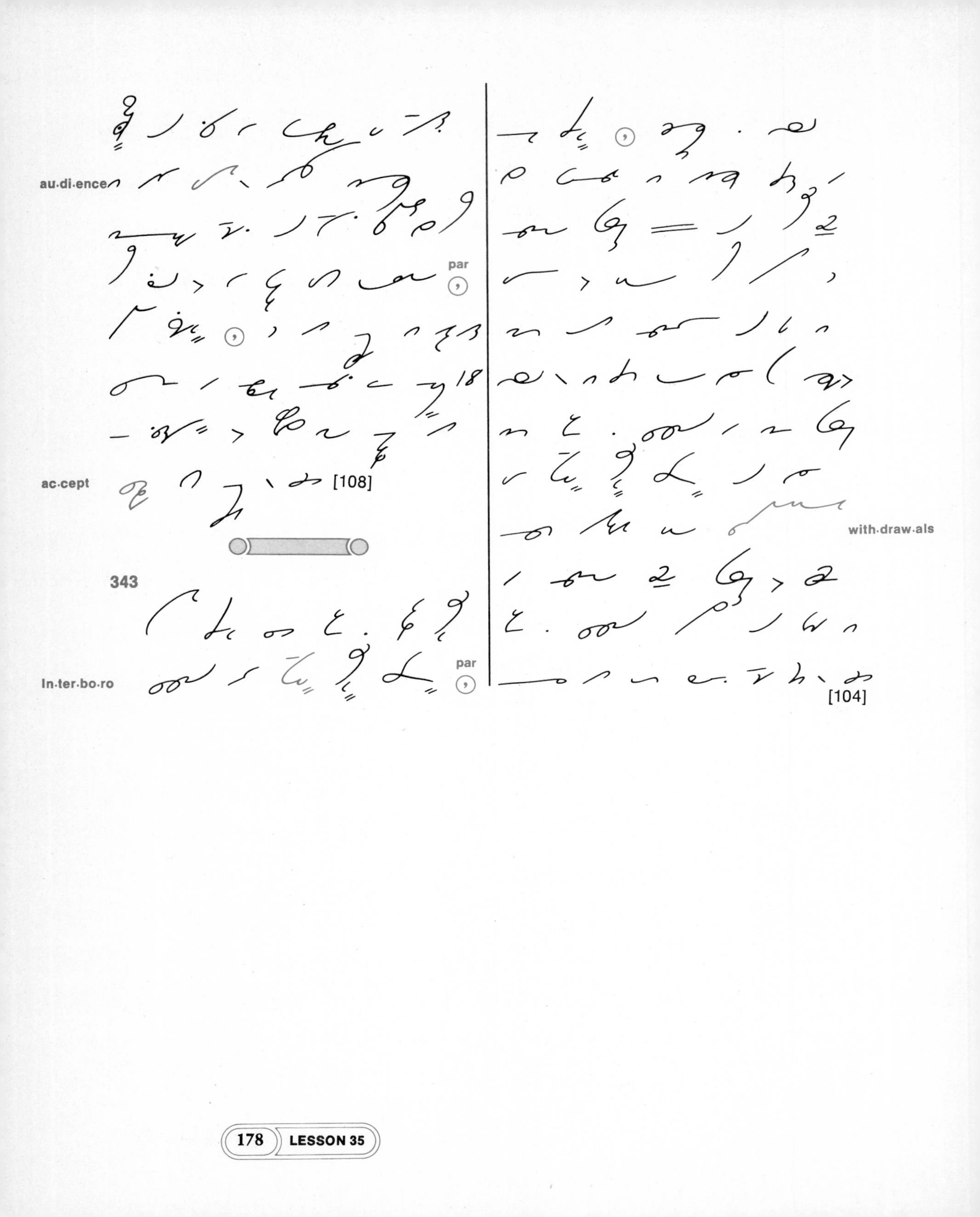

au·di·ence

par

[108]

ac·cept

343

par

In·ter·bo·ro

with·draw·als

[104]

RECALL

Lesson 36 is another breather. In Lesson 36 you will find a chart that contains a review of shorthand devices you studied in Lessons 1 through 35 and a Reading and Writing Practice that you should find interesting as well as informative.

344 Recall Chart

This chart contains illustrations of shorthand principles you studied in previous lessons. There are 12 brief forms and derivatives, 12 phrases, and 66 words in the chart.

Can you read the entire chart in 5 minutes?

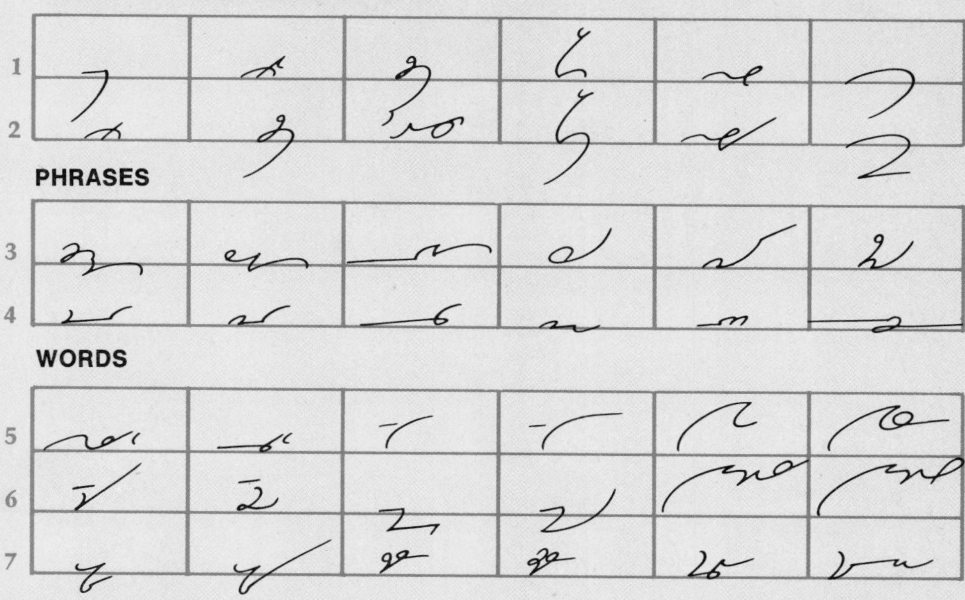

8						
9						
10						
11						
12						
13						
14						
15						

Building Transcription Skills

345 Business Vocabulary Builder

effecting Bringing about; resulting in.

capacity Ability.

accord *(verb)* Give to.

Reading and Writing Practice

346 The Secretary in Business

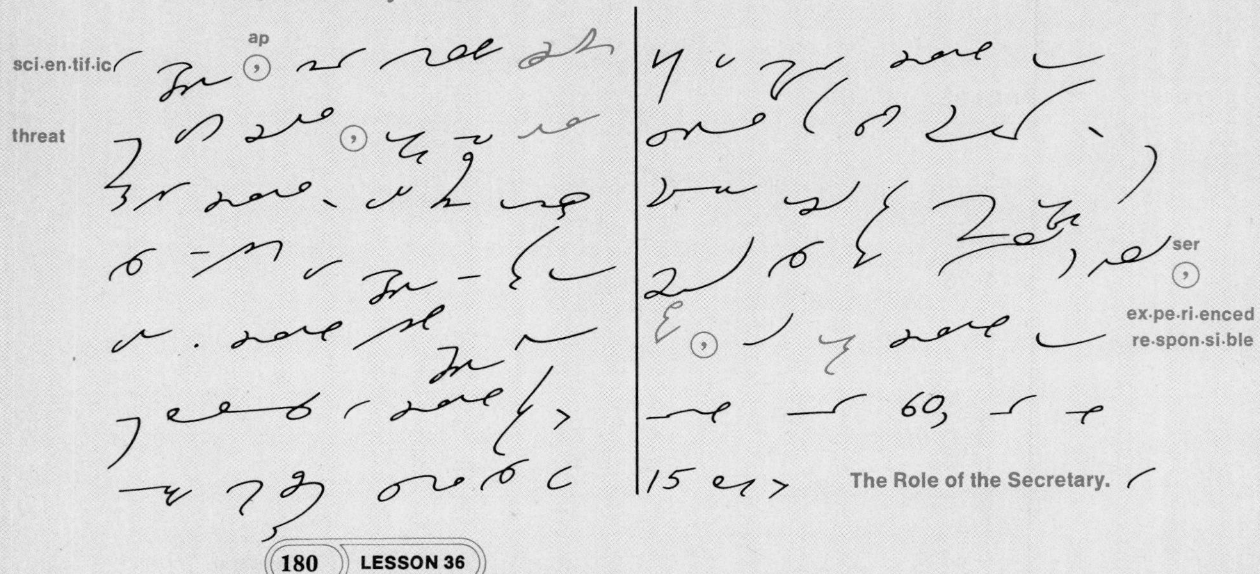

role
ad·di·tion
par
ser
chal·leng·ing

The secretary's job

cor·re·spon·dence
par
ser
ef·fect·ing

ar·eas

The secretary and

par

Secretarial Positions Differ.

af·fect·ed
ser
or·ga·ni·za·tion
en·ter·prise

[486]

347 Courtesy and Success

primar·i·ly

calm

odd

par

iden·ti·cal

ser

co·op·er·a·tion

Our courtesy

ser

an·swer

con·scious

[216]

348 Sleep and Diet

snack

ser

weight

cal·o·ries

ser

[113]

CHAPTER

7 The Secretary Takes Dictation

The ability to take dictation is the core of the secretary's job, but just being able to write shorthand is not enough. Success in this important part of the secretary's work will depend upon writing good, sensible notes which can be transcribed easily and quickly with accuracy.

Handling dictation may be the secretary's most important task. The secretary must be ready to take dictation whenever the employer wants to give it. When the boss is ready to dictate, all other work must be put aside.

Many secretaries form the good habit of checking—the first thing in the morning—to be sure that their dictation tools are in order. "I wouldn't think of answering my employer's call without a shorthand notebook and my pen," says one secretary. When summoned to the boss's office, the secretary is ready to answer promptly with an open shorthand notebook and a pen.

During the dictation session, the secretary makes it possible for the employer to get the work done as expeditiously as possible. All dictation and instructions are recorded accurately. Nothing is done to divert or annoy the dictator.

The dictating habits of employers vary greatly. For some, dictating is hard work and ideas come slowly. Some employers may pause for long periods during a difficult letter or report, but once they clarify the idea they want to express, they are likely to reel it off very rapidly. Other employers, more gifted at expressing themselves, dictate at a fairly regular or brisk pace.

Employers expect their secretaries to be proficient shorthand writers, able to keep up with the dictation no matter how fast the pace becomes. True, if the dictation speed of an entire letter is average, it may seem fairly slow; yet during every dictation period there are many times when a high shorthand speed is required to keep up.

To maintain your shorthand skill, use it outside the office too. Try using it for all personal notes and instructions. Create opportunities to practice reading and writing shorthand whenever you can.

Following a dictation session, the secretary should get all the instructions and clarifications needed before leaving the boss's office so that it will not be necessary to interrupt later. All instructions should be written so that there is no need to rely on memory alone.

Much of the business conducted today takes the form of letters and other written communications. To expedite communicating information, today's secretary must be able to take and transcribe dictation both quickly and accurately.

Principles

349 Word Ending -ingly

The word ending *-ingly* is represented by a disjoined *e* circle.

Spell: *in-k-r-e-s-ingly, increasingly*

Increasingly, exceedingly, convincingly, amazingly, willingly, interestingly, accordingly.

350 Word Beginning Im-

The word beginning *im-* is represented by *m*.

Spell: *im-p-r-e-s, impress*

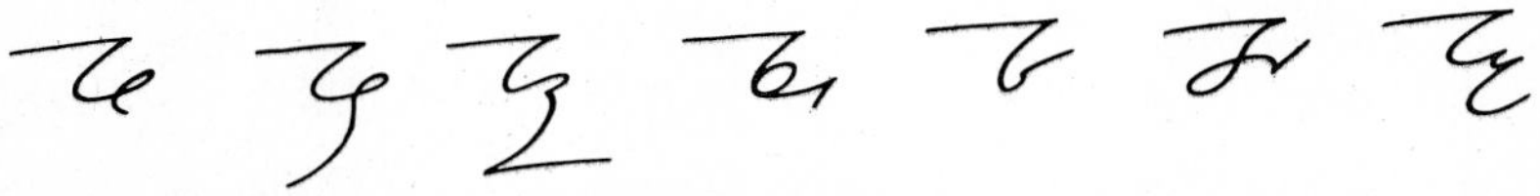

Impress, impressive, improvement, impartial, import, impact, improper.

351 Word Beginning Em-

The word beginning *em-* is also represented by *m*.

Spell: *em-p-ī-r, empire*

Empire, embarrass, emphatically, embraced, employee, employer.

352 Omission of Minor Vowel

When two vowel sounds come together, the minor vowel may be omitted.

Various, serious, previous, period, genuine, ideal, situate, situated, situation.

Building Transcription Skills

353 PUNCTUATION PRACTICE , if clause

A subordinate (or introductory) clause followed by a main clause is separated from the main clause by a comma. A subordinate clause is often introduced by subordinating conjunctions including *if, as, when, though, although, because,* and others. In this lesson you will consider only subordinate clauses introduced by *if*.

If you complete the work before 5 o'clock, *you may leave.*

If I cannot come, *I will call you.*

If John is ill, *he should stay home.*

Each time a subordinate clause beginning with *if* occurs in the Reading and Writing Practice, it will be indicated thus in the shorthand: if ⦅,⦆

354 Business Vocabulary Builder

impartially Fairly.

emphatically Forcefully.

reimbursed Paid back.

Reading and Writing Practice

355 Brief-Form Review Letter

ap

un·usu·al

par

ser

pe·ri·od·i·cals

if

re·quest

[181]

356

ser

the·o·ries

par

[146]

re·im·bursed

357

if ap

16 25

em·ploy·ee

25 el·i·gi·ble

ser

im·pres·sive

par

won

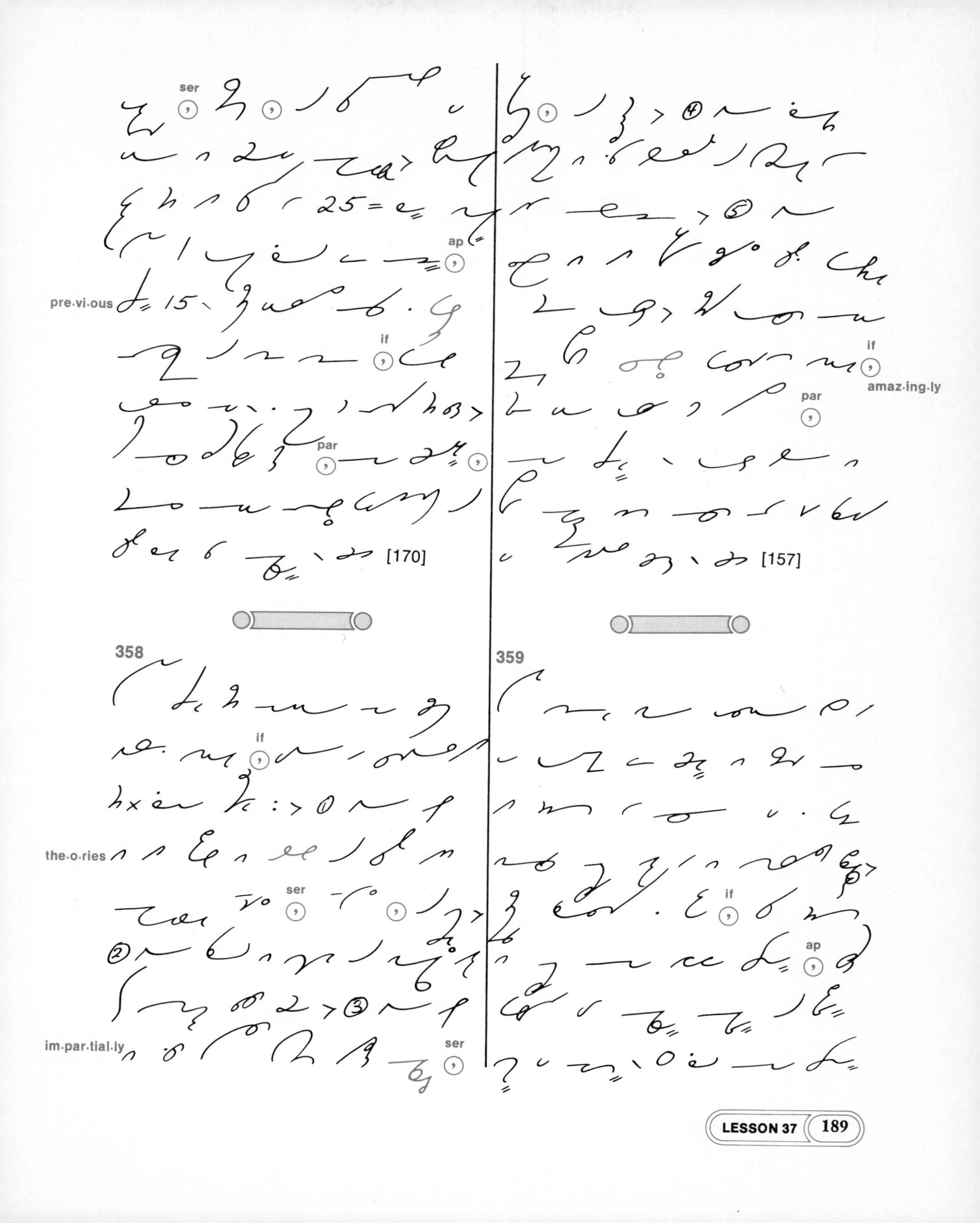

ser

ap

pre·vi·ous 15

if

par

[170]

if

amaz·ing·ly

par

[157]

358

if

the·o·ries

ser

im·par·tial·ly

ser

359

if

ap

Em·ploy·ee

ser

if

[121]

360

too

par

par

[106]

361

ap

thor·ough·ly

brought

cal·en·dar

if

[130]

hon·ored

Principles

362 Word Ending -ship

The word ending *-ship* is represented by a disjoined *ish*.

Spell: s-t-e-m-ship, steamship

Steamship, friendship, membership, relationships, fellowship, leadership.

363 Word Beginning Sub-

The word beginning *sub-* is represented by *s*.

Spell: sub-m-e-t, submit

Submit, subscribe, subscription, subdivide, subdivision, substantial, suburbs, subway.

364 Word Ending -ulate

The word ending *-ulate* is represented by a disjoined *oo* hook.

Spell: r-e-gay-ulate, regulate

Regulate, stimulate, congratulate, formulate, tabulator, calculated.

365 Word Ending -ulation

The word ending *-ulation* is represented by *oo-shun*.

Spell: r-e-gay-ulation, regulation

Regulation, insulation, accumulation, circulation, stimulation, congratulations.

366 Word Ending -rity

The word ending *-rity* (and a preceding vowel) is represented by a disjoined *r*.

Spell: m-a-j-rity, majority

Majority, security, prosperity, sincerity, charity, authorities, minority.

Building Transcription Skills

367 PUNCTUATION PRACTICE , as clause A subordinate clause introduced by *as* and followed by a main clause is separated from the main clause by a comma.

As you know, *you have not yet paid your June bill.*

As I cannot attend the meeting, *I will send my assistant.*

Each time a subordinate clause beginning with *as* occurs in the Reading and Writing Practice, it will be indicated thus in the shorthand: as (,)

368 Business Vocabulary Builder

prosperity Economic well-being.

subsidiary A company owned by another.

proceeds *(noun)* Income.

Reading and Writing Practice

369 Brief-Form Review Letter

ser (,) ex·pe·ri·enced

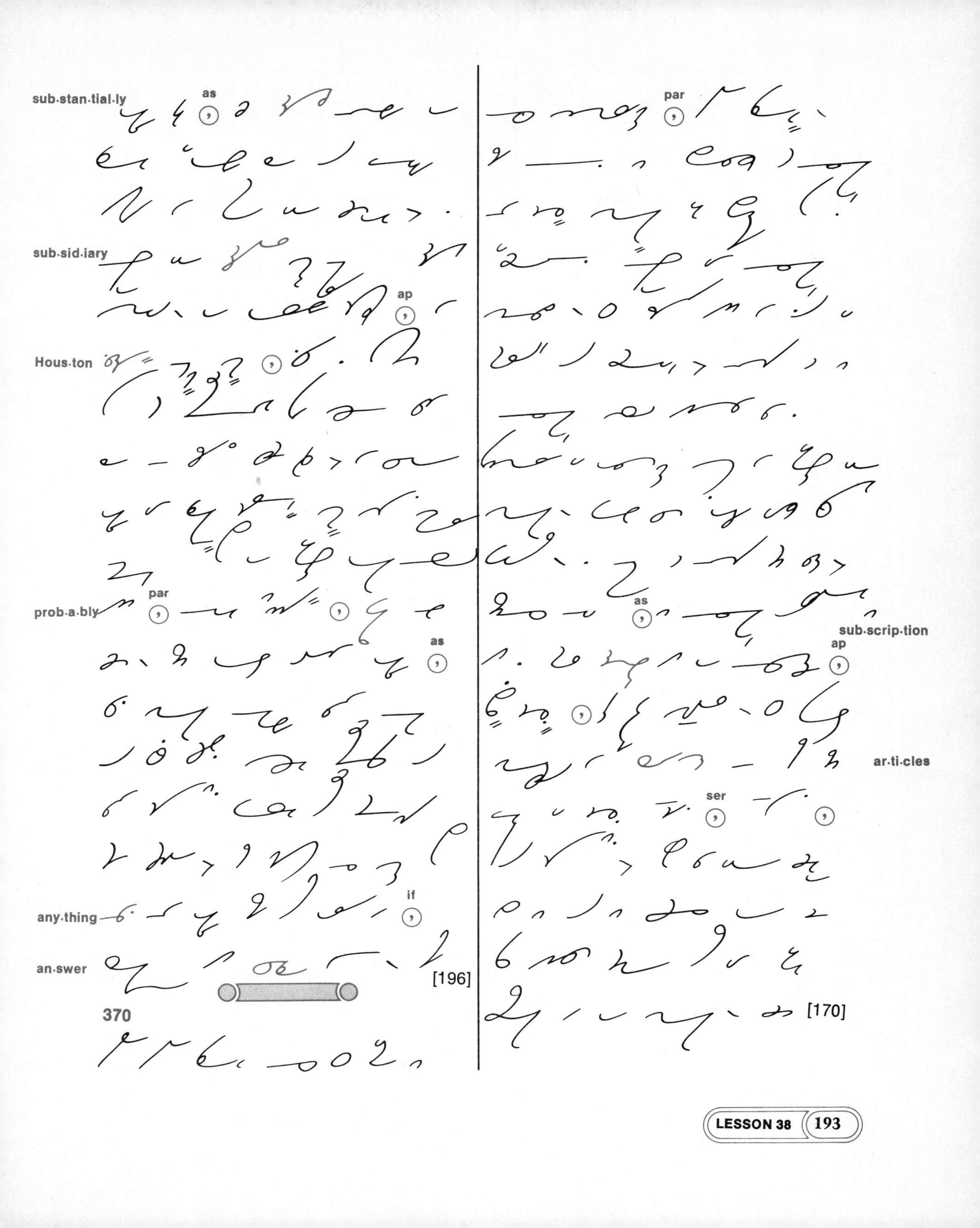

sub·stan·tial·ly

as

sub·sid·iary

ap

Hous·ton

par

prob·a·bly

as

any·thing

if

an·swer

[196]

370

par

as

sub·scrip·tion

ap

ar·ti·cles

ser

[170]

371

char·i·ty

ap

pro·ceeds

ap

gen·er·os·i·ty

[118]

372

as

pleas·ant

[104]

373

ad

cal·cu·la·tors

if

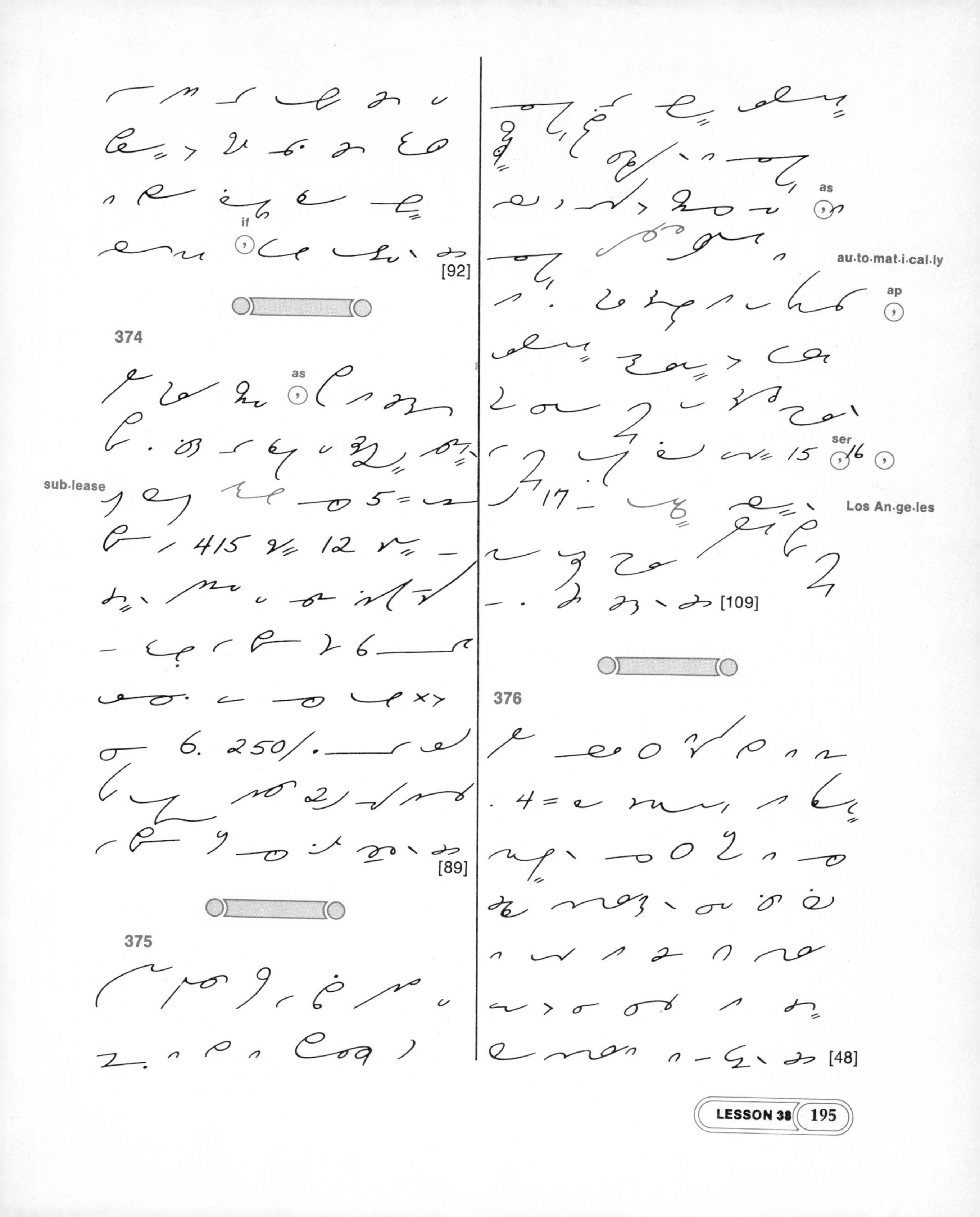

if

[92]

374

as

sub·lease

[89]

375

as

au·to·mat·i·cal·ly

ap

ser

Los An·ge·les

[109]

376

[48]

Principles

377 Word Ending -lity

The word ending *-lity* (and a preceding vowel) is represented by a disjoined *l.*

Spell: a-b-lity, ability

Ability, facility, possibility, dependability, locality, realities, qualities.

378 Word Ending -lty

The word ending *-lty* (and a preceding vowel) is also represented by a disjoined *l.*

Spell: f-a-k-ulty, faculty

Faculty, penalty, royalty, loyalty.

379 Word Endings -self, -selves

The word ending *-self* is represented by *s*; *-selves* is represented by *ses.*

Spell: h-e-r-self, herself; them-selves, themselves

Herself, itself, himself, yourself, myself, oneself; themselves, ourselves, yourselves.

Building Transcription Skills

380 PUNCTUATION PRACTICE , when clause A clause introduced by *when* and followed by the main clause is separated from the main clause by a comma.

When I was in Dallas, *I attended three meetings.*

When you do not pay your bills, *you are endangering your credit.*

Each time a subordinate clause beginning with *when* occurs in the Reading and Writing Practice, it will be indicated thus in the shorthand: when ⊙

381 Business Vocabulary Builder

individuality Total character distinguishing a person or thing from another.

stability Firmness.

integrity Honesty.

Reading and Writing Practice

382 Brief-Form Review Letter

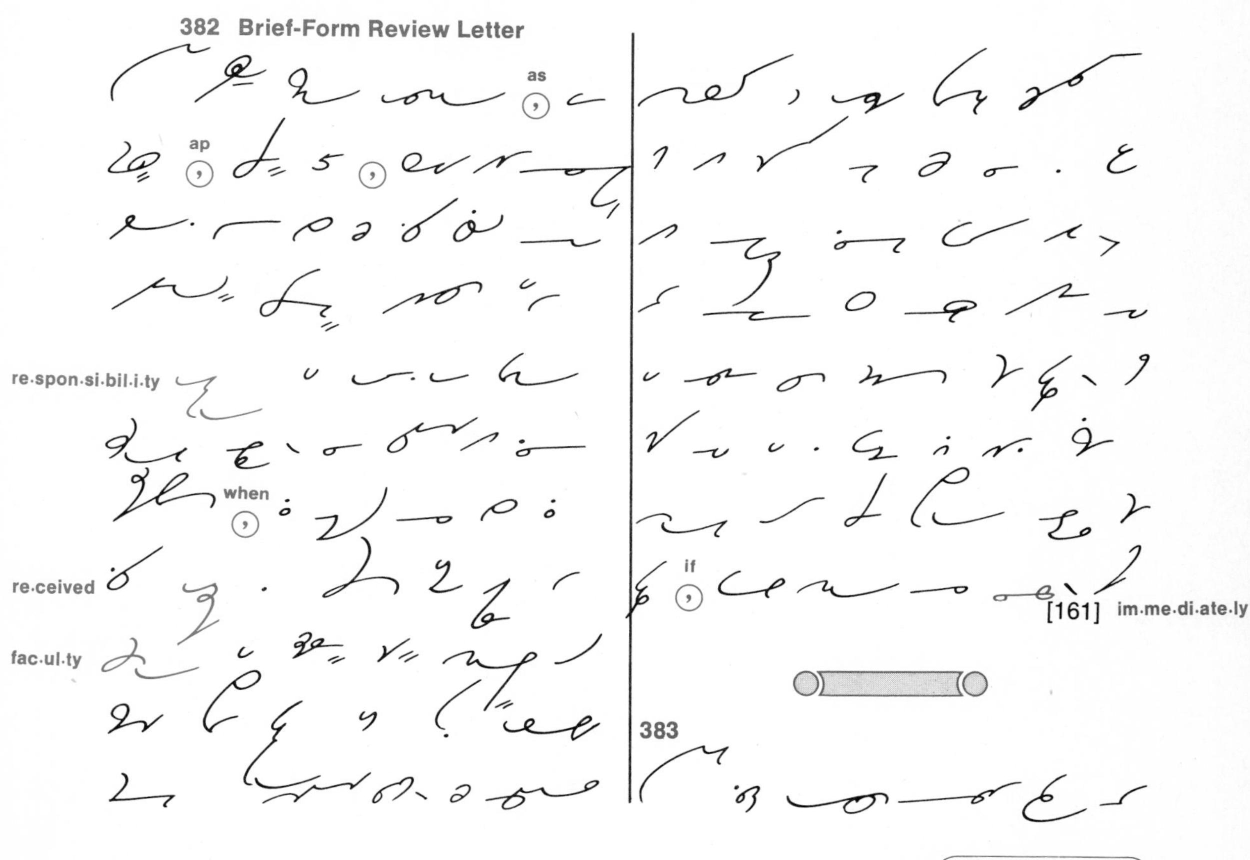

ser

prac·ti·cal

par

var·i·ous

20

12

ser

qual·i·ty

when

ar·ea

dis·cuss

par

[182]

384

ap

cus·tom·er

due

ap

sub·stan·tial

prompt·ly

par

par

if

re·mit·tances

[135]

385

route

gov·ern·ment

par

par·tic·u·lar·ly

as

text

be·lieve

when

pro·ceed

as

[150]

386

par

re·place·ment

phases

oc·curred

[124]

387

par

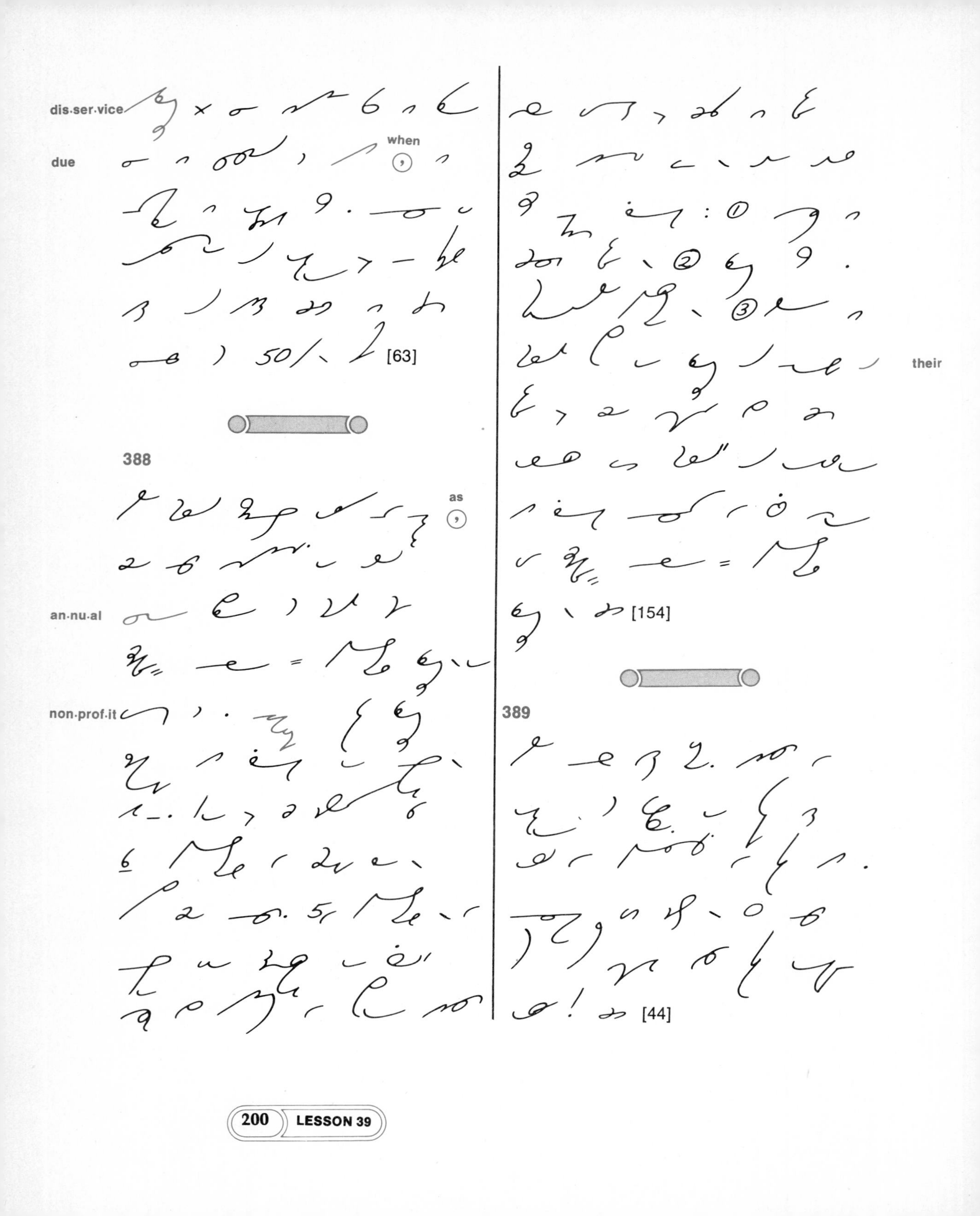

dis·ser·vice

due

when

[63]

388

as

an·nu·al

non·prof·it

their

[154]

389

[44]

Principles

390 Abbreviated Words—in Families

Many long words may be abbreviated in shorthand by dropping the endings. This device is, of course, used in longhand, as *Jan.* for *January.* The extent to which you can avail yourself of this device will depend on your familiarity with the words and with the subject matter of the dictation. Whenever you are in doubt as to whether you should abbreviate a word or write it out, write it out!

The ending of a word is not dropped when a special shorthand word-ending form has been provided, such as *-cal* in *practical.*

Notice how many of the words written with this abbreviating device fall naturally into families of similar endings.

-quent

Frequent, frequently, consequent-consequence, consequently, subsequent, subsequently, eloquent, eloquently.

-tribute

Attribute, contribute, contributed, contribution, distribute, distributed, distributor.

-quire

Require, requirement, required, inquiry, inquiries, inquired, esquire.

-titute

Substitute, substituted, substitution, institute, institution, constitute, constitution.

-titude

Aptitude, gratitude, attitude, altitude, latitude.

Building Transcription Skills

391 PUNCTUATION PRACTICE , introductory A comma is used to separate a subordinate (or introductory) clause from a following main clause. You have already studied the application of this rule to subordinate clauses introduced by *if, as,* and *when*. Here are additional examples:

While I understand the statement, *I do not agree with it.*

Although it was only 3 o'clock, *he closed the office.*

Before you sign the contract, *discuss it with your lawyer.*

A comma is also used after introductory words or phrases such as *furthermore, on the contrary,* and *for instance.*

Furthermore, *the report was incomplete.*

On the contrary, *you are the one who is responsible.*

For your convenience in sending your check, *I am enclosing an envelope.*

Each time a subordinate word, phrase, or clause other than one beginning with *if, as,* or *when* occurs in the Reading and Writing Practice, it will be indicated thus in the shorthand: intro (,)

▶ Note: If the subordinate clause or other introductory expression follows the main clause, the comma is usually not necessary.

I am enclosing an envelope for your convenience in sending your check.

---

392 Business Vocabulary Builder

atlas A bound collection of maps.

maintenance The upkeep of property or equipment.

endeavor *(noun)* A serious, determined effort.

Reading and Writing Practice

393 Brief-Form Review Letter

con·fer·ence

intro

ex·cel·lent

intro

ban·quet

ap

intro

in·quired

par

oc·ca·sion

ar·ea

intro

[176]

394

lease

when

ser

fu·el

intro

intro

ve·hi·cle

if

if

as

re·al·ize

[138]

395

re·ferred

as

intro

re·quests

par

readi·ly

par

un·pleas·ant

par

par

en·deav·or

[139]

ap

ur·gent

intro

co·op·er·a·tion

sat·is·fied

par

[138]

396

397

Man·u·al

ap

ap

com·mer·cial

col·ors

piece

intro

in·qui·ries

[132]

398

wom·en

par

com·plete·ly

intro

fur·ther·more

ser

par

[135]

Principles

399 Abbreviated Words—in Families (Continued)

-graph

Phonograph, paragraph, telegraph, photograph, photographic, autographed, stenographer.

400 Abbreviated Words—Not in Families

The ending may be omitted from long words even though they do not fall into a family.

Anniversary, convenient-convenience, memorandum, significant-significance, statistic, statistics, statistical.

Reluctant-reluctance, equivalent, privilege, privileged, privileges.

401 Word Beginning Trans-

The word beginning *trans-* is represented by a disjoined *t*.

Spell: trans-a-k-t, transact

Transact, transaction, transportation, transmitted, translation, transistor, transfer, transcribe, transplant.

Building Transcription Skills

402 SIMILAR-WORDS DRILL assistance, assistants

assistance Help.

Thank you for the assistance *you gave me with my term paper.*

assistants Helpers.

One of my assistants *will discuss the matter with you.*

403 Business Vocabulary Builder

transmitted Forwarded; handed over.

reluctant Unwilling.

autographed Signed by hand.

Reading and Writing Practice

404

par

Gov·er·nor

when

as·sis·tance

grat·i·tude

intro

[129]

per·son·al

405

an·ni·ver·sa·ry

intro

priv·i·lege

par

wouldn't

intro

if

ser

en·ve·lope

[173]

406

ap

oc·ca·sion

as

max·i·mum

intro

[165]

407

Guide

ap

when

stud·ied

intro

ex·ceed·ing·ly

ser

gen·er·ous

intro

un·bi·ased

intro

[121]

408

ad·ver·tise·ment

as

as·sis·tants

[91]

409

intro

per·mis·sion

[89]

410

prac·ti·cal

ser

intro

at·mo·sphere

par

priv·i·lege

[70]

411

par

var·i·ous

past

25

if

[152]

TRANSCRIPTION CHECKLIST *Are you getting the full benefit from the spelling and punctuation helps in the Reading and Writing Practice by—*

- 1 Encircling all punctuation in your notes as you copy each Reading and Writing Practice?
- 2 Noting the reason for the use of each punctuation mark to be sure that you understand why it was used?
- 3 Spelling aloud at least once the spelling words given in the margin of the shorthand?

RECALL

There are no new shorthand devices for you to learn in Lesson 42. However, it does contain a review of the word beginnings and endings you have studied thus far. The Reading and Writing Practice contains some suggestions that you should heed carefully if you wish to get ahead in business.

412 Recall Chart

There are 90 word beginnings and word endings in the following chart. Can you read the entire chart in 4 minutes or less?

WORD BEGINNINGS AND ENDINGS

1						
2						
3						
4						
5						
6						
7						
8						
9						
10						

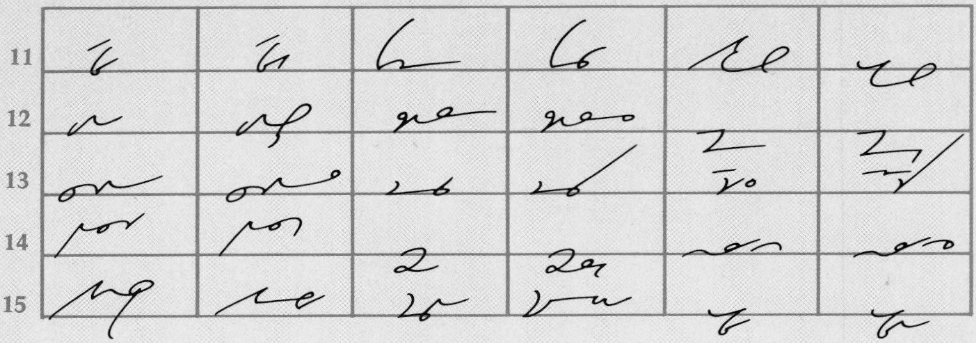

11						
12						
13						
14						
15						

Building Transcription Skills

413 Business Vocabulary Builder

tribulations Trying experiences.

comprehend Understand.

similarities Likenesses.

significantly Considerably.

Reading and Writing Practice

Reading Scoreboard The last time you measured your reading speed was in Lesson 30. See how much your reading speed has grown since Lesson 30. The following table will help you measure your reading speed on the *first reading* of Lesson 42.

Lesson 42 contains 632 words

If you read Lesson 42 in **17 minutes** your reading rate is **38 words a minute**
If you read Lesson 42 in **20 minutes** your reading rate is **32 words a minute**
If you read Lesson 42 in **23 minutes** your reading rate is **28 words a minute**
If you read Lesson 42 in **25 minutes** your reading rate is **25 words a minute**
If you read Lesson 42 in **29 minutes** your reading rate is **22 words a minute**
If you read Lesson 42 in **32 minutes** your reading rate is **20 words a minute**

If you can read Lesson 42 through the first time in less than 17 minutes, you are doing well. If you take considerably more than 32 minutes, perhaps you should:

- 1 Pay closer attention in class while the shorthand devices are being presented to you.
- 2 Spend less time trying to decipher outlines that you cannot read after spelling them.
- 3 Review, occasionally, all the brief forms you have studied through the chart at the back of the book.

414 Evaluate Yourself

if

in·ven·to·ry

traits

ser

at·ti·tudes

intro

se·ri·ous

bawl

their

em·bar·rass

trib·u·la·tions

if

hon·es·ty

[193]

415 Words, Words, Words

as

un·fa·mil·iar

intro

com·pre·hend

achieve

par

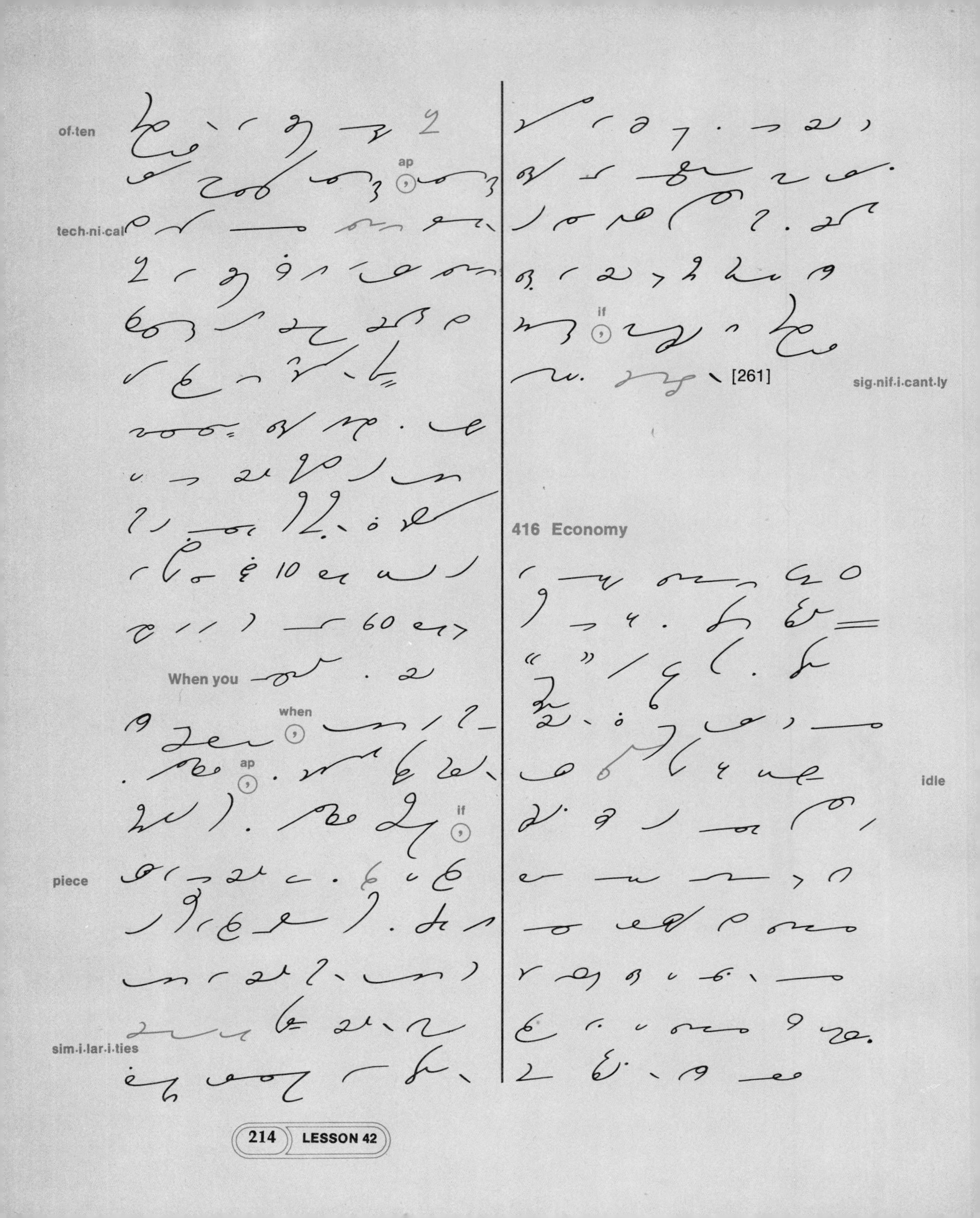

of·ten

ap

tech·ni·cal

When you

when

ap

if

piece

sim·i·lar·i·ties

if

[261]

sig·nif·i·cant·ly

416 Economy

idle

stin·gi·ness

intro

if

intro

intro

intro

[178]

BRIEF-FORM CHECKLIST *Are you making good use of the brief-form chart that appears on page* 447? *Remember, the brief forms represent many of the commonest words in the language; and the better you know them, the more rapid progress you will make in developing your shorthand speed.*

Are you—

- 1 Spending a few minutes reading from the chart each day?
- 2 Timing yourself and trying to cut a few seconds off your reading time with each reading?
- 3 Reading the brief forms in a different order each time—from left to right, from right to left, from top to bottom, from bottom to top?

CHAPTER

The Secretary Interacts With Others

No one in the business world needs greater skill in both human and public relations than the secretary. From the beginning to the end of the working day, the secretary must deal with people—instructing, asking, requesting, persuading, explaining, reminding, listening, cooperating.

Only when the principles of good human relations are observed in an office, can members of the business team work together successfully. Working well with others involves much more than merely getting along with people. It involves a conscious effort to exercise good judgment and tact, to feel concern for the problems and reactions of others, to show consideration for them and for their viewpoints, and to develop the personal character traits of loyalty, trust, and fairness.

Many situations arise every day in which the secretary will need the cooperation of co-workers. There will be other instances when the secretary will be asked to lend a hand to workers in other departments. These situations may involve working with other secretaries, receptionists, mailroom clerks, messengers, or copy-machine attendants. In addition, good working relationships must be developed with people outside the office. For example, the secretary might deal with a temporary personnel agency, a duplicating service, a machine-maintenance service, or even a florist.

It is necessary to maintain good human relations with all office personnel, but those with the employer are of paramount importance to the secretary. The successful secretary must have an excellent working relationship with the employer. This relationship must be based on mutual respect and understanding of the rights and responsibilities of each person.

Another of the secretary's important functions in human interactions is to maintain good relations with other company executives and, of course, with their secretaries. A secretary can contribute substantially to the employer's success by maintaining good human relationships between company offices.

Although the terms *human relations* and *public relations* are often used interchangeably, they do not mean the same thing. Human relations is based on understanding and responding to an individual or a group. Public relations is the technique of developing and keeping the goodwill of the public and the people with whom the company deals for the company and its employees.

The secretary's role as a public relations representative for the company is vital. It is the secretary to whom most customers and visitors first speak, either in person or by telephone. It is the secretary's voice or typed correspondence that says, "We are pleased to work with you."

Whether the situation involves dealing with another employee, a customer, a supplier, or a visitor, the secretary's skill in dealing with people is very important. The secretary's manner with co-workers, executives, or outside contacts has much to do with the overall success of the business.

Many secretaries consider the opportunities to meet and help others—whether from outside or within the firm—the most important job they do.

Principles

417 Word Beginning Mis-

The word beginning *mis-* is represented by *m-s*.

Spell: mis-t-a-k, mistake

Mistake, mistaken, misapprehension, misplaced, misunderstood, mystery.

418 Word Beginning Super-

The word beginning *super-* is represented by a disjoined right *s*.

Spell: super-v-ī-s, supervise

Supervise, supervisor, supervisory, supervision, superintendent, superior, superb.

419 U Represented by OO

The *oo* hook may be used after *n* and *m* to represent the sound of u, as in *music*.

Spell: m-oo-s-e-k, music

Music, musical, mutual, communicate, communication, continue.

Building Transcription Skills

420 PUNCTUATION PRACTICE , conjunction

A comma is used to separate two independent clauses that are joined by one of these conjunctions: *and, but, or, for, nor.*

An independent clause (sometimes called a main or a principal clause) is one that has a subject and a predicate and that could stand alone as a complete sentence.

There are 15 people in my department, but *only 11 of them are here now.*

The first independent clause is:

There are 15 people in my department

And the second independent clause is:

Only 11 of them are here now.

Both clauses could stand as separate sentences, with a period after each. Because the thoughts of the two clauses are closely related, however, the clauses were joined to form one sentence. Because the two independent clauses are connected by the conjunction *but,* a comma is used between them and is placed before the conjunction.

Each time this use of the comma occurs in the Reading and Writing Practice, it will be indicated thus in the shorthand: conj (,)

---

421 Business Vocabulary Builder

misapprehension Misunderstanding.

strikingly Impressively.

suitability Fitness.

Reading and Writing Practice

422 Brief-Form Review Letter

ad·ver·tis·ing

ser

mis·ap·pre·hen·sion

conj

com·pa·nies

when

ser

dis·cussed

than

par

bud·get

[150]

423

su·per·vi·sors

ap

su·perb

ser

han·dling

conj

so·lu·tions

conj

cou·pon

[194]

424

manu·script

conj

su·pe·ri·or

ac·cept

intro

if

re·view·er's

[139]

425

Mys·tery

conj

intro

as

sci·en·tif·ic

yours

conj

ar·ea

par

prompt·ly

[137]

426

re·spon·si·ble

as

ap

conj

ac·knowl·edg·ment

intro

quite

if

any·one

[98]

427

ti·tles

ap

conj

cop·ies shipped

ap

Pol·i·tics

off

when

par

[129]

428

edi·tion

ap

ad·di·tion

par

com·ple·tion

conj

[147]

429

en·light·en·ing

ap

as

when

intro

per·mis·sion

par

[123]

Principles

430 Word Beginning Self-

The word beginning *self-* is represented by a disjoined left *s*.

Spell: self-m-a-d, self-made

Self-made, self-confidence, self-reliance, self-addressed, self-improvement, self-assurance, selfish, unselfish, selfishness.

431 Word Beginning Circum-

The word beginning *circum-* is also represented by a disjoined left *s*.

Spell: circum-s-ten-s, circumstance

Circumstance, circumstances, circumstantial, circumnavigate, circumvent.

432 Word Ending -ification

The word ending *-ification* is represented by a disjoined *f*.

Spell: k-l-a-s-ification, classification

Classification, specification, justification, notification, gratification, identification, modifications, qualifications.

Building Transcription Skills

433 PUNCTUATION PRACTICE , and omitted

When two or more adjectives modify the same noun, they are separated by commas.

A stamped, addressed *envelope is enclosed.*

However, the comma is not used if the first adjective modifies the combined idea of the second adjective plus the noun.

The book was bound in an attractive brown *cloth.*

Note: You can quickly determine whether to insert a comma between two consecutive adjectives by mentally placing *and* between them. If the sentence makes good sense with *and* inserted between the adjectives, then the comma is used. For example, the first illustration would make good sense if it read:

A stamped and *addressed envelope is enclosed.*

Each time this use of the comma occurs in the Reading and Writing Practice, it will be indicated thus in the shorthand: and o (,)

---

434 Business Vocabulary Builder

merger The combining of two or more business organizations.

upright Honest; conscientious.

trying *(adjective)* Difficult.

tedious Boring.

Reading and Writing Practice

435 Brief-Form Review Letter

prob.a.bly

as

gov.ern.ment

par

conj

and o

cour.te.ous

ser

priv.i.leges

con.ve.niences

if

[161]

436

stud·ied

when

an·noyed

ap

su·per·in·ten·dent

[111]

437

and o

up·right
cit·i·zens

ser

prin·ci·ples

par

and o

en·ve·lope

[117]

438

para·graph

par

intro

valu·able

intro

poise

ser

when

con·vinc·ing·ly

par

en·roll·ing

if

156-1171 [166]

439

as

for·mal·ly

ap

ap·pre·ci·ate

and o

conj

te·dious

[124]

com·mit·tee

440

ap

15

[33]

441

if

fer·vent·ly

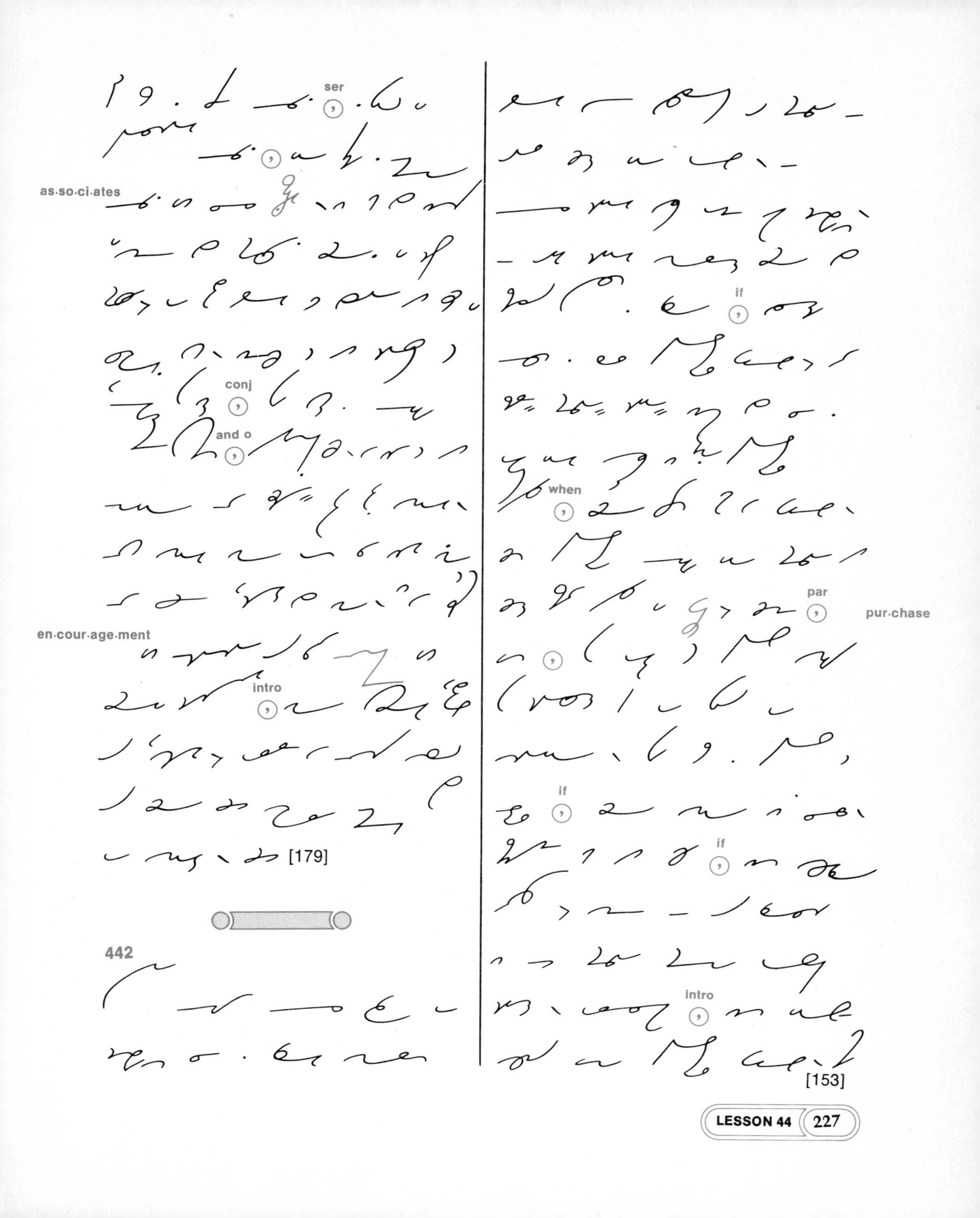

ser

as·so·ci·ates

conj

and o

en·cour·age·ment

intro

[179]

442

if

when

par

pur·chase

if

if

intro

[153]

Principles

443 Word Ending -hood

The word ending *-hood* is represented by a disjoined *d*.

Spell: n-a-b-r-hood, neighborhood

Neighborhood, childhood, boyhood, girlhood, parenthood, likelihood.

444 Word Ending -ward

The word ending *-ward* is also represented by a disjoined *d*.

Spell: o-n-ward, onward

Onward, backward, afterward, awkward, rewarding, forward, forwarded.

445 Ul

Ul is represented by *oo* when it precedes a forward or upward stroke.

Spell: re-s-ul-t, result

Result, consult, adult, ultimately, multiply, culminate.

446 Quantities and Amounts

Here are a few more helpful abbreviations for quantities and amounts.

500; $500; $5,000,000; $5,000,000,000; a dollar, a million, several hundred, 5 pounds, 8 feet.

▶ Notice that the *n* for *hundred* is written under the figure as a positive distinction from *million,* in which the *m* is written beside the figure.

Building Transcription Skills

447 SPELLING FAMILIES -tion, -sion, -shion An effective device to improve your ability to spell is to study words in related groups, or spelling families, that contain a common problem; for example, words ending in the sound *shun.* This sound is sometimes spelled *tion,* sometimes *sion,* and occasionally *shion.*

Practice each spelling family in this way:

- 1 Spell each word aloud, pausing slightly after each syllable.
- 2 Write each word once in longhand, spelling it aloud as you read it.

You will find many *shun* words in the Reading and Writing Practice.

Words Ending in -tion

ed·u·ca·tion	**no·ti·fi·ca·tion**	**pub·li·ca·tion**
in·for·ma·tion	**cir·cu·la·tion**	**po·si·tion**
or·ga·ni·za·tion	**op·er·a·tions**	**re·la·tions**

Words Ending in -sion

oc·ca·sion	**pro·fes·sion**	**ex·ten·sion**
di·vi·sion	**dis·cus·sion**	**pro·vi·sion**
ses·sion	**de·ci·sion**	**re·vi·sion**

Words Ending in -shion

fash·ion	**cush·ion**

448 Business Vocabulary Builder

ultimate Maximum; final.

prone Having a tendency or inclination.

insecure Uncertain.

Reading and Writing Practice

449 Brief-Form Review Letter

ses·sion

ap

com·put·er·iz·ing

conj

ar·ea

prof·it·able

and o

or·ga·ni·za·tion

neigh·bor·hood

par

if

ad·van·tage

[181]

450

when

phys·i·cal·ly

conj

prone

ser

in·se·cure

awk·ward

and o

intro

ex·er·cise

stead

intro

intro

bod·ies

[157] —*Physical Fitness Council*

451

and o

par as

ser

mis·cel·la·neous

due conj

re·mit·tance intro

and o

intro en·ve·lope prompt·ly

[183]

452

and o

intro

rise

ex·ceed·ing·ly

intro

spe·cial if [158]

col·ors conj pro·fes·sion·al

453

intro intro oc·ca·sion [113]

SHORTHAND NOTEBOOK CHECKLIST

Your shorthand notebook is another important tool of your trade. Do you:

- **1** Use a notebook with a spiral binding so that the pages always lie flat as you write?
- **2** Write on the front cover your name and the first and last dates on which you use the notebook?
- **3** Place a rubber band around the used portion of your notebook so that it opens automatically to the first blank page?
- **4** Date the first page of each day's dictation at the bottom of the page for quick and convenient reference—just as a stenographer in an office would do?
- **5** Check before class to see that there are sufficient pages remaining in your notebook for the day's dictation and, if not, supply yourself with a second notebook so that you will not run out of paper in the middle of dictation?

Principles

454 Word Ending -gram

The word ending *-gram* is represented by a disjoined *gay*.

Spell: t-e-l-gram, telegram

Telegram, diagram, cablegram, program, programs, programmed.

455 Word Beginning Electric-

The word beginning *electric-* (and the word *electric*) is represented by a disjoined *el*.

Spell: electric-l, electrical

Electric, electrical, electrically, electric typewriter, electric wire, electric motor.

456 Word Beginning Electr-

The word beginning *electr-* is also represented by a disjoined *el*.

Spell: electro-n-e-k, electronic

Electronic, electronically, electricity, electrician.

457 Compounds

Most compound words are formed simply by joining the outlines for the words that make up the compound. In some words, however, it is desirable to modify the outline for one of the words in order to obtain an easier joining.

Anyhow, anywhere, thereupon, someone, worthwhile, however, within, withstand, notwithstanding.*

*The dot may be omitted in *however*.

458 Intersection

Intersection, or the writing of one shorthand character through another, is sometimes uesful for special phrases. This principle may be used when constant repetition of certain combinations of words in your dictation makes it clearly worthwhile to form special outlines for them.

A.m., p.m., vice versa, Chamber of Commerce.

Building Transcription Skills

459 SIMILAR-WORDS DRILL prominent, permanent

prominent Notable; standing out.

He took lessons from a prominent *musician.*

permanent Not subject to change; lasting.

He was offered a permanent *job with the company.*

---

460 Business Vocabulary Builder

consultant One who gives professional advice or services; an expert.

primarily Chiefly.

priority Something meriting first attention.

● Reading and Writing Practice

461 Brief-Form Review Letter

con·sul·tant

ap

plane

for·tu·nate·ly

intro

par

Mu·nic·i·pal

ap

prom·i·nent

if

par

[174] fee

462

when

some·one

per·ma·nent

elec·tri·cal

ser

ap

neigh·bor·hood

par

con·ve·nient

[141]

463

Su·pe·ri·or

as

shelves

ser

man·u·als

par

pri·mar·i·ly

intro

and o

pro·fes·sion·al

ap

15

10

en·joy·able

conj

sou·ve·nir

[176]

464

intro

pro·gram·ming

intro

em·ploy·ees

[106]

465

ap

sched·uled

15

con·fi·dent

par

[111]

466

ap

con·trol·ling

par

par

its

[129]

467

ap

ser

if

[87]

Principles

468 Geographical Expressions and Names

In geographical expressions and names, *-burg* is expressed by *b; -ingham,* by a disjoined *m; -ington,* by a disjoined *ten* blend; *-ville,* by *v.*

-burg

Spell: h-a-r-e-s-berg, Harrisburg

Harrisburg, Pittsburgh, Greensburg, Bloomsburg, Newburgh.

-ingham

Spell: b-oo-k-ingham, Buckingham

Buckingham, Cunningham, Framingham, Nottingham, Birmingham.

-ington

Spell: l-e-x-ington, Lexington

Lexington, Wilmington, Washington, Burlington, Huntington.

-ville

Spell: n-a-ish-ville, Nashville

Nashville, Jacksonville, Evansville, Brownsville, Louisville, Danville.

Building Transcription Skills

469 GRAMMAR CHECKUP Most executives have a good command of the English language. Some rarely make an error in grammar. There are times, though, when even the best dictators will perhaps use a plural verb with a singular noun or use the objective case when they should have used the nominative. They usually know better. In concentrating intently on expressing a thought or idea, however, they occasionally make a grammatical error.

It will be your job as a stenographer to catch these occasional errors and correct them when you transcribe.

From time to time in the lessons ahead you will be given an opportunity to brush up on some of the rules of grammar that are frequently violated.

GRAMMAR CHECKUP comparisons The comparative degree of an adjective or adverb is used when reference is made to two objects; the superlative degree is used when reference is made to more than two objects.

comparative

Of the two girls, Jane is the taller.

Which boy is more *efficient, Jim or Harry?*

Is Mr. Smith or Ms. Green better *qualified to do the job?*

superlative

Of the three boys, John is the tallest.

Which of the girls is the most *efficient, Jane, Mary, or Arlene?*

Is Mr. Smith, Ms. Green, or Mrs. Brown the best *qualified to do the job?*

---

470 Business Vocabulary Builder

fallacy A false idea.

unsurpassed The best; second to none.

extraordinary Remarkable; unusual.

Reading and Writing Practice

471 Brief-Form Review Letter

as

conj

suits

ap

principle

client

ser

courteous

and o

pleasant

neighborhood

when

and o

unsurpassed

par

[187]

472

par

naturally

intro

intro

extension

par

debts

[138]

473

enough

par

par

trans·ferred

pass·book

if

par

[118]

474

intro

ex·traor·di·nary

and o

sim·ple

li·brary

[78]

475

intro

conj

al·ready

intro

ef·fect

ap

conj

ser

par

fa.cil.i.ties

en.ve.lopes

and o

ap

and o

par

when

[167]

[102]

476

SPELLING AND PUNCTUATION CHECKLIST

Are you careful to punctuate and spell correctly when—

- **1** You write your compositions in English?
- **2** Prepare your reports for your social studies classes?
- **3** Correspond with friends to whom you must write in longhand?

In short, are you making correct spelling and punctuation a habit in all the longhand writing or typing that you do?

RECALL

In Lesson 47 you studied the last of the new shorthand devices of Gregg Shorthand. In this lesson you will find a Recall Chart that reviews all the word-building principles of Gregg Shorthand and a Reading and Writing Practice that contains some "food for thought."

477 Recall Chart

This chart contains illustrations of alphabetic characters, word-building principles, and phrasing principles of Gregg Shorthand.

WORDS

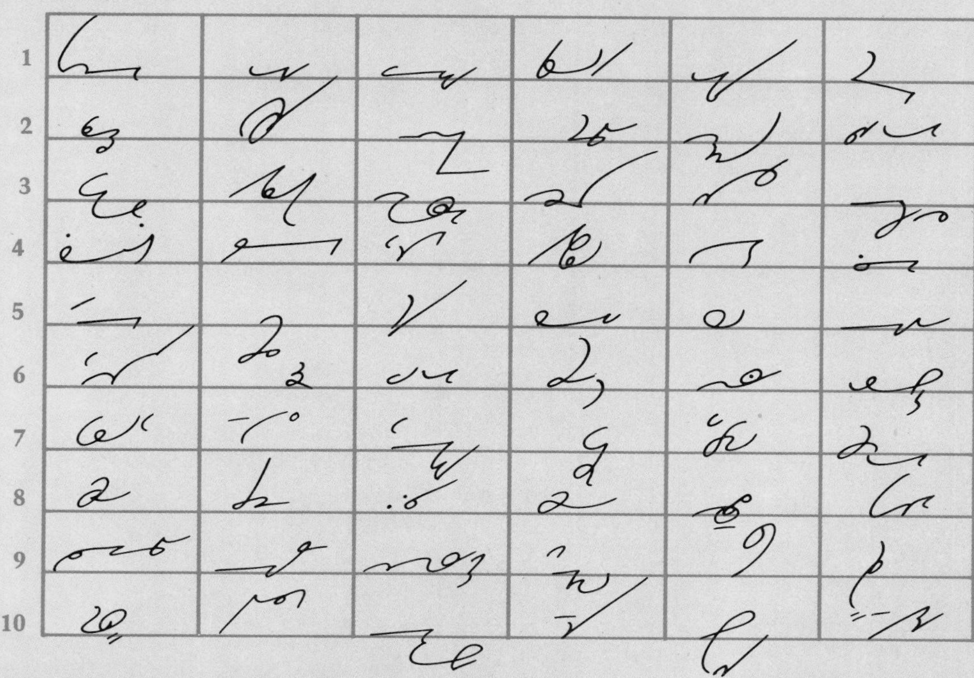

11						
12						
13						
14						

PHRASES AND AMOUNTS

15						
16						
17						

Building Transcription Skills

478 Business Vocabulary Builder

accomplishments Achievements.

phase Aspect; side; part.

extensive Considerable.

Reading and Writing Practice

479 Reading

if

lev·el

conj

intro

Reading for Pleasure.

wheth·er

dai·ly

ser

intro

worth·while

and o

cit·i·zen

conj

well

Reading in School.

es·sen·tial

as

phase

if

col·lege

30

Reading on the Job.

ser

mis·cel·la·neous

intro

sur·vey

ap

par

ad·di·tion

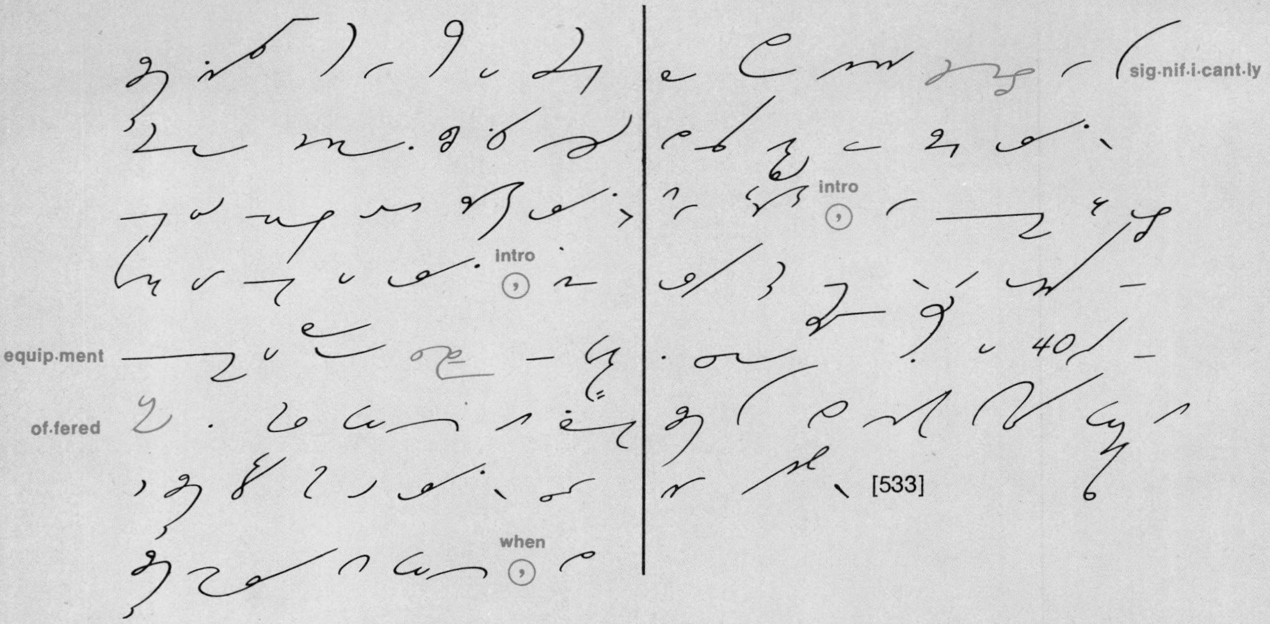

intro

equip·ment

of·fered

when

sig·nif·i·cant·ly

intro

[533]

DID YOU KNOW THAT—

- *President Woodrow Wilson was an expert shorthand writer and that he drafted all his state papers in shorthand?*
- *Samuel Pepys wrote his famous diary in shorthand? He wrote so legibly that students of literature had no difficulty making an accurate transcript of his notes.*
- *George Bernard Shaw did all his composing in shorthand and then had his secretary transcribe his notes?*

PART

Reinforcement

CHAPTER

The Secretary's Day

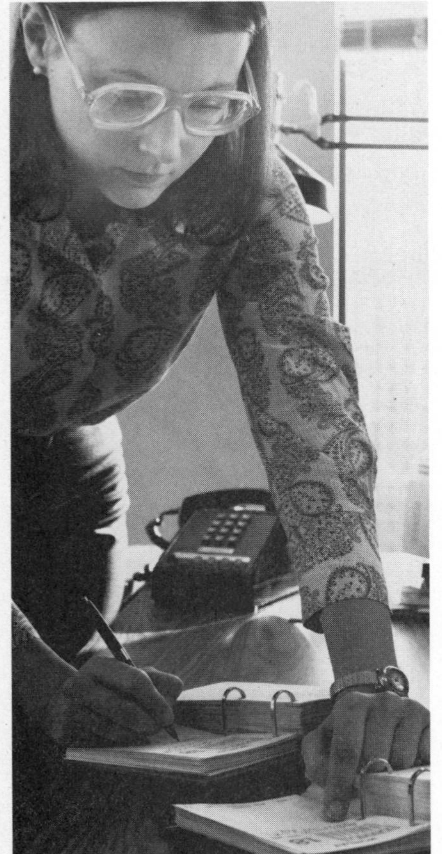

There are as many secretarial job descriptions as there are employer-employee teams, and each job varies considerably from day to day. Although taking dictation and typing are an important part of the day's work, the secretary does many other things as well.

To give you an idea of what a typical day in the life of a secretary is like, imagine that you are secretary to Mrs. Ellen Garcia, marketing manager for a large textile company.

9:00 Arrive at the office. Check Mrs. Garcia's appointment calendar to make sure it agrees with yours. You notice that she has an 11 o'clock staff meeting, a luncheon appointment at 12:30 with Mr. Washington at the Cedar Inn, and a 3 o'clock appointment with Miss Rosen to go over the special department store promotion. A few minutes later, Mrs. Garcia arrives and you remind her of the meetings and appointments for the day. She gives you a corrected draft of a report to type for the staff meeting.

9:15 The morning mail is delivered. You open and sort it and bring it to Mrs. Garcia along with previous correspondence related to the incoming mail. Then you start typing the report.

9:30 Mrs. Garcia calls you in to take dictation.

9:45 You return to your desk to finish typing the report. The telephone rings several times and you provide information to those callers who don't need to speak to Mrs. Garcia personally. Mrs. Garcia asks for some information that must be obtained from the files. The company library calls and asks if Mrs. Garcia is finished with the book she borrowed. Someone else needs it. You check with Mrs. Garcia, and since she no longer needs the book, you take it back to the library.

10:30 You bring the completed report to Mrs. Garcia. While she is reading it, you check to make sure the conference room is ready for the meeting. Mrs. Garcia returns the report with no changes, so you make copies and distribute them for the meeting.

11:00 You make sure that all the materials are ready for the meeting. Then you begin transcribing. And the interruptions begin:

- You answer several telephone calls and take messages.
- Mrs. Garcia calls to ask you to bring a copy of this year's marketing plan to her in the conference room.
- You greet one caller who has come without an appointment. After checking the calendar, you set up a tentative appointment for 10 o'clock tomorrow.

11:45 The meeting is over and Mrs. Garcia stops at your desk to ask you to arrange a two-day trip to the Chicago office Monday and Tuesday of next week. You tell her about the appointment for tomorrow and when she agrees, you call the person and confirm.

12:00 You remind Mrs. Garcia of her luncheon date and then go to lunch yourself, after letting the receptionist know that you are leaving.

1:00 Return from lunch. You make all the necessary arrangements for Mrs. Garcia's trip, including transportation to and from the airports, plane and hotel reservations, and a rental car in Chicago. You type the itinerary and then you return to transcribing.

1:45 Mrs. Garcia returns with Mr. Washington and asks you to give him some papers he needs before he leaves. You get the papers and show him out.

2:00 Mrs. Garcia calls you in so she can start dictating a lengthy report. There are several interruptions; people stop to ask questions and the telephone rings.

2:50 The receptionist calls to say that Miss Rosen has arrived. You go to the reception area and escort her to the office.

3:00 You finish transcribing the morning's dictation.

3:15 Mrs. Garcia buzzes and asks you to bring in the samples of the new line.

3:30 Mrs. Garcia asks you to show Miss Rosen out and then bring your book so that she can continue dictating the report.

4:30 Mrs. Garcia decides to continue the report tomorrow. You prepare the correspondence for her signature. After she has signed the letters, you get them ready for the mail.

5:00 You clear your desk and tell Mrs. Garcia that you are leaving. You go home, knowing that you have worked hard today and that you will work just as hard tomorrow—but that tomorrow's schedule will be entirely different.

The letters in this lesson concentrate on the shorthand principles you studied in Chapter 1. You should have no difficulty reading them.

480 BRIEF FORMS AND DERIVATIVES

1. *I, Mr., have, having, are-hour-our, ours-hours, will-well, willing, a-an, am, at-it, but.*
2. *In-not, increase, invite, indeed, is-his, that, can, cannot, you-your, yours, Mrs., of, with.*

Reading and Writing Practice

481

[57]

482

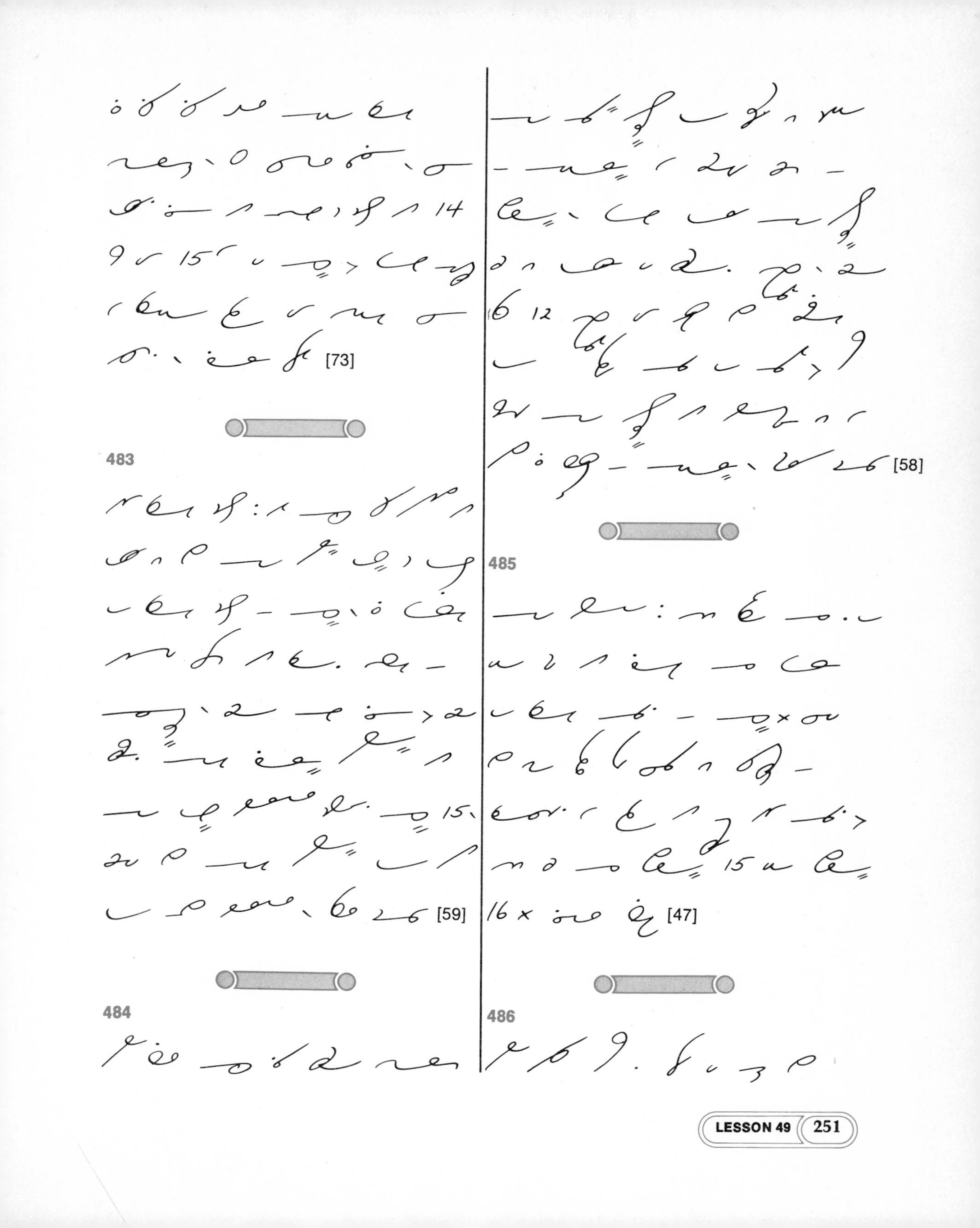

[73]

483

[59]

484

[58]

485

[47]

486

[64]

487

[53]

488

[64]

489

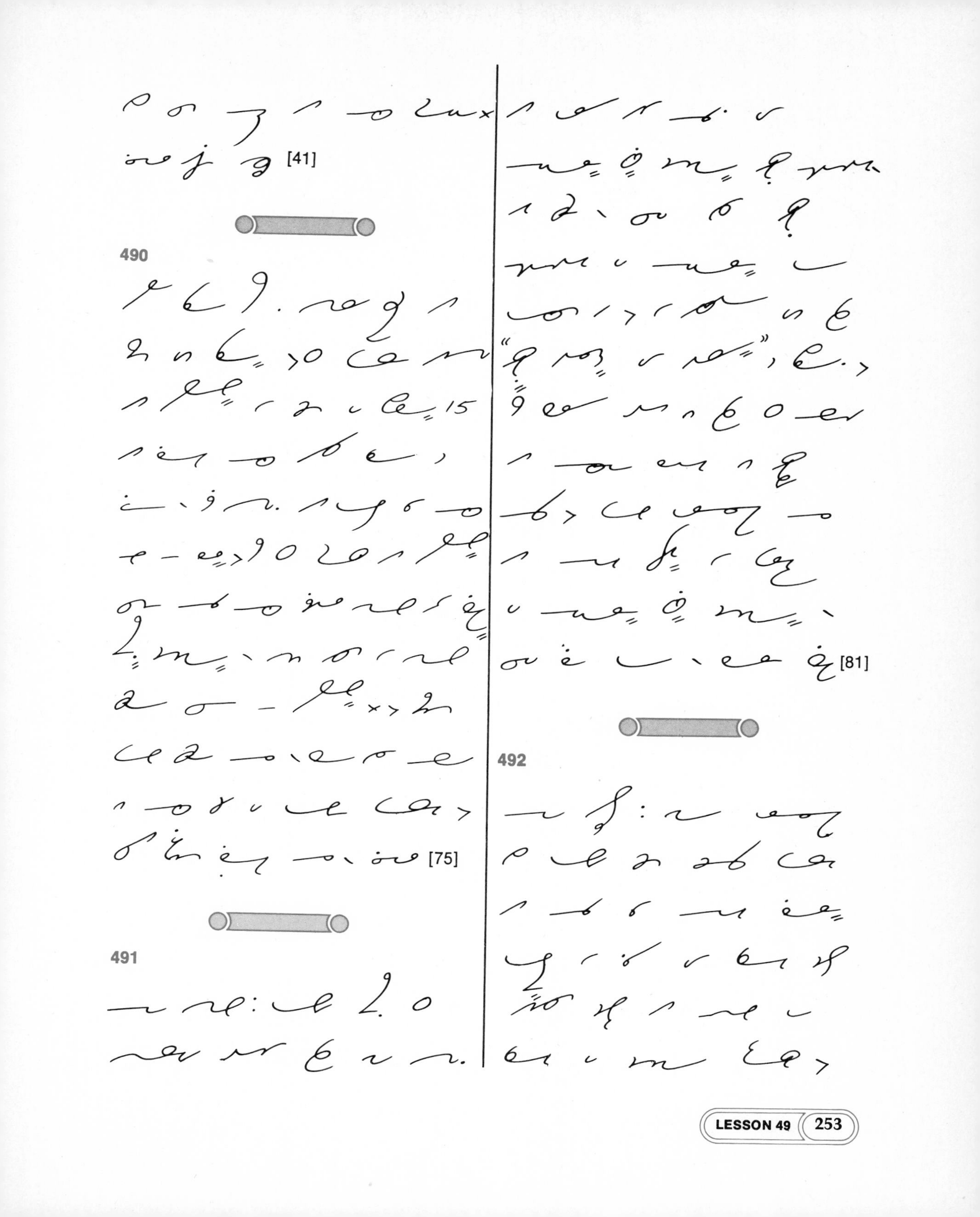

[41]

490

15

[75]

491

[81]

492

[85]

493

[50]

DICTATION CHECKLIST *When you take dictation, do you—*

- 1 Make every effort to keep up with the dictator?
- 2 Refer to your textbook whenever you are in doubt about the outline for a word or phrase?
- 3 Insert periods and question marks in your shorthand notes?
- 4 Make a real effort to observe good proportion as you write—making large circles large, small circles small, etc.?
- Do you write down the first column of your notebook and then down the second column?

The practice material in this lesson concentrates on the shorthand principles you studied in Chapter 2.

494 BRIEF FORMS AND DERIVATIVES

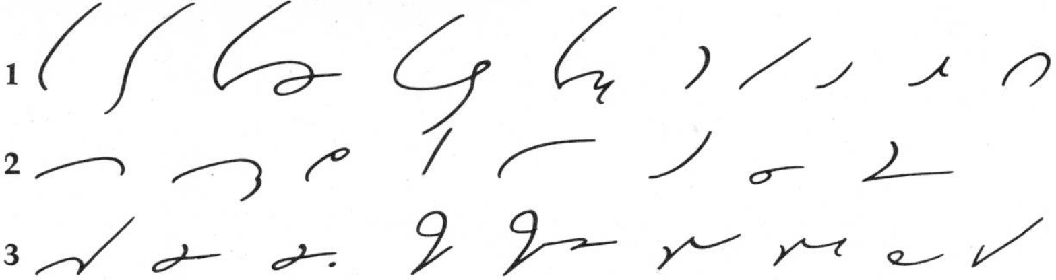

1. *Be-by, before, began, believe, because, for, would, there (their), theirs, this.*
2. *Good, goods, they, which, them, and, when, from.*
3. *Could, send, sending, after, afternoon, street, streets, were, should.*

Building Transcription Skills

495 Business Vocabulary Builder

inspired Motivated.

fatal Causing death.

role Part.

Reading and Writing Practice

496

[75]

497

[95]

498

[81]

499

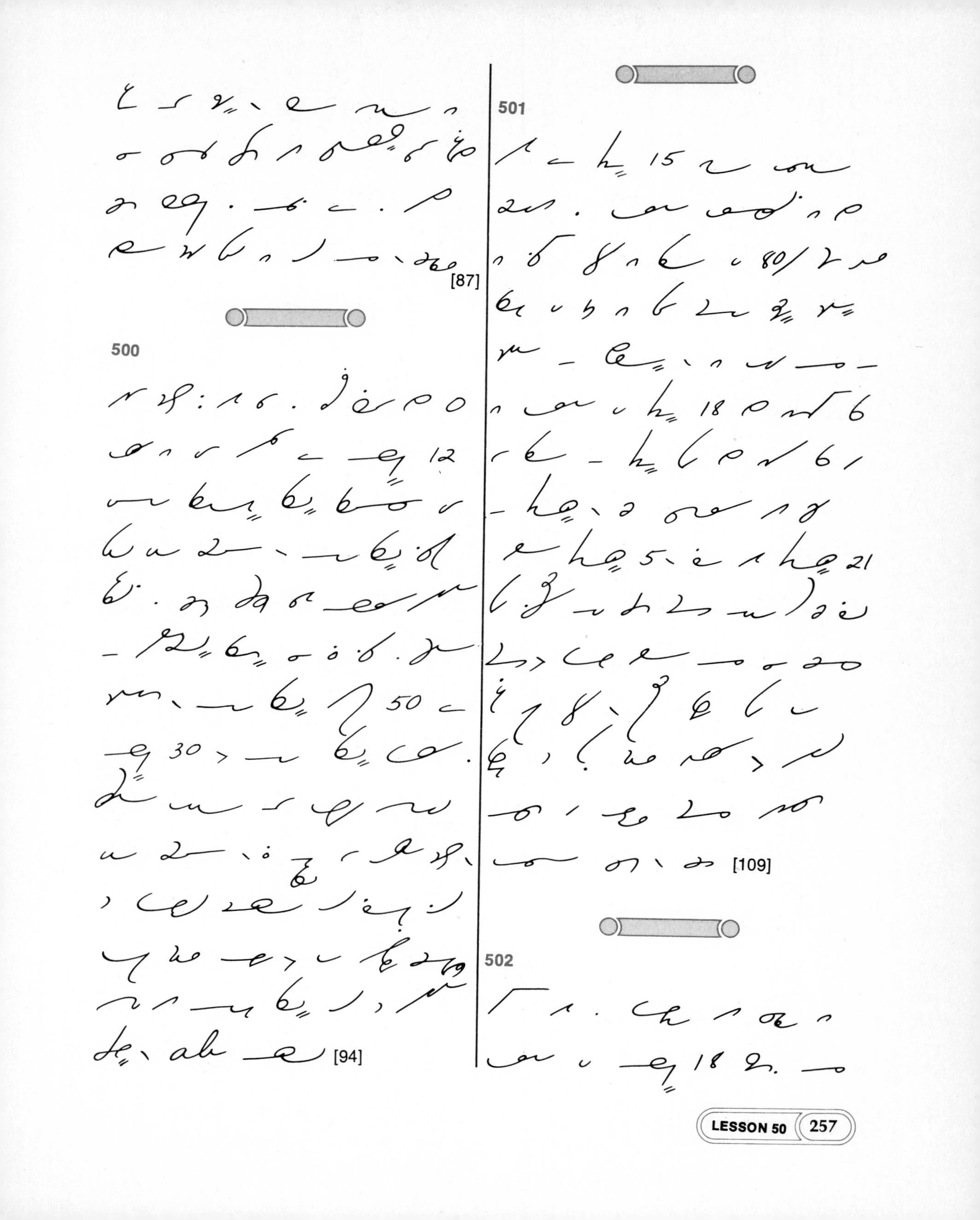

[87]

500

[94]

501

[109]

502

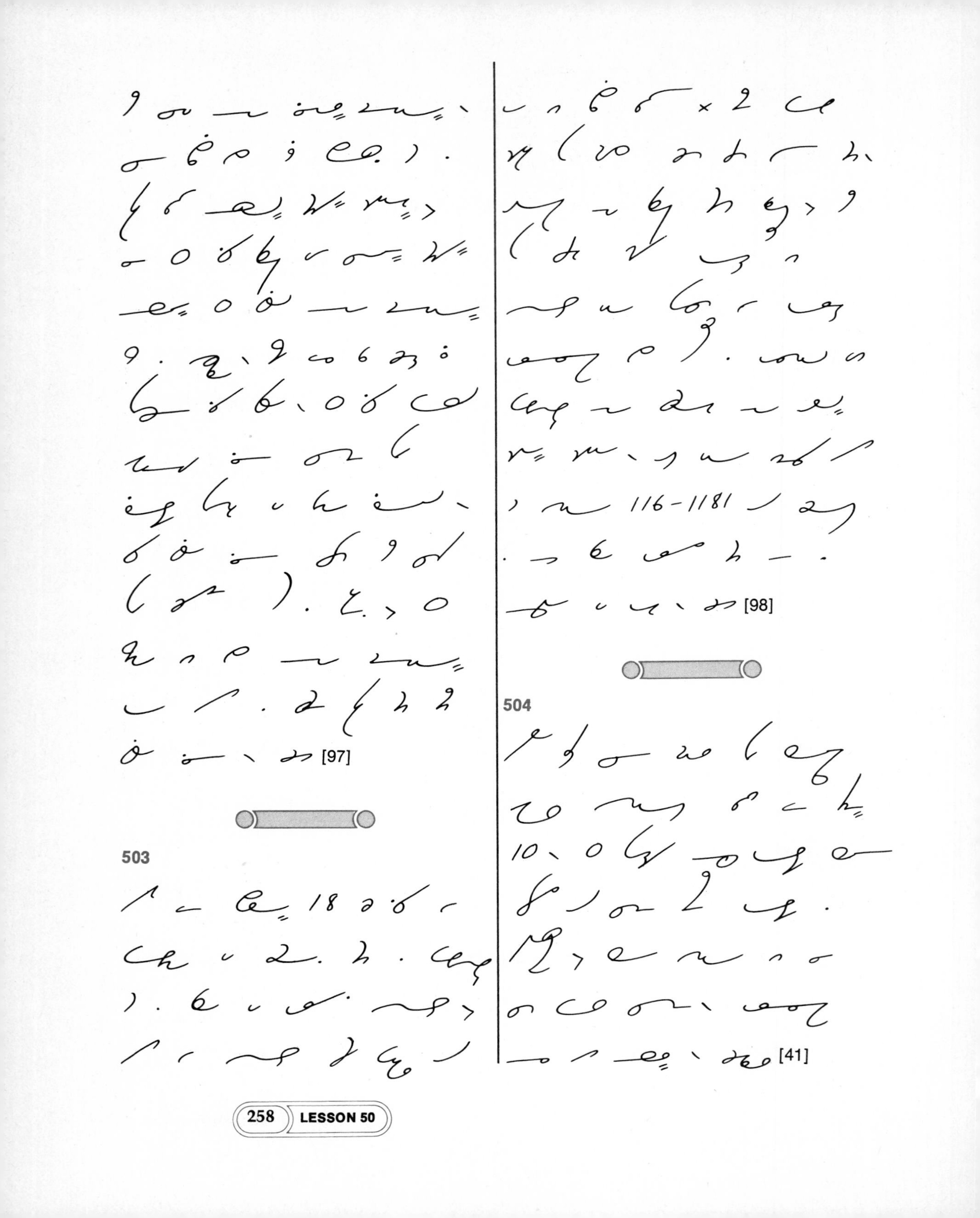

[97]

503

18

116-1181

[98]

504

10

[41]

Lesson 51 concentrates on the shorthand principles you studied in Chapter 3.

505 **BRIEF FORMS AND DERIVATIVES**

1. *Gladly, worked, yesterday, circular, ordered, sooner, thank, enclosed, was.*
2. *Valuable, one (won), once, than, what, about, thing-think, thinks, businesses, doctor, anything.*
3. *Gentlemen, morning, important-importance, where, company, manufacturer, next, shortly.*

Building Transcription Skills

506 **Business Vocabulary Builder**

suitable Adapted to a use or purpose.

launching Originating or setting in motion.

Reading and Writing Practice

507

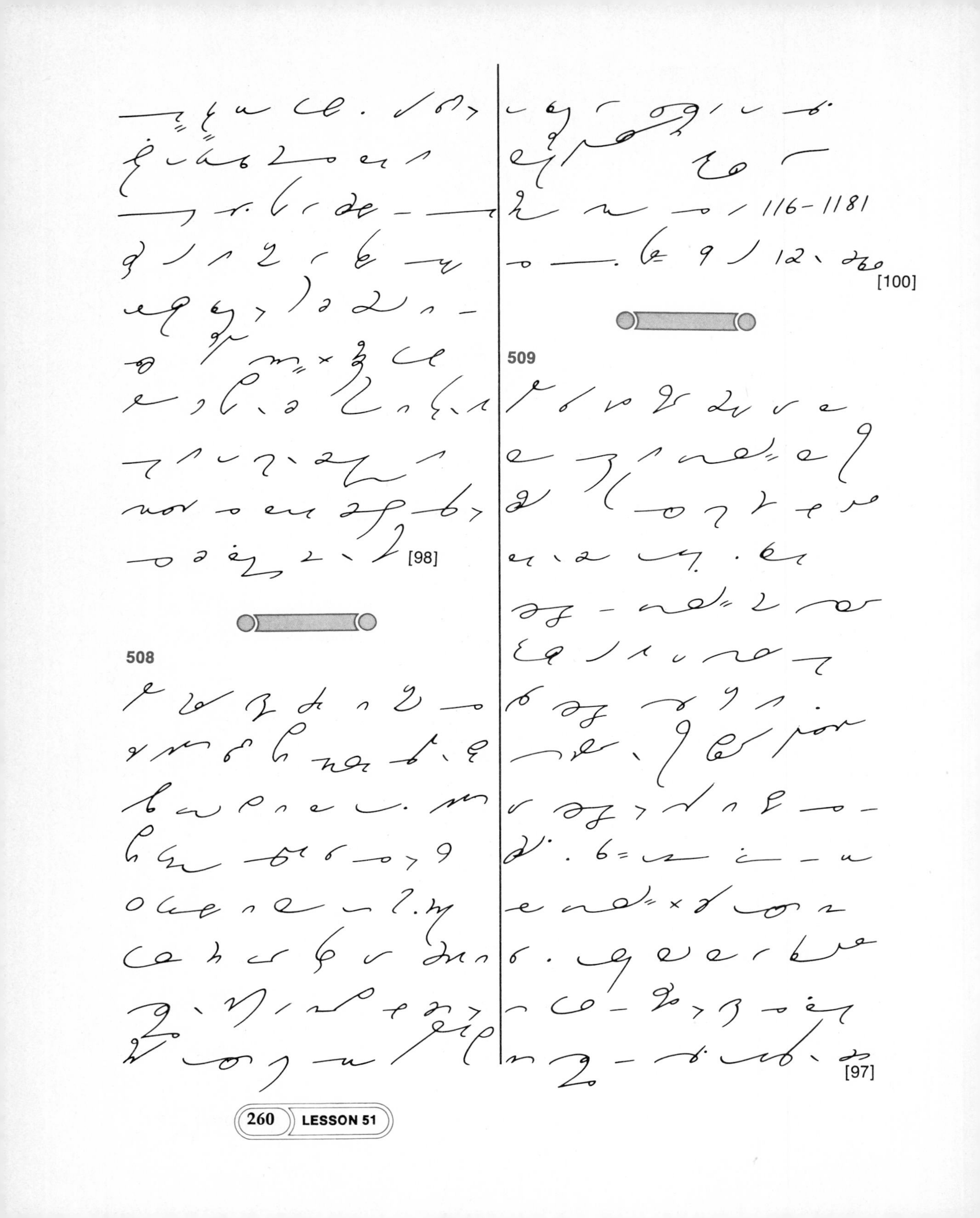

[98]

508

116-1181

12

[100]

509

[97]

510

[114]

511

[126]

512

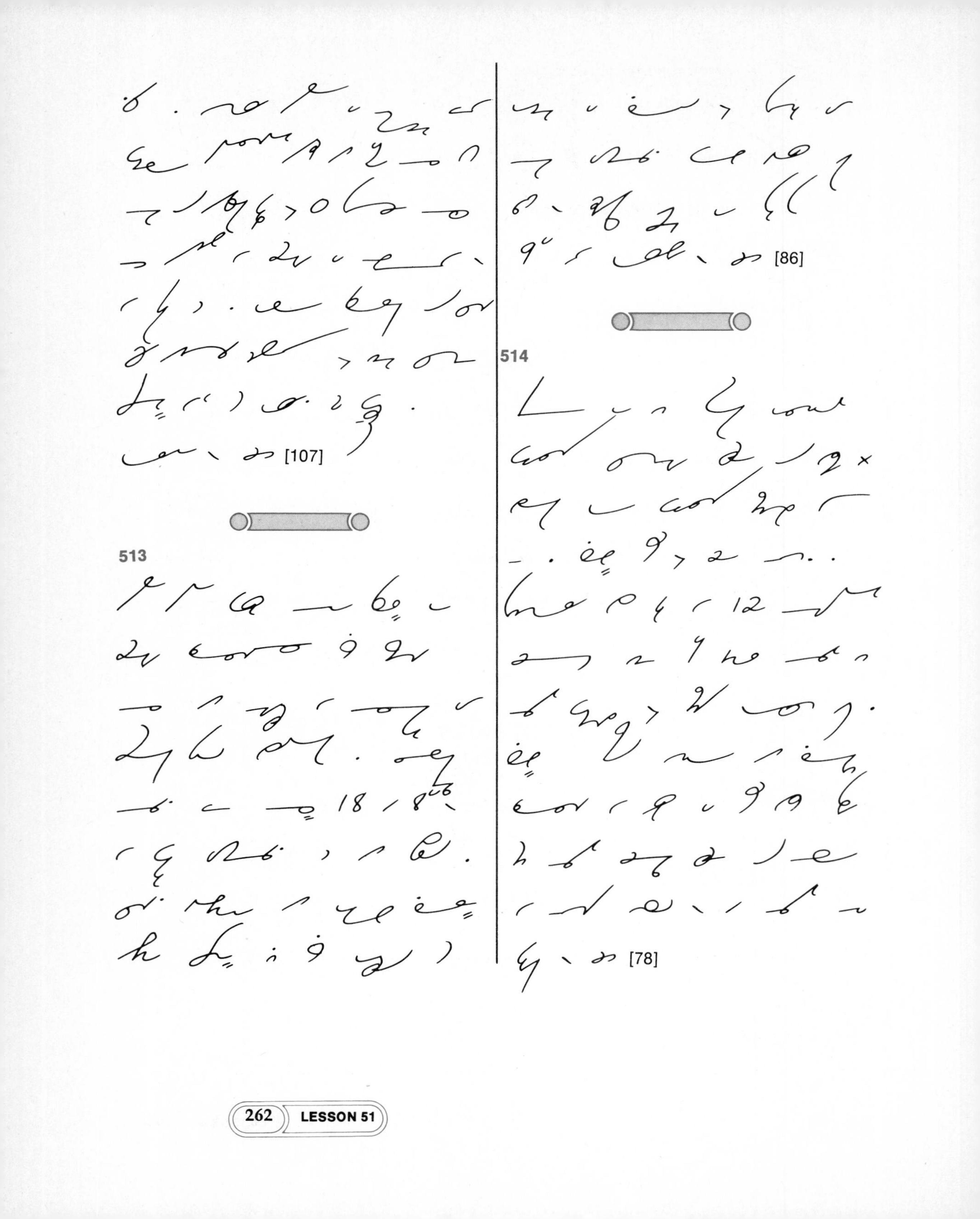

[107]

513

[86]

514

[78]

In this lesson you will receive a concentrated review of the shorthand principles you studied in Chapter 4.

515 **BRIEF FORMS AND DERIVATIVES**

1. *Presently, presents, part, parted, partly, advertise, advertisement, Ms., immediately, opportunities.*
2. *Advantage, advantages, suggestions, several, out, outside, ever-every, whenever, very.*
3. *Time, timed, acknowledgment, acknowledged, generally, questions, organization, overdue, overtime.*

Building Transcription Skills

516 **SPELLING FAMILIES silent e dropped before -ing**

Words in Which Silent E Is Dropped Before -ing

ad·ver·tis·ing	**en·clos·ing**	**in·creas·ing**
de·sir·ing	**ex·am·in·ing**	**pro·duc·ing**
de·cid·ing	**forc·ing**	**pur·chas·ing**
dic·tat·ing	**guid·ing**	**re·ceiv·ing**

517 **Business Vocabulary Builder**

occur Happen.

appropriate *(adjective)* Especially suitable or fitting.

competent Able.

Reading and Writing Practice

518

dic·ta·ting

wheth·er

sim·ply

de·cid·ing

ac·knowl·edge

[158]

519

per·son·nel

ad·ver·tis·ing

30

[117]

520

me·di·um

pur·chas·ing

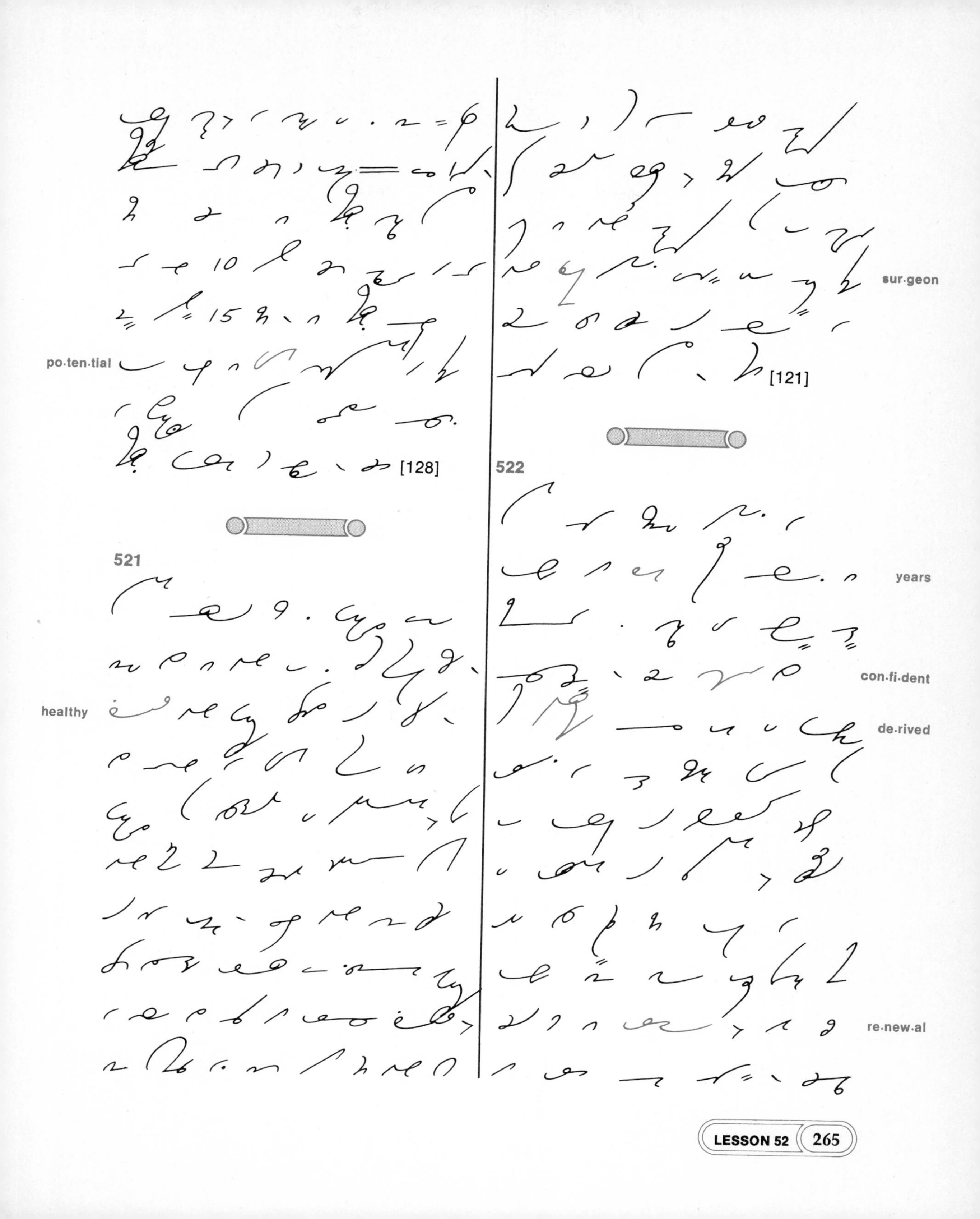

po·ten·tial

[128]

521

healthy

[121]

522

sur·geon

years

con·fi·dent

de·rived

re·new·al

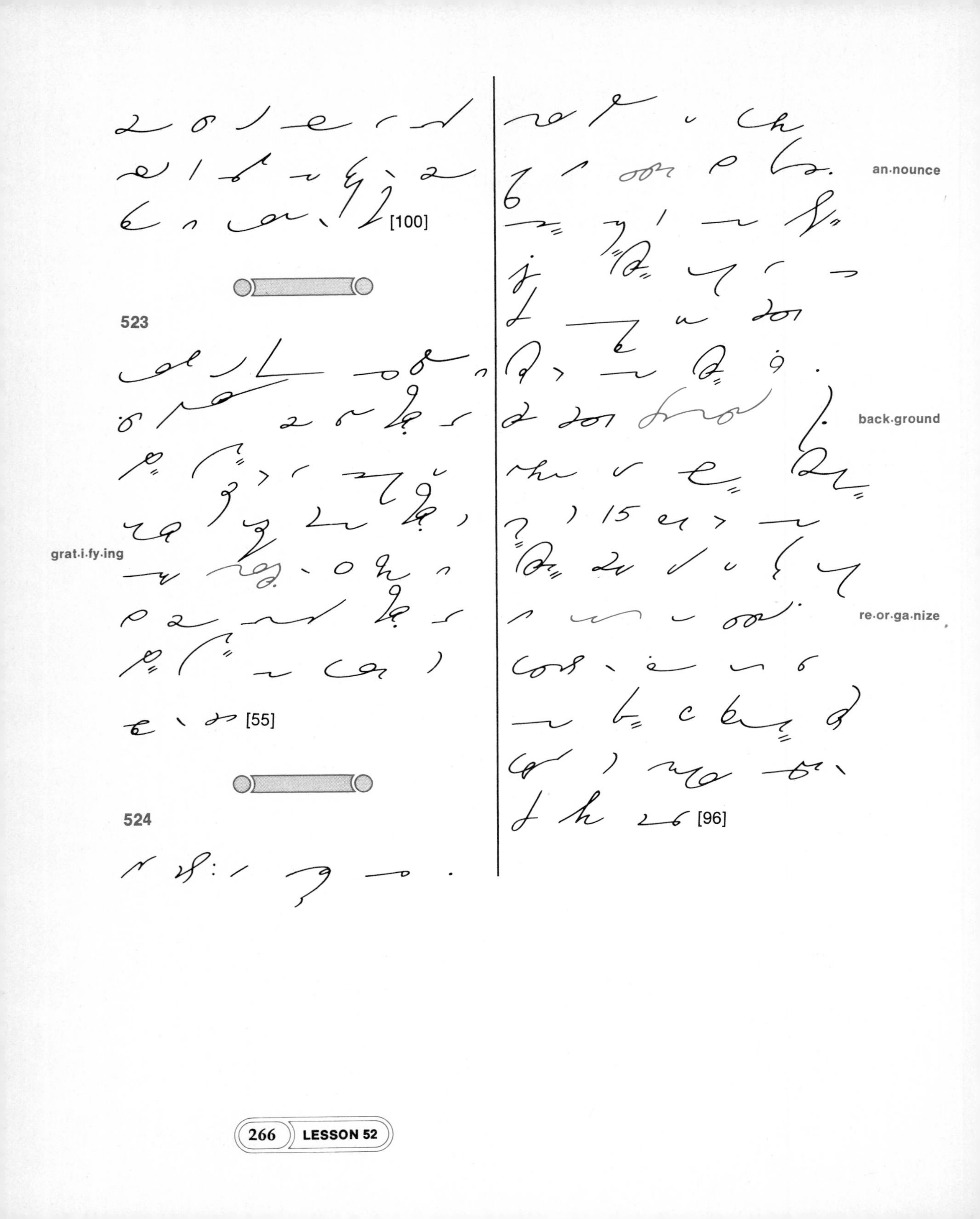

[100]

523

grat·i·fy·ing

[55]

524

an·nounce

back·ground

re·or·ga·nize

[96]

In Lesson 53 you will practice many words and phrases that are written according to the principles you studied in Chapter 5.

525 BRIEF FORMS AND DERIVATIVES

1. *Difficulty, envelope, progressed, success, satisfy-satisfactory, state, statement, requested, underneath, wishing.*
2. *Particularly, probably, regularly, speaks, ideas, subject, regarded, newspaper, newspapers, opinions.*
3. *Responsible, worthy, publicly, publications, ordinary, ordinarily, experience, experienced, usually, world, recognized.*

Building Transcription Skills

526 Business Vocabulary Builder

pressman The operator of a printing press.

petition A formal written request.

depot A building for railroad or bus passengers or freight; a station.

Reading and Writing Practice

527

rec·og·nized

prob·a·bly

ap·pre·ci·ate

en·ve·lope

[116]

528

120

ar·ea

de·pot

shop·ping

[113]

Coun·cil

529

le·gal

whose

phases

li·brary

[156]

530

phys·i·cal·ly

[94]

531

de·vot·ed

prac·ti·cal

[120]

532

trav·el·ing

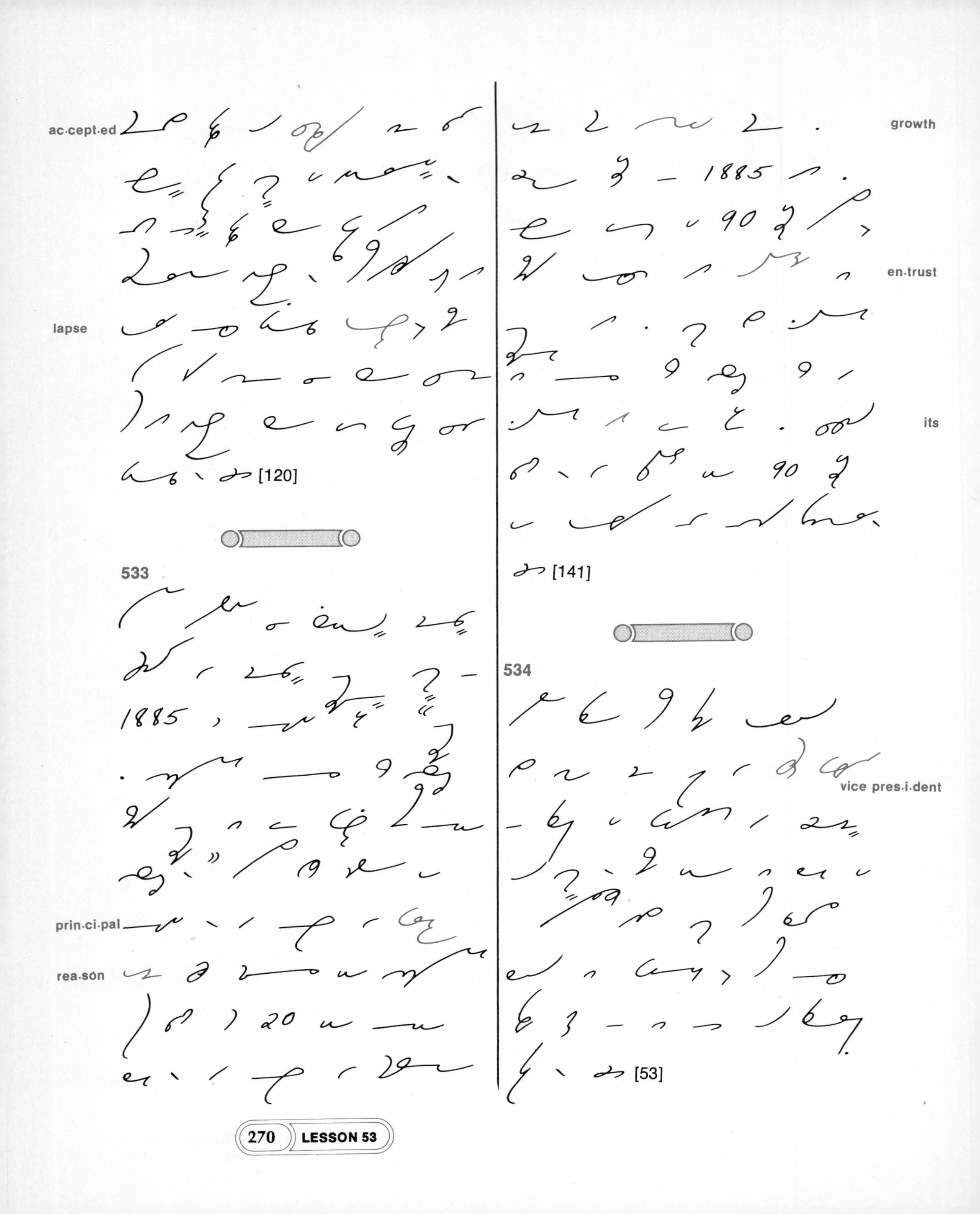

ac·cept·ed

lapse

[120]

533

1885

prin·ci·pal

rea·son

growth

1885 90

en·trust

its

90

[141]

534

vice pres·i·dent

[53]

In this lesson you will have an opportunity to brush up on shorthand principles you studied in Chapter 6.

535 BRIEF FORMS AND DERIVATIVES

1. *Never, quantity, quantities, executive, throughout, object, objective.*
2. *Character, characters, governor, government, corresponded.*

Building Transcription Skills

536 SIMILAR-WORDS DRILL vacation, vocation

vacation A holiday; a period devoted to rest or relaxation.

I will take a short vacation *in June.*

vocation A regular occupation or profession.

My vocation *is teaching.*

---

537 Business Vocabulary Builder

creative Imaginative.

novel Original; new.

sites Places; locations.

Reading and Writing Practice

538

Phoe·nix

vo·ca·tion

par

wheth·er

de·scribed

ap

ser

knowl·edge

cre·ative

par

ref·er·ence

[144]

539

ap

cop·ies

de·spite

par

par

re·ceive

[94]

540

par

nov·el

va·ca·tion

ser

sites

the·aters

ap

world's

ser

com·fort·able

[132]

541

par

ex·pe·ri·ence

par

[138]

542

equal

par

no one

than

ap 15

mod·ern

ad

par

sched·ule

[108]

543

ap

380

par

fur·ther

[103]

544

ap

26

rec·re·ation·al

new·com·er's

mer·chan·dise

coun·sel·ing

[133]

545

par

par

re·cip·ro·cate

[63]

TRANSCRIPT OF SHORTHAND CHECK LIST

Are you using the Transcript of Shorthand to best advantage?

- You *are* if you refer to it immediately when you cannot read a shorthand outline after you have spelled it.
- You *are not* if you spend several minutes trying to decipher an outline and refer to the transcript only as a last resort.
- You *are* if you keep your place in the shorthand with your left index finger each time you refer to the transcript.
- You *are not* if you must hunt for your place each time you return to the shorthand after referring to the transcript.

In Lesson 55 you will review shorthand principles you studied in Chapter 7.

546 BRIEF-FORM DERIVATIVES

1. *Suggested, corresponded, timed, organized, governed, manufactured.*
2. *Particularly, successfully, immediately, presently, gladly, partly, generally.*
3. *Sooner, manufacturer, speaker, sender, governor, timer, shorter.*

Building Transcription Skills

547 GRAMMAR CHECKUP the infinitive The infinitive is the form of the verb usually introduced by *to—to see, to be, to have, to do.*

Careful writers try to avoid "splitting" an infinitive, that is, inserting a word or phrase between *to* and the following verb.

no

To properly do *the job, you need better tools.*

yes

To do *the job properly, you need better tools.*

no

He was told to carefully prepare *the report.*

yes

He was told to prepare *the report carefully.*

548 Business Vocabulary Builder

durability Ability to withstand wear; sturdiness.

inherited Received property by will.

reality The quality of being actual or true.

Reading and Writing Practice

549

trans·fer·ring

if

be·com·ing

ap·ti·tude

ser

re·ceive

if

phase

sal·a·ry

par

ser

ex·ceed·ing·ly

if

ser

pho·to·graph

[154]

550

intro

intro

sta·tis·ti·cal

ser

de·pend·abil·i·ty

du·ra·bil·i·ty

pur·chase

when

intro

[130]

551

as

in·her·i·ted

intro

div·i·dend

trans·mit·ting

par

par

ti·tle

[123]

552

intro

re·al·i·ty

ser

18

19

20

if

grat·i·tude

priv·i·lege

ap

[158]

553

es·tate

ser

intro

clas·si·fied

[137]

554

an·nu·al

ap

dy·nam·ic

415-1177

10

[63]

LESSON 56

The practice material in Lesson 56 will give you an opportunity to review shorthand principles you studied in Chapter 8.

555 BRIEF-FORM DERIVATIVES

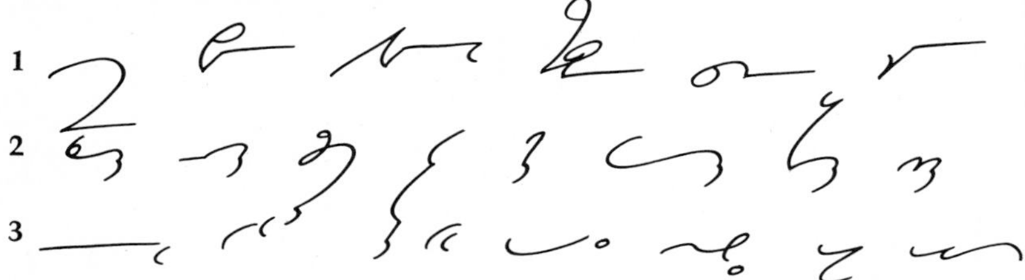

1. *Government, apartment, departments, advertisement, acknowledgment, statement.*
2. *Circulars, encloses, executives, publications, wishes, progresses, objects, worlds.*
3. *Mornings, thanks, thinks, willingly, correspondingly, represent, reorganize.*

Building Transcription Skills

556 COMMON PREFIXES super- In the English language there are many common prefixes. An understanding of the meanings of these prefixes will often give you a clue to the meaning of words with which you may be unfamiliar.

For example, you may never have encountered the word *superfluous.* However, if you knew that *super* meant *more than,* you probably could figure out that *superfluous* means *more than enough.*

In each "Common Prefixes" exercise you will be given a common prefix, its meaning, and a list of words in which the prefix is used.

Read each definition and study the illustrations that follow. Several *super* words are used in the Reading and Writing Practice of this lesson.

super- over, more than

superior Over in rank; higher.

supervise To oversee.

supervisor One who oversees.

superfluous More than enough.

557 **chore** A routine task or job.

Business Vocabulary Builder

clarification The act of making clear or understandable.

Reading and Writing Practice

558

te·dious

as

and o

chore

par

kitch·en

ser

conj

[124]

559

ap

lo·cal

par

con·fi·dent

if

ser

neigh·bor·hood

when

con·ve·nient

[178]

conj

[146]

560

manu·script

worth·while

and o

intro

rec·om·men·da·tion

par

561

ap

col·li·sion

ap

intro

su·ing

intro

[107]

562

fa·mil·iar

par

as·sis·tant

ex·ten·sion

par

Coun·cil

[117]

563

ser

bal·ances

par

past

[117]

564

10

cre·ation

en·gi·neers

qui·et·er

ser

fair

intro

ap

par

[196]

565

guest

if

par

[73]

PART

Shorthand & Transcription Skill Building

CHAPTER

The Secretary Advances

Your first job is important because it will give you an opportunity to use the skills you have developed and to gain experience in making them work for you. Your ability to handle more important responsibilities will be gauged by the way you handle the duties assigned to you. In order to move up, you must first earn a reputation for reliability.

Promotion in secretarial work consists of moving up to jobs that are successively more important. A secretary may begin to work for a junior executive, advance to be secretary to a department head, then become secretary to a corporate officer, and finally, advance to a position of secretary to the president of a company or chairman of the board of directors.

From the outset it is important to establish a good record. Remember, you are your own best friend when it comes to progressing on the job. By doing your best work on every assignment, by sharpening and improving your skills, and by welcoming new responsibilities as chances to prove your abilities, you will open doors for promotion for yourself.

In order to generate new opportunities for yourself, you must keep adding to your inventory of professional abilities. Continue to learn, and you will increase your value to your employer. Improve your

work procedures and accuracy, and take advantage of opportunities for extra service.

Keep up with changes in the business world. Participate in professional activities outside the job by taking additional training and joining a professional secretarial association. These and similar activities will enhance your value in the office and in the company.

If you want to move ahead, you have to think ahead. Achieving excellence and earning promotions rarely occur by chance; they are likely to occur when you look ahead, choose your goals, and then work hard to achieve them.

Lesson 57

Lesson 57 is a "brief form" lesson. It contains one or more illustrations of *every* brief form in Gregg Shorthand. Counting repetitions, there are 526 brief forms or derivatives. Because you have seen and written all of these brief forms many, many times, you should be able to complete this lesson in record time!

Building Transcription Skills

566 SPELLING FAMILIES -able, -ible A difficult spelling problem for stenographers is deciding whether a word ends in *-able* or *-ible.* Unfortunately, there is no rule that tells us when to use *-able* and when to use *-ible.* In a majority of English words the ending is spelled *-able,* but it is spelled *-ible* in a sufficient number of words that you should think twice before you type an *a* or an *i.* In the following list dots are placed in the words where they may be divided on the typewriter.

Words Ending in -able

avail·able	**prob·a·ble**	**re·li·able**
com·fort·able	**prof·it·able**	**suit·able**
de·sir·able	**rea·son·able**	**valu·able**

Words Ending in -ible

de·duct·ible	**im·pos·si·ble**	**re·spon·si·ble**
flex·i·ble	**pos·si·ble**	**sen·si·ble**

---

567 Business Vocabulary Builder

defray To provide for the payment of.

administer Supervise; manage.

forcefulness Effectiveness.

Reading and Writing Practice

568

if

chil·dren

fam·i·ly

if

suc·cess·ful

and o

re·spon·si·ble

and o

suit·able

re·quest

when

intro

par

[177] fu·ture

569

ap

Op·por·tu·ni·ties

busi·nesses

ser

siz·able

intro

par

com·pa·ny's

im·me·di·ate·ly

par

prof·it·able

par

en·ve·lope

[158]

570

gov·ern·ment

if

intro

ap·pli·ca·tion

han·dling

conj

intro

yours

par

[147]

sat·is·fy·ing

571

ap

Tues·day

10

[79]

572

ser

1850

im·pres·sive

2 3

twelfth

12

if

[125]

573

ser

dis·sat·is·fied

if

and o

[89]

574

16

18

[64]

575 Transcription Quiz In Lessons 31-56 you have studied nine rules for the correct use of the comma. In Lessons 57-69 you will have an opportunity to test your mastery of these rules through a "Transcription Quiz"—a letter in which no commas are indicated in the shorthand.

It will be your job, as you copy the letter in shorthand in your notebook, to insert the commas in the proper places and to give the reasons why the commas are used.

The shorthand in your notebook should resemble the following example:

As you probably know, (, as) I will be in Dallas on Friday, (, ap) August 4.

At the head of each Transcription Quiz you will find the number and types of commas the letter calls for.

The correct punctuation of the following letter calls for 5 commas—1 comma *as* clause, 1 comma conjunction, 2 commas series, 1 comma *if* clause.

[133]

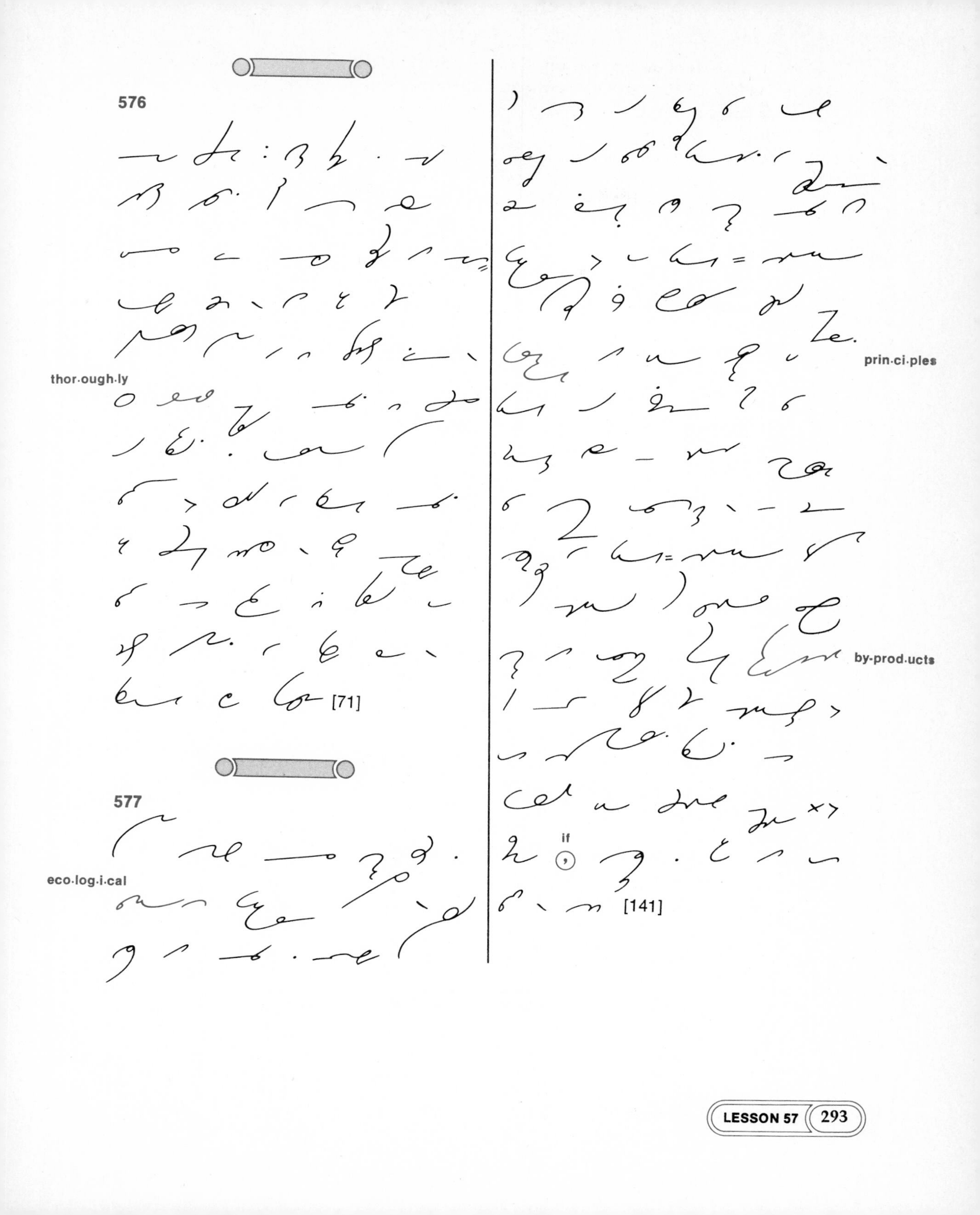

576

thor·ough·ly

[71]

577

eco·log·i·cal

prin·ci·ples

by-prod·ucts

if

[141]

This lesson provides you with an opportunity to increase your phrasing skill. It contains many illustrations of the phrasing principles of Gregg Shorthand. All told, it contains 156 phrases, counting repetitions.

Building Transcription Skills

578 GRAMMAR CHECKUP sentence structure Parallel ideas should be expressed in parallel form.

no

I hope our relationship will be long, pleasant, *and* of profit *to both of us.*

yes

I hope our relationship will be long, pleasant, *and* profitable *to both of us.*

no

As soon as we receive the necessary information, your account will be opened *and* we will ship your order.

yes

As soon as we receive the necessary information, your account will be opened *and* your order will be shipped.

It is especially important to keep parallel all ideas in a tabulation.

no

The secretary's main duties were:

1. *Taking dictation and transcribing*
2. *Answering the telephone*
3. *To take care of the files*

yes

The secretary's main duties were:

1. *Taking dictation and transcribing*
2. *Answering the telephone*
3. *Taking care of the files*

579 Business Vocabulary Builder

complications Difficulties.

county A territorial division for local government within a state.

geared Adjusted in order to satisfy something.

Reading and Writing Practice

580

Christ·mas

par

par

owe

as

pur·chased

and o

en·ve·lope

[127]

581

when

115-1118

conj

cour·te·ous

shipped

40,

if

per·son·al

intro

[121]

582

Coun·ty

if

pol·i·cies

if

to·mor·row

ser

if

ex·pe·ri·enced

ap

world's

par

[118]

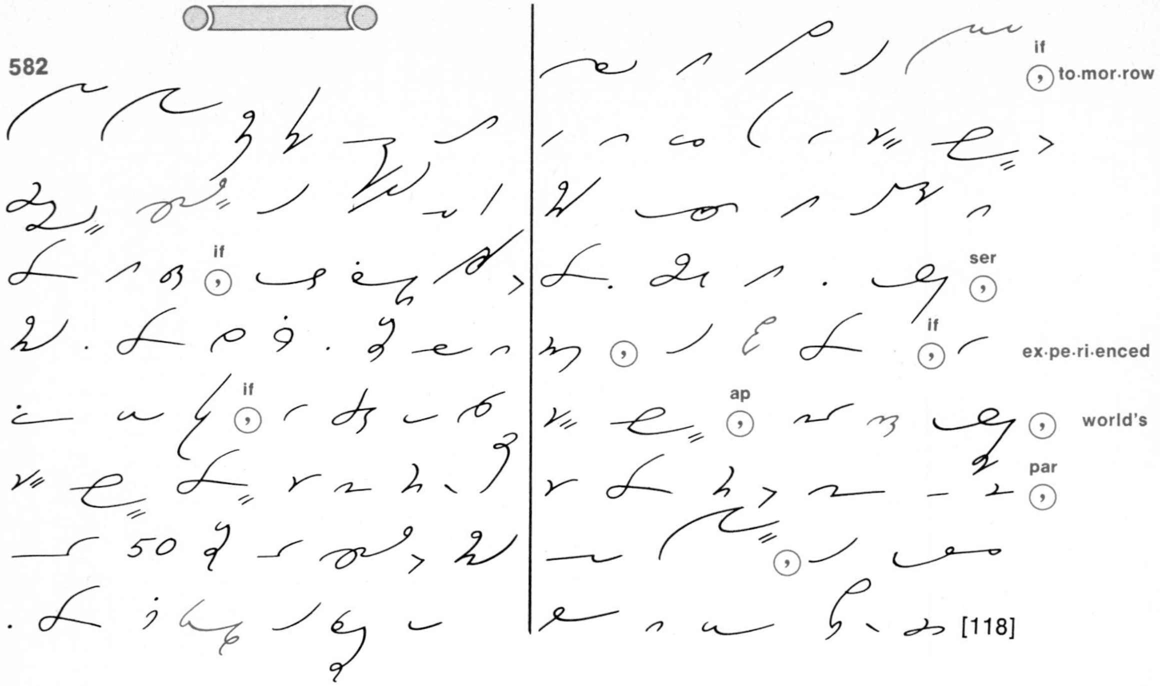

583 **Transcription Quiz** The correct punctuation of the following letter calls for 5 commas—1 comma *when* clause, 2 commas parenthetical, 2 commas series.

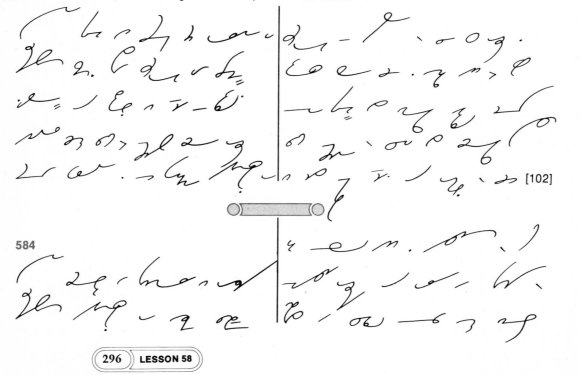

[102]

584

Feb·ru·ary

ap

Chi·ca·go

as

if

[134]

585

22

yours

and o

strict

[101]

586

ap

12

ser

ac·ces·so·ries

[93]

Lesson 59 provides an opportunity for you to brush up on the joined word beginnings of Gregg Shorthand. In the letters of this lesson there are 106 words containing joined word beginnings.

Building Transcription Skills

587 SPELLING FAMILIES -cial, -tial Be very careful when you transcribe words ending in the sound of *shul*. The ending is sometimes spelled *-cial,* sometimes *-tial*.

Words Ending in -cial

ben·e·fi·cial	**fi·nan·cial**	**so·cial**
com·mer·cial	**of·fi·cial**	**spe·cial**

Words Ending in -tial

es·sen·tial	**ini·tial**	**po·ten·tial**
in·flu·en·tial	**par·tial**	**sub·stan·tial**

588 Business Vocabulary Builder

conversion Something changed from one use to another.

colleagues Associates; co-workers.

exhausted Used up.

convalesce To recover health gradually after sickness.

Reading and Writing Practice

589

un·for·tu·nate·ly

par

ap

de·spite conj

em·ploy·ees intro

sub·stan·tial and o

en·cour·ag·ing if

com·mer·cial

con·ver·sion when

apol·o·gize

[153]

590

ap

li·brary

thor·ough·ly conj

par de·light·ed

[100]

591

ap spe·cial

intro

ini·tial ex·haust·ed

par

conj per·son·al

ser ad·ver·tis·ing

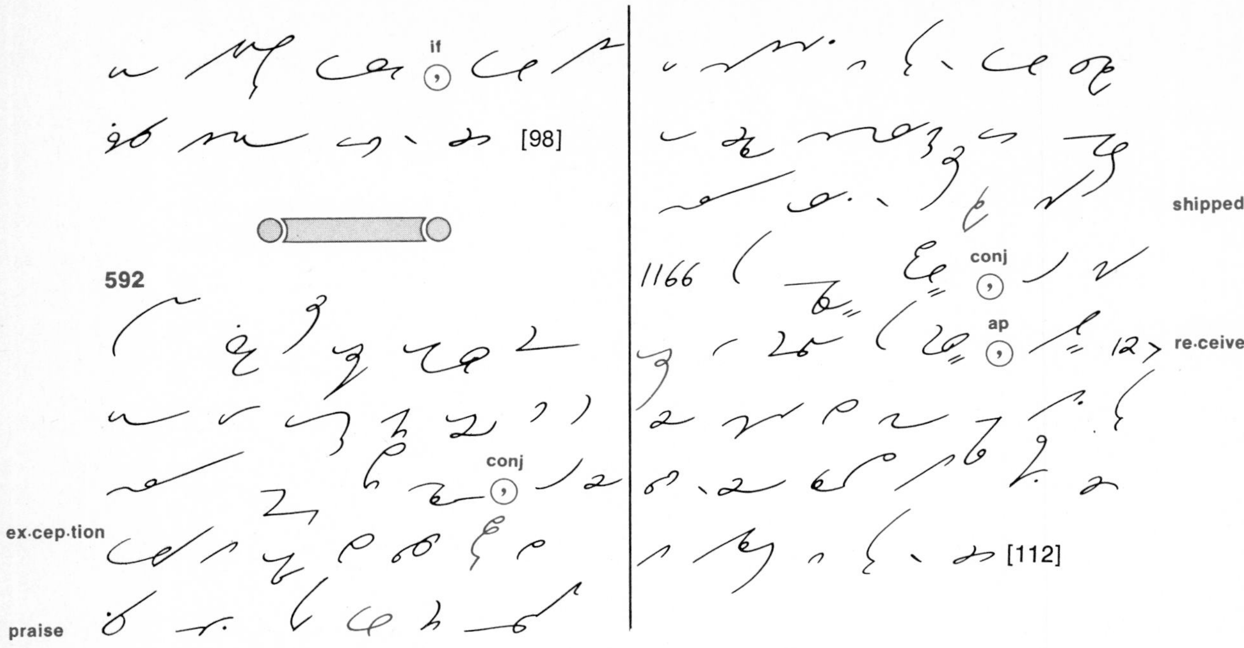

593 Transcription Quiz The correct punctuation of the following letter calls for 6 commas—2 commas conjunction, 2 commas parenthetical, 1 comma *as* clause, 1 comma introductory.

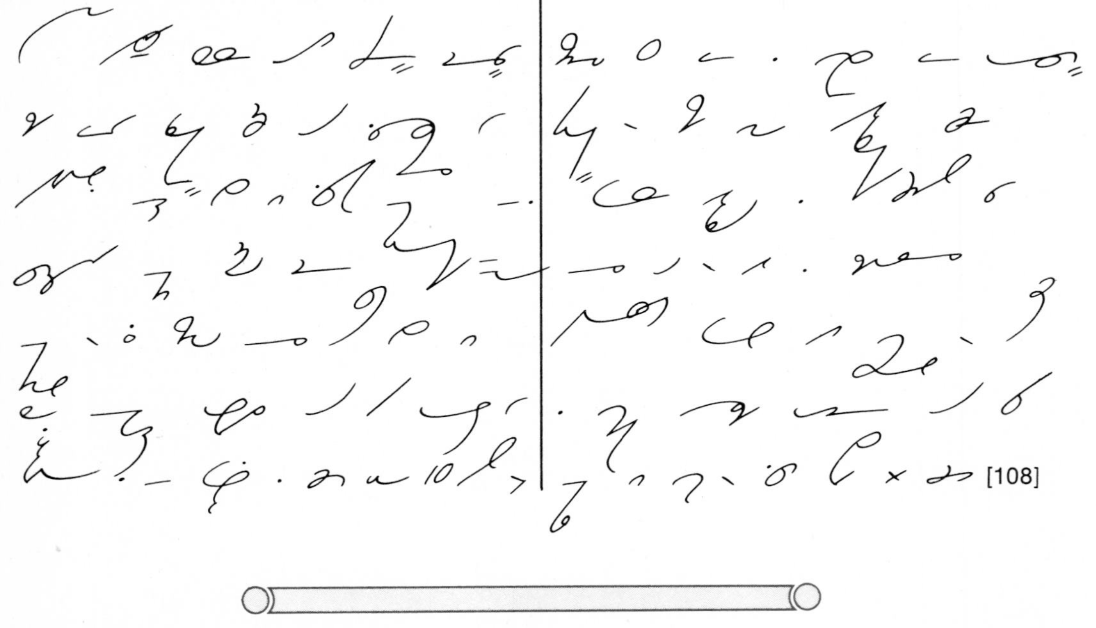

594

Flight

116

intro

116

conj

flown

par

oc·ca·sion·al·ly

conj

in·curred

15

par

[156]

595

if

en·cour·ag·ing

conj

10

sup·plies

[122]

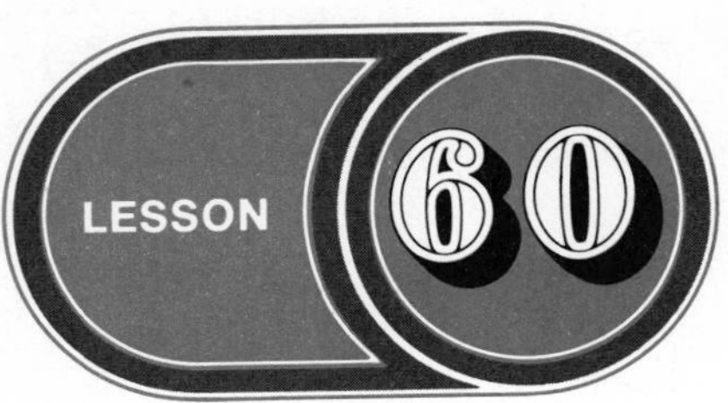

Lesson 60 concentrates on joined word endings. There are 100 words containing them in this lesson.

Building Transcription Skills

596 COMMON PREFIXES re-

re- again

replenish To fill or supply again.

repeat To say or do again.

reconsider To take up again.

reconfirm To assure again.

renew To make like new again.

---

597 Business Vocabulary Builder

mark down *(verb)* Reduce the price of.

portable Capable of being carried or moved about.

humid Moist.

Reading and Writing Practice

Reading Scoreboard Here is your chance to determine how much your reading speed has increased over your first score in Lesson 18.

Lesson 60 contains 1,003 words

If you read Lesson 60 in **22 minutes** your reading rate is **46 words a minute**
If you read Lesson 60 in **25 minutes** your reading rate is **40 words a minute**
If you read Lesson 60 in **29 minutes** your reading rate is **35 words a minute**

If you read Lesson 60 in **32 minutes** your reading rate is **31 words a minute**
If you read Lesson 60 in **36 minutes** your reading rate is **28 words a minute**
If you read Lesson 60 in **38 minutes** your reading rate is **26 words a minute**

598

rep.u.ta.ble

intro

debt

cred.i.tors

conj

if

ser

leath.er

re.plen.ish

ward.robe

par

[157]

599

as

if

rep.e.ti.tion

ser

hu.mid

and o

de.pend.able

when

won't

par

intro

[140]

600

par

intro

sig·na·ture

24 48 36

ser

and o

if

worth·while

[113]

601

par

en·vi·able

intro

intro

ef·fi·cient·ly

ser

when

[127]

602

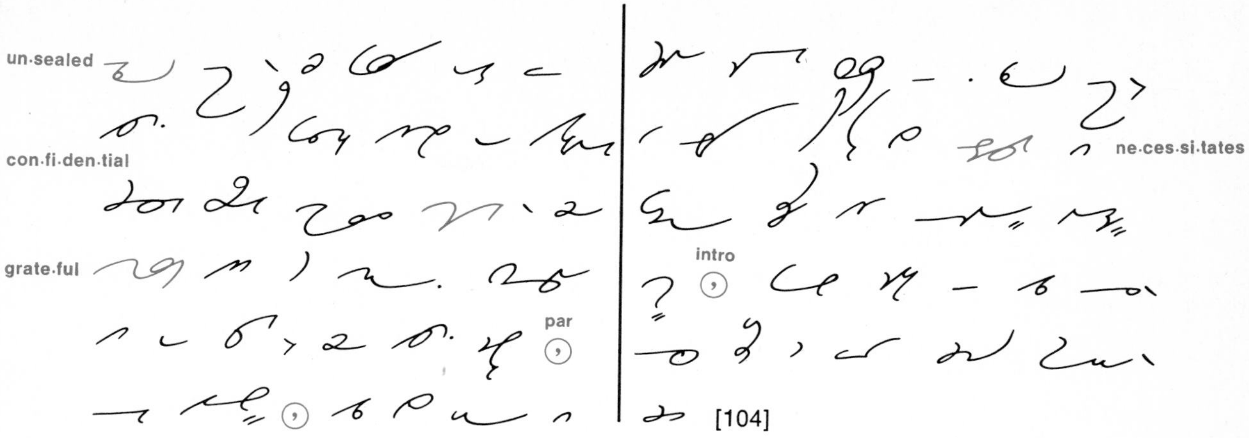

un·sealed

con·fi·den·tial

grate·ful

par

intro

ne·ces·si·tates

[104]

603 Transcription Quiz As you copy the following letter in your notebook, be sure to indicate the necessary commas at the proper points and to indicate the reason for the punctuation.

The letter calls for 5 commas—2 commas series, 1 comma apposition, and 2 commas parenthetical.

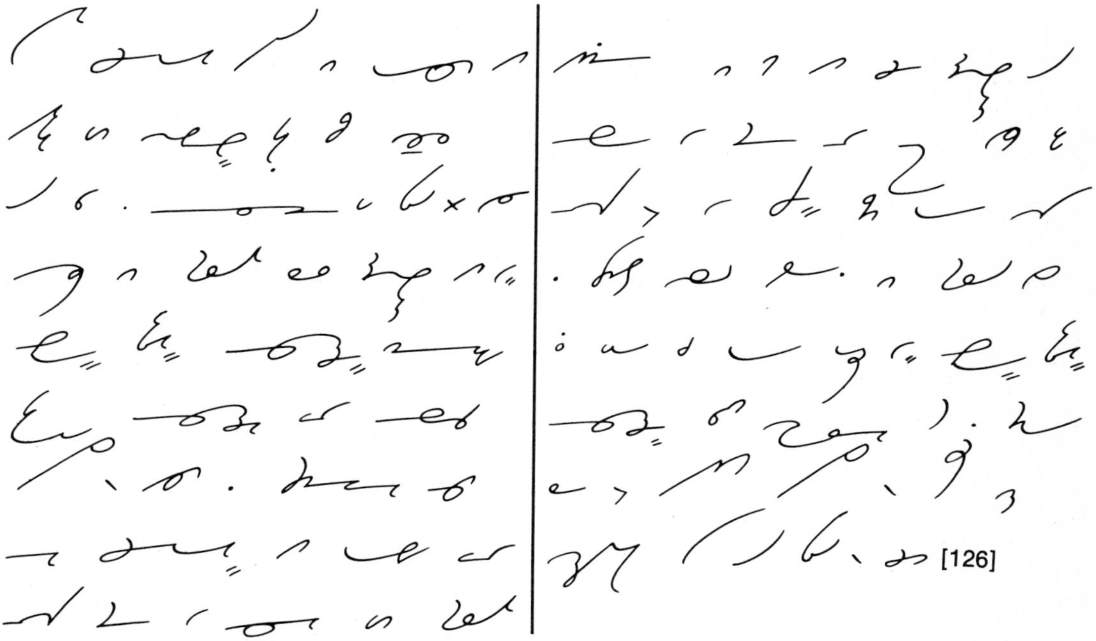

[126]

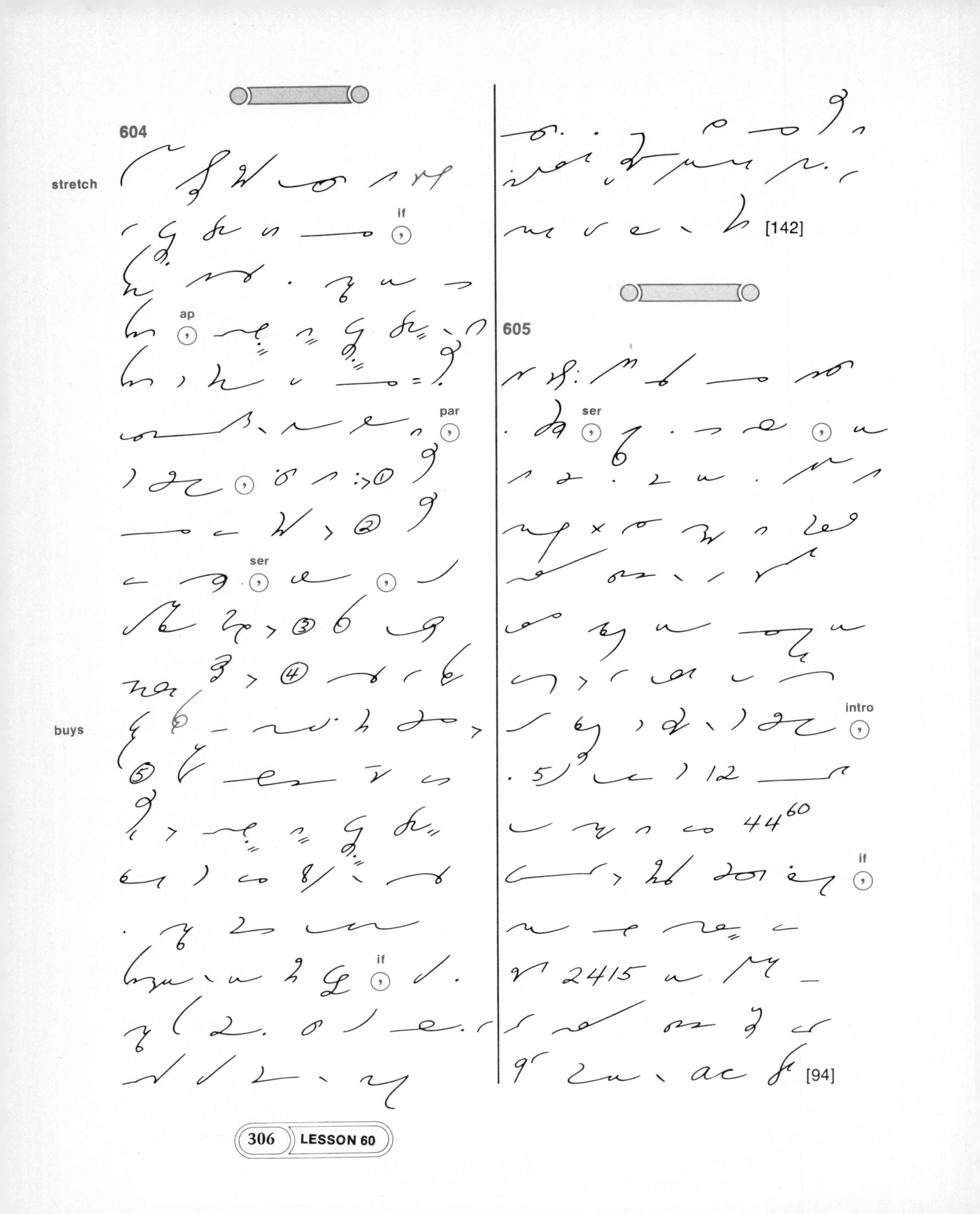

604

stretch

if

ap

par

ser

buys

if

[142]

605

ser

intro

if

[94]

The disjoined word beginnings of Gregg Shorthand are treated extensively in Lesson 61. In the Reading and Writing Practice of this lesson, you will find 77 words containing disjoined word beginnings.

Building Transcription Skills

606 GRAMMAR CHECKUP subject and verb

A verb must agree with its subject in number.

Our representative is *taking care of your needs.*

Your bills *for April* are *enclosed.*

The inclusion of a phrase such as *in addition to, as well as,* or *along with* does not affect the number of the verb. If the subject is singular, use a singular verb; if the subject is plural, use a plural verb.

Our representative, *as well as our managers,* is *looking forward to the pleasure of serving you.*

Your canceled checks, *along with your statement,* are *mailed to you each month.*

---

607 Business Vocabulary Builder

effects *(noun)* Physical property; goods.

buffet A counter for refreshments.

frustrating Disappointing.

Reading and Writing Practice

608

ap

re·cent·ly

su·per·vi·so·ry

if

ed·i·to·ri·al

ap

[134]

609

ap 15

adopt·ed

de·sir·able

when

ser

ef·fects

as

em·ploy·ee

[114]

610

14

buf·fet

14

14

par

8-9

bro·chure

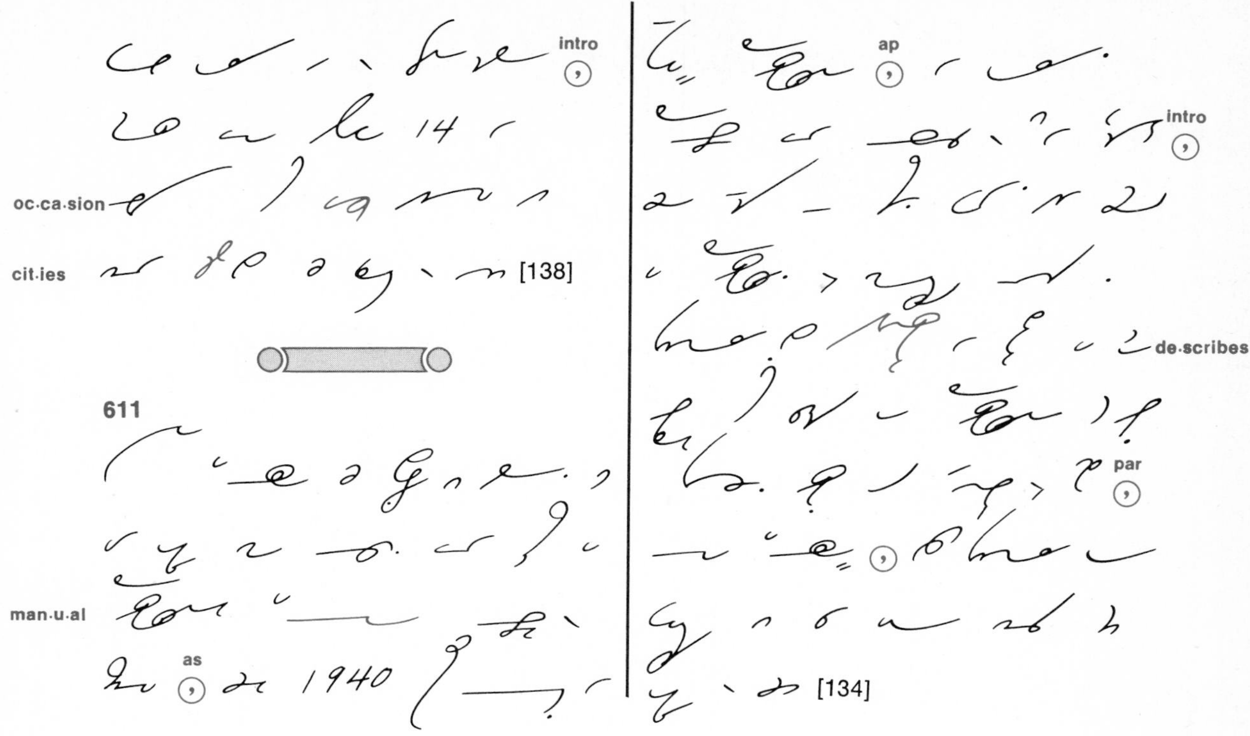

612
Transcription Quiz

In the letter that follows you must supply 4 commas to punctuate it correctly—1 comma conjunction, 1 comma introductory, 1 comma *and* omitted, 1 comma *if* clause.

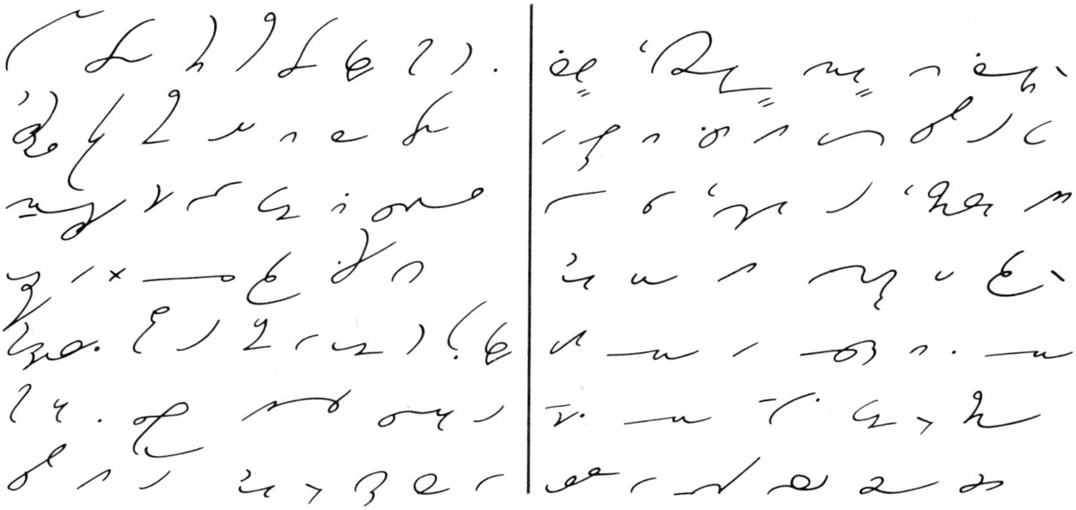

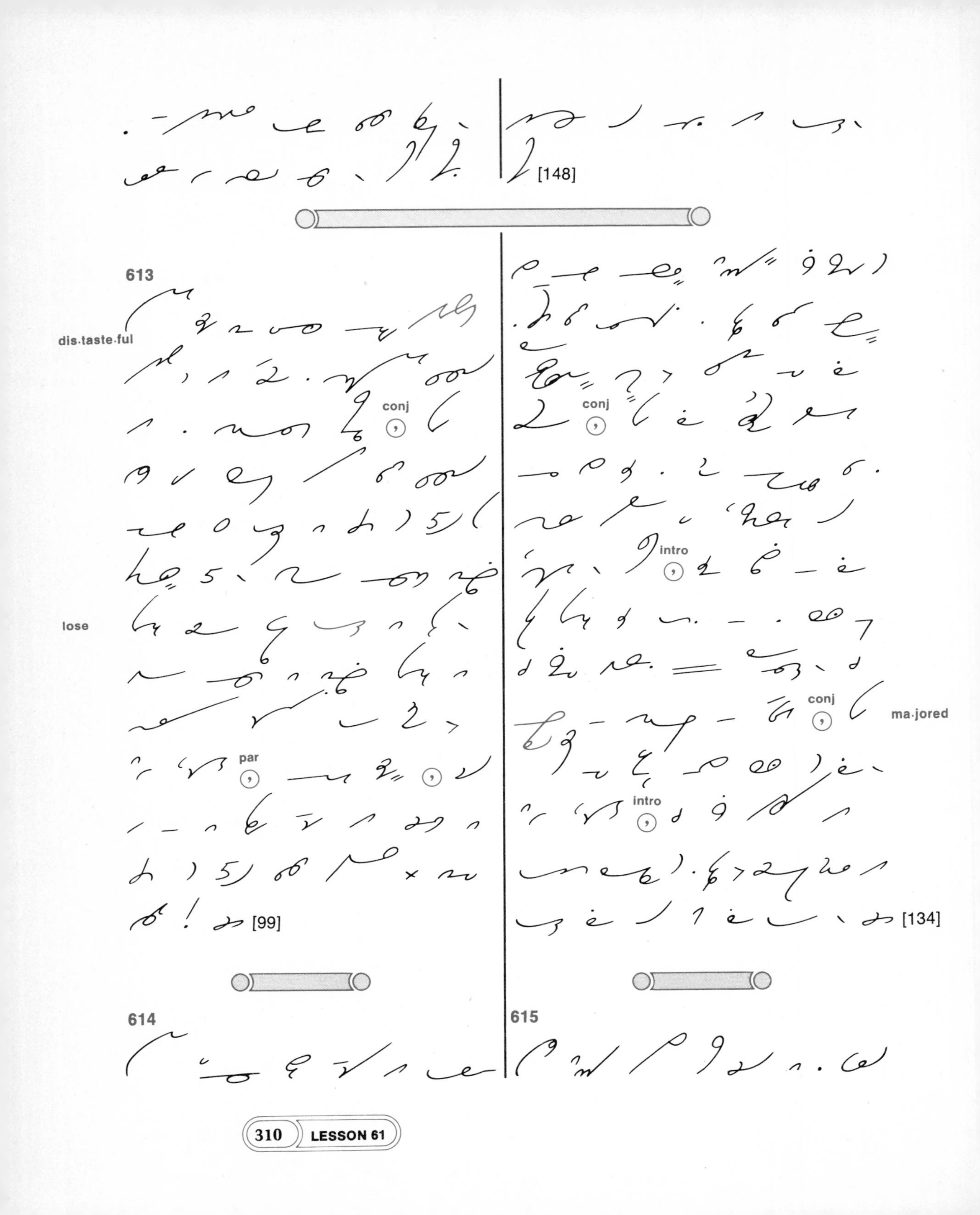

[148]

613

dis·taste·ful

conj

lose

par

[99]

conj

intro

conj

ma·jored

intro

[134]

614

615

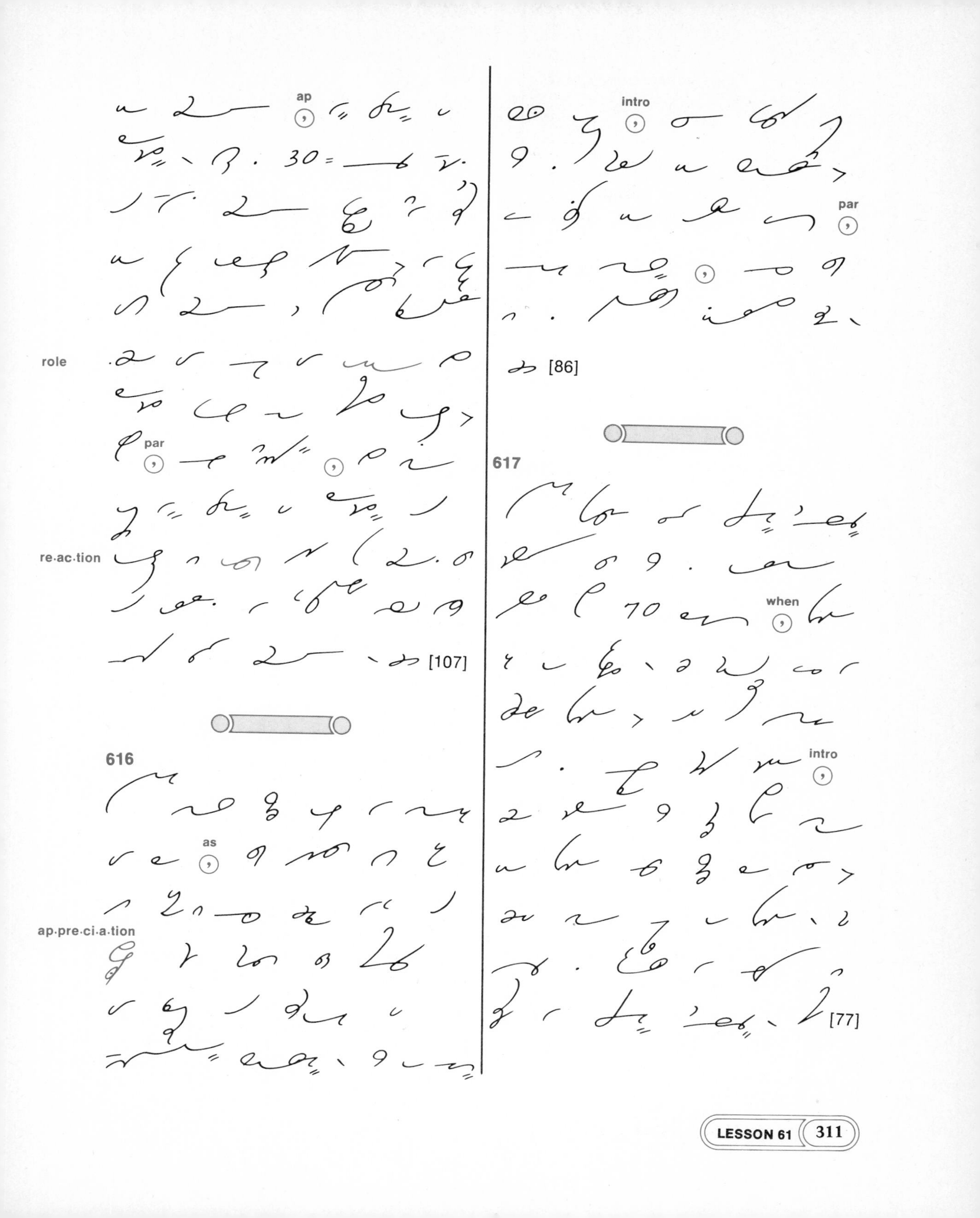

ap

role

par

re·ac·tion

[107]

616

as

ap·pre·ci·a·tion

intro

par

[86]

617

when

intro

[77]

Here is an opportunity for you to improve your grasp of disjoined word endings in Gregg Shorthand. In this lesson there are 92 words containing disjoined word endings.

Building Transcription Skills

618 SIMILAR-WORDS DRILL their, there, they're

their Belonging to them.

Some people make their *own clothes.*

there In or to that place.

The students went there *at my request.*

they're Contraction for *they are.*

They're *always ready to serve you.*

---

619 Business Vocabulary Builder

discomfort Annoyance.

purification The act of cleaning.

impartial Fair; showing no favoritism.

Reading and Writing Practice

620

their
neigh·bor·hood
ap
conj
jus·ti·fied
rec·om·men·da·tions
and o
intro
par
par
pro·ceed
conj
they're
par

when
[157]

621

conj
veg·e·ta·ble
conj
whole
as
chem·i·cals
pu·ri·fi·ca·tion
if
en·gi·neers
intro

623 Transcription Quiz The following letter requires 6 commas—2 commas parenthetical, 2 commas series, 1 comma apposition, 1 comma introductory. Can you supply these commas?

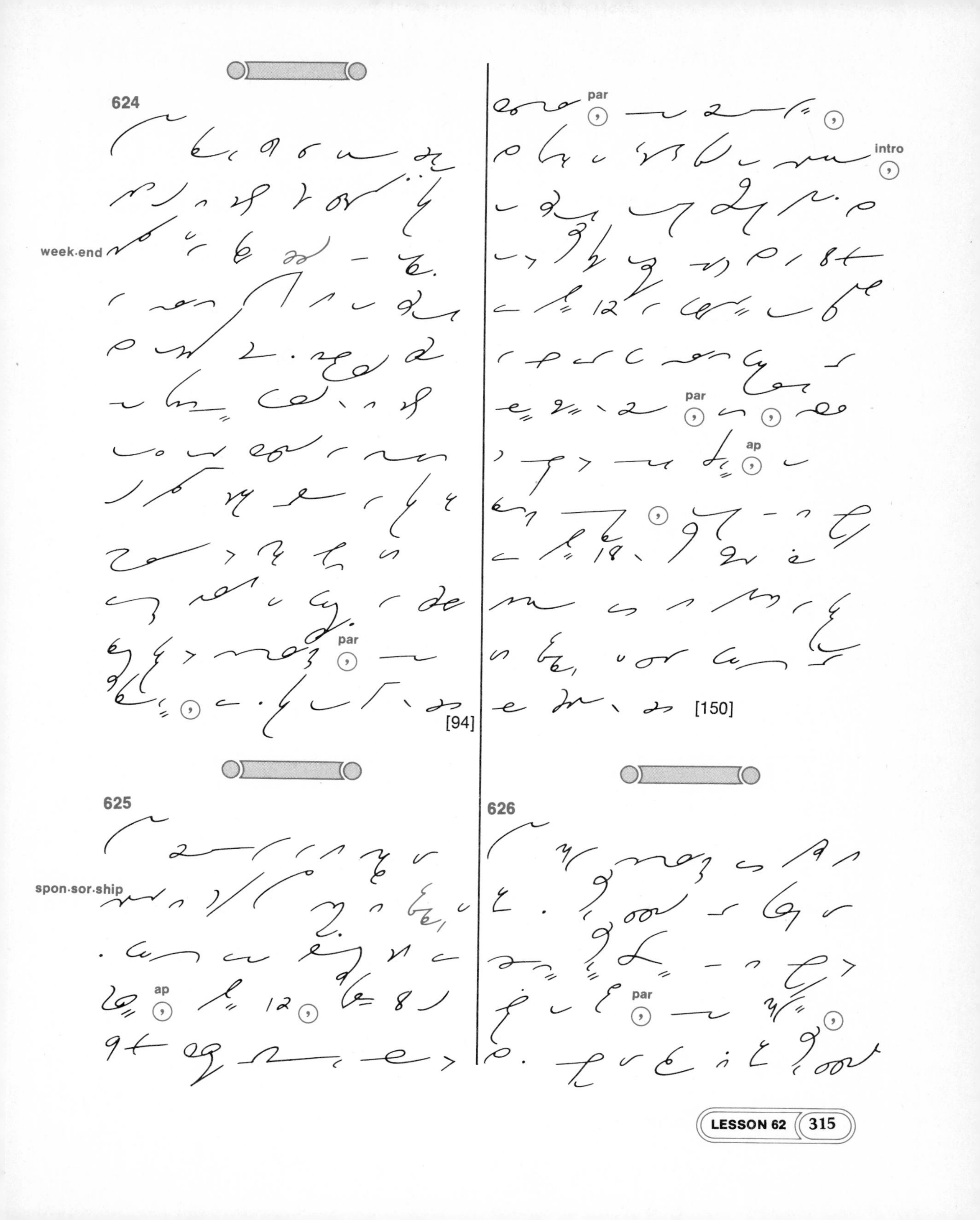

624

week·end

par

[94]

par

intro

par

ap

[150]

625

spon·sor·ship

ap

626

par

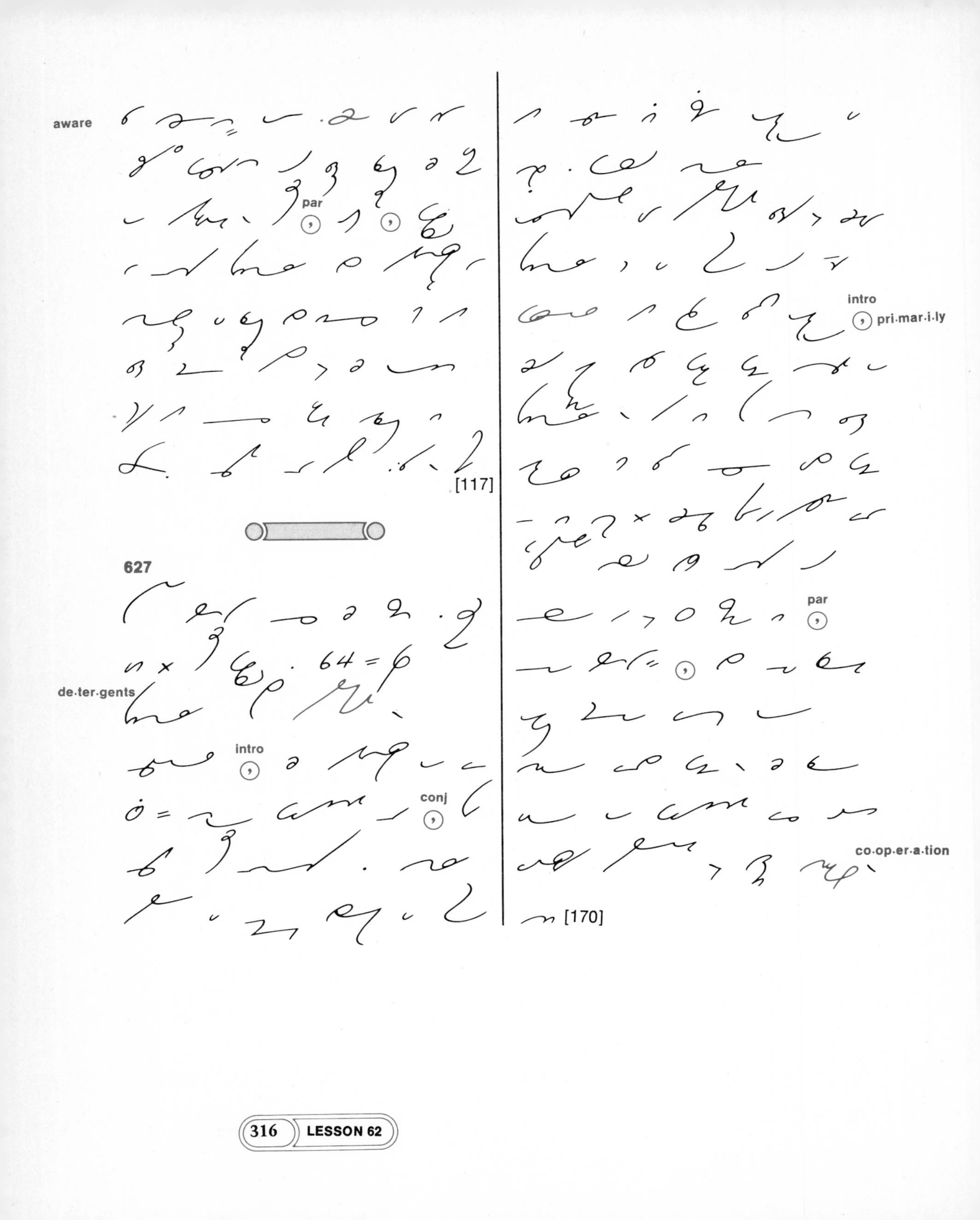

aware

par

[117]

627

de·ter·gents

intro

conj

intro

pri·mar·i·ly

par

co·op·er·a·tion

[170]

In dictation your employer will frequently use numbers. Because of the great importance of accuracy in transcribing numbers, you should take special care to write numbers legibly in your notes. The material in this lesson will help you fix more firmly in your mind the various devices for expressing numbers and quantities in Gregg Shorthand.

Building Transcription Skills

628 COMMON PREFIXES un-

un- not

unusual Not ordinary; rare.

uncertain Not sure.

unprecedented Not having been done before.

unnecessary Not needed.

unquestioned Not disputed.

629 Business Vocabulary Builder

processed *(verb)* Moved along.

pledged Guaranteed; promised.

depressed *(adjective)* Suffering from low economic activity.

Reading and Writing Practice

630 Tons of Food

70 14

weight

loaves

ser

her·ring ser

veg·e·ta·bles ser

ser

ad·di·tion intro

ser

cheese

—*Your Health* [144]

631

pro·cessed ap

as

conj pur·chased

par plea·sure

pleas·ant and o

[136]

632

un·ques·tioned

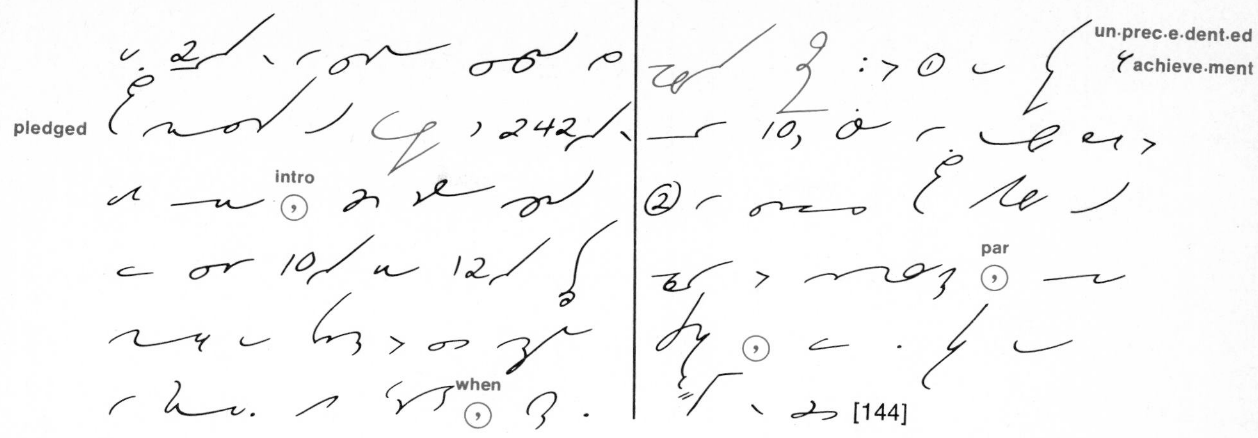

633 Transcription Quiz The following letter requires 6 commas—1 comma *if* clause, 4 commas parenthetical, 1 comma *when* clause. Remember to indicate these commas in your shorthand notes and to give the reason for their use.

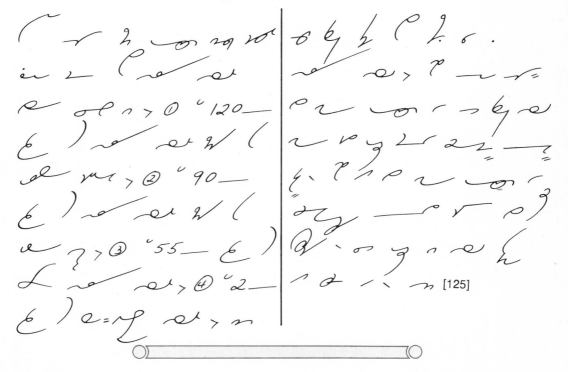

[125]

634

whether

conj

believe

if

questionnaire

par

[113]

635

conj

accessories

par

par

realize

conj

when

won't

[109]

636

intro

appreciate

when

conj

un·in·ten·tion·al·ly

if

[98]

637

conj

1890 conj

roast·ing

if

[88]

638

intro

ap

[86]

As you learned during the early stages of your study of Gregg Shorthand, vowels may be omitted in some words to help you gain fluency of writing. In this lesson you will find many words illustrating the omission of vowels.

Building Transcription Skills

639 SPELLING FAMILIES -er, -or, -ar

Words Ending in -er

bak·er	cus·tom·er	re·mind·er
con·sid·er	of·fi·cer	speak·er

Words Ending in -or

col·or	gov·er·nor	op·er·a·tor
doc·tor	ma·jor	pro·fes·sor

Words Ending in -ar

dol·lar	pop·u·lar	schol·ar
gram·mar	reg·u·lar	sug·ar

640 Business Vocabulary Builder

enviable Highly desirable.

dynamic Forceful.

constructive Promoting improvement or development.

Reading and Writing Practice

641

wheth·er

ide·al

if

ser

ad·di·tion

ap

if

intro

par

cour·te·ous

and o

[133]

642

en·vi·able

of·fer·ing

ser

intro

stretch

intro

and o

ap

gen·u·ine

par

aware

conj

com·pli·ments

when

[133]

643

as

guest

ap

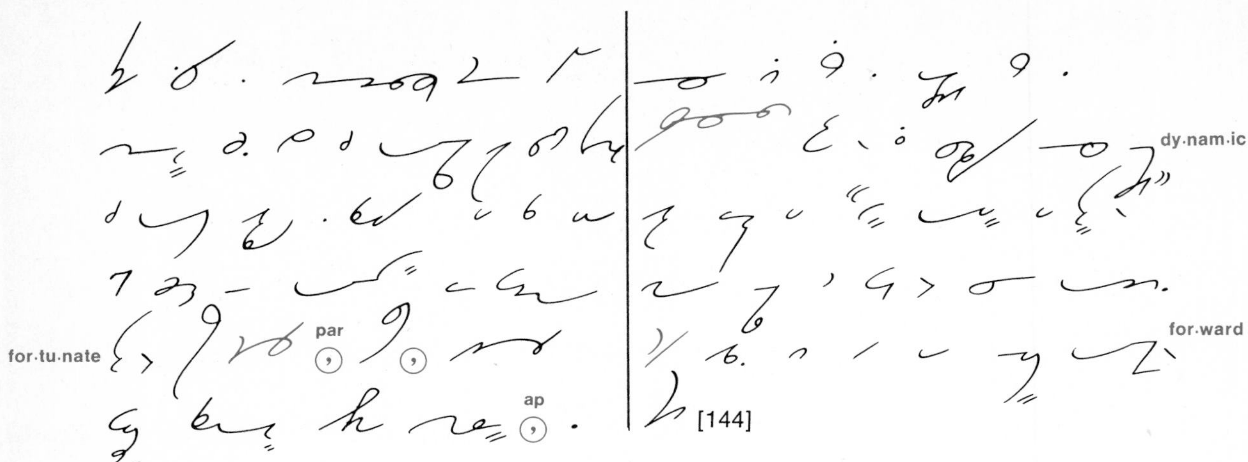

644 Transcription Quiz For you to supply: 5 commas—1 comma *if* clause, 1 comma introductory, 2 commas series, 1 comma *when* clause.

[131]

645

intro

and o

conj

cop·ies

conj

rec·re·ation·al

for·eign

swim·ming

if

[114]

[135]

646

when

sub·scrip·tion

647

ap

hap·pi·er than

conj

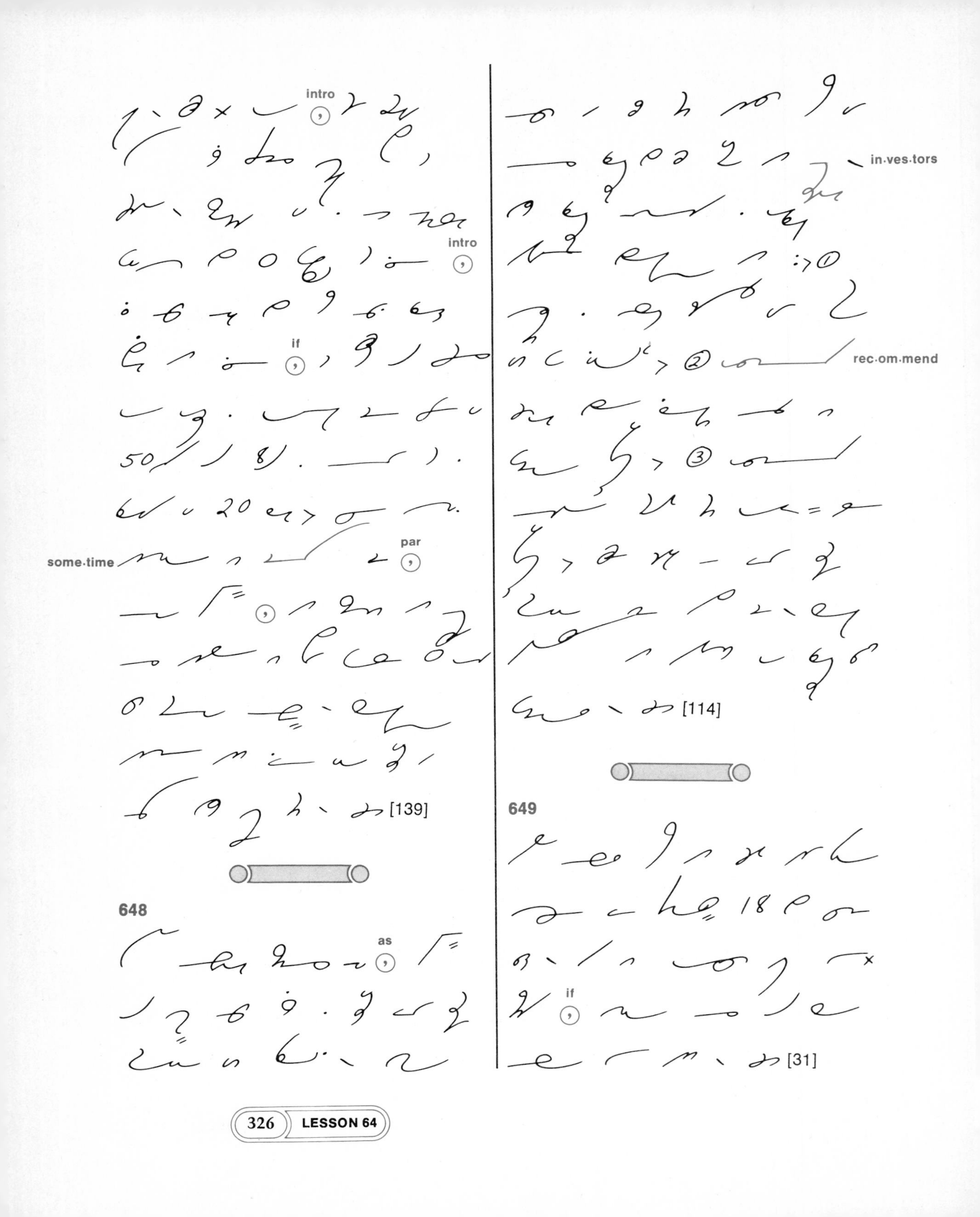

intro

intro

if

some·time

par

[139]

648

as

in·ves·tors

rec·om·mend

[114]

649

if

[31]

One of the reasons why Gregg Shorthand can be written so fluently and rapidly is its blends—single strokes that represent two or more sounds. In the Reading and Writing Practice of this lesson you will find 113 words containing blends.

Building Transcription Skills

650 SIMILAR-WORDS DRILL brought, bought

brought The past tense and past participle of *bring.*

They brought *the books back after they had read them.*

bought Purchased.

Thousands of companies have bought *our Model 116 computer.*

651 Business Vocabulary Builder

intense Considerable.

refineries Plants for purifying oil.

commendation Praise.

Reading and Writing Practice

652

en·er·gy

ex·am·ple

intro

de·vel·op·ment

ser

if

par

and o

vi·tal

ur·gent·ly

[136]

653

as

mer·chants

com·men·da·tion

ap

bought

intro

brought

conj

lo·cal

when

conj

ex·cel·lent

[118]

654

res·i·dence

par

prompt·ly

au·to·mat·i·cal·ly

ap

par

151-1161 [109]

655

114

intro

hours

114

intro

enough

de·spite

ser

intro

114

ap

114 brought

intro

bought

if

114

[173]

656

ap

Man·age·ment

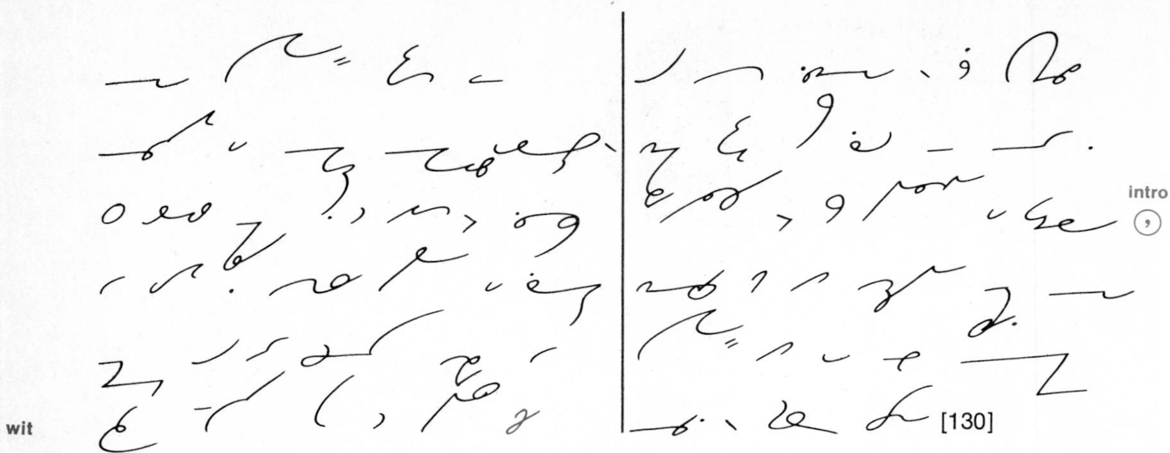

657 **Transcription Quiz** For you to supply: 7 commas–2 commas apposition, 4 commas series, 1 comma *if* clause.

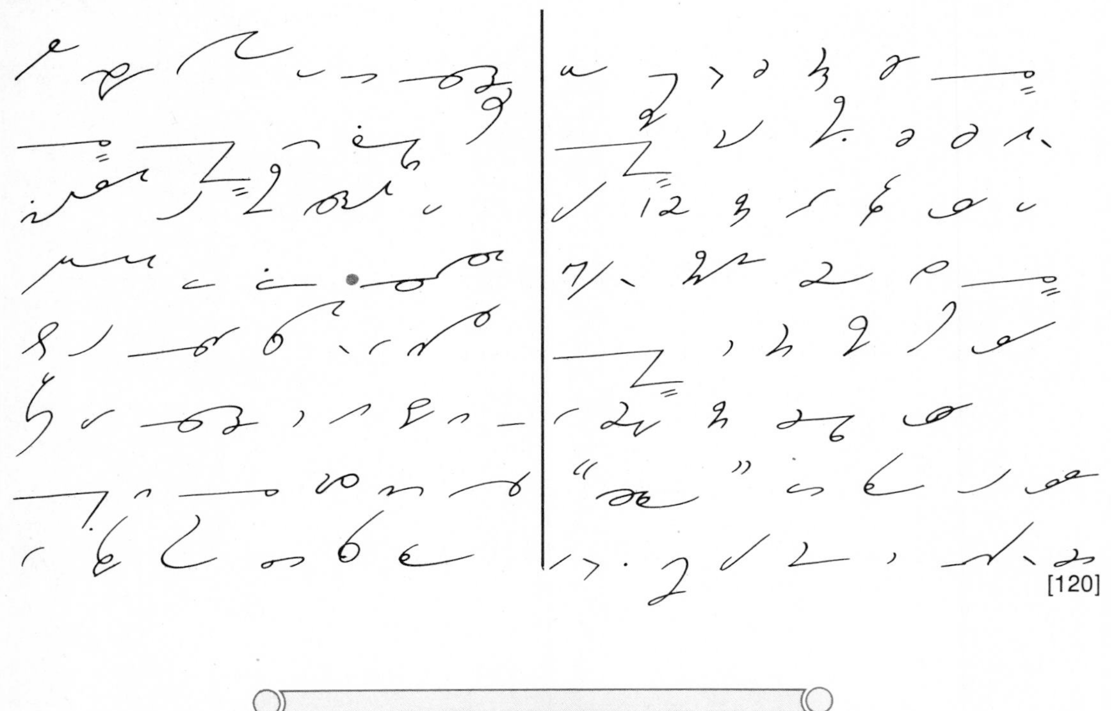

This is another lesson that concentrates on brief forms. Counting repetitions, it contains 651 brief forms and derivatives.

Building Transcription Skills

658 COMMON PREFIXES pro-

pro- in many words *pro-* means *before, ahead, forward,* or *future.*

proceed To go ahead.

progress A forward movement.

prospect A possible future customer.

promotion The act of moving ahead.

procedure A manner of going ahead.

---

659 Business Vocabulary Builder

anticipation The act of looking forward.

in arrears Behind in payment; overdue debt.

Reading and Writing Practice

660

its

intro

conj

im·me·di·ate·ly

intro

and o

log·i·cal

trans·fer·ring

[146]

661

ac·knowl·edge

15

ap

pro·ceed

conj

re·mit·tance

any·one

when

ar·rears

if

en·ve·lope

pro·ceed

[134]

662

as

prob·a·bly

ap·pli·cants

conj

ser

qual·i·ties

par

conj

duties

worth·while

conj

and o

chal·leng·ing

[178]

663 **Transcription Quiz** For you to supply: 5 commas—3 commas introductory, 1 comma conjunction, 1 comma *if* clause.

[141]

664

if

ex·pe·ri·ence

Per·suad·ing

gov·ern·ment

ser

conj

lo·cal

[134]

when

of·fered

par

hap·pi·er

ca·pac·i·ty

[161]

665

ap

intro

666

intro

per·son·nel

par

[87]

667

as

ap

conj

intro

Chi·ca·go

15

[157]

668

ser

af·fect

30

80

in·stalled

ser

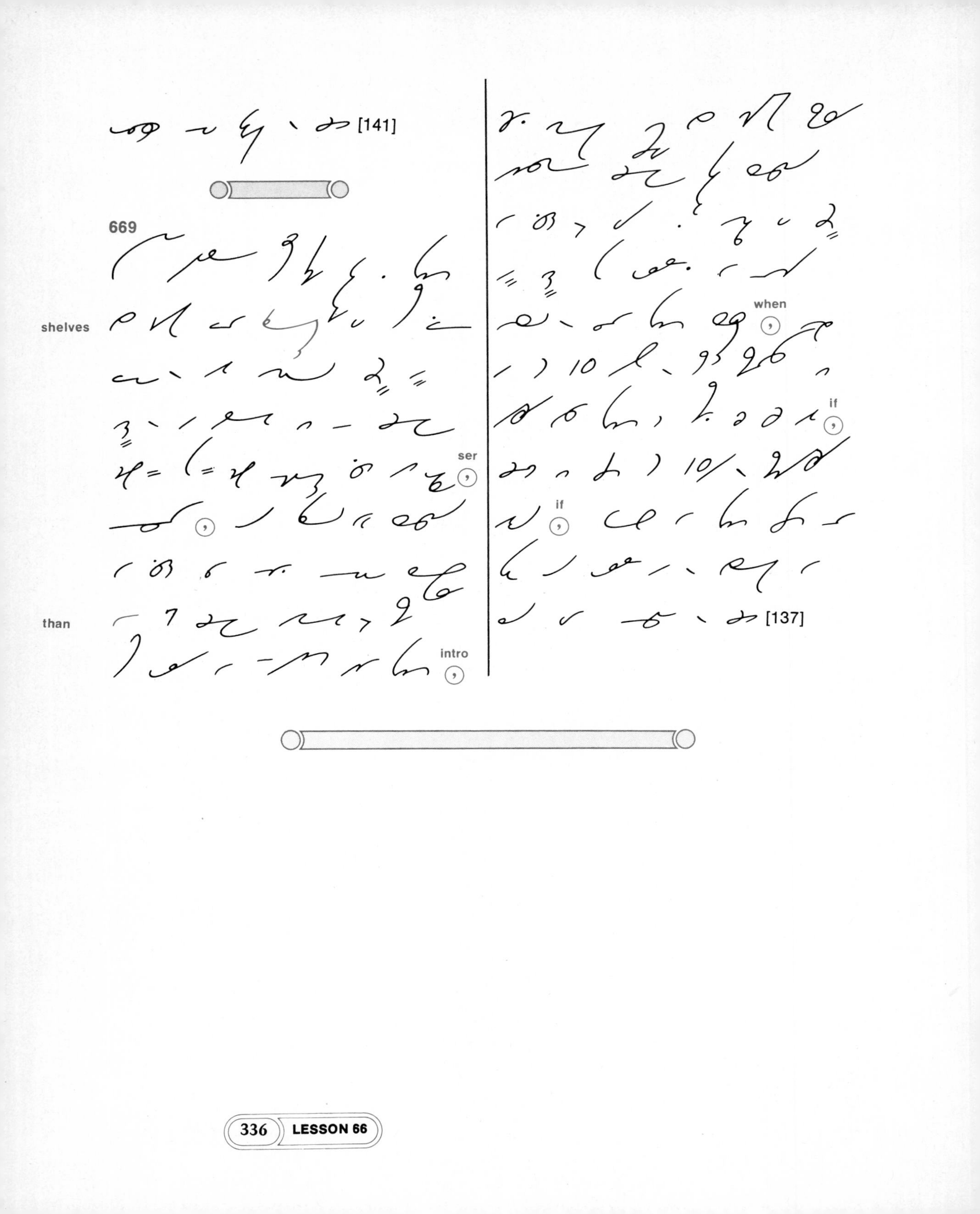

[141]

669

shelves

ser

than

intro

when

if

if

[137]

Here is another opportunity for you to increase your skill in writing phrases. In this lesson there are 158 phrases.

Building Transcription Skills

670 GRAMMAR CHECKUP verbs with "one of"

■ **1** In most cases, the expression *one of* takes a singular verb, which agrees with the subject *one.*

One of *the people on the staff* is *ill.*

One of *our typewriters* does *not work.*

■ **2** When *one of* is part of an expression such as *one of those who* or *one of the things that,* a plural verb is used to agree with its antecedent in number.

Kay solved one of the problems that have (*not* has) *been annoying us for years.*

Lee is one of the students who drive (*not* drives) *to school.*

---

671 Business Vocabulary Builder

bearable Capable of being borne.

eventful Momentous; full of events.

milestones Significant points in development.

Reading and Writing Practice

672

par

bi·cy·cle

re·lieved

as

con·va·les·cence

bear·able

if

[87]

673

ap·pre·ci·ate

ap

15

conj

re·ceive

when

else·where

par

im·pressed

par

than

[130]

674

ap

15

an·ni·ver·sa·ry

16

par

conj

mile·stones

ser

suc·cess·ful

conj

intro

won't

[134]

675

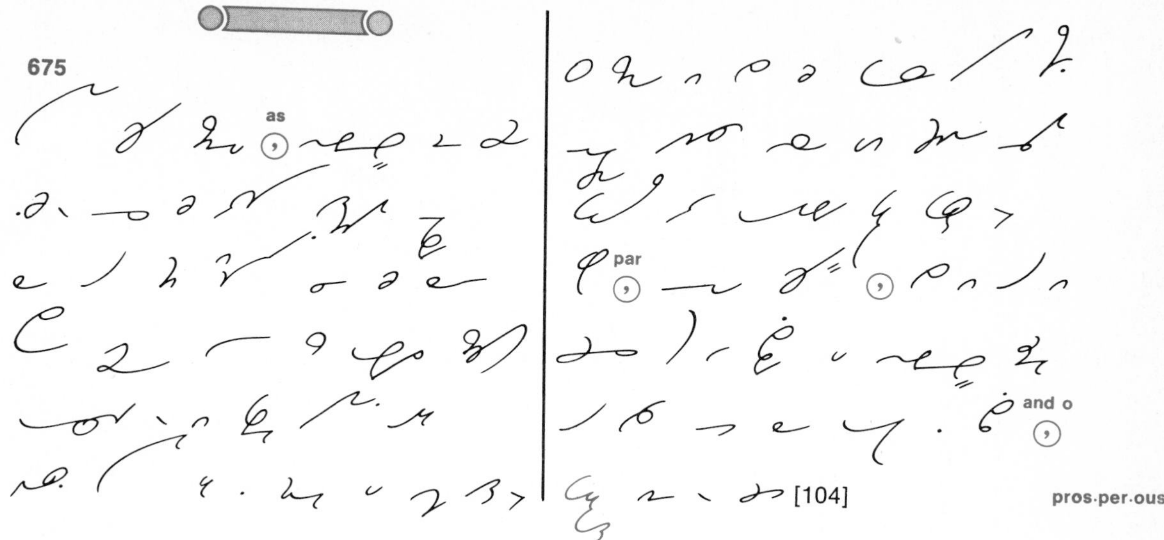

676 Transcription Quiz For you to supply: 6 commas—1 comma conjunction, 1 comma *as* clause, 1 comma apposition, 1 comma *and* omitted, 2 commas parenthetical.

[129]

677

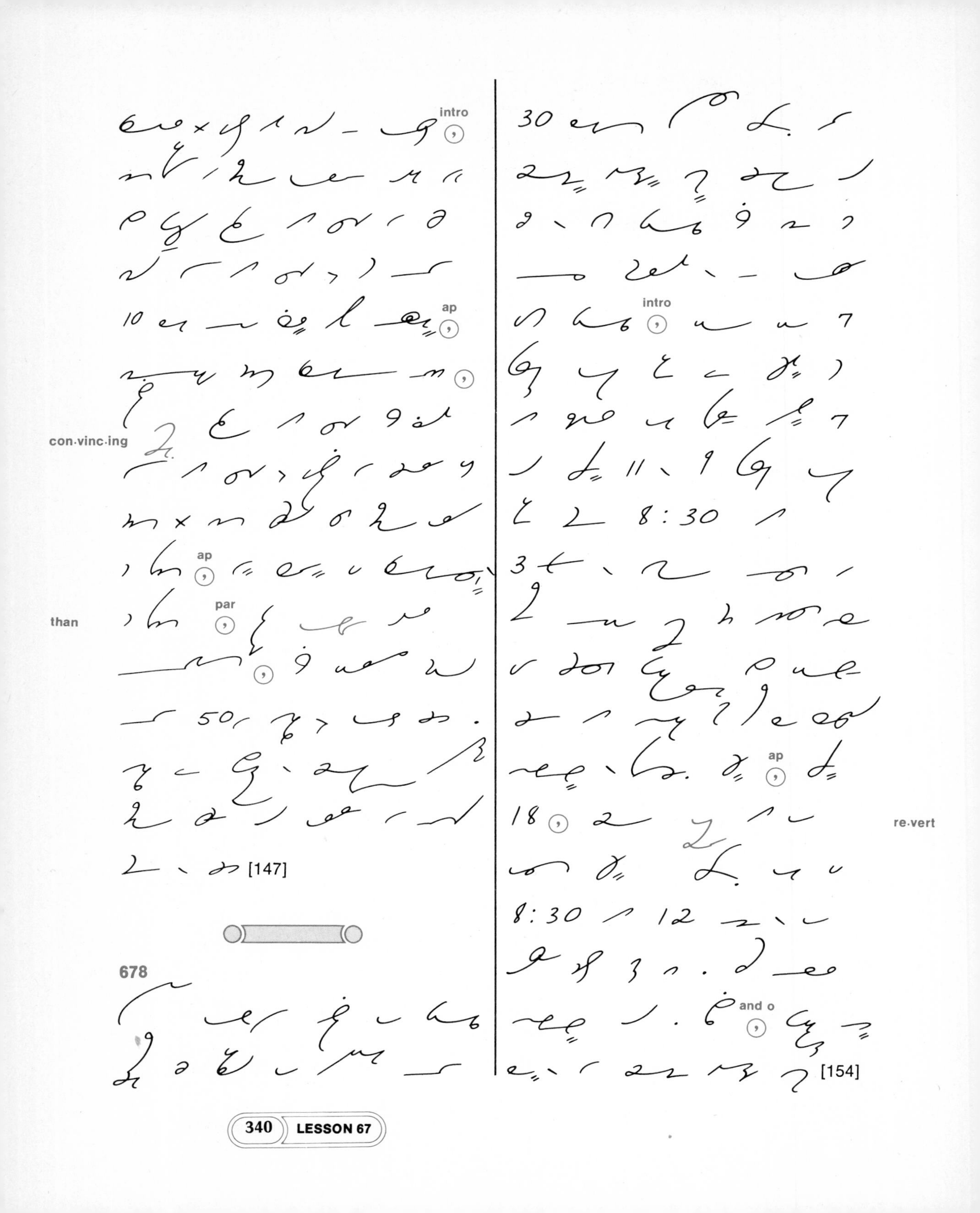

con·vinc·ing

than

[147]

678

re·vert

[154]

Lesson 68 contains a general review of many of the major principles of Gregg Shorthand.

Building Transcription Skills

679 SIMILAR-WORDS DRILL some, sum

some A portion.

Have some *of our services displeased you?*

sum Amount; total.

You owe us the sum *of $500.*

---

680 Business Vocabulary Builder

incredibly Hardly believable.

judicious Having sound judgment; wise.

net income Earnings remaining after expenses.

frankness Honesty.

Reading and Writing Practice

681

par

in·cred·i·bly

sum

ju·di·cious

en·gi·neers

ser if ser

[127]

682

ap intro and o

its

eco·nom·i·cal than

of·fer·ing

conj if ap

[142]

683

as

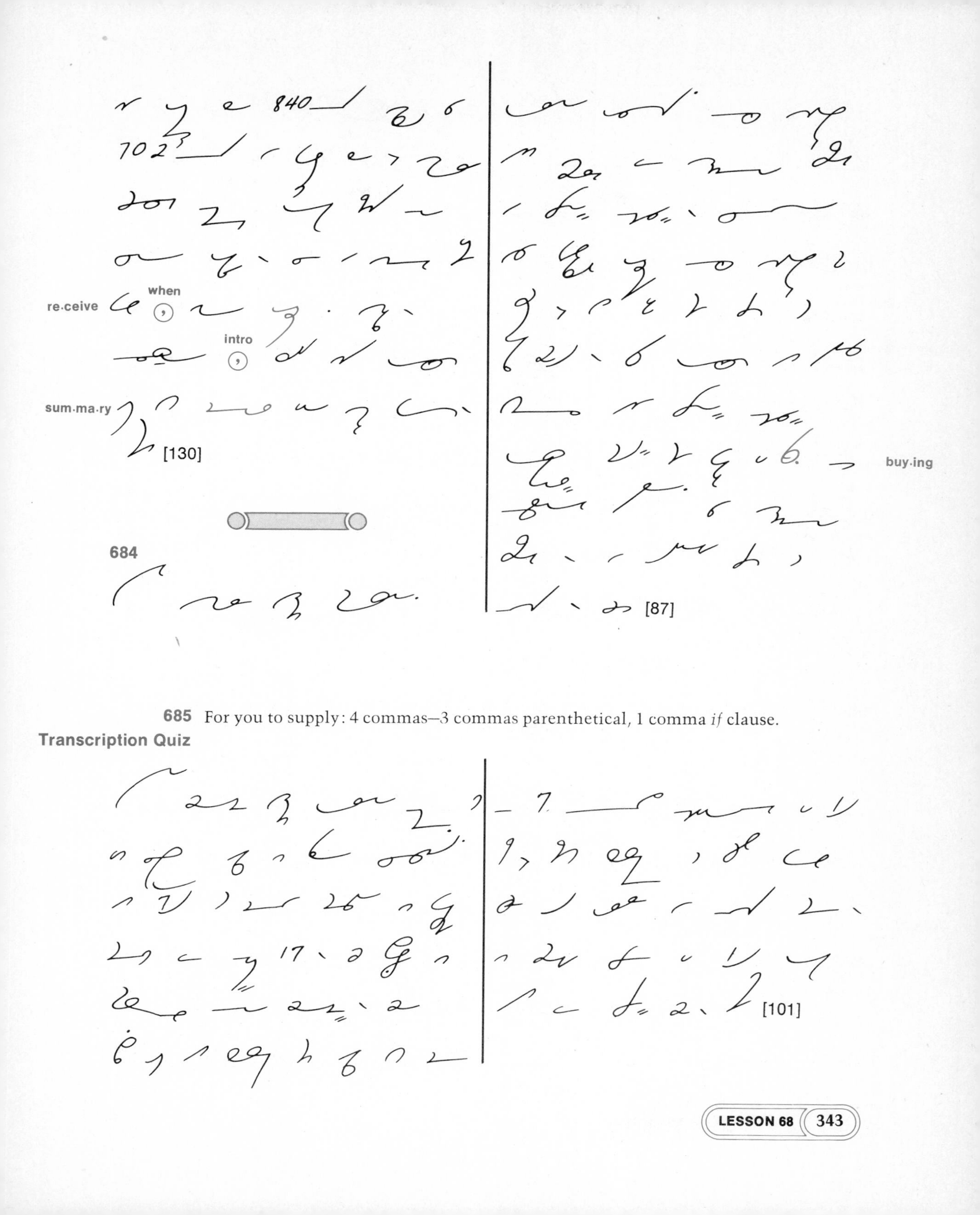

re·ceive

when

intro

sum·ma·ry

[130]

buy·ing

[87]

684

685 For you to supply: 4 commas—3 commas parenthetical, 1 comma *if* clause.

Transcription Quiz

[101]

686

conj

intro

an·swers

man·u·al

and o

[135]

687

conj

conj

pa·tient

[110]

688

their

conj

intro

ser

intro

[144]

dog·sleds

intro

125

125

its

[108]

689

125

intro

prin·ci·ple

leads

690

if

[38]

You probably won't be able to refrain from chuckling as you read the "hotel" letters in the Reading and Writing Practice. They are an exchange of letters by the manager and a guest with a sense of humor.

Building Transcription Skills

691 COMMON PREFIXES pre-

pre- before; beforehand.

- **predict** To tell beforehand; to prophesy.
- **preliminary** Coming before the main business.
- **premature** Happening before the proper time.
- **presume** To assume to be true before proof is established.

---

692 Business Vocabulary Builder

- **desolated** Sad; unhappy; disappointed.
- **conceivably** Possibly.
- **establishment** Place of business.

Reading and Writing Practice

693

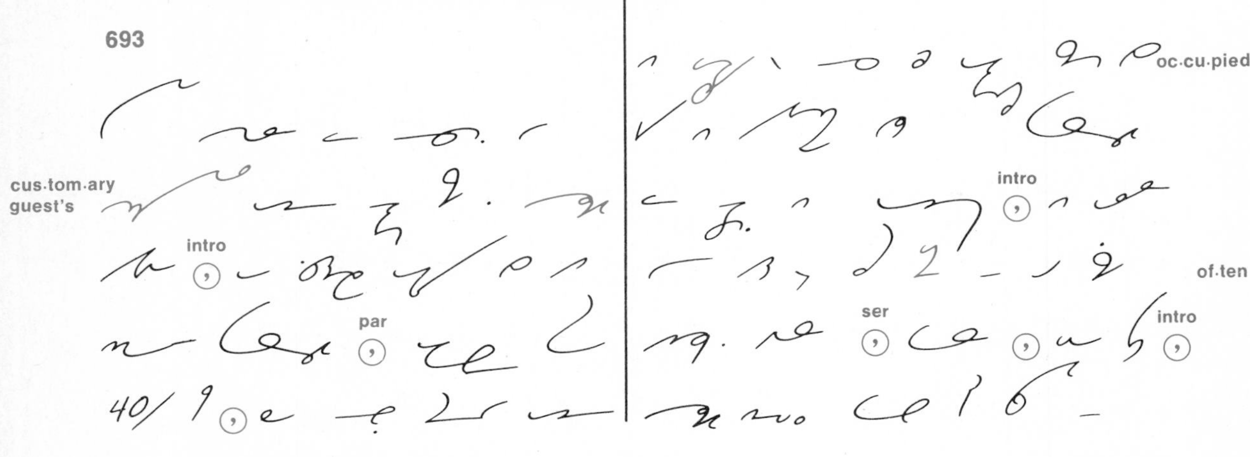

par

[95]

694

des·o·lat·ed

ap

sou·ve·nirs

vis·i·tor

zoo

con·ceiv·ably

par

par

run·ning

as

thought·ful·ly

draw·er

intro

maid

when

if

es·tab·lish·ment

[258]

695 Transcription Quiz For you to supply: 5 commas—1 comma *and* omitted, 1 comma introductory, 1 comma conjunction, 2 commas parenthetical.

[141]

696

when

bought

per·for·mance

par

intro

[124]

697

in·su·lat·ing

[108]

VOCABULARY CHECKLIST *Has your command of words improved since you began your study of Gregg Shorthand? It has if you—*

- 1 Studied all the words in the Business Vocabulary Builders and added them to your everyday vocabulary.
- 2 Paid careful attention to the Similar-Words Drills, so that you know the difference between *addition, edition; some, sum,* etc.
- 3 Learned the meanings of the common prefixes presented in a number of the lessons of your textbook.

When you are employed in a business office, you will have occasion to use the telephone frequently. The information in the Reading and Writing Practice will help you use the telephone efficiently.

Building Transcription Skills

698 SPELLING FAMILIES -ize, -ise, -yze

Be careful when you must type a word ending with the sound of *iz.* The ending may be spelled *-ize, ise,* or *-yze.*

Words Ending in -ize

apol·o·gize	**re·al·ize**	**uti·lize**
or·ga·nize	**rec·og·nize**	**vi·su·al·ize**

Words Ending in -ise

ad·ver·tise	**com·prise**	**rise**
ad·vise	**en·ter·prise**	**su·per·vise**

Words Ending in -yze

an·a·lyze	**par·a·lyze**

---

699 Business Vocabulary Builder

moderate *(adjective)* Reasonable.
offensive *(adjective)* Giving unpleasant sensations.
visualize To form a mental image of; to see.
commending Praising.

Reading and Writing Practice

Reading Scoreboard Now that you are on the last lesson, you are no doubt very much interested in your final shorthand reading rate. If you have followed the practice suggestions you received early in the course, your shorthand reading rate at this time should be a source of pride to you.

To get a picture of how much your shorthand reading rate has increased with practice, compare it with the reading rate in Lesson 18, the first time you measured it.

Lesson 70 contains 1,028 words

If you read Lesson 70 in 21 minutes your reading rate is 50 words a minute
If you read Lesson 70 in 25 minutes your reading rate is 41 words a minute
If you read Lesson 70 in 29 minutes your reading rate is 35 words a minute
If you read Lesson 70 in 34 minutes your reading rate is 30 words a minute
If you read Lesson 70 in 38 minutes your reading rate is 27 words a minute
If you read Lesson 70 in 43 minutes your reading rate is 24 words a minute

---

700 The Telephone

par

uti·lize

when

born

conj

an·a·lyze

Fast or Slow?

if

too

intro

ap

mod·er·ate

120 150

Pitch.

intro

de·scribed

than

rise

conj

breath·ing

Volume.

of·fen·sive

intro

em·pha·sis

A Pleasant Voice.

par

and o

agree·able

Telephone Courtesy.

re·al·ize

ex·ten·sion

if

than

vi·su·al·ize

ser

in·ter·rupt

if

rec·og·nize

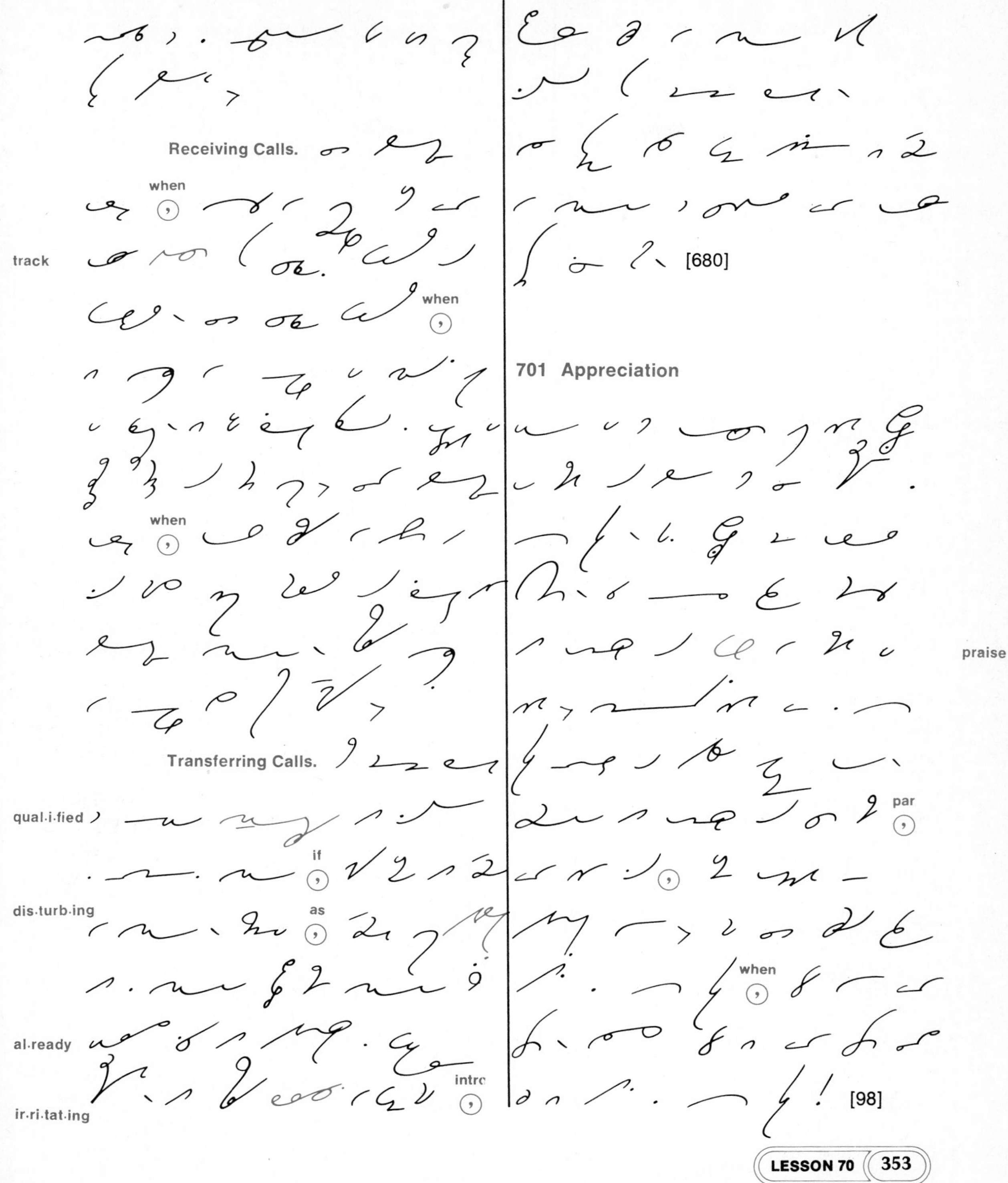

Receiving Calls.
when
track
when
when
Transferring Calls.
qual·i·fied
if
dis·turb·ing
as
al·ready
ir·ri·tat·ing
intro
[680]
701 Appreciation
praise
par
when
[98]

702 Judgment

mere·ly
de·cid·ing
conj
be·gin·ning
ex·er·cise
nev·er·the·less
intro
in·valu·able

weighed
rea·son·ing
im·pulse
ax·i·om
when
conj
conj

[250]

Appendix

States

The abbreviations in parentheses are those recommended by the Postal Service.

Alabama [AL]

Alaska [AK]

Arizona [AZ]

Arkansas [AR]

California [CA]

Colorado [CO]

Connecticut [CT]

Delaware [DE]

Florida [FL]

Georgia [GA]

Hawaii [HI]

Idaho [ID]

Illinois [IL]

Indiana [IN]

Iowa [IA]

Kansas [KS]

Kentucky [KY]

Louisiana [LA]

Maine [ME]

Maryland [MD]

Massachusetts [MA]

Michigan [MI]

Minnesota [MN]

Mississippi [MS]

Missouri [MO]

Montana [MT]

Nebraska [NE]

Nevada [NV]

New Hampshire [NH]

New Jersey [NJ]

New Mexico [NM]

New York [NY]

North Carolina [NC]

North Dakota [ND]

Ohio [OH]

Oklahoma [OK]

Oregon [OR]

Pennsylvania [PA]

Rhode Island [RI]

South Carolina [SC]

South Dakota [SD]

Tennessee [TN]

Texas [TX]

Utah [UT]

Vermont [VT]

Virginia [VA]

Washington [WA]

West Virginia [WV]

Wisconsin [WI]

Wyoming [WY]

Selected Cities of the United States

Akron
Albany
Anchorage
Atlanta
Baltimore
Baton Rouge
Birmingham
Boston
Bridgeport
Buffalo
Cambridge
Camden
Charleston
Charlotte
Chattanooga
Cheyenne
Chicago
Cincinnati
Cleveland
Columbia
Columbus
Dallas

Dayton
Denver
Des Moines
Detroit
El Paso
Fairbanks
Fargo
Fort Worth
Grand Rapids
Hartford
Honolulu
Houston
Indianapolis
Jacksonville
Jersey City
Kansas City
Knoxville
Laramie
Las Vegas
Lincoln
Little Rock
Los Angeles

Louisville
Memphis
Miami
Milwaukee
Minneapolis
Montpelier
Nashville
Newark
New Orleans
New York
Norfolk
Oakland
Oklahoma City
Omaha
Philadelphia
Phoenix
Pittsburgh
Portland
Providence
Richmond
Rochester
Sacramento

St. Louis

St. Paul

Salt Lake City

San Antonio

San Diego

San Francisco

Seattle

Shreveport

Spokane

Springfield

Syracuse

Tacoma

Tallahassee

Tampa

Toledo

Trenton

Tucson

Tulsa

Washington

Wichita

Wilmington

Common Geographical Abbreviations

America

American

United States

England

English

Great Britain

Canada

Canadian

Puerto Rico

The Metric System

If you take dictation in which there are many occurrences of metric measurements, you will have frequent use for the abbreviated forms given below. It is not wise to attempt to learn these forms until you know you will have use for them.

The metric system was devised by France and adopted there by law in 1799. Since that time its use has become almost universal except in Great Britain and the United States. It is rapidly coming into use in those two countries and, therefore, it is possible that you will need these special outlines. If the terms occur only infrequently in your dictation, it is better to write them in full.

The following abbreviations will be useful to those who must frequently take metric measurements in dictation.

		meter	liter	gram
kilo-	1,000			
hekto-	100			
deka-	10			

		meter	liter	gram
deci-	1/10			
centi-	1/100			
milli-	1/1,000			
micro-	1/1,000,000			
nano-	1/1,000,000,000			

ADDITIONAL METRIC MEASUREMENTS

Celsius

centigrade

cubic centimeter

kilobit

kilocalorie

kilocycle

kilohertz

kiloton

kilovolt

kilowatt

kilowatt-hour

megabit

megahertz

megaton

megawatt

megohm

micromicron

micron

microsecond

milliampere

millibar

millifarad

millihenry

millimicrosecond

millivolt

milliwatt

nanosecond

Recall Drills

JOINED WORD ENDINGS

1 -ment

2 -tion

3 -tial

4 -ly

5 -ily

6 -ful

7 -ble

8 -ther

9 -ual

10 -ure

11 -self, -selves

12 -ort

13 -tain

14 -cient, -ciency

DISJOINED WORD ENDINGS

15 -hood

16 -ward

17 -ship

18 -cal, -cle

19 -ulate, -ulation

20 -ingly

21 -ings

22 -gram

23 -ification

24 -lity

25 -lty

26 -rity

JOINED WORD BEGINNINGS

27 Per-, Pur-

28 Em-

29 Im-

30 In-

31 En-

32 Un-

33 Re-

34 Be-

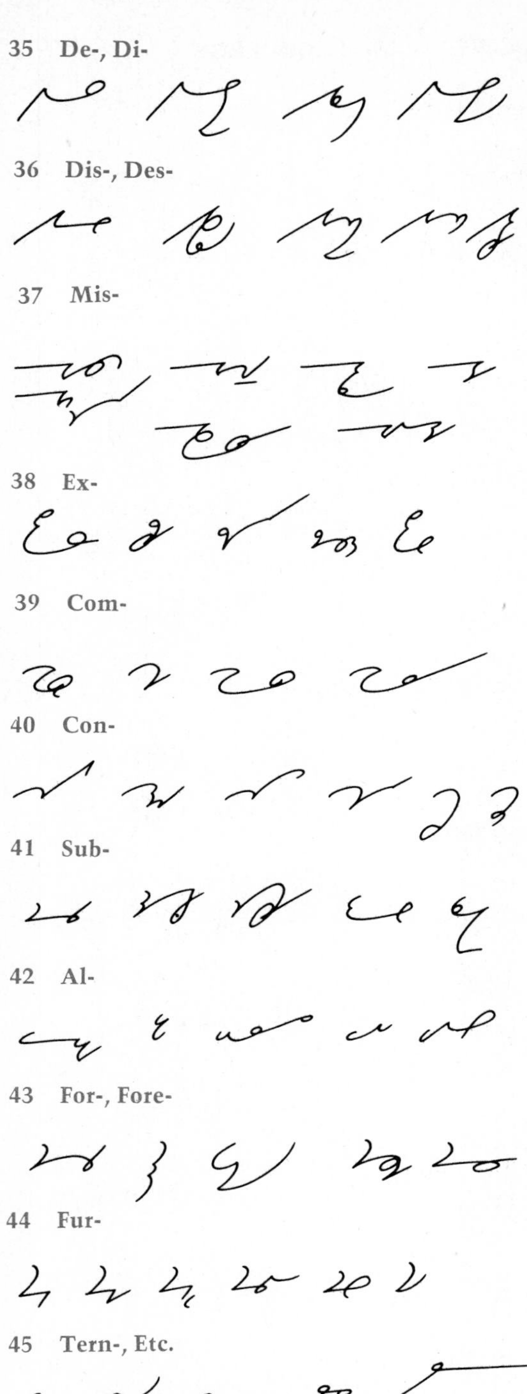

35 De-, Di-

36 Dis-, Des-

37 Mis-

38 Ex-

39 Com-

40 Con-

41 Sub-

42 Al-

43 For-, Fore-

44 Fur-

45 Tern-, Etc.

46 Ul-

DISJOINED WORD BEGINNINGS

47 Inter-, Etc.

48 Electr-, Electric

49 Super-

50 Circum-

51 Self-

52 Trans-

53 Under-

54 Over-

Transcript of Shorthand

(The material is counted in groups of 20 standard words or 28 syllables for convenience in timing the reading or dictation.)

CHAPTER 1

LESSON 2

10 *Alphabet Review*
A, e, n, m, t, d, v, f, s.

LESSON 3

15 *Alphabet Review*
T, d, n, m, v, f, s, e, a, o, r, l, h, i.

Group A

1 I have not seen our neighbor, Mr. Leo Bates, nor have I seen Mr. Peter Price.
2 I will leave home in an hour.[1] Our plane leaves at nine.
3 Please place my will inside our safe at home.
4 I am leasing a mail meter. I will sign a lease[2] in a day or so.
5 Our people are meeting in Moline. Please invite Mr. Bright. I know Mr. Bright well indeed.[3] [60]

Group B

6 At least four main pipes in my home are frozen. I have no heat at home.
7 Mr. Stone will hire at least four people[1] in a retail store he will open in Mobile.
8 I am having my main meal in Taylor's Diner. I am not eating[2] at home.
9 I need more filing space. May I have it?
10 Our sales rose in May. I am indeed pleased. [57]

Group C

11 I am preparing my brief. I will type it later.
12 My neighbor will not drive. He needs a spare tire. He will buy it[1] at Post's Tire Store.
13 I realize I am at least an hour late.
14 I am not feeling well. I have a pain in my right[2] ear.
15 Mr. Bates raised my pay. I am well pleased. [48]

Group D

16 I am not failing in typing. I will type an hour at home at night.
17 Sales in our Reno store are high. Sales in our[1] Erie store are not so high.
18 I will see Ray in an hour or so in my library.
19 My neighbors are well-known polo[2] players.
20 It seems he will not buy my boat at my price. I will not lease it.
21 I read in my spare hours. I read well.[3] [60]

Group E

22 I will meet my niece in an hour.
23 Mr. Taylor typed my name.
24 Please drive slower. I am not well.
25 I wrote my will in[1] May. I placed it inside my safe at home.
26 I will not drive in a snowstorm. [33]

LESSON 4

20 *Alphabet Review*
A, f, s, v, e, m, n, d, t; l, r, o, h, i, b, p, s.

Group A

1 We are flying home in May.
2 We will move to Maine in a week or so.
3 Our new home will have five rooms. We really

need [1] seven rooms.

4 Mr. Green will take my two girls to a polo game while I am in White Plains.

5 Kate will wear a new blue [2] ski suit to school. [43]

Group B

6 It will take Mr. Sweet at least an hour to grade our typing papers.

7 He swears he gave me my wife's coat.

8 Please place my [1] will in a safe place.

9 We have a fine stereo in our game room.

10 I do not like people to smoke in my room at [2] home. [41]

Group C

11 I have an hour to read my evening paper.

12 Mr. Bates will buy a new stereo at White's Radio Store.

13 I [1] have not paid my dues.

14 He will open a new retail store at 25 Post Road in Moline.

15 Pay rates at Baker's [2] Tire Store are low indeed. I need a pay increase. [48]

Group D

16 I am inviting Mr. Fine to our sales meeting in Mobile in May.

17 We may reduce our dues in May.

18 Please see [1] Mr. Wade at noon. I know Mr. Wade well.

19 We will buy a new ice maker. We need an ice maker in our store. [2]

20 Mr. Green's wife will bake a fine cake. We will eat it at noon. [51]

Group E

21 We try to keep our room at home tidy.

22 Mr. Drew will not drive to our sales meeting in Green Bay. I presume he [1] will take a plane. I will take a train.

23 It will take me an hour or more to clean our boat well.

24 Our fruit trees are doing [2] well.

25 Our sales decreased a great deal in May. [47]

Group F

26 I may buy our food at Dover's Food Store.

27 I am going riding.

28 It will take me at least an hour to read my evening [1] paper.

29 I placed a "No Smoking" sign in my room. [29]

LESSON 5

26 *Alphabet Review*
A, s, v, f, e, m, n, t, d, o; l, r, h, i, b, p, s, oo, k, g.

32 Mrs. Day: Do you know that you have a new Smith car dealer in your city? His name is Mr. Harry West. His [1] store is at 16 Park Avenue.

Mr. West is a fine mechanic who can provide your car with the type of [2] service it needs. His service is the best, but his rates are not high.

Visit Mr. West. While you are at his store, see [3] the latest line of Smith cars. I know that the cars you see will please you. Henry Gray [74]

33 Mrs. Keith: Last evening I read the draft of the sales letter that you are planning to mail to our clothing dealers [1] in the North. I am well pleased with the smooth style of your writing as well as with the nice tone of the letter.

But your [2] typist made three typing errors in the draft. I have marked those errors in red.

Can you have the final letter ready [3] to mail in May? If you can, you will make our sales staff happy indeed. Ruth Grace [74]

34 Mrs. West: As you will remember, Mr. Baker had hoped to meet with you during the first week of May, but he [1] regrets that he will have to cancel his plans. Mr. Baker is flying to Dallas to help settle a strike that [2] has arisen in our clothing factory.

Mr. Baker will telephone you later to set a new

meeting[3] date with you.

Mrs. Mary Sweet, Secretary to Mr. Baker [73]

35 Mrs. Moon: As you know, I had made plans to go with you to the sale of girls' clothing at the Keith Hotel during[1] the first week of April, but I am afraid that I cannot do so.

Last night while skiing in Maine, I broke my right[2] leg. The leg is in a cast. It will remain in a cast at least three weeks. My wife will drive me home in a week or[3] so.

Please accept my sincere regrets. Ed Blue [68]

LESSON 6

36 *Alphabet Review*
D, p, s, n, th, o, b, s; h, e, k, r, f, l, t, i; v, m, g, a, oo, th.

37 *Recall Chart*
1 Throw, throws; swim, sweet; wait, waiter.
2 Do, duty; park, parked; go, goes.
3 Increase, increased; wire, while; act, actor.
4 Neighbor, neighbors; then, theme; move, moved.
5 Serve, served; fact, factor; know, knows.
6 Head, heading; late, latest; gleam, cream.
7 I, Mr., have, are-our-hour, will-well, a-an.
8 Am, it-at, in-not, is, his, the, that.
9 Can, you-your, Mrs., of, with, but.
10 I will, I am, I can, I cannot, I may, we can.
11 You will, you can, you are, of the, of our, of your.
12 In the, in that, in these, in our, it will, it will not.
13 He is, he is not, it is, here is, with the, with our.
14 To the, to that, to get, to you, we are, we will.

38 Mrs. Drew: Last evening Mr. White gave me the sad news that he plans to leave our sales staff in the middle of April.[1] He need not retire, but he feels it is best since his health is poor.

His leaving means that we will have a sales staff[2] vacancy in April. Can you give me names of people who might fill the vacancy? If you can, please phone me.[3] If we can hire a man while Mr. White is still here, he will help train him. Harvey Smith [75]

39 Dear Neighbor: During the past six or seven weeks Mrs. Edith Harper, who is a well-known artist, has had people[1] ask her to start an art class in the West Haven Evening School. Mrs. Harper will start a class in April if[2] at least 20 people agree to take the course.

The class will meet three hours a week starting April 18.

If the[3] course appeals to you, phone me at 118-1161. I will give you the whole story. Harry Sweet, Principal,[4] West Haven Evening School [84]

40 Dear Fred: May I ask a big favor of you, Fred.

Our salesman here in the West, Mr. Henry Smith, will have to move[1] to White Plains with his wife Beth in May. We are assigning him to head the new clothing factory we are opening[2] in that city.

Can you or a member of your staff help the Smiths locate a five- or six-room home in or near[3] White Plains? The Smiths will buy or lease.

If you can help, please phone me at my home at 116-1181. Ed Bates[4] [80]

41 Dear Neighbor: May I invite you to the opening of the new West Side Ladies' Clothing Store at 14 Park Place.[1] The date is May 15. Please make a note of the date. The hours are nine to five.

In our new store we will have more room[2] so that we can carry an even bigger supply of the latest styles in ladies' wear.

May we plan to greet you[3] opening day?

The West Side Ladies' Clothing Store [69]

42 Mrs. Lee: I have read the proof of the ad that we plan to include in the May *Travel Magazine.* The proof is[1] fine, but you will notice that I have supplied a new heading. The heading I have supplied is clearer.

Please mail a[2] proof to Miss Green. Miss Green will file it. Fred Harper [49]

43 Dear Edith: Last night I met Bill Smith at a

sales meeting in the Harper Hotel. He said that you had broken your [1] left arm while skating in the park but that the break is healing well. That is indeed fine news.

Telephone me at [2] 118-1161 if I can help you while you are in bed at home. Mary Gates [55]

CHAPTER 2

LESSON 7

48 Dear Madam: The Hall College evening travel agency course will start on March 20. The course trains people to meet [1] the problems involved in operating an agency. It is a 15-hour course that meets three nights each week.

The [2] teacher of the course is Mr. James Shelly, who has his own travel agency in Great Falls.

If operating [3] a travel agency appeals to your fancy, call our evening school dean, Mrs. Helen Small, at 118-1151. [4] She can provide you with all the facts. But hurry—we have to limit the class to 25 people. [5] Yours very truly, [104]

49 Dear Sir: Will the Red River High School need a teacher of French in the fall? If it will, I can supply you with a [1] fine teacher—Mrs. Shirley James, who moved to Red River last week with her three daughters. She bought a home on Church [2] Avenue.

Mrs. James has taught French in grade schools as well as in high schools. She is the author of two French readers that [3] are selling well.

I am sure Mrs. James can do a fine job teaching French in your school.

Her data sheet is attached. [4] Yours very truly, [84]

50 Dear Sir: It takes a lot of copies of all types of papers to keep a large insurance firm like yours going. That [1] is why it is vital that you watch the cost of making those copies.

The cost of making copies on the new Model [2] 18 White copier is small. It is so small that it will surprise you.

May we have a member of our sales [3] staff show you our copier in your own office? The call will not obligate you to install our copier. [4] Sincerely yours, [83]

51 Mrs. Jack: It is a pleasure to tell you that the sales in Mr. Small's territory increased in March. The March [1] increase is not large, but it shows that Mr. Small is learning the art of selling.

Please drop Mr. Small a note telling [2] him that we are pleased with the job he is doing. Paul C. Page [51]

52 Mr. Thomas: On June 20 we are losing Mrs. Jerome Shaw, who has had charge of our mailing room since [1] 1977. She is leaving to accept a job with an insurance firm in East Chester. We will miss her. [2]

Do you have a girl on your lists whom we can promote to Mrs. Shaw's job? If you do, please have her call me. Henry [3] G. Gates [61]

LESSON 8

57 Dear Sir: Suppose your wife tells you that she would like to take a two-week motor trip with you early in June, but your [1] teenage daughters do not care to go. If this happens, leave them at Camp James By-the-Sea, which is a well-known camp for [2] girls. There they will have an active two weeks with girls their own age.

All that Camp James By-the-Sea has to offer is shown [3] in the attached brochure.

Have a good trip with the knowledge that your daughters are totally happy at Camp James By [4]-the-Sea. The cost for both girls for two weeks would be only $550. Sincerely, [97]

58 Dear Sir: My face is indeed red. In my letter of June 10 I wrote you, "I am attaching two checks, totaling [1] $160, which take care of my bill for the dry goods I bought early in April."

At 7 [2] o'clock last night, while going through a fairly large pile of papers on my desk, I came across the two checks. I had not [3] attached them to my letter. I will be positively sure that they are attached to this letter before I mail [4] it.

I am sincerely sorry for this error. Yours very truly, [93]

59 Mrs. Hall: I have good news for you. Two hundred thousand copies of our brochure arrived at this office at 6 [1] o'clock last evening.

They will be shipped by the middle of the week to our three branches as follows: 100,000 [2] to Mobile; 50,000 to Erie; 20,000 to White Plains. We will keep the remaining 30,000 [3] copies here in Dallas.

There is more good news. I thought the cost of the 200,000 brochures would not be [4] below $4,000, but the bill for them came to only $2,000, which is 50 percent less. [5] Harry Gates [102]

60 Dear Sir: Last week at a teachers' meeting in Moline my wife saw you give a group of girls their first lesson in typing [1] with the aid of cassettes.

There are five clerks on my staff who would like to learn to type, but we have no teacher. Are [2] your cassettes for sale? If they are, we may buy a set. Sincerely, [52]

61 Mr. Best: As you know, our sales on the West Coast are not good. In June they dropped to only $500,000, [1] which is a decrease of nearly 10 percent since May. I believe that our sales will be below $300,000 [2] by July.

I feel we are losing sales because the packaging of our goods is poor. Would you please check [3] on this matter of packaging with our sales staff. Charles H. Bates [71]

62 Mr. Mills: Last night, while glancing through our latest catalog, I came across an error that has me worried. I [1] sincerely hope it will not cause problems for our sales staff.

On page 18 we list the price of our Model 18 [2] desk as $80. The price for this model is $140.

Please see that the $80 [3] price is changed neatly in pencil to $140 in all of the catalogs remaining in our [4] shipping room. George Harper [84]

63 Dear Sir: Are you able to heat all the rooms in your home properly? Is your gas heater burning lots of costly [1] gas but not heating your rooms evenly? If so, you need to get your heater checked by members of our service staff. [2] They can help you lower your heating costs by 20 percent or more. We have helped your neighbors reduce their heating [3] costs; we can help you reduce your costs.

The price of our service? Our fee is only $75. Yours very [4] truly, [81]

LESSON 9

68 Mrs. Chase: On the advice of his physician, Mr. Green has asked me for a leave beginning early in April. [1] Mr. Green is not well, nor is his wife. His physician feels that a vacation in a warm climate will be [2] good for both of them.

As this is the slow season in our operations, my staff is not too busy. They would, therefore, [3] have no problem taking care of Mr. Green's duties proficiently. He plans to be back by June, which is the [4] beginning of our major selling season.

May I authorize Mr. Green to plan for his leave? James J. Smith [5] [100]

69 Mr. Day: Attached are the vacation plans of the members of my section. I am staggering the vacation [1] dates of my people to be sure that there will be two of them on the floor to answer the telephones at all hours [2] of the day.

I would like to begin my own two-week vacation on July 4. But before I can do this, I [3] will have to ask you to fill in for me as chairman of a sectional meeting of National Retail Store Owners [4] in Dallas on July 6.

Can you do it for me? Henry L. Barnes [93]

70 Dear Sir: June 15 can be a happy day or it can be a sad day for you. If I have your check for [1] $1,000 in my possession by 5 o'clock on June 15, your March bill will be marked "Paid." You will then have the [2] good feeling of knowing that you have met your obligations efficiently. If I do not have your check in my [3] possession by June 15, I will have to place this matter with the National Collection Agency.

Is June [4] 15 going to be a happy day or a sad day? Make it a happy day by mailing me your check for [5] $1,000. I am waiting for it patiently. Yours very truly, [107]

71 To the Staff: It is my sad duty to write you that Mr. James Bright will retire as chief of the planning section [1] of our corporation, a section that he ran with efficiency since 1977.

As you may [2] know, Mr. Bright had a slight stroke last May. He plans to follow his physician's advice to retire early at the [3] age of 62.

We do not plan to fill Mr. Bright's position before July 15, the date on which the [4] officers of the corporation will meet in Dallas. David L. Klein [93]

72 To the Staff: Last week I wrote you that the marketing section would be moved to the first floor on which there is more room. [1] The moving date will be June 18. On that day the movers will arrive at 9 o'clock.

Please see to it that all [2] your moving preparations are made by June 17.

If no problems arise, the marketing section will be [3] operating efficiently in its new location by June 19 or 20 at the latest. James G. Gray [4] [80]

73 Dear Ned: I am sorry to have to write you that I cannot play golf with you on July 18.

You may recall [1] that I had a sore arm on June 15. That same day my physician gave me a shot in that arm, which helped a little, [2] but it is still sore. My physician thought it would be best to rest the arm for at least two weeks, which I will do. [3]

I have asked Jim Henry to fill in for me. He plays a fine game of golf. In fact, he shoots in the 80s. Sincerely, [4] [80]

74 Mrs. Small: As you may know, Bill Harper is not in good health. His physician advised him to take a 30-day [1] vacation in Maine. Bill has, therefore, asked for a leave in July. I did not give Bill a final answer so that [2] I might have a chance to talk to you first. July is our slow season; therefore, we would not sorely miss Bill during [3] his leave.

May I authorize Bill to take a 30-day leave? Mary Harper [74]

LESSON 10

80 Mrs. Grant: Can you be at my offices on June 15 by 10 o'clock for a brief meeting? There are three people [1] I would like you to meet. They seem to be fairly good prospects for the sales positions which we have open in [2] the West. They sent me their data sheets; you will find them attached. Please read them with care.

If you like these people as well [3] as I do, I will hire them at the end of this meeting. Jerry Best [73]

81 Dear Sir: Would you like to reduce your printing costs by 50 percent or more? We can show you the way you can do [1] this by making an analysis of your printing needs. On the basis of this analysis, our trained people [2] can offer you a plan that will enable you to buy printing efficiently. Because they have a thorough knowledge [3] of printing processes, they can select those processes that will give you the most for the dollars you spend on [4] printing.

Give our people a chance to assist you. There is no charge for their services. Sincerely yours, [98]

82 Dear Sir: I am sorry to learn that the National Insurance Agency has not paid your claim for $240. [1] We processed the claim on June 15. As the National Insurance Agency is known for the [2] fine service it renders in settling claims, we are surprised that your check has not arrived.

We will check into the [3] matter. Sincerely yours, [64]

83 Dear Sir: I telephoned the National Insurance Agency to ask if they had processed your claim for [1] $240. Mr. Randy Moses said that he sent you a check for $240 on June [2] 18, but apparently the check went astray in the mail. The agency has sent you a new check.

As I wrote [3] you in my letter of June 25, this agency is well known for its efficiency in settling claims. [4] I am happy that they have given your claim their best service. Sincerely yours, [94]

84 Mr. Trent: My secretary tells me that the current issue of the *Auto Guide* is not in the library [1] files. Did you borrow it or do you know who did?

This issue has a list of car rental firms to which I

would [2] like to mail our latest catalog. Bill Smith [48]

85 Dear Evelyn: On June 6 a man by the name of Don Bond applied for a position on our staff. On his [1] application he wrote that he knows you well. I would like to hire him, but before I do so, I need more facts which [2] I sincerely hope you can supply.

1. Did Mr. Bond sell for your firm?
2. Would you hire him again if you [3] had an opening?
3. Why did he leave you?

Your answers will help me greatly. Sincerely yours, [76]

86 Dear Grant: My sister Mary says that last evening she left her reading glasses on your desk in Room 25. Did [1] you find the glasses there? If you did, please phone me at 181-5516. I will then arrange to have a [2] clerk call for them before school closes at 3 o'clock. Sincerely yours, [53]

LESSON 11

93 Dear Sir: On July 18 my wife and I were on Flight 10 from Grand Island to Dallas. When we arrived in Dallas, I could [1] not find my glasses. I called your baggage section, and a Mr. Leonard answered. I told him of my plight, and he [2] assured me that he would search for the glasses. Two hours later he called to tell me that he had been able to find the glasses [3] and that he would send them by messenger to my hotel on West Street. He said I should have them by 3 [4] o'clock in the afternoon, and I did.

I am well pleased with efficient services of this type; they are hard to [5] beat. Mr. Leonard is indeed an asset to your airline. Sincerely yours, [114]

94 Dear Shareholder: We held our meeting on April 16 at the Golden Motel on East 14 Street in Garden [1] City. We were happy to be able to greet the 2,000 people who came to the meeting. They heard talks from [2] our officers on the operations of the firm. They were given a chance to visit the showrooms after the [3] meeting to see the new projects which we have "on the drawing boards" and which we should be able to place on the market [4] in July.

A brochure has been prepared for those who could not be at the meeting so that they can have a [5] record of our actions. When it is ready, we will send you a copy. Very truly yours, [115]

95 Mrs. Wilder: When I called at the Flint Children's Store on West 18 Street this afternoon, the owners told me that [1] they were not pleased with the services they have been getting from our salesman, Mr. Childs. He has not been in to see [2] them for weeks. In fact, he failed to send them the samples they asked for after his last visit. I told them that we were [3] sorry they felt they had been ignored but that I should be happy to check into the matter.

Could you talk to Mr. [4] Childs and get his side of the story for me? A. C. Golden [92]

96 Dear Sir: When you have a meeting to plan and arrange, you can do the job with a phone call to Coastal Airlines. We [1] have a staff of people who have been trained to help you choose a good hotel for your meeting.

We will fly your people [2] to and from the meeting place and arrange rooms for them. We will even plan athletic events for them while they are [3] there.

For more facts, mail the attached card. We will send you our meeting-planning brochure. Sincerely yours, [77]

97 Dear Jim: I am sending you by parcel post a series of eight large charts that I have prepared for our sales meeting [1] on March 15. Please hold them for me till the day of the meeting. The charts show the growth in our children's line since [2] 1975.

Will you be free for an hour or so before the meeting? I have a new project on which I [3] need your advice. Sincerely, [65]

98 Dear Fred: Your charts arrived last evening, and I have placed them in my private storage room. They will be there when you get [1] here.

I will be happy to spend an hour or two with you before the sales meeting on March 15. If you can get [2] here by 7 o'clock, we can have breakfast at the National Hotel. Sincerely yours, [56]

LESSON 12

99 *Recall Chart*

1 Be-by, for, would, there [their], this, good.

2 They, which, them, and, when, from.

3 Should, could, send, after, street, were.

4 To be, to have, to pay, to see, to say, to plan.

5 Have been, I have been, I have been able, I have not been able, he will be able, would be able.

6 Sincerely yours, Yours truly, Dear Sir, Dear Madam, Very truly yours, Yours very truly.

7 $8; 800; 800,000; $800,000; 8 percent, 8 o'clock.

8 Share, shared; fold, folder; patient, efficiency.

9 Caution, cautioned; became, began; increase, increases.

10 Brand, branded; print, printer; age, aged.

11 Ship, shipping; change, changed; throw, thrown.

12 Thick, thicker; arise, arises; neatly, namely.

13 We, way; swim, swam; to, do.

14 Fast, vast; shop, job; arm, farm.

101 Dear Madam: You will be happy to learn that your application for a charge card in Gordon's Fifth Street Ladies' Shop [1] has been approved. It gives me pleasure to send you the attached card.

When you buy dresses or accessories from our [2] store and charge them, please be sure to have your card with you and hand it to the clerks who are serving you. When you do this, [3] they will be able to serve you rapidly and efficiently.

If you should drive from your home to our store, you can [4] park your car in the lot which is on the west side of the store. There is no parking fee for our cardholders.

I am [5] sure you will find shopping at Gordon's a real pleasure. Sincerely yours, [113]

102 Dear Jane: Mary and I were happy to learn of your marriage to Bill. We know you will both be happy.

As you know, [1] we have not met Bill, but we feel we know him after reading the glowing letters you wrote Mary and me while you [2] were in college.

Could you and Bill drop by for a visit when you are both home during the Christmas holidays? It will be [3] good to see you again and to meet Bill. Our neighbors, Mr. and Mrs. Green, would like to meet you as well. [4] Sincerely, [82]

103 To the Staff: During the week of July 18, our record shop will hold a sale for members of the staff. At this [1] sale you will be able to buy the records shown in the attached leaflet for only $2, or 30 percent [2] below retail prices. You will be able to buy cassette tapes for only $4.50, or 50 [3] percent below retail prices.

Plan to visit the record shop during the week of July 18. It will [4] be open from 9 to 5 o'clock. A. R. Barnes [89]

104 Dear Sir: We have prepared a little brochure on life insurance that we feel you should read. It provides all kinds of [1] insurance facts that you and people in your walk of life should be familiar with. It has seven fact-filled chapters [2] in all.

Would you like to have a copy of this brochure? We will send it to you if you will sign and mail the [3] attached card. It needs no postage. Sincerely yours, [69]

105 To All Dealers: Because of sharply rising costs, we will have to raise the price of our Model 18 filing [1] cabinet by 10 percent. This will mean that the price to you as a dealer will be $286 a [2] cabinet, an increase of $26.

We do not plan to raise the prices on our office desks and chairs, [3] but if costs keep rising, we may have to raise prices on them too.

We are sorry we have to take this step, but we [4] cannot go on operating at a big loss. James L. Harris [92]

106 Dear Ben: My wife and I spent last night in the city. While we were there, I stopped at the Mets ball park and bought the two [1] tickets you asked me to get for you for the night game with the Reds on July 18. The seats are in the third row [2] of Section 18.

They are good seats, and you should be able to see well from them. I paid $4 apiece for [3] them.

Should I mail the tickets to you, or would you prefer to have your clerk call for them at my office? Sincerely, [4] [80]

107 Dear Fred: I have all the papers relating to the home I bought for you on Fifth Avenue and 18 Street [1] in Salem in my office. Please stop in on your way to your office and sign them.

Our fee for handling this [2] matter for you is $180. Sincerely yours, [51]

CHAPTER 3

LESSON 13

111 Dear Sir: Thank you for the order you gave Mr. Cook yesterday for the printing of 10,000 four-color [1] circulars. We were glad to get it as it was the first order you have placed with us since you opened your bookstore.

We [2] will begin work on these circulars soon and notify you when they are ready.

I am enclosing a number [3] of circulars we prepared as promotion pieces for our own products. These circulars are illustrations of [4] the type of work that we can do.

Again, thank you for the chance to serve your printing needs. Sincerely yours, [98]

112 Dear Madam: We are sorry that we have not been able to fill the order enclosed with your letter of June 5 [1] for the printing of circulars and booklets. The work crews at our Third Street plant went on strike, and all production there [2] was stopped on June 6. But I am glad to write you that the strike was settled yesterday by arbitration and that [3] we will be able to go into full production again soon.

To speed up the filling of orders that arrived [4] in our plant after the strike began, we must put our entire staff to work nights.

Thank you for your patience. Sincerely [5] yours, [101]

113 Dear Bud: Thank you for the 30 illustrations you prepared for our book entitled *Drugs in Industry.* They arrived [1] yesterday, and I was glad to get them.

The bill you enclosed with your illustrations was for $480. [2] I clearly remember that when we placed the order with you for these illustrations, we agreed to [3] pay you $15 an illustration, in which case your bill should be for $450.

If you [4] will send us a correct bill, I will see that it is paid in full soon after I get it. Sincerely yours, [98]

114 Dear Ned: I am glad that you are well pleased with the illustrations I prepared for your book, *Drugs in Industry.*

My [1] bill for $480 is correct. Two weeks after Mrs. Cook, the author, had approved my sketches, [2] she asked me if I could make a number of major changes on three of the illustrations. For this type of work, [3] I charge $15 an hour. It took me two hours.

My original bill is enclosed. Sincerely yours, [78]

115 Mr. Butler: As you will see by reading the enclosed letter from Mr. Green, our shipping clerks made an error [1] in filling his order of June 15. They shipped him 100 copies of Moore's *Chemistry* when they should have shipped him [2] 100 copies of Wilson's *Applied Chemistry.*

Would you be good enough, therefore, to see that Mr. Green gets [3] the books he ordered. A. B. White [66]

116 Mrs. Swift: I am afraid I have bad news for you. Yesterday I had a telephone call from Mr. Cook of [1] the West Printing Corporation in which he told me that the two big presses on which they print our books caught on fire [2] and that all work on our books had to be stopped. He feels that the presses will not be back in operation before [3] March or April.

This means that we will not be able to place the books I am listing on the enclosed sheet on the [4] market before June. This makes me feel sick because we will lose at least $100,000 in sales.

Please [5] notify our sales staff of our problem. A. J. Smith [109]

LESSON 14

121 Mrs. Baldwin: I was glad to get the circular you drafted to push the sale of our hardware products. Thank you [1] for finishing the job so soon. You must have worked on it day and night.

Yesterday I placed an order with Broadway [2] Printshop to print 10,000 copies of the circular. They quoted us a price of only $1,000 [3] for the job and were the lowest bidders. A copy of the order is enclosed for your files. Edwin Quinn [78]

122 Dear Madam: As you may know, the National credit card is not issued to all who apply for it. It is issued [1] to an applicant only after the application has been studied and investigated with great care. [2] It is a pleasure to tell you that you have qualified for a National credit card; your application has [3] been accepted by our board.

We are sending you your card today from our Dallas offices, and you should have it [4] soon. Always carry it with you.

Take a half hour or so to read the enclosed brochure. There you will find listed in [5] detail all the services to which your card entitles you.

In July you will get your first copy of our free [6] magazine, *Travel.* We know you will like it when you get it. Yours very truly, [134]

123 Mrs. Queen: Mr. Harry Smith, who teaches an art class at the Broadway School of Fine Arts, would like us to take his [1] class on a guided tour of our Park Street studios. I invited him and his class to visit us on July [2] 10 between 9 and 10 o'clock.

Could you arrange your plans for this day so that you can take them on a quick guided [3] trip through our studios? James Mild [66]

124 Dear Sir: You may remember me as the salesman who often waited on you at the Park Square Clothing Store.

On June [1] 15 I left the Park Square Clothing Store, and I am today opening my own shop on Broadway and Third Street. At [2] this shop I will be able to take care of all your clothing needs and give you service that is quick and efficient. [3] My clothing is well tailored, but my prices are the lowest in the city.

Stop in to see me soon. You will be [4] well pleased with the good buys I offer. Sincerely yours, [90]

125 Dear Madam: You will recall that on July 15 you asked me to quote you a price on the installation of [1] pine paneling in the library of your home at 16 Cooper Square. On July 17 a member of [2] my staff visited your home and made a study of your library. On the basis of his study, we quoted [3] you a price of $2,000, provided we could begin the work on or before July 25. Today [4] is July 23, and we have not heard from you.

If we must wait beyond July 25 before [5] beginning the work, we will have to raise the price we quoted you by at least 10 percent.

Why not call us today and [6] authorize us to proceed with the paneling. Our number is 116-1188. Sincerely yours, [139]

126 Dear Helen: Thank you for the snapshots of your children. I was glad to get them.

I sincerely hope, Helen, that I [1] will soon be able to spend a week or so with you and the children in your cottage on Lake George. Sincerely, [39]

127 Mrs. Corwin: I have a bit of news that should make you happy. Yesterday I learned that Trent College in Atlanta [1] adopted our book entitled *Writing Effective Credit Letters.* Their first order was for 500 copies. [2]

With his order Mr. Smith included a letter in which he says, "I selected your book after a thorough [3] study of all the books on credit collections that I could find."

I know you will be as elated with this [4] news as I am. Helen Cooper [86]

128 Miss Cooper: I was indeed elated with the news that Trent College adopted *Writing Effective Credit Letters.* [1]

I will drop a line to Mr. Davis, the author. I know that he, too, will be glad to have this good news. Mary [2] Corwin [42]

LESSON 15

134 Dear Dr. Baldwin: If you lease your car from us, there is one thing you will not have to worry about, and that is [1] car repairs.

If your car stalls on the road, you simply call our business office. When we receive the call, we will send [2] our capable, reliable mechanics to take care of any repair work that is needed. If they cannot [3] find what the trouble is quickly, they will call our business office, and we will send a new car to replace the stalled [4] one.

What does our leasing service cost? It costs less than you might think.

May we call on you soon, Dr. Baldwin, and tell [5] you in detail about our valuable leasing plan that has won us hundreds of friends? Sincerely yours, [118]

135 Dear Dr. White: Yesterday we received an application from Mrs. Alice James for the position of research [1] analyst that we have available. She indicated that she had worked for you and listed your name as [2] a business reference.

Could you answer these queries about her?

1. Was she a valuable member of your staff? Was [3] she reliable?

2. Do you think you would hire her again if a vacancy arose in your business?

3. Were you paying [4] her more or less than $150 a week when she resigned?

Please tell us anything else about [5] Mrs. James which will enable us to rate her fairly. Thank you, Dr. White, for any help you can give us. [6] Sincerely yours, [122]

136 Dear Jim: Our new salesman, Mr. Charles Best, wrote me about the pleasant reception he received from you on his first [1] visit to your Third Street offices. He enclosed with his letter his first order from you for our tables.

I [2] remember well when I broke in as a new salesman in this business, and I know what a good feeling it is for a [3] beginner to receive a warm reception from one of his most valuable buyers.

If there is anything we [4] can do to be of service to you, please call us. We will be glad to help. Sincerely yours, [96]

137 Mr. Grace: I have been trying to reach you by phone at the office since June 16, but I have not been able [1] to catch you. Therefore, I am writing you this note.

Would it be possible for me to get about 5,000 copies [2] of the enclosed circular by July 10? I need them for a mailing I will make to insurance agents [3] less than two weeks from today. I should have them by 2 o'clock the afternoon of July 10 at the latest. A. [4] C. Smith [81]

138 Dear Dr. Nolan: If you ask anyone who operates a business what asset is most valuable, I think [1] the reply would quickly be "a good credit rating."

You have a favorable credit rating, but you will lose it if you [2] do not soon pay us the $450 you owe us.

If you cannot pay the whole bill, at least pay us [3] half and tell us when you will take care of the rest.

Of one thing you may be sure—we are patient and we are reasonable. [4] Sincerely yours, [84]

139 Dear Dr. Blair: Will you be available for a brief meeting in my office on the afternoon of June 15 [1] at 3 o'clock? I would like to talk to you about a research project that I think will enable us to [2] increase our business by at least 20 percent.

If you cannot make it on June 15, would June 18 be better? [3] Please call my secretary and let her know the day you can be here. Sincerely yours, [76]

LESSON 16

145 Dear Dr. Royal: When servicing is needed on your car or when anything has to be repaired on it, you [1] do not call in just anyone. What do you do? You call in capable craftsmen who know all about your car.

We [2] at the Yale Garage like to think of our men as skilled craftsmen because they have had years of valuable factory [3] training.

If you have not yet had your car serviced this year, drive it to the Yale Garage on Doyle Street soon. We will have[4] your car ready in less than an hour. We have been in business here in West Point for a decade, and we guarantee[5] all our work. Sincerely yours, [105]

146 Dear Dr. Coyne: Does the grass in your yard always get yellow and full of weeds by the middle of July? If your[1] answer is yes, let our trained men spread rich topsoil and Sawyer's grass seed on your lawn this year in March. This will give you[2] not only a good green lawn but one that will be free of weeds for many years as well. You will have a lawn that will[3] be a joy instead of an eyesore.

Place an order for our service today. You will be glad you did. Sincerely[4] yours, [81]

147 Dear Joyce: I am enclosing the circular about the West Point Boys' Camp which I mentioned to you after your meeting[1] yesterday. I have known the manager, Mr. Roy Moses, for many years. He was a classmate of mine at[2] Yale.

He operates his camp efficiently. My own boys spent their vacations there during their high school years and were[3] happy there. I think your boys would like it too.

Thank you for inviting me to be your guest at your meeting. You have[4] nice friends. It was a pleasure meeting them. Sincerely, [90]

148 Dear Dr. Baker: The old year is leaving us, and the new one will be here in less than three weeks. This year has been[1] a good one for us in the toy business. We kept most of our old friends and won many new ones. We should be able[2] to finish this year with a net profit of $100,000, which is 10 percent above last year.

Thank[3] you for helping us make this fine year possible. We received many sizable orders from you, and you always[4] paid your monthly invoices when they were due.

We are sending you two of our new calendars and hope that you like[5] them. Sincerely yours, [104]

149 Mrs. Roy: Could you send me the name of the woman who was appointed credit manager of the Boyd Toy Shop[1] in West Point last week? I made a note of her name, but I cannot find the piece of paper I made it on. I would[2] like to write her a nice note. C. C. Jones [47]

150 Dear Roy: You will recall that last year you rented me your cottage on Lake Doyle during the months of June and July.[1]

Would you be willing to rent it again this year?

Last year you charged me $250 for the two months.[2] I realize that this year you may want to charge more.

At any rate, please advise me if your cottage will be[3] available. Sincerely yours, [65]

151 Mr. Royal: At its meeting in April the board established a new vacation policy. Beginning at[1] once all members of the firm who have been with us for ten years or more will receive one month's vacation.

I am[2] enclosing a list of the members of your staff who are eligible. Charles Green [54]

LESSON 17

157 Gentlemen: Early next year the Royal Manufacturing Company will open a branch in Detroit, where we[1] have won many important and valuable friends.

We have most of the permanent personnel which will staff this branch,[2] but shortly there will be two new, important positions open that we will have to fill. We will need a dependable[3] sales director and a purchasing agent. These desirable positions will pay good salaries.

The[4] persons we are after must have worked at least five years for a manufacturing company and must be able[5] to provide good personal references. If you know of any persons who you think can handle these positions[6] of importance, please have them call Mr. Green, our personnel director, at 116-1117 any[7] morning next week between 9 and 11 o'clock. Sincerely yours, [153]

158 To the Staff: I am delighted to be able to tell you that this morning the directors of our company [1] decided to purchase the Yale Paper Manufacturing Company, which is perhaps the most important and [2] best-known paper manufacturer in the West.

The final papers should be delivered to our officers about [3] March 15. Dr. Roy Tracy, who has had many years of valuable training in the paper business, will [4] shortly take direct and personal charge.

We believe that this purchase is a step of great importance to our [5] operations in the West, where we do from a third to one-half of our business. Lee Baldwin [116]

159 Gentlemen: The purpose of this letter is to tell you that yesterday the directors of our company [1] decided to halt work on the manufacture of the No. 118 jetliner because of rising costs. If [2] we were to proceed with the work, our costs would be far greater than we had anticipated.

The directors regret [3] having to take this action because we had 200 orders for these planes which were to have been delivered [4] this year and next. We are canceling these orders.

Full details about the board's decision will appear shortly in [5] the daily papers. Sincerely yours, [107]

160 Gentlemen: Your business records are of great importance to your manufacturing business. If one morning you [1] should arrive at your office and find that your records had been burned, could you reopen for business? The chances are [2] you could not. What would you then do?

Do not let anything happen to your records. Deposit them in a well-built [3] Harris safe, where you will know that they are protected.

To learn all about Harris safes, send for a copy of our [4] circular. We will be glad to send it to you if you will sign and mail the enclosed card. Why not do this soon. [5] Sincerely yours, [102]

161 Mrs. Drake: Thank you for writing me about the plan you are preparing for our next meeting. When it is ready, [1] will you be good enough to mail it by registered mail to my West Point address at 116 Main Street. I will [2] be staying there from July 15 to July 31.

Our last meeting was not too inspiring. I am sure, though, [3] that our next meeting will be a good one. A. B. Baker [70]

162 Mr. Best: This morning I saw the design prepared by Mr. James for our book, *The History of Rome*. I like it. [1]

Mr. James has prepared a number of fine cover designs for us. Perhaps we might be smart to invite Mr. [2] James to join our permanent staff. We could pay him about $15,000 a year.

When you again see Mr. [3] James, ask him if a permanent job with us appeals to him. Charles C. Doyle [74]

163 Gentlemen: At the last meeting of the board of managers, we decided to add three people to our sales staff [1] to sell our manufactured products on the East Coast. If you know of any ambitious men or women who would like [2] a career in marketing with our company, please ask them to call our personnel director any weekday [3] morning between nine and twelve. Very truly yours, [70]

164 Gentlemen: We are looking for two people to sell our manufactured goods on the East Coast. We haven't had [1] anyone in that important territory since we closed our office in Lynn in 1975.

Do you [2] have any people on your lists who could fill these positions? If you do, please have them call me at 116-1181. [3] Sincerely yours, [65]

165 Dear Dr. Cook: Our car business has increased so rapidly in the last five years that our showroom and garage are [1] too small for us to render our friends the kind of service to which we feel they are entitled.

We have, therefore, purchased [2] the building at 14 Harper Square. This building has two large floors where we will be able to take care of about [3] 20 cars on any given day.

We plan to move into our new building on March 18 and open on [4] March 19. Why not stop in and help us celebrate opening day. Sincerely yours, [95]

LESSON 18

166 *Recall Chart*

1 Glad; work, worked; circular; order, ordered.
2 Thank, enclose, was, value, than, one [won].
3 What, about, thing-think; business, businesses; any.
4 Gentlemen, morning, important-importance; company; manufacture, manufacturer.
5 Short, where, yesterday, soon, next, doctor.
6 Dear Sir, Dear Madam, Sincerely yours, Yours very truly, Yours truly, Very truly yours.
7 To pay, to find, to buy, I have been, I have not been, I have not been able.
8 $5; 400; 8 o'clock; 12,000; 120,000; 4 percent.
9 Direction, directory; desire, desirable; repeat, repeated.
10 Salesmen, women; appoint, appointed; spoil, spoiled.
11 Invoice, invoices; purchase, purchases; begin, beginner.
12 Efficient, efficiency; land, landed; month, monthly.
13 Quote, quoted; white, whiter; just, adjust.
14 Book, booked; swimming, swimmer; shared, sharing.
15 Persist, persisted; thin, thinner; health, healthy.
16 Yellow, yard; graded, traded; chair, charm.

168 *Marketing*

What do you think of when you hear the word *market*? If you are like most people, you think of a place where one purchases [1] meats and groceries. That is a market to be sure. In business, though, the word means many more things. It may be [2] a measure of sales. Manufacturers might say that there is no market for a product or a service. They mean [3] that the product or service does not sell well.

On occasion, the word *market* refers to a selected group of [4] buyers like the "teenage market." This refers to buyers who are from 13 to 19 years old.

If a person [5] tells you that there is a new product on the market, he means that a company is manufacturing and [6] offering a new thing for sale.

Then again the word may refer to the place in which goods or services are sold. It [7] may be said that a company was producing goods for a "local market." That means it will sell its goods mostly [8] to those living in or adjacent to the city where the business is located.

Firms that produce for a [9] national market sell their goods nationwide.

The Importance of Marketing. Why is marketing of great importance? [10] It is important because business firms produce goods and services to sell them, and marketing helps sell goods. A [11] firm that does not sell what it produces will often remain in business for less than a year. But buyers are not [12] always easy to please. They have many kinds of wants, and the producer must supply those wants. Many buyers want [13] credit, free parking space, delivery service, and trading stamps. Quite often they have to be persuaded that a product [14] is valuable and that they should order it.

Selling goods and services is the primary purpose of [15] marketing, and marketing involves activities like packaging, storing, shipping, and sales promotion. All of [16] these things help producers to sell their goods and services.

You can see, therefore, that marketing plays a vital role [17] in the operation of a business. [347]

169 *A Worker's Creed*

I will be loyal to the company I work for and will not talk about its operations even with my [1] best and closest friends.

I will be kind and patient when I deal with the people I work with.

I will learn all I can [2] about the company's business so that I will be able to relieve my boss of as many routine details [3] as possible.

I will try hard to be alert so that my boss will not have to repeat any instructions.

I [4] will always be tidy and neat and watch my health.

I will spend my company's money as though it were my own. [5] [100]

170 *The Importance of Good Health*

Good health is by far your most valuable asset. Good health can assist you in gaining promotions to more important [1] jobs. Bad health can cause you to fail in business.

You should do all you can to guard your health.

Health is a personal [2] thing. To protect it learn what you must do to stay fit.

If you can honestly say yes to the following queries, [3] your chances of keeping fit are good:

1. Do you get at least eight hours sleep daily?
2. Do you eat what is good for [4] you and not just what you like?
3. Do you see a doctor once a year for a checkup?
4. Do you have a hobby [5] from which you derive pleasure?

Remember, people cannot do their best work when they do not possess reasonably [6] good health. Your health is priceless. Take good care of it. [129]

CHAPTER 4

LESSON 19

177 Dear Dr. Hugo: After reviewing the applications of about 30 applicants, the board of trustees [1] this morning offered Ms. Eunice James the position as director of the Utica School of Financial [2] Management. She accepted the assignment, and her appointment is effective immediately. She will move to [3] Utica shortly.

Ms. James was head of the advertising department of Baker College for ten years and has [4] the unique talents that we feel are desirable to help us reach our present ambitious goals.

So that you may [5] have an opportunity to meet Ms. James socially, we will hold a special party at the school on July [6] 27. Refreshments will be served between the hours of 5 and 7 o'clock. Please use the enclosed card to [7] tell us if you can be with us at the party. Sincerely yours, [152]

178 Gentlemen: Would you like to increase your company's business immediately? This is what you can do if you [1] place an advertisement for your motel in the next issue of the *United Travel Magazine.*

Many heads [2] of advertising departments have told us that their initial advertisement in our magazine immediately [3] increased their business from 20 to 25 percent.

The *United Travel Magazine* is presently [4] read by 200,000 people who travel for social or business reasons. They are important and [5] valuable prospective users of your motel. Yet the cost of reaching them through advertising is less than you might [6] think.

Take this opportunity to get an immediate increase in your business. Advertise in the *United* [7] *Travel Magazine.* Yours very truly, [148]

179 Dear Dr. Bond: Thank you for referring Ms. Edith Hughes to Mrs. Hugo of our manufacturing department. [1] Mrs. Hugo had a good opportunity to talk with her yesterday and to present her to a number [2] of department heads and company officials.

There are three departments in which we presently have vacancies. [3] Up to this moment I have not been able to decide where Ms. Hughes will initially work, but of one thing [4] I am quite sure—she will be part of our staff beginning June 5. We are glad to add her to our staff. Yours very [5] truly, [101]

180 Mr. Moses: Please place an immediate purchase order for 15,000 copies of the attached circular. [1] It is a matter of especial importance that these circulars be mailed to our dealers as soon after [2] July 15 as possible. If they were to be mailed later than July 30, we could lose a good deal of [3] our fall business.

Is there anything you can do personally to speed up the printing of these circulars? C. [4] C. George [81]

181 Mr. Allen: When I visited Bill Smith in his new store on East 15 Street, he told me that he could use a [1] few of our posters advertising our line of men's clothing.

Please send him the three posters which we prepared in July. [2] These should be sufficient for his needs. A. B. Casey [50]

182 Mrs. Hughes: This morning I received a letter from the James Printing Company saying that they have finished printing [1] and binding our book, *Opportunities in Advertising,* and that we will have 10,000 copies in our [2] shipping room on or before July 15. This is good news indeed.

Please have the advertising department begin [3] work immediately on the preparation of suitable advertising copy that we can use in [4] the major national magazines shown on the enclosed list.

I think that with the right kind of promotion, we should [5] be able to sell at least 9,000 copies of *Opportunities in Advertising* in the first year. If [6] you or the advertising department need more data about the book, please call me. Harry C. Smith [138]

LESSON 20

188 Ms. Powers: May I take this opportunity to compliment you and the other members of your committee [1] on the important part you played in the preparation of the advertisement announcing the new No. [2] 118 computer we will place on the market shortly.

The advertisement was well placed and immediately [3] caught my eye when I opened the May issue of the *Accountants' Monthly.* It presents concrete facts about the [4] computer, which should have considerable appeal to company comptrollers and other financial people.

Keep [5] up the good work, Ms. Powers. Mary C. Powell [109]

189 Dear Dr. Brown: Because of the business we have received from you and our many other friends in past years, we have [1] found it desirable to move our leather goods shop from our present crowded store to a considerably larger [2] one. This morning we are moving to 14 South Third Street, where we will occupy four complete floors.

We invite [3] you to visit us at your first opportunity to see how we have utilized the space in our new store. While [4] you are there, see the thousands of leather products we have gathered from all parts of the globe.

We think you will be as [5] delighted with our new store as we are. Yours very truly, [110]

190 Gentlemen: When you appoint a person to an important position that makes it necessary for him to [1] move to another city, arrange for Brown Brothers to handle his moving.

Brown Brothers specializes in working [2] with companies that must make personnel moves. We work with more companies of this type than any other moving [3] concern. Each move is planned and controlled in one central place by our staff. They are backed by the industry's most [4] comprehensive computer operation.

May we send you a complimentary booklet that tells you how we can [5] serve your moving needs? It is called *Easy Moving.* A copy is yours for the asking. Very truly yours, [118]

191 Mr. Bates: As you will learn when you read the next issue of our company newsletter, I was promoted [1] yesterday to the position of manager of our concrete manufacturing plant in South Bend. I plan to move [2] there with my father and mother, but I do not know just when. It will be in either June or July, depending [3] on how soon I will be able to complete all the things that are presently on my desk.

I must now decide whether [4] to buy or rent a house in South Bend. What do you recommend? You know that I always value your advice. Charles [5] H. James [101]

192 Mrs. Davis: Thank you for the circular you enclosed with your last letter. I am glad that you were able to [1] include an order coupon on the back.

Could you send me 2,000 copies of the circular not later than [2] next week? I would like to use them in a special mailing I will make to building contractors shortly after the [3] first of the year. James C. Hughes [65]

193 Dear Bill: Perhaps you have heard that on July 15 I will take charge of our leather processing plant in Utica. [1] I plan to move to Utica with my mother and father in May or June.

I think I have a purchaser [2] for my house here, but I am faced with the problem of finding a place to live in Utica. Can you contact a [3] reputable agent in Utica and ask him or her to send me a list of available six- or [4] seven-room houses that are for sale in the $30,000 range.

Thanks for any help you can give me in getting [5] settled in Utica. Sincerely yours, [108]

LESSON 21

199 Gentlemen: We have written you several letters asking you to send us a remittance to pay for the [1] advertising circulars we printed for you last July. Evidently they were lost or they escaped your attention [2] because we have not yet received any remittance from you.

I am sure everyone would agree that it is [3] to a company's advantage to maintain a good credit standing with its creditors. You have had a very [4] good credit standing ever since you placed your first order with us, but you are in danger of losing it.

I suggest, [5] therefore, that you send us a check for $2,000 without delay. Do not wait—every day is very [6] important. Yours very truly, [125]

200 Dear Dr. Fenton: Enclosed is your personal copy of our tennis catalog. It contains just about [1] everything that any tennis player could ever need. We suggest that you browse through it and then take advantage of [2] our very low prices. In the back of the catalog you will find several order cards.

We are proud to announce [3] that next month we are opening a women's department, where we will carry a complete line of women's tennis [4] outfits. After all, today as many women are playing tennis as men. We feel, therefore, that we should make [5] our services available to them.

Whenever you need tennis equipment, give us an opportunity [6] to serve you. We are confident that no other tennis shop can maintain our high standard of service and meet our [7] very low prices. Sincerely yours, [147]

201 Dear Dr. Brandon: We are very sorry that we cannot send you 50 copies of our bulletin entitled [1] *Pointers for the Business Typist.* This bulletin has been out of print ever since April, and we have no [2] immediate plans to manufacture any more copies.

But perhaps I can be of assistance to you. I have [3] several file copies and would be glad to lend you one which you may duplicate. Thus your students will be able [4] to take advantage of the many valuable suggestions that this well-planned bulletin contains.

All we ask is [5] that you place a special credit line on every copy saying that it has been reproduced with our approval. [6]

What do you think of this suggestion? Sincerely yours, [130]

202 Ms. Landon: At 10 o'clock on the morning of June 15 we will have a short meeting of managers and [1] assistant managers in the main conference room. At this meeting our president, Mr. Baker, will give us his [2] views on salary increases for next year.

I know that you are very busy and have lots of work on your desk, [3] but I assure you that the meeting will last less than an hour. This meeting is of great importance to every one [4] of us, so please try to be present. Allen Cobb [89]

203 Mrs. Gaston: Thank you for inviting me to the President's Dinner on June 15. I would like to attend, [1] but I cannot.

Yesterday I was invited by Dr. Jones to talk to the student body of the West Street [2] High School in Trenton on June 15, and I accepted. If only you had invited me one day sooner! Mary [3] L. Hughes [62]

LESSON 22

211 Dear Ms. Moses: No doubt every so often you would like to make a live presentation of your product to an [1] important potential customer but cannot do so. Whenever that happens again, make your demonstration [2] with a Temple sound projector. Simply set it up in your prospect's office, press a button, and watch it demonstrate [3] your product very effectively in full color.

The enclosed circular outlines several advantages [4] of the Temple system. We suggest that you read it, Ms. Moses. And after you have read it, give our [5] representative an opportunity to demonstrate a Temple at your place of business. Sincerely yours, [118]

212 Dear Mr. Temple: I am sorry for the annoyance you were caused because your morning paper was not delivered [1] on Tuesday, Wednesday, and Thursday. The boy who had been assigned to your street resigned from his job on Monday, and [2] we could not find even a temporary replacement before Friday. You will be glad to know that we have now [3] been able to hire a permanent replacement. Commencing tomorrow, August 5, a boy by the name of Edwin [4] Hughes will serve your street. He is a personable chap, and I am certain you will like him.

Incidentally, [5] Mr. Temple, if you know of any boys or girls who would like to obtain paper routes, please refer them to me. [6] They will be put to work immediately. Cordially yours, [131]

213 Gentlemen: Thank you for the estimate of $350 to repair the damage our company [1] car sustained on Sunday, September 6, when a 16-year-old driver of another car lost control and ran [2] into our car.

I am rather surprised at the size of your estimate. It is about 50 percent higher [3] than I had anticipated. Would you be good enough, therefore, to make a complete itemized list of the work [4] and parts that your estimate covers and send it to me by Saturday of next week. I will give you a decision [5] as to whether to proceed with the work shortly after I receive your itemized list. Yours very truly, [6] [120]

214 Mrs. Smith: You will be glad to know that the demand for our manufactured goods in the East increased considerably [1] during the months of November, December, and January. The first two weeks of February are good [2] too. I estimate that we have added about 500 new customers since November. This indicates one [3] thing to me—the well-planned advertising campaign which we launched in the East is paying off.

I think we should begin [4] to make plans soon for a similar campaign in the West, where our business has not been doing so well. What do you [5] think? A. C. Temple [104]

215 Dear Dr. Landon: As I am sure I need not tell you, we value your business. That is why we were so happy [1] to receive an order from you for hospital supplies yesterday, the first we have received since last February. [2] The supplies will be shipped tomorrow morning, and you should have them by Monday, October 15.

Thank you for your [3] business, Dr. Landon. Yours sincerely, [67]

216 Dear Mr. Bennett: In our business, the months of August, September, and October are very busy months. We [1] estimate that these months account for at least 60 percent of our entire year's business.

In order to take [2] care of our customers' needs efficiently during these months, we hire temporary help. This year we will need two [3] secretaries, two typists, and three filing clerks.

Last year your agency supplied us with the temporary help [4] we needed. Can you do so again this year?

I am available to see anyone you refer to me on [5] any Tuesday, Thursday, or Friday between ten and four. Sincerely yours, [113]

217 Dear Mr. Beane: Thank you for helping us obtain temporary help for our busy season in August, September, [1] and October. Of the eight people you sent us, we hired six. The other two decided they would not be happy [2] working in our type of business. Very truly yours, [50]

218 Dear Mr. Smith: On December 30 we will release our year-end issue of the *Financial Daily.* In this [1] issue we will review briefly what happened in business during the year and take a look at what is in store for [2] business next year. About 800,000 people will read this issue. Our readers have learned to depend on this [3] issue to help them make good financial decisions.

The December 30 issue provides a [4] good medium for advertisers to reach investors with their advertising message. So make your space reservation [5] now for our year-end issue. A reservation card is enclosed. Sincerely yours, [116]

219 Dear Mr. Temple: Our credit manager is a little worried. He says that your account is six weeks past due [1] and that he has not heard from you even though he has written you five friendly letters.

If your business is having [2] financial problems and you cannot pay the $186 you owe us, please tell us. We will help [3] you find a way to pay your bill. But please write us. Cordially yours, [72]

LESSON 23

226 Gentlemen: This will acknowledge your letter of Monday, October 23, to our general manager, [1] Ms. Gloria Landon, asking several questions about the advertising practices of our [2] organization. Ms. Landon left yesterday afternoon on a short business trip, and your letter has been referred to me. [3] Here are answers to your questions:

1. We place our advertising through outside agencies. They create our [4] advertisements and place them in whatever media they feel will develop our sales best.
2. This year we plan to devote [5] between 25 and 30 percent of our revenue to advertising.
3. At this time we do not [6] contemplate an increase in our advertising appropriation for next year. There has been a very definite [7] drop in the demand for our goods recently while there has been a sharp increase in our company's overhead, [8] which is too high. We may, in fact, soon have to make a cut in the appropriation for our advertising [9] division.

If I can answer any other questions for you, I will be glad to have you call me. Sincerely yours, [10] [200]

227 Dear Mr. Doyle: We suggest that this Christmas you give your wife a really different and valuable present. [1] Give her a General piano, which is without question the acknowledged leader in its field. The General [2] organization manufactures the finest piano on the market.

Our upright model can be placed [3] in any living area, where it will completely fill your home with brilliant sound over the years. Your wife will [4] appreciate your special gift every day of the year and thank you for it. Take advantage of this opportunity [5] to make her happy.

If you place an order for a General piano immediately, we [6] definitely guarantee to have it in your home in time for Christmas. Sincerely yours,

PS. A circular about [7] General pianos is enclosed. [147]

228 Mrs. Hughes: Last November my associate, Captain John Quinn, and I devised a plan to merge the sales division [1] with the advertising division. We think the plan will enable our organization to make an [2] important saving in overhead costs over the next two years.

Would you be able to spare about two hours of [3] your time to see Captain Quinn and me on Friday morning, January 3, to go over the general plan [4] with you and to answer any definite questions you may have about it? I am free on that day; Captain Quinn [5] is too.

May I please have an acknowledgment of this note by Tuesday, December 15, Mrs. Hughes. Charles L. Bond [6] [120]

229 Dear Dr. Purcell: There are different types and different sizes and different makes of pianos. But when a [1] piano bears the name of Baker, you may be sure that it was built to the work standards set by Joseph Baker in [2] 1853, the year he organized the Baker Piano Company.

His policy was "Build a better [3] piano than anybody else and sell it at the lowest price." We have not departed from that policy. [4]

Should you be in the market for a piano, stop in at our Main Street showrooms and look over our entire [5] line. Sincerely yours, [104]

230 Dear Mr. Devine: I have a question I would like to ask you. What value do you place on the confidence of [1] your creditors? You know that their confidence means a great deal to you and to your organization. If you lose [2] that confidence, you will not be able to obtain merchandise on credit and your business will be in deep trouble. [3]

You realize, I am sure, that you are about to lose our confidence in you by not paying your bills and by [4] not even acknowledging our friendly reminders.

It may be that your customers are slow in paying your bills; [5] therefore, you cannot pay ours. If that is the case, please tell us. We have been in that position. We have always found, [6] though, that our creditors were ready to meet us halfway when we told them of our problems. We, too, are ready to [7] meet you halfway but we must hear from you.

Don't jeopardize your present fine credit rating. Once you lose it, you may [8] not be able to regain it. Sincerely yours, [170]

LESSON 24

231 *Recall Chart*

1 Present, part, advertise, Ms., immediate, opportunity.
2 Advantage, suggest, several, out, ever-every, very.
3 Time, acknowledge, general, question, organize, over.
4 To me, to know, to make, Dear Mr., Dear Mrs., Dear Ms.
5 Dear Miss, Cordially yours, Yours sincerely, several months, to put, I have been able.
6 Divide, division; create, creation; different, difference.
7 Demand, demanded; estimate, estimated; wet, sweet.
8 Contains, containing; ounce, ounces; believe, believed.
9 Other, another; unite, united; replaces, replaceable.
10 Persist, persisted; years, yards; special, specially.
11 Month, monthly; appoint, appointment; efficient, efficiency.
12 Just, justly; persuade, persuaded; decide, decided.
13 Thrill, thrilled; challenge, challenged; shot, shots.
14 Comply, complain; deny, denied; intend, intended.
15 September, February, August; Sunday, Wednesday, Saturday.

233 *Safe Driving*

Here are ten general suggestions for safe driving. If you cannot answer yes to all of them, I suggest that [1] you are not a good driver.

1. Do you use a safety belt every time you drive no matter how short your trip?
2. Do you [2] always insist that anyone riding with you immediately fasten his or her safety belt?
3. Do you [3] signal whenever you are going to change over to another lane?
4. Do you check your rearview mirror every [4] few moments while you are driving?
5. Do you always observe posted speed limits?
6. Do you always reduce [5] your speed by several miles an hour when you are driving in an area where the pavement is wet?
7. [6] Do you stop for a rest when you begin to feel very tired?
8. Do you constantly drive defensively, always [7] assuming that the other person might commit a dangerous driving error?
9. Do you always lower [8] your headlights at night when another car approaches?
10. Do you always check your tires before you set out [9] on a trip?

How about it? Can you answer yes to these ten questions? If you can, you are a good driver. [198]

234 *Advertising*

Advertising is all around us during our waking hours, whether it is the sign on the diner that simply [1] says "Eats," the pamphlets and circulars that many companies send out through the mail, or the commercials we hear [2] every few minutes on radio and television. We are in constant contact with advertising messages [3] of one kind or another.

It was estimated recently that the average home listens to or sees [4] 2,000 advertising messages a day—and that is a conservative estimate.

If you walked a few blocks [5] to get to school, you could have passed 100 shop signs and advertising posters on the way. If you stopped in a [6] drugstore, you could have seen cards and packages printed with advertising messages. Glancing through a monthly [7] magazine, you would see at least 100 ads.

Every advertisement is intended to persuade the consumer [8] to take positive action that is favorable to the advertiser. But each consumer responds to only [9] a very small part of the advertising he hears or sees. His mind rejects what it does not want to be concerned [10] with.

Who Pays for Advertising? The advertiser pays the bill for preparing and spreading the advertising [11] message. This is just one part of the many costs he faces in manufacturing an item or organizing [12] a service that he desires to sell.

The consumer, when he buys the product or service, pays for the cost [13] of making and selling it. The cost of advertising can be high in one industry and low in another. [14] One business may advertise a great deal while another may invest very little in advertising.

Truth in [15] *Advertising.* The words contained in ads are often those that a sales representative would use while attempting [16] to make a sale to a potential customer. These words praise a product or service being sold. They deal with the [17] nice things that the consumer would derive from the use of the product or service.

Advertising cannot be balanced. [18] Its job is to present the views of the sponsor who pays for the opportunity to persuade the [19] consumer to buy his product or service.

Ads can be inspiring and attractive. They can be annoying, [20] boring, and confusing. But 99 percent of them tell the truth. [404]

CHAPTER 5

LESSON 25

239 To the Staff: Now that the end of the year is approaching, I wish to take the time to do two things:

1. Wish you a [1] very happy holiday season.

2. Compliment you on making possible a satisfying year for our [2] division.

Of course, it was not one of outstanding sales progress in all areas, but it was one in which we had [3] considerable success holding our own, especially in the states of Michigan, Illinois, and [4] Massachusetts.

Our competitors, on the other hand, had to work under great difficulties.

I make only one request: [5] Let us all do our best next year. If we do this, the new year could be an even more satisfactory one [6] for our division than last year.

I hope you like the Christmas present you will find in the attached envelope. A. B. [7] Smith, President [144]

240 Dear Dr. Overman: We have a request to make of you. On the morning of Thursday, February 15, a [1] representative of our New York State service department called at your home to take care of the difficulty [2] you were having with your ice-making unit.

We would appreciate it, Dr. Overman, if you would answer [3] the questions on the enclosed list about his visit. If you care to make any general statements or suggestions [4] about his visit, please write them on the reverse side of the list.

Your answers will give us an invaluable [5] opportunity to find out what success we are having in satisfying the wishes of our customers. [6] I hope you will fill out and mail the list as soon as possible. A stamped envelope is enclosed. Thank you for your [7] cooperation.

There will, of course, be no charge for our services. Under your agreement with our organization, [8] these services are covered by your warranty. Sincerely yours, [173]

241 Ms. Boyle: My trip to the state of Missouri in November was a difficult but satisfying one. While [1] I was in St. Louis, I took advantage of the opportunity to visit Mr. Harvey Underwood [2] and several other officers of the St. Louis Envelope Manufacturing Company. I believe [3] I made very satisfactory progress with them, and I am confident we will soon obtain quite a bit of [4] business from them.

They requested me to send them samples of our latest paper products and, of course, I plan to [5] do this immediately. I will include in the package five or six of our advertising circulars.

I [6] think my trip was a definite success. I will be glad to tell you all about it as soon as I get back to [7] Boston, which should be shortly after the first of the year. A. C. Baird [153]

242 Gentlemen: There are many moving companies in the state of California, and we acknowledge the fact that [1] they all offer the same services that we do. But we realize that we will not be able to increase our business [2] by being only as good as our competitors; we have to be better. Therefore, we have developed a moving [3] code that outlines the important things you need to know in order to move smoothly—things like where to look for a [4] reliable moving company and how to read estimates.

No one can promise that every move will be perfect. [5] But we do think that our code is a progressive step in the right direction.

Whenever you must move again, [6] I hope you will call us and let us show you how we can satisfy your moving needs. Yours very truly, [138]

243 Dear Mr. Underwood: This is a difficult letter for me to write for reasons that I am sure you will [1] understand. The Los Angeles Envelope Company has not paid its bills since June. They are 90 days overdue, [2] and we must insist that you pay them without any more delay. The four letters we have written you have not been [3] answered, including the one we sent by registered mail.

You will admit, I am sure, that we have been patient, but [4] I hope, Mr. Underwood, that you will send us a check for $85 today. An envelope that does [5] not need any postage is enclosed. Please use it to help us close our books on this matter. Sincerely yours, [118]

LESSON 26

248 To the Staff: I wish to tell you how well satisfied the management of your organization is with the [1] progress we made in the sale of our office appliances last year. Our success was especially notable in [2] the states of Missouri, Pennsylvania, and Illinois, where we encountered difficult sales resistance. Only [3] in one state in the South were sales unsatisfactory and below our estimates.

Under another cover [4] I am sending you an envelope containing a list of marketing questions. After his department meeting [5] on Wednesday morning, the general manager requested that every sales representative answer these questions. [6] They are short questions, and you should be able to answer them in about 15 minutes. Please get this list back [7] to us as soon as possible.

Thank you for your cooperation. A. B. Crowley [155]

249 Dear Mrs. Ryan: We are proud to announce a completely new magazine devoted entirely to science. [1] We think that science is too important a part of our lives to be left to scientists. Yet most magazines [2] that deal with science are too difficult for most people to understand. Therefore, our editors have created [3] the *Science Magazine*, which is written for laymen. It endeavors to give an unbiased presentation of [4] the developments in each field of science.

What is more, it contains no advertising. *Science Magazine* will [5] enable you to enrich your life and provide you with many hours of unbeatable enjoyment.

Place your [6] order for a full year of *Science Magazine* on a trial basis, Mrs. Ryan. Attach your check for $6 [7] to the enclosed coupon and mail both to us in the business reply envelope we have provided. Yours [8] very truly, [163]

250 Dear Dr. O'Brien: It is always a very unpleasant task to have to threaten a client with legal [1] action because of an unpaid bill, but you leave me no choice.

I have written you several letters asking you [2] to pay for the appliances you ordered in August, September, and October, but I have received neither [3] a payment nor an acknowledgment from you. Your payment of $1,000 is now more than four months overdue,[4] and unless you let me have your check immediately, I will refer your account to our lawyer.

Do not[5] do anything to endanger your valuable credit rating. It is a precious thing. Take the time at once[6] to make out your check and mail it. A stamped envelope is enclosed for your use. Yours very truly, [137]

251 Dear Ms. Wilde: Because of the outstanding engineering and manufacturing skill of the National[1] Appliance Company, you can be sure that the color television set you purchased from our West Street dealer on[2] Saturday, December 26, is the finest receiver ever made.

Yesterday we mailed you our circular[3] of instructions. We urge you to read it before you plug in your set and take advantage of the suggestions[4] it contains.

You may be truly proud of your new National. It is an instrument unmatched in beauty and[5] precision. From it you will be able to derive many years of good viewing enjoyment.

The next time you need an[6] appliance of any kind, we hope you will give us an opportunity to serve you. Yours very truly,[7] [140]

LESSON 27

257 Dear Ms. Banks: I wish your invitation to speak at your regular spring meeting on Saturday, April 15,[1] had arrived just a day sooner. Yesterday I accepted an invitation for that date to speak at the banquet[2] of the National Newspaper Editors Conference at the State Street Hotel in Long Beach, California.

May I[3] suggest to you as a speaker my good friend, Dr. Frank Strong. I regard Dr. Strong as a pioneer in[4] computer research. In my opinion, he probably knows more about the subject of computers than any other[5] person working in our particular field.

In addition, he has a fine reputation as a speaker.[6] He will bring to your audience many new and enlightening ideas. You can reach Dr. Strong at[7] 101-5151 until next Sunday, January 3.

I hope, Ms. Banks, that your meeting is a great success.[8] Very truly yours, [163]

258 Gentlemen: The *Lincoln Times* is no longer just a morning newspaper. It is now a 24-hour[1] newspaper with regular editions every morning, afternoon, and evening. Each edition brings fresh news and ideas[2] regarding many subjects.

What does this particular change in our policy mean to your advertising[3] department? In our opinion, it means that each day you have several opportunities to reach potential[4] customers rather than just one. Your advertising in the *Lincoln Times* will probably bring you more orders than[5] your advertising in any other medium.

Don't you think a progressive organization like the Franklin[6] Manufacturing Company should be advertising its products and services in the three editions of[7] the *Lincoln Times*? Frankly, we think there is no question that it should. Sincerely yours, [154]

259 Dear Mr. Long: The National Bankers Association will hold its next regular banquet at 7 o'clock[1] on Wednesday, November 15, at the Franklin Hotel in Des Moines. More than 500 bankers belong to[2] our association and probably half of them will be present.

Of course, we wish to have the strongest possible[3] speaker, and in my opinion, you are indeed well qualified. No one is more highly regarded in the banking[4] business than you, Mr. Long. If you are free on this particular evening, we would be honored to have you speak[5] to us on the topic "Automation—A New Idea in Banking." I know this is a subject on which you have[6] very definite ideas.

You understand, of course, that we would take care of your travel and hotel bills. We will,[7] in addition, pay you our regular speaker's fee of $350.

We hope that you will be[8] able to say yes to our invitation. Sincerely yours, [171]

260 Dear Mr. Frank: As a newly married man, you will be glad to know that the General Insurance Company[1] has a special plan for young married couples on their car insurance. This plan could save you over 40 percent [2] of the premium you would have to pay if you were young and single.

Of course, it is probable that we are not [3] the only company that offers a special rate to young married couples, but we do offer today's most [4] satisfactory claim service.

To obtain a copy of our circular, which outlines the important advantages [5] of this valuable plan, simply request it by filling out the enclosed short questionnaire and send it to us [6] in the envelope we have provided. Sincerely yours, [130]

261 My dear Mayor: On December 5 and again on January 15 I wrote the roads commissioner of [1] the town about the difficult condition that prevails on the corner of Baker Road, where my house is located. [2] I have not had an acknowledgment or reply from him to my letters.

In the middle of the road there are [3] two large holes. Since January, they have caused two minor accidents and one major one.

I am writing you with [4] the hope that as mayor you will take whatever action is necessary to have this road repaired immediately. [5]

Thank you for your cooperation. Sincerely yours, [111]

262 Mrs. Long: When you have a few minutes to spare, stop in to see me. I would like to chat with you about the printing [1] and binding quotations you sent me for the third edition of our book, *Our Banking System.* I have an idea [2] that the quotations are probably wrong. In my opinion, they are 20 percent too high.

Call me and let [3] us arrange a time when we can get together. Sincerely yours, [72]

LESSON 28

267 Gentlemen: I am sorry I will not be able to keep my engagement with you in Lincoln on Tuesday, [1] December 15, to talk about the idea of your handling our summer line of cotton goods.

Perhaps you [2] read in yesterday's newspapers that our treasurer, Mr. Max Strong, suffered a particularly severe stroke [3] while he was speaking before a group of income tax accountants in Los Angeles. His doctor regards his [4] immediate condition as unsatisfactory, and it is his opinion that he will probably be away [5] from the office for several months.

While he is away, I will take over much of his work as well as handle [6] my regular duties.

I will be glad to bring up the subject of your handling our summer line of [7] cotton goods again when Mr. Strong gets well. Yours very truly, [151]

268 Dear Mrs. Rush: As you are perhaps very much aware, income tax time is not far away, and you will shortly [1] have to complete and send in your state income tax blanks. We suggest that before you touch the blanks, you peruse *Dixon's* [2] *Income Tax Guide.*

This guide covers most of the essential areas of income tax filing which you may need. The [3] few hours it will take you to go through the guide, Mrs. Rush, may save you much time and a good deal of money in tax [4] payments.

The guide is indexed so that you can quickly find a satisfactory answer to any difficult [5] tax question you may have. All you have to do to order a copy is fill out the coupon at the bottom of [6] the enclosed circular, attach your check for $7, and mail both to us in the envelope we have [7] provided. Yours very truly, [145]

269 Dear Staff Member: Have you found the perfect place where you would like to go this coming summer for your vacation but [1] decided after some thought that your budget could not stand it? Then you should come to us, your company's credit [2] organization. Some 2,000 staff members took advantage of the opportunity to borrow for a [3] vacation, to pay their taxes, or to buy something they have always wished to own. Their requests were generally granted [4] by us in under 48 hours.

Find out how easy it is to become a member of our organization [5] and to take advantage of our services. Fill out the enclosed blank and bring it to our business office [6] in Room 41 on the second floor. We are open every working day from nine to four.

I hope you will come [7] in soon. You have a warm welcome ahead of you. Max H. Brush [151]

270 Ms. Myers: This will acknowledge receipt of your letter asking what progress we have made in filling the vacancy [1] in our advertising department. Thank you for your concern about our problem.

Up to the present time, we [2] have had no success whatever. We have had two applicants, but neither one had the talents necessary for [3] this important and desirable job.

Next Tuesday morning I have an appointment with another candidate [4] who I hope will be able to meet our standards. As soon as I have something definite to tell you, I will get [5] in touch with you. Rex Smith [104]

271 Dear Mrs. Dunne: Do you think that you are overpaying taxes on your investments? If you do, send for a copy [1] of our valuable booklet, *Investment Taxes.* The sooner you do this the better because you are going [2] to have to make a lot of tax decisions between now and the end of the year.

The suggestions in the booklet [3] can help you reduce your taxes and still enable you to keep your investment in an industry you like.

To [4] get your copy of *Investment Taxes,* Mrs. Dunne, simply fill out and mail the enclosed card. Sincerely yours, [99]

272 Mr. Dunn: During the month of August, while you were away on vacation, my staff and I went ahead with the [1] complex job of preparing the budget for the coming year. We have just about completed the job. Harry Smith [2] [40]

LESSON 29

279 Dear Mr. Lang: When you buy a suit, you expect it to look good and to fit perfectly. But what you ordinarily [1] expect in a suit and what you usually get are two very different things.

It's not that way when you buy [2] from us. We have been serving the public for years and have been recognized in fashion publications as the state's [3] most successful and progressive men's clothing manufacturer.

Our experienced and responsible tailors [4] are extremely careful to see that you get your money's worth.

The next time you wish to purchase articles of clothing, [5] Mr. Lang, get exactly what you wish at exactly the prices you wish to pay. Visit the World Men's Clothing [6] Center at its Worth Street branch, where you will receive a warm welcome.

We hope to see you soon. Very truly yours, [7] [140]

280 Dear Mrs. Lincoln: *Why People Fail* is the title of a recent publication by Ms. Mary Garden, who [1] has earned a reputation around the world for her unusual experimental work in the field of general [2] personnel development. The book is published by the Worth Publishing Company of Boston, Massachusetts.[3]

In this book Ms. Garden carefully analyzes the reasons why many experienced people with recognized [4] talent do not ever reach their potential either in business or public life. She then offers some practical [5] and logical suggestions to help people reach out and attain their potential.

This book will be of maximum [6] usefulness to present-day holders of responsible jobs. It will be valuable as well to those who aspire [7] to more important positions.

Why People Fail ordinarily sells for $9, but if you order [8] ten copies or more, the price drops to $6.50.

Use the enclosed stamped envelope to place your order. [9] Sincerely yours, [183]

281 Dear Dr. Diamond: Thank you sincerely for the enjoyable presentation you made yesterday morning before [1] the World Conference on Technical Publishing. I am sure you are aware that you were responsible for [2] our large attendance, which far exceeded our fondest expectations. I think we had more than 500 people.[3] Ordinarily we have under 200.

Your speech on the public relations problems of a

publisher [4] of technical and medical magazines was extremely practical and well worth hearing. The members of the [5] audience immediately recognized that you were an expert on your particular subject. After the [6] meeting I heard several of them say that hearing you was a completely delightful experience. In fact, [7] I have had ten requests for copies of your speech.

I am enclosing our usual speaker's fee of $250. [8] I will send you a check for your expenses as soon as I receive your statement.

Thank you again for [9] making our World Conference on Technical Publishing such a successful event. Sincerely yours, [198]

282 Dear Mr. Overman: If you are like most people, you probably like the satisfaction and freedom that go [1] with owning your own business. Here is your opportunity. Our organization now has newspaper home [2] delivery franchises available in several areas in Long Island. For quite a modest investment [3] you can have such a franchise. The work is not difficult and no experience is necessary. In addition, [4] the income potential is, in our opinion, extremely high.

If this idea appeals to you and you [5] have any questions regarding the advantages of our regular newspaper franchises, call us at [6] 151-1171 and ask for Department D. Our offices are open until 6 o'clock every [7] day except Sunday. Very truly yours, [147]

LESSON 30

283 *Recall Chart*

1 Difficult, envelope, progress, success, satisfy-satisfactory, state.

2 Request, wish, under, particular, probable, regular.

3 Speak, idea, subject, regard, newspaper, opinion.

4 Responsible, worth, public, publish-publication, ordinary, experience.

5 Usual, world, recognize, recognizes, ordinarily, regarded.

6 We hope, your order, more than, as soon as, to do, let us.

7 To us, you ordered, of course, as soon as possible, I hope, let me.

8 Explain, explanation; flexible, inflexible; critical, critically.

9 Doubtful, undoubtedly; direct, direction; becoming, influential.

10 Frank, frankly; endeavor, endeavored; create, creation.

11 Meant, mental; king, kingdom; contained, containers.

12 Compliment, complimentary; brother, brothers; review, reviewed.

13 Yard, yield; unite, united; resist, resistant.

14 Quiet, quietly; purchase, purchased; print, printed.

15 Ahead, aware; divide, division; soil, soiled.

285 *The Value of Exercise*

Nobody, of course, can promise you that regular physical exercise will guarantee you a longer life. [1] But exercise can help put the odds in your favor.

Exercise is one satisfying thing you can do to get [2] your body in good physical condition. You should check with your doctor first, and then decide on the type of [3] exercise you prefer. You will be able to choose from swimming, tennis, jogging, handball, and many other enjoyable [4] and healthful pastimes.

Exercise is good for your weight, your lungs, and the 600 muscles in your body, [5] including the most important one—your heart. [108]—*Physical Fitness Council*

286 *Good Listening*

Many people regard hearing and listening as the same thing, but there is a great difference between the two. [1] Hearing is dependent only upon the ears, but listening utilizes the mind and often the eyes. Your [2] ears permit you to hear sounds; the mind enables you to decipher those sounds into words and then changes them into [3] thoughts and ideas.

You may not have considered the eyes to be an important tool in listening. Yet what [4] you see when a person is speaking could sometimes be of as much importance as what you hear. A speaker's facial [5] expression may completely change the meaning of the words he is saying.

Listening in Business. Efficient [6] listening habits play a part in a person's success in all areas of life but particularly in business. [7] So important are habits of listening that a number of the world's most progressive organizations [8] find it worth their while to provide short listening courses for many of their managers.

Effective listening [9] is valuable to managers. Successful and experienced managers don't just give orders. They do a lot [10] of listening. They listen to their people to find out what they think about the company and about their jobs [11] so that they can establish good relations. They listen to staff members. They recognize that staff members often [12] are glad to express their ideas on many subjects when they have a good audience.

Good listening is [13] important to clerical people, too. They must rely on good listening in order to carry out their ordinary [14] assignments. The telephone operator certainly must listen carefully in order to handle [15] requests of hundreds of public callers every day. The sales representative must listen carefully to deal [16] responsibly with the wishes of his clients. All people who provide services of any kind to the general [17] public are dependent to some extent on their listening habits to carry out their duties satisfactorily. [18]

We All Listen a Lot. Listening probably demands more of the time a person is awake than [19] any other activity. One recently published opinion survey states that approximately one-third [20] of a person's waking hours are spent in listening—in school, in the home, or at work. People listen about three [21] times as much as they read such publications as newspapers, magazines, books, circulars, and other advertising [22] matter. The advantages of good listening are acknowledged to be great. They include increased learning, increased [23] job opportunities and promotions, and better understanding and appreciation of the spoken [24] word.

On the other hand, poor listening habits may bring difficulties and trouble in life. Often school dropouts [25] fail in their studies because they do not know how to listen.

Listening on the Job. The advantages of good [26] listening habits are quite tangible when you hold a job. They often mean a bigger paycheck! Beginners must [27] listen to instructions and directions from managers and others in the organization. They must listen [28] to suggestions and frank criticism in order to do their job efficiently. To get ahead in a job, [29] they must know what is going on in their department and in the company, and they can learn what is going on [30] best by listening intelligently. [607]

287 *Decisions, Decisions*

All of us have to make decisions of one type or another just about every day. Being human, we will [1] sometimes make a poor decision. The important thing is that we make many more good decisions than bad ones.

Here [2] are some things to remember to keep bad decisions to a minimum: Don't make any really vital decisions [3] when you are under the influence of emotion. Put off making a painful decision until you have [4] "cooled off" and can think rationally. When you are angry or irritated you may make a snap decision that [5] you may later regret. Don't make important decisions when you are in an unusually jubilant frame of [6] mind.

Successful people are aware that they can make the best decisions when they are relaxed and have complete control [7] of their emotions.

A good rule to follow is this: When you are upset, stay away from people, and if [8] possible, put off making all decisions—important or unimportant. The most complicated problems may not [9] look so difficult to solve the next day. [187]

CHAPTER 6

LESSON 31

293 Dear Ms. Samuels: The regular company or government letterhead serves satisfactorily, of course, [1] for most of an executive's correspondence. But it should never be used for correspondence of a social [2] nature, such as letters of sympathy and goodwill. Correspondence of this type, we feel, calls for a personal [3] executive letterhead that is friendly and that actually reflects the executive's individual [4] character. It calls, in short, for Johnson stationery.

Johnson is recognized throughout the world as the leading [5] manufacturer of executive letterheads. In the enclosed folder, Ms. Samuels, you will find samples [6] in miniature of our executive letterheads. Examine them objectively and critically. Then [7] select the one which appeals to you most, and place your order for a quantity on the blank that is included [8] in the folder.

You can use the enclosed envelope to send your order to us. Very truly yours, [178]

294 Gentlemen: It gives me great pleasure to be a character reference for Mr. Max O'Brien who, I [1] understand, is applying for an executive position with the State Department of the federal government. [2]

Mr. O'Brien was chief correspondent with the Century Motion Picture Company for some time. Throughout [3] the years he was with us, he never objected to taking over difficult and challenging ventures. We [4] were often amazed at the quantity of work he was able to handle in his department.

Mr. O'Brien [5] resigned, as I recall, in 1978 to take a responsible position with the National [6] Insurance Company, of which he eventually became a vice president.

I think that Mr. O'Brien [7] could have a great future ahead of him working for the government. I am glad, therefore, to recommend him [8] without reservation. Sincerely yours, [167]

295 Dear Mrs. Quinn: The National Bank and Trust Company first opened its doors to the public in 1785. [1] We had offices on what is now Fifth Street in Philadelphia. Our correspondence files revealed that [2] National granted the government the first loan it ever obtained. It was for slightly more than $200,000. [3]

Since that time we have seen our gross national product gradually grow to its present size, and through [4] the years our primary objective has been to grow along with it. Our successful progress, though, has not been achieved [5] at the expense of the friendly character of our bank. We have never confused size with excellence, Mrs. [6] Quinn.

The future of our bank, I am happy to say, looks very bright. Unless something happens to our economy, [7] we expect to enjoy another satisfactory year.

If you have any questions about our business [8] operations, do not hesitate to write us. Very truly yours, [173]

296 Mr. Worth: This morning I learned that the stock of the third edition of our publication, *The Correspondent's* [1] *Manual,* will shortly be exhausted. I estimate that we are down to 3,000 copies. This quantity [2] will, in my opinion, last us only through October. The book has been selling extraordinarily well [3] since we published it last year, thanks to the good work of the advertising department.

May I request, therefore, that [4] you manufacture another 20,000 copies immediately. We know from experience that it [5] usually takes several months to print that quantity.

I would appreciate it, Mr. Worth, if you would [6] acknowledge this request as soon as you receive it. A. B. James [131]

297 Ms. Lopez: The president of the National Newspaper Editors' Association told me yesterday [1] afternoon that you would soon be asked to speak at their next general meeting on a subject of your choice. The meeting [2] will probably be held in December.

I wish you would accept this particular assignment, Ms. Lopez. [3] I regard it as a fine opportunity for you to give that organization some idea of the [4] problems we face in the advertising industry.

Please let me know when you receive the invitation. Allen [5] H. West [101]

298 Dear Mr. Strong: Yesterday afternoon I sent you 45 copies of our sales-training manual. Please accept [1] them, Mr. Strong, with our compliments.

This manual, written by a well-known sales executive, has been used[2] throughout our selling organization with great success.

A revision of this manual is scheduled to come[3] off the press shortly. I will send you a quantity as soon as I receive copies.

I hope that you will never[4] hesitate to let us know when our organization can be of assistance to you at some future time.[5] Sincerely yours, [102]

299 Dear Mr. Case: During the past year our executives had many occasions to ask for special service[1] from your correspondence department. On every occasion they received it from Miss Mary Samuels of your[2] staff.

People like Miss Samuels are a great credit to your organization, Mr. Case, and make it a real pleasure[3] to do business with your organization. Sincerely yours, [72]

LESSON 32

305 Dear Dr. Samuels: Our organization, the Albany Power Company, has never been more heavily[1] involved in the control of air pollution, a problem that is troubling governments throughout the world. We[2] are presently at work building 18 plants in this country that will create almost no fumes. These plants will not destroy[3] or even alter the character of the area in which they are being built.

We have prepared a special[4] circular that describes our activities in pollution control and also discusses our objectives for[5] the future. It was written by Mr. Charles H. Dixon, an executive in our correspondence department.[6]

Would you like to obtain a quantity of these descriptive circulars, Dr. Samuels, for use in your classes?[7] If so, simply tell us on the enclosed card how many you wish and we will be glad to send them to you.[8] Sincerely yours, [162]

306 Dear Mrs. Long: One way to help your executives accomplish more in less time is to put at their disposal[1] a Wilson jet, the finest business jet manufactured today.

This sturdily built jet can fly your people[2] easily, quietly, and speedily to their destinations. It is so efficient that it is actually more[3] economical to operate than an ordinary standard-sized automobile.

In addition to saving[4] expensive fuel, the Wilson will also save thousands of valuable and useful hours for your executives[5] over a year's time.

The enclosed booklet, *Today's Business Jet*, describes the features of the Wilson and discusses[6] its advantages. After you have had an opportunity to read it, Mrs. Long, you will readily[7] understand why we have already filled orders for more than 3,000 of these planes. Yours very truly, [158]

307 Dear Ms. Worth: In recent months there has been altogether too much discussion in the newspapers about voter[1] apathy. We know that the responsible citizens of Albany do not believe in voter apathy.[2] They recognize the fact that this year's election is unquestionably the most critical one in years.

On the[3] state level we will vote for a governor. We will, in addition, vote for a senator to represent us[4] at the national level.

Be sure that the persons you wish to have speak for you in government have your endorsement[5] by voting for them.

Although voting is vital, Ms. Worth, it is not enough. You must encourage your friends and[6] your family to come out to vote. This year's public election on Tuesday, November 3, is everybody's[7] concern because the issues are of such importance. Sincerely yours, [153]

308 Mr. Banks: Yesterday I read over hastily your summary of the difficulties we are experiencing[1] in the publications division of our West Street office. Thank you for supplying me with all the facts.[2]

I was particularly disturbed by the resignation of our assistant manager, Mr. Short, on Monday,[3] December 15. I regarded him as a progressive and practical person and had considered the[4] idea of promoting him to the position of general publisher of the division.

The publications[5] division should, in my opinion, be completely reorganized immediately. I suggest[6] that we talk about the subject at the next regular meeting of the board, which will probably be held on the [7] morning of Wednesday, January 15. Fred C. Baxter [151]

309 Dear Mr. Smith: All of us like to make new friends, but we think old friends are the best friends. Therefore, when an old friend has [1] stopped seeing us, we usually begin to wonder why.

That is how we feel about you, Mr. Smith. For several [2] years we received orders from you regularly. But suddenly they stopped, and we are wondering why.

Could it [3] be that something has happened to disturb our pleasant and successful business relations? If that is the case, I [4] have a request. Please tell us where we have failed. We will be very glad to make whatever adjustment will be [5] satisfactory to you.

Please use the enclosed envelope to write us. Yours very truly, [116]

310 Mr. Dwyer: Your letter of Friday, December 15, regarding the steadily declining sales in our [1] Albany branch is disturbing. I think we must make an immediate change in the management of that store. Mr. [2] Green, the present manager, is a good man, but I am afraid we will have to inject some new talent in [3] that store if we are to make it a profitable operation. I would like to discuss this matter with you [4] when you are in Albany. G. H. Shaw [87]

LESSON 33

316 Dear Ms. Sexton: The object of this letter is to invite you to see the display of executive office [1] furniture we will hold throughout the week of January 15 in the Government Exhibit Center in [2] Miami.

We started planning this display a long time ago. Never before have we been able to assemble [3] for the public such a large quantity of office furniture that has charm, character, and style.

During this [4] sale, Ms. Sexton, special low prices will be in effect. You will be able to obtain entire suites at [5] reductions of 30 to 40 percent. This would be a good time, therefore, to refurnish your office.

We hope to [6] see you at our display. We think you will enjoy it. Sincerely yours, [133]

317 Dear Mr. Doyle: Several days ago we opened our second office furniture showroom at 15 Worth Street [1] in Albany, New York. It is designed to enable business executives to see office furniture in [2] a comfortable setting.

Come in and inspect the construction and design of the chairs, desks, correspondence files, [3] and many other items of furniture and equipment in one room. Then step into the next room, where you can [4] study our office equipment in another setting. We have ten beautifully furnished offices.

Our [5] responsible, experienced, and devoted sales force is ready to serve you and give you any information [6] you may wish about our furniture. Furthermore, Mr. Doyle, you will undoubtedly be pleased with our prices. While [7] prices in general have been steadily rising, you will find out that ours are actually lower than they were [8] two years ago. Sincerely yours, [166]

318 Gentlemen: On Friday, October 15, or exactly six weeks ago, I sent you a two-year renewal [1] to your publication, *The Factory Foreman.* With the renewal form, I sent you my personal check for [2] $12.

Although my canceled check came back from the bank several days ago, I have not yet received the issues [3] published in November, December, and January. Please check into this matter soon so that I may once again [4] receive my copies.

If there is any further information you need to locate my order, I will, of [5] course, be glad to furnish it.

Please be good enough to acknowledge receipt of this letter. Yours very truly, [119]

319 Dear Mrs. Howard: Forty years ago the Johnson Furniture Company, a recognized world leader in its [1] field, met and conquered the challenge of space—office space, that is. But we have done much more than just fill that space. We have [2] made it work.

Time and again we have proven that office furniture can be comfortable, practical, and [3] efficient.

We have furnished the offices of hundreds of well-known companies. Furthermore, Mrs. Howard, we are [4] one of about five organizations in the state which create, manufacture, and sell their own furniture.

The [5] next time you wish to furnish an ordinary, informal office or a large formal suite, come to Johnson's and [6] save. Cordially yours,]124]

320 Dear Mr. Jackson: Here is an unusual offer that you cannot afford to pass by. Purchase any suit, jacket, [1] or overcoat in our men's department at our advertised price and we will sell you another one just like [2] it for only $1. Why are we doing this? We have large quantities of men's clothing in stock that we [3] necessarily must dispose of before our spring stock comes in.

But this opportunity is good only during [4] the week of February 15. Make plans immediately to come in and take advantage of this unusual [5] offer. Cordially yours, [104]

321 Mr. Day: I recently read a copy of a new publication, *World Events,* published by Wilson and [1] Company. This publication is extraordinarily well written.

Please be responsible for purchasing [2] copies for all our representatives. C. R. Brown [50]

322 Dear Mr. Ford: About two weeks ago we mailed you the Monday, December 12, issue of our magazine, *World* [1] *News.* That was the third issue we mailed to you beyond your expiration date. We did this because we were sure you [2] would not want to miss this issue.

Unfortunately, Mr. Ford, we cannot send you any further copies unless [3] we receive your renewal. Sincerely yours, [69]

LESSON 34

329 Mr. Worth: For some time I have been corresponding with our sales representatives with the object of determining [1] what quantity we should print of the first edition of our new publication, *Modern Science of the* [2] *World.* The estimates I received from them varied widely, as usual, and most of them were unsatisfactory [3] and undependable.

On the basis of our past experience in publishing and marketing a book of [4] this character, I believe we should be able to sell 50,000 copies in the first year.

Could you be [5] responsible, Mr. Worth, for placing a manufacturing order for this quantity promptly? In addition, [6] please place an immediate order for 200,000 copies of the attached circular describing the [7] features of the book. Have them delivered to Mr. Smith, head of the advertising department, at our Franklin [8] Street office when they are ready.

Thank you very much for your cooperation. Lydia C. Long [178]

330 Dear Dr. Stern: I understand, Dr. Stern, that several days ago you joined the large family of shareholders [1] of the Eastern Sporting Goods Company. May I take advantage of this opportunity to welcome you. [2] You will be informed of the operations and progress of our organization through quarterly and annual [3] reports and by executive bulletins whenever we have something that we want to tell you promptly about [4] the company.

You will shortly receive a copy of this year's report and also a copy of our house [5] magazine, *Sports Today.* It is issued four times a year, in January, April, August, and December. If [6] you want to receive this valuable magazine regularly, please fill out the enclosed form and return it in [7] the envelope we have provided.

As president of the Eastern Sporting Goods Company, I am inviting [8] you officially to visit our modern plant in Chicago, Illinois, and our headquarters in Philadelphia, [9] Pennsylvania. You will be warmly welcomed by our staff. Yours very truly, [196]

331 Gentlemen: It makes no difference whether your executives wish to fly 200 miles, 10,000 miles, or [1] farther. The modern Star jet will promptly take them where they want to go and when they want to go.

When your executives[2] must travel somewhere on public, private, or government business, they can take off on a Star jet from any[3] one of almost 1,000 airports throughout the country. They never have to worry about confirmed or unconfirmed[4] reservations.

The Star jet provides speed, economical operation, and distance. It can cruise comfortably[5] at 500 miles an hour.

If you want helpful information about the Star jet, we will be glad to[6] have our well-informed Star jet engineer visit you on request. Yours very truly, [135]

332 Dear Ms. Lopez: We can understand your extreme annoyance with the letters you have been receiving asking for[1] payment of your account after it has been fully paid.

Your personal check was received on Friday, December[2] 10, and passed through for collection. But no one seemed to recognize the importance of giving this information[3] to the computer. Yesterday we informed the computer in no uncertain terms that it should not send you any[4] more collection letters.

Please accept our sincere regrets, Ms. Lopez. Next time we will keep our computer informed[5] about the status of your account. Sincerely yours, [110]

333 Mrs. Overmeyer: This morning I read Mr. Green's report about the difficulties our Boston office[1] has been experiencing selling our sporting goods successfully in the states of New York, Massachusetts, and[2] Maine.

I suggest, Mrs. Overmeyer, that you give this matter your personal attention and have a conference[3] with every sales representative in these states soon.

We must work out this problem very promptly at all costs.[4] A. R. Smith [82]

LESSON 35

338 Mr. Hastings: I am particularly disturbed by the number of men and women we have lost throughout the[1] international division of Billings Enterprises in the last three or four years. Some of them left after[2] working only one or two months.

You are aware, of course, of the expense this turnover represents. Whenever[3] one of these people resigns, we lose our valuable investment in time, money, and training.

To solve this perplexing[4] and difficult problem, we will use this hiring procedure in the future:

1. An executive will first[5] speak to a candidate.

2. If on the basis of this interview the executive decides that the candidate[6] can readily fill one of the openings on the staff, he or she will be asked to take an objective test.[7]

3. In order to be eligible for the job, the candidate would have to make a grade of at least 85[8] percent.

I hope, Mr. Hastings, that with this procedure we will be able to solve successfully one of[9] our most critical problems. Max Quill [187]

339 Dear Mr. Cummings: In yesterday morning's newspaper I read the report of the death of your president, Sanford[1] H. Jennings. I want to extend to you, Mr. Cummings, the deepest sympathies of the members of my[2] organization, International Enterprises.

I was introduced to Mr. Jennings three or four years ago[3] and enjoyed the pleasure of his company at our annual professional meetings. I also corresponded[4] with him occasionally about private and government business matters.

Mr. Jennings will long be[5] remembered as a man of wide interests, good ideas, and high principles. I personally think that he[6] was one of the best-informed men on the subjects of entertainment and recreation.

He may be gone, but he[7] will never be forgotten. Sincerely yours, [148]

340 Dear Mr. Franks: You will be interested to know that eight domestic airlines check their crews into Intercontinental[1] Hotels, the finest hotels in the world. The airlines know that we do everything we can to see that[2] each guest gets comfortable and nicely furnished lodgings, is well fed, and enjoys an uninterrupted night's sleep.[3]

When a crew has a long layover in a city between flights, the airlines do not want them to be bored. That is [4] why they choose a hotel that provides for their recreation and that makes available interesting entertainment [5] in the evenings. These are things you probably look for too.

When you have a reservation at one of our [6] hotels, our limousine picks you up at the terminal and takes you right to the entrance of the hotel.

When you [7] have to make another business trip to one of the cities we serve, Mr. Franks, we suggest that you dial [8] 118-1161 for a reservation. Sincerely yours, [172]

341 Gentlemen: This is an acknowledgment of your letter of Monday, November 18, in which you ask three questions [1] regarding our dealings with Mrs. Mary Jones. I am sorry I could not write you sooner.

1. She has had [2] a general checking account at the State National Bank for more than 15 years. At no time has she overdrawn [3] her account.

2. She also has a regular savings account in which her current balance is $5,000. [4]

3. Several years ago we granted her a loan of $3,000 to purchase a quantity [5] of building supplies. We arranged a special repayment plan for her on which she made every payment promptly.

In [6] our opinion, Mrs. Jones is a person of fine character and a very satisfactory credit risk. [7] We are glad to be able to list her as a customer. Cordially yours, [154]

342 Dear Dr. Hastings: Perhaps you may remember that about two or three years ago I was the chairman of one [1] of the meetings of the International Business Education Association and had the pleasure of [2] introducing you to the audience. At that time you gave one of the most interesting and entertaining [3] addresses that I have ever heard.

The purpose of this letter, Dr. Hastings, is to invite you to speak to [4] us again at next year's meeting on November 18 in Houston.

I hope that you are in a position to [5] accept this invitation. Sincerely yours, [108]

343 Dear Ms. Jennings: When you open a special savings account at the Interboro Savings Bank, Ms. Jennings, we [1] give you a card that permits you to cash checks at any one of our branches—and we have 200 of them.

All [2] you have to do is walk into any one of them and show your card. Your check will then be cashed.

You can open an account [3] at one branch of the Interboro Savings Bank and then make deposits or withdrawals at any one of [4] our 200 branches.

Why not open an account today and put your money to work earning interest for [5] you. Sincerely yours, [104]

LESSON 36

344 *Recall Chart*

1 Never, quantities, executives, object, correspond-correspondence, govern.

2 Quantity, executive, throughout, objective, corresponded, government.

3 Weeks ago, years ago, months ago, I want, you wanted, if you want.

4 Some of the, one of the, many of the, one of our, in the world, men and women.

5 Greetings, meetings; entertain, entertainment; temper, temperament.

6 Interested, interfered; information, informed; demonstrate, demonstration.

7 Report, reported; eastern, western; furniture, furthermore.

8 Term, termination; steady, steadily; alter, alteration.

9 Desired, desirable; brother, mother; article, medical.

10 Efficient, efficiency; explain, explanation; come, income.

11 Tax, taxation; contain, container; bank, banquet.

12 Long, belong; appreciate, appreciated; unfair, unless.

13 Discover, discovered; divide, division; comply, compliance.

14 Encounter, encountered; credential, credentials; human, humanly.

15 Purchase, purchases; yellow, yield; joy, joyful.

346 *The Secretary in Business*

The computer, one of the greatest scientific inventions of this century, represents no threat to the [1] secretary. Although everyone recognizes that the introduction of the computer in business will [2] alter a secretary's duties in the future, it will never eliminate the secretary's job.

Most [3] company executives agree that the present shortage of competent secretaries will actually be [4] with us for a long time. Furthermore, recent published government reports have confirmed that the demand for trained, [5] experienced, and responsible secretaries will increase more than 60 percent in the next 15 years.

The [6] *Role of the Secretary.* The secretary has always been the keeper of the secrets of the boss and of [7] the business. Today's secretary must also fill this role. In addition, though, the secretary will be [8] expected to work shoulder to shoulder *with* rather than *for* an executive. The executive's job has become [9] more difficult, more complex, and more challenging. The secretary's job has also become more demanding. [10] The secretary must, therefore, take over much of the boss's correspondence and routine tasks and do so with [11] a minimum of direction. This will enable the executive to devote more time to achieving [12] important objectives, such as discovering new ways to increase the company's business, forming valuable [13] plans for the future, and effecting savings in all areas of the company's operations.

The secretary [14] and the boss should operate as a team, with the executive making most of the decisions and the [15] secretary following through on the details of carrying out the decisions.

Today, more than ever before, [16] the secretary and the executive must pull together.

Some years ago secretaries emerged as [17] members of management teams. They are vital links between the making and the carrying out of business plans. [18]

Secretarial Positions Differ. No two secretarial positions are alike. Each position is [19] affected by five factors:

1. The size and special nature of the business organization, profession, or other [20] enterprise.

2. The character and status of the executive's position.

3. The executive's [21] willingness to turn over quantities of work to others.

4. The capacity of the secretary to assume [22] duties for which the executive is primarily responsible.

5. The intelligence and general [23] interests of the secretary.

These are factors that will be of interest to you if you want to enter [24] the secretarial field. [486]

347 *Courtesy and Success*

In every office people must work together, and where people work together, it is only natural that [1] there will occasionally be annoying friction. All it usually takes, though, to calm things down is a little bit of [2] ordinary courtesy.

Courtesy is an odd thing. We enjoy extending it to complete strangers. Yet the better [3] we know people, the more likely we are to be rude to them. This is unfortunate because extending [4] courtesy—the identical kind that we gladly accord strangers—is the logical way to win and maintain [5] cooperation, goodwill, and understanding from the people we work with.

Our courtesy shows up in many [6] different ways. It shows up in the way we say "hello" to the public bus driver, to the police officer on [7] the street, and to our friends. It shows up in the cheerful tone we use when we talk to a person on the telephone. [8] It shows up in the thoughtful and considerate way we answer questions.

People are very conscious of courtesy [9] and immediately recognize its presence.

Remember courtesy costs you nothing, but it is worth a [10] good deal. It is extremely important to you if you want to get ahead in this world. [216]

348 *Sleep and Diet*

Proper sleep and diet are basic to good health. Most young people need seven or eight hours of sleep to keep their minds [1] alert and their bodies refreshed.

Poor eating habits cause physical deficiencies. If

you skip breakfast, gulp down [2] a snack for lunch, and then eat heavily in the evening, you may not be able to get through a day's work comfortably, [3] and you may develop weight problems. Find out from your doctor how many calories you should have each day [4] for your age, height, and body build. Then divide these calories among three balanced meals.

This plan will assure you of [5] the energy and "pep" you need for a happy and productive day. [113]

CHAPTER 7

LESSON 37

355 Gentlemen: Our organization, the Overmyer Toy Company, is planning an unusual line of toys [1] for which we will need large quantities of the particular type of plastic you manufacture. In our opinion, [2] these toys will have a natural appeal to youngsters and will probably sell readily.

We would like to [3] establish a regular line of credit with you to purchase the plastic we will need. Our organization, [4] established more than 100 years ago, is well known and highly regarded throughout the toy manufacturing [5] world.

Enclosed are the following items:

1. Our latest bank statement.
2. A list of the various organizations [6] with which we ordinarily do business on credit.
3. A list of the newspapers, periodicals, [7] and other publications in which we generally advertise our goods.

If there is any other [8] information you wish about us, all you have to do is request it. We will willingly furnish it. Sincerely [9] yours, [181]

356 Dear Ms. Stern: I want to express to you my genuine appreciation for the part you played in our union [1] conference in Miami yesterday afternoon. All of us felt that you presented your theories on [2] management convincingly, emphatically, and impartially. I am sure, Ms. Stern, that everyone benefited [3] from the presentation of your subject. You certainly had the audience's undivided attention.

We [4] were also quite impressed with your sense of humor. We seldom have an opportunity to hear a public speaker [5] who has a serious message to bring and can present it entertainingly.

Could you send me in the next [6] few days a statement of your expenses for the conference? When I receive it, I will see that you are reimbursed [7] for them promptly. Sincerely yours, [146]

357 Dear Mr. Santos: If my memory serves me correctly, on Friday, December 16, you will complete [1] 25 years as an employee of the Empire Import and Export Company and will be eligible to [2] join our 25-Year Club.

Your progress with Empire has indeed been unusual, impressive, and successful. [3] Throughout the years your impact on our sales has been an exceedingly powerful one. You have, in addition, won [4] the genuine respect, affection, and admiration of all your fellow employees.

I hope it will be [5] possible for you to attend the 25-Year Club dinner, which will be held on Monday, January 15. [6] If you have already made a previous engagement and cannot come, please let me know. An envelope is enclosed [7] for your use.

You have my very best wishes, Mr. Santos, for many more increasingly productive and [8] satisfactory years with Empire. Sincerely yours, [170]

358 Dear Mr. Jennings: If you enroll in our executive training course, what will it actually do for you? Here [1] are several things:

1. It will teach you to express your theories and ideas to your employers [2] interestingly, entertainingly, and convincingly.
2. It will build your confidence, and you will be able to [3] speak before groups without fear.
3. It will teach you how to make difficult decisions impartially, objectively, [4] and forcefully.
4. It will help you discover your hidden talents and develop them to the maximum. [5]
5. It will enable you to obtain exceedingly satisfying pleasures from life.

If you would like more [6] information about this amazingly practical course, phone or write us today,

Mr. Jennings. Let us tell you [7] about the improvement you can make in the short period of two or three weeks. Sincerely yours, [157]

359 Dear Ms. Cummings: You will recall that at our luncheon on Wednesday you asked me to suggest the name of a person [1] you might invite to speak at your graduation exercises.

If you have not yet selected a speaker, I [2] would suggest you invite Mr. C. C. Baker, vice president of the Empire Import and Export Company [3] of New York. I heard Mr. Baker make a speech yesterday on the subject of "Improving Employee Relations." [4] He spoke interestingly, entertainingly, and convincingly. If you want to get in touch with Mr. [5] Baker, call him at 116-1171. Tell him that you are calling him at my suggestion. Sincerely [6] yours, [121]

360 Dear Mrs. Best: We were exceedingly pleased to read your letter of November 18 telling us of the [1] courteous service you received from our employees on Flight 166. We often receive letters from passengers [2] who are unhappy with our service. We seldom receive letters complimenting us on a job well done.

I am [3] sending copies of your letter to the members of the crew of Flight 166. I know that they, too, will be pleased [4] to read it.

I hope, Mrs. Best, that we will again have an opportunity to serve you on flights to the cities [5] that we serve. Sincerely yours, [106]

361 Dear Mr. Green: Our representative, Mr. C. C. Baker, tells me that he thoroughly enjoyed the talk on [1] improving employee relations that you gave at the National Manufacturers Association meeting. [2] He was so impressed by the information that you brought to the meeting that he suggested I invite you [3] to speak at our monthly management meeting on the same subject.

Would you consider making a one-hour presentation [4] at our December 10 meeting? We begin our meetings with a luncheon at twelve o'clock, and the speaker [5] usually makes a presentation from one until two.

If your calendar is free on that day and you can be [6] with us, we would be honored to have you. Cordially yours, [130]

LESSON 38

369 Dear Mrs. Underwood: It is my delightful duty to write you that the Suburban Steamship Company has [1] just experienced another year of prosperity, success, and progress. As our latest report shows, we [2] substantially increased our sales over last year and almost doubled the value of our securities.

A majority [3] of our subsidiary companies enjoyed substantial growth. Our latest subdivision, the Houston [4] Insulation Company, had a difficult time for several months but came out of the year in exceedingly [5] fine shape.

The annual report of the Suburban Steamship Company containing complete information [6] about our operations will be mailed to you, Mrs. Underwood, probably next week. As you leaf through the report, [7] I think you will be impressed with the important and highly satisfying gains we have made and with the [8] stimulating plans we have formulated for the future.

If you should have any questions about anything in [9] the report after you have read it, I will be glad to answer them. Yours very truly, [196]

370 Dear Dr. Billings: May I offer you my congratulations, Dr. Billings. Yesterday morning your application [1] for membership in the Ski Club was approved by an overwhelming majority of the membership [2] committee. I extend to you the hand of friendship and fellowship.

Enclosed is your membership card together [3] with a booklet of regulations governing the operations of our club. Please acknowledge receipt of these [4] items promptly. An envelope is enclosed for your use.

As you may know, your membership entitles you to a [5] free subscription to our magazine, *Happy Skiing*, which is published quarterly. I believe you will find the [6] articles in each issue on the subject of skiing interesting, entertaining, and stimulating.

I hope [7] with all sincerity that you and your

family will soon be able to take full advantage of the [8] opportunities available at our club. Sincerely yours, [170]

371 Dear Captain Brown: We sincerely appreciate your kindness in subscribing to the annual charity ball [1] to be held on Friday, October 29, at the Western Hotel on Fifth Street.

The proceeds of this affair [2] will be devoted to the purchase of Thanksgiving baskets for serious hardship cases in Franklin Township. [3] Your subscription of $50 will help make Thanksgiving Day a happy one for some worthy family.

Your [4] ticket to the charity ball was mailed to you several days ago by our corresponding secretary. [5] Perhaps you have already received it.

Thank you for your generosity, Captain Brown. Sincerely yours, [118]

372 Ms. Strong: Would you be responsible for ordering approximately 100,000 copies of the [1] circular describing our line of Suburban fire security equipment. I suggest that you have Diamond Brothers [2] do the work unless you would like to place the work elsewhere for any reason. As you know, our relationships [3] with them have been pleasant whenever we dealt with them in the past. They have never failed to meet their delivery [4] promises.

The owners are men of character, and they have long been recognized for their leadership in the printing [5] field. Charles H. Perez [104]

373 Dear Mr. Baker: In the May issue of several national magazines we will run a full-page ad [1] featuring Mason calculators. This advertising should greatly stimulate sales for our dealers.

Would you like to [2] have reprints of this ad for use in your local advertising? If you would, tell us how many you want and we [3] will deliver them to you in the last week of April.

If there is anything we can supply you that will help [4] you sell Mason calculators, please let us know. Sincerely yours, [92]

374 Dear Fred: As you know, about two weeks ago I bought a house in the suburb of Westfield Township. Therefore, I will [1] have to sublease my five-room apartment at 415 East 12 Street in Chicago. Do you know of anyone [2] who would be interested in subleasing the apartment for the six months remaining on my lease?

I am paying [3] $250 a month rent but will be glad to take $200 in order to get the [4] apartment off my hands quickly. Sincerely yours, [89]

375 Dear Mr. Drake: I have the happy duty of informing you that your application for membership in the [1] National Retailers Association has been accepted. Your membership card is enclosed.

As you may know, [2] your membership automatically entitles you to a free subscription to our bulletin, *Retailers* [3] *Newsletter.*

Plans for our annual convention are substantially complete. The convention will be held October [4] 15, 16, and 17 in Los Angeles, California. You will receive complete details about [5] the convention in a few weeks. Sincerely yours, [109]

376 Dear Mary: I understand that you won a four-year scholarship to Billings College. May I offer you my sincere [1] congratulations. I know how hard you worked to win this great honor.

When I get to Chicago, I will [2] congratulate you in person. Sincerely yours, [48]

LESSON 39

382 Dear Mr. Dwyer: As you will recall, on Friday, January 5, I wrote to the membership telling them [1] that we had hired Mr. Donald Banks to take over the responsibility of running our pool facilities [2] next year. When I talked to him several days ago, he informed me that he had received a very good [3] offer to join the faculty of Western State College and asked about the possibility of his being released [4] from his contract with us. We naturally granted his request because we did not wish to stand in his way when [5] an opportunity to improve himself presented itself.

At the moment, I myself do not know of [6] anyone I can suggest for the position. If you should know of a person who you think has the qualities and [7] the general ability necessary for the position, please call me immediately. Yours very [8] truly, [161]

383 Dear Mrs. Hughes: Like many other people in the decorating business, we at Brown and Company employ [1] designers who have ability, individuality, and exceedingly practical ideas. Unlike [2] most other people in this business, though, we actually manufacture the various furnishings that we [3] design. We have been doing this for more than 20 years.

Our organization is not the largest in the world. [4] There are only 12 of us. We do all the work ourselves, and we enjoy what we are doing.

By working together, [5] we steadily maintain the integrity, the quality, and the dependability of our [6] services.

When business or pleasure brings you to the area of Albany Street, stop in to see us. We want you to [7] examine our facilities and see for yourself what we have to offer. We want you to meet our employees [8] and speak to our executives.

We are always ready to discuss decorating with you, Mrs. Hughes. Very [9] truly yours, [182]

384 Dear Mr. Short: The credit departments of many organizations ordinarily concern themselves with [1] only one type of customer, the one who usually does not pay his bills when they are due.

Here at Interboro [2] Enterprises our credit department also concerns itself with another type of customer, the one [3] who regularly buys substantial quantities of our imported sporting goods and pays every bill promptly. You, [4] of course, are the second type of customer.

Congratulations, Mr. Short, on the thoughtful way you meet your [5] financial responsibilities. If all our customers were as prompt in sending in their remittances as you [6] are, my job would be a comfortable and easy one indeed. Very truly yours, [135]

385 Gentlemen: By now you have probably read the reports published in the newspapers regarding the route exchange [1] we have arranged with International Airlines. This exchange is still subject to general review by government [2] authorities. In our opinion, though, they will not object to it and will approve it soon.

As you can well [3] imagine, we do not particularly enjoy giving up any market. We have built up for ourselves a [4] reputation for quality and loyalty in the cities we have served throughout the years. But the financial [5] realities leave us no choice. When the text of this agreement has been completed, we believe we will be able [6] to achieve financial stability.

As our discussions with the government and other public officials [7] proceed, we will keep you posted. Sincerely yours, [150]

386 Dear Mr. Sanchez: Last evening I received the unhappy news that our advertising manager has resigned. [1] We are, therefore, in the market for his replacement. The person we want must possess the following qualities: [2]

1. A familiarity with all phases of advertising.
2. A pleasing personality.
3. The [3] ability to inspire loyalty in a large staff of assistants.

It occurred to us that with your extensive [4] experience in advertising, you might know of some person who can meet our needs and who would be interested [5] in joining our organization.

We will quickly arrange an interview for any person you suggest. [6] Sincerely yours, [124]

387 Dear Mr. Gray: Do you realize, Mr. Gray, that you are doing yourself a disservice? When you do not pay [1] your bill when your account is due, you endanger your reputation as a man of integrity and [2] responsibility.

In justice to us and to yourself, send us your check immediately for $50. Yours [3] very truly, [63]

388 Dear Friend: As you may have read in the newspapers, we are now conducting our third annual appeal for funds for [1] the Westport meal-delivery service. Our organization is a nonprofit public service established to [2] help our neighbors. It is not a charity.

We started with 600 deliveries the first year. Today we are [3] making 5,000 deliveries. The majority of our subscribers are hardship cases that do not have the [4] ability to take care of themselves.

We need your support if we are to go on. There are three ways in which you [5] can help: (1) Give your financial support. (2) Serve as a volunteer driver. (3) Tell your friends about our service [6] and enlist their support.

We are confident that we can rely on your friendship and loyalty to help maintain [7] the high quality of the Westport meal-delivery service. Sincerely yours, [154]

389 Dear Max: Thank you for offering to take the responsibility for preparing our budget yourself rather [1] than delegating the job to a member of your staff. I now have every confidence that the job will be done [2] right! Sincerely yours, [44]

LESSON 40

393 Dear Dr. Myers: From all indications, our conference at Interboro Institute on aptitude testing [1] was an outstanding success. In my estimation, this success can be attributed directly to the [2] excellent contributions of speakers like yourself.

Your address at the banquet on Friday, November 6, set an [3] ideal tone for all the other meetings. In fact after your presentation yesterday, several members [4] of our own faculty inquired whether they could obtain copies of it. Do you have any extra copies [5] I can distribute to them?

I am sending you under another cover a copy of the *New World Atlas* [6] as a token of our appreciation. I hope, Dr. Myers, that you have occasion to use it frequently [7] and that it will remind you of the gratitude of Interboro Institute for your valuable contribution. [8]

The next time you are in this area, please stop in to see us. Sincerely yours, [176]

394 Dear Mr. Samuels: When you lease a truck from the Empire Township Rental Company, you get more than an [1] ordinary truck. You get everything you need for an exceedingly efficient distribution system. You get [2] a new truck, maintenance, fuel, and insurance. Consequently, your only responsibility is to provide [3] a driver.

Whenever you require a substitute vehicle, we will be glad to supply it. If you require [4] emergency road service at any time, we will provide it.

If you are interested in leasing a [5] truck for your business, return the enclosed card informing us when one of our experienced representatives [6] may call. As I am sure you realize, this will place you under no obligation. Sincerely yours, [138]

395 Dear Mrs. Dix: Your letter asking the Strong Calculator Company to contribute to your scholarship fund [1] was referred to me a few days ago by our Albany office.

As you may be aware, we have offices [2] all over the country. Consequently, we frequently receive requests for contributions to worthy and [3] recognized charities. We wish we could contribute to all of them. You can readily see, though, that this would be [4] impossible. We have decided to limit our contributions to causes that affect our home state of Illinois. [5] It is my unpleasant duty, therefore, to report to you that we cannot contribute to your fund.

We hope, [6] Mrs. Dix, that you are successful in your endeavor to raise $100,000. Sincerely yours, [139]

396 Dear Mr. Mild: I know how much trouble I caused you when I asked you to deliver our order for 20 [1] calculators a month earlier than the delivery date we had agreed on. But on Wednesday, January 15, [2] I received an urgent call from a difficult but important customer saying that he required 20 [3] calculators for his advertising department in Detroit without delay.

The calculators arrived on [4] Monday morning, and we delivered them to him on Tuesday. Because of your cooperation, we have been able [5] to make him a satisfied customer, and we will unquestionably get more business from him in the [6] future.

I want to thank you, Mr. Mild, for your help. You have my sincere gratitude. Yours very truly, [138]

397 Ms. Smith: We are making progress in the preparation of the circular promoting our new publication,[1] *The Correspondence Manual.* It should be completed shortly after the first of the year. It will be illustrated[2] by Charles Brown, an acknowledged leader in the field of commercial art. It will be printed in four colors,[3] which is something we have never done before.

We will mail the circulars in yellow envelopes. Both the circulars[4] and the envelopes will be printed by Doyle Brothers, where we always get the advantage of special prices.[5]

I think the circular will be an advertising piece that has character and pulling power. Consequently, it[6] should bring in thousands of inquiries and orders. James B. Ryan [132]

398 Mr. Billings: Last Friday morning I interviewed two enterprising young women who, in my opinion,[1] are excellent prospects for the sales positions we have available in the international division[2] of Jennings Enterprises. I am enclosing their data sheets. You will notice that both of them meet our requirements[3] completely, and I think they can make a definite contribution to our organization. Furthermore,[4] they both speak German, French, and Spanish.

I suggest, Mr. Billings, that you study the data sheets carefully, and[5] then invite the women to come in for an interview with you and with a member of the personnel department.[6]

Let me have a report on these women as soon as possible. Harry L. Smith [135]

LESSON 41

404 Dear Mr. Doyle: Thank you again, Mr. Doyle, for your memorandum of introduction to Governor Day.[1] Governor Day welcomed me courteously at the entrance to the Executive Mansion, and I had the privilege[2] of spending almost one hour with him.

I had a very good opportunity to submit to him my views[3] on the subject of general public transportation and to make a plea for more assistance to the big cities.[4] When I was finished, he expressed his gratitude for my interest and promised to do what he could to improve[5] mass transit facilities throughout the state.

Without your assistance, I probably could not have obtained a[6] personal interview with him. Sincerely yours, [129]

405 Dear Mrs. Hughes: A check of our records indicates that you have been a regular cash customer of the State[1] Street Photographic Institute for a long time. In fact, today marks the fifth anniversary of your first[2] transaction with us. It has been a privilege to serve your photographic requirements, Mrs. Hughes. My assistants[3] and I have enjoyed our business relationship with you.

Because you buy from us so frequently, wouldn't you like[4] to open a charge account with us? A majority of our customers enjoy the practical convenience[5] that a charge account affords. It enables them to do their shopping without having to carry large amounts[6] of cash. They also appreciate the convenience of being able to transact business by mail or telephone.[7]

If you like the idea of a charge account with us, fill out, sign, and return the enclosed form in the[8] envelope we have provided for your convenience. Very truly yours, [173]

406 Mr. Dwyer: The treasurer transmitted to me your memorandum requesting permission to purchase a[1] transistor radio and phonograph combination. I understand that this is to be used as a present[2] for Mr. Frank Gold, manager of our statistics department, on the occasion of his twenty-fifth[3] anniversary with the Billings Transportation Company.

As you may know, company regulations specify[4] that the maximum that can be spent on an employee's twenty-fifth anniversary is $150.[5] The transistor radio and phonograph combination you want to purchase actually costs about[6] $250.

I am reluctant to approve this request, but in view of the significant[7] contribution Mr. Gold has made to the Billings Transportation Company and management's high regard for him,[8] I will do so. James C. French [165]

407 Dear Ms. Clinton: Thank you for the autographed copy of your latest publication, *The Transportation Executive's*[1] *Guide.* When I received it a few days ago, I immediately sat down and studied it. As usual,[2] you did an exceedingly fine job.

I particularly like the organization of the book, the[3] generous quantity of photographs, and the useful tables of statistics that you have provided. In my unbiased[4] opinion, *The Transportation Executive's Guide* is easily your most valuable and significant[5] work. You have every reason to be proud of yourself.

Again, thank you for my autographed copy. Sincerely[6] yours, [121]

408 Gentlemen: I read your advertisement in yesterday's newspaper describing a new type of paint your engineers[1] developed after many years of study. As we are manufacturers of high-quality furniture,[2] we were naturally attracted by your advertisement and would like to learn about the special advantages[3] of your paint over other types.

Please suggest a date when it will be convenient for one of my assistants[4] to discuss your paint with your engineers. Sincerely yours, [91]

409 Dear Mr. Mann: Last night I read with interest your translation of the article on transistors that appeared[1] in a recent issue of a French magazine. You have done an excellent job.

With your permission, I would like[2] to share your translation with our staff of engineers. The article contains many significant facts that I[3] know will be of interest to them.

A stamped envelope is enclosed for your convenience in letting me know[4] whether I have your permission. Sincerely yours, [89]

410 Dear Ms. Tresh: I have just received a memorandum from our credit manager that you have opened a charge account[1] with us. I know you will find your charge account a quick, convenient, and practical way to purchase your clothing[2] needs. In addition, you will enjoy shopping in the friendly atmosphere that prevails in our store.

It will be[3] a privilege to serve you, Ms. Tresh. Sincerely yours, [70]

411 To the Staff: For several years we have been suffering for lack of working space on the three floors of the Transportation[1] Building that we occupy. We have, in fact, had to transfer several departments to various parts[2] of the city. This has caused considerable inconvenience for many of us.

It is my privilege[3] to tell you that in about eight or ten months our space troubles will be a thing of the past. We have just signed a contract[4] with National Builders to build a modern 25-story office building for us on Fifth Avenue[5] and State Street. This building will easily accommodate all our departments and will also provide ample room[6] for future expansion.

If all goes well, we will be able to move into this building in December.

I will[7] keep you informed on the progress of our new building. C. R. Green [152]

LESSON 42

412 *Recall Chart*

1 Efficient, patient; myself, themselves; tabulate, tabulation.

2 Faculty, royalty; deficiency, proficiency; confidential, confidentially.

3 Available, valuable; termination, determination; eastern, western.

4 Detaining, containing; comfortable, uncomfortable; brother, mother.

5 Thoughtful, thoughtfully; feature, nature; readily, steadily.

6 Exceedingly, unwillingly; facility, reliability; sincerity, majority.

7 Steamship, relationship; meetings, ratings; entertainingly, entertainment.

8 Introduce, introduction; employ, employee; improve, improvement.

9 Debate, debated; pursue, pursued; repeat, repeated.

10 Performer, performance; person, impersonal; enforce, enforced.

11 Transport, transportation; become, beneath;

displace, replace.

12 Alter, alterations; extreme, extremely; inform, information.

13 Actual, actually; submit, submitted; interestingly, uninterested.

14 Direct, direction; confer, conference; critical, critically.

15 Describe, dismissed; furniture, furthermore; report, reporter.

414 *Evaluate Yourself*

Would you like to become a better and more interesting person? If you would, your first step should be to take an [1] inventory and identify those personality traits, attributes, and attitudes that require substantial [2] improvement.

To begin with, you might ask yourself such serious questions as:

1. Can I always be depended [3] on to do what I say I will do?
2. Do I frequently go out of my way cheerfully and willingly [4] to help others?
3. Do I try not to show off how much I know?
4. Do I "bawl out" people who do things that displease [5] me?
5. Do I avoid making fun of others behind their backs?
6. Am I careful not to make comments that [6] embarrass others?
7. Are my relationships with my fellow employees pleasant?
8. Do I keep my [7] personal tribulations to myself?
9. Do I listen carefully when others are speaking?
10. Do I smile [8] pleasantly and often?

If you answer these questions with sincerity and honesty, you will no doubt discover [9] some areas where you can improve and thus become a better person. [193]

415 *Words, Words, Words*

There are some writers who like to use long words to convey the meaning of a number of shorter words. As everyone [1] will agree, looking up unfamiliar words in the dictionary slows down reading considerably. [2] Consequently, the more words you know, the faster you will be able to read and comprehend.

Any person who [3] hopes to achieve a position of leadership must, of course, develop a large vocabulary. The executive [4] must often read complicated regulations, regulations that contain many technical terms. Often [5] the executive has to translate technical paragraphs into simple sentences that ordinary [6] people can understand. John Wanamaker used to keep a list of new words each day and look up their meanings every [7] evening. He started the habit when he was ten years old and kept at it for more than sixty years.

When you [8] encounter a word that is unfamiliar, look it up in a dictionary, a student's best friend. If you don't [9] have a dictionary available, write the new words on a piece of paper and save the paper until you [10] have a chance to look the words up. Look for similarities between words. This will help you remember them better. [11] Study the way in which a new word is used in the material you are reading, and then try to make up a [12] sentence using the word.

If you follow these suggestions, you will find your vocabulary growing significantly. [13] [261]

416 *Economy*

The most economical person I ever knew was a big spender—"investor" would probably be a better [1] word. He never let his money lie idle but was always finding ways and means to make it earn more income. [2]

This man realized that economy is the careful use of anything. Many people think of economy [3] as refraining from spending. That is merely stinginess.

To be truly economical, you must learn to [4] spend wisely. Once you learn to do this, you are on the road to becoming truly economical.

There are more [5] kinds of economy than economy of money. There is economy of time and economy of [6] energy. These are most important. If you do not use time and energy properly, you will have no money [7] on which to practice economy!

To economize on time means to use your time to best advantage. To do [8] this, you must economize on energy. In turn, this means that you must work on a plan and a schedule. [178]

CHAPTER 8

LESSON 43

422 Dear Ms. Harding: It is a strange thing about institutional advertising. Much of it is designed to correct [1] the public's misinformation, misapprehension, and mistaken ideas about an organization. [2] Yet somehow the advertising never seems to reach the people for whom it is intended, and companies [3] frequently continue to communicate with other companies.

When you tell the facts about your organization [4] in an advertisement in the *Readers Monthly,* this will not happen. Statistics prove that our publication [5] is read, discussed, and trusted without question by more successful persons than any other publication [6] in the world.

Plan to include advertising in the *Readers Monthly* in your next advertising budget, Ms. Harding. [7] You will be making no mistake. Sincerely yours, [150]

423 Dear Mr. Mild: There is nothing more satisfying to an individual in a supervisory [1] position than to be able to analyze a difficult task and then make the right decision. Supervisors [2] and superintendents who read Dr. Newton's superb book, *Executive Supervision,* improve their chances [3] of making important decisions correctly and of preventing misunderstandings and misconceptions on [4] the part of employees.

Executive Supervision discusses the supervisor's special job of [5] communicating with people, working with machines, and handling himself or herself. It presents stimulating case [6] problems of human relationships that require objective judgment, and it then suggests satisfactory [7] solutions for them. The book is strikingly illustrated with a generous quantity of beautiful photographs. [8]

Executive Supervision sells for $9, and you can order your copy by filling out and [9] returning the coupon at the bottom of the enclosed circular. Cordially yours, [194]

424 Dear Mr. Banks: Several days ago we had transmitted to us a manuscript entitled "The World of Music." [1] Our music editors and supervisors have examined the manuscript, and they report that the author [2] has done a superior job and that the manuscript contains many good features. Before we accept the [3] manuscript, we want to have a music authority with your recognized reputation and experience give [4] a critical opinion of its accuracy and suitability for our market.

If you are interested [5] in reviewing this manuscript for us, we will be glad to pay you our regular reviewer's fee of [6] $70. A stamped envelope is enclosed for your convenience in writing us. Sincerely yours, [139]

425 Dear Mr. Long: Thank you for submitting to us the manuscript for your collection of short stories entitled [1] "The Mystery of the West." I read the manuscript this morning, and I think it is superb.

Unfortunately, [2] we cannot publish it to our mutual profit. As you will see by the enclosed catalog, we publish books and [3] periodicals of a scientific and technical character that are ordinarily sold to schools. [4] Books such as yours must be sold almost entirely to the general public, and that is an area which [5] we cannot readily reach with our sales force or through correspondence.

I hope, Mr. Long, that you will promptly find [6] a publisher for your manuscript. I am sending it back to you by express. Sincerely yours, [137]

426 Dear Fred: As you know, I am responsible for obtaining a speaker for the Progressive Executives [1] Association meeting on Saturday, December 18. I wrote to Mrs. Mary Worth inviting her to [2] be our speaker, but I have not even had an acknowledgment of my letter.

Because the time is getting quite [3] short, I must definitely look elsewhere for a speaker. If you should know of anyone you think our members would [4] enjoy hearing, I wish you would let me have his or her name as soon as possible. Sincerely yours, [98]

427 Dear Mr. Banks: Thank you for your order of November 16 for a number of books. Only one of the titles [1] on your list is our publication, *International*

Misunderstandings. The 20 copies you ordered [2] of this title have been shipped, and they should reach you shortly. The other titles on your list are published by the [3] National Communications Company of Los Angeles.

You will be interested to know that in January [4] we will publish another title in the area of international relations, *International* [5] *Politics.* When this volume comes off the press, we will send you a circular describing it.

Again, Mr. [6] Banks, thank you for your order. Sincerely yours, [129]

428 Dear Mr. Castro: In this morning's mail I received your manuscript for the third edition of your book, *The* [1] *Supervisor in Business.*

I wish to congratulate you on two things:

1. You have done a superb job bringing [2] the material up to date. You have, in addition, added many features that will appeal to business [3] executives.

2. You have improved by two weeks the schedule that we set last July for the completion of the [4] manuscript. I realize that this required a superhuman effort on your part, and I sincerely [5] appreciate it.

We have high hopes for this third edition. We expect to sell a minimum of 30,000 [6] copies of *The Supervisor in Business* in the first year of publication and 150,000 [7] copies in five years. Sincerely yours, [147]

429 Dear Mr. Day: Many thanks for your enlightening and entertaining presentation at our management meeting [1] on Friday, December 10. I can understand Mr. Baker's enthusiasm when he suggested that [2] I invite you to speak to us.

As you no doubt noticed, we had your presentation taped along with the question- [3] and-answer period. When everything is transcribed, I will send you a copy.

With your permission, we would like [4] to print in our house organ that portion of your presentation relating to employee incentives. This house [5] organ goes to all employees at the supervisory level. May we have your permission, Mr. Day? Very [6] truly yours, [123]

LESSON 44

435 Dear Depositor: As you probably read in the newspapers a few days ago, the West Street Manufacturers [1] Trust Company has, with government approval, taken over all branches of the State Security Bank [2] throughout the city. At the same time we have acquired all its assets and assumed the responsibility [3] for handling all classifications of its accounts.

There is no immediate action required on your [4] part because of this transaction, and all your regular business will continue to be handled in the usual [5] courteous, helpful manner.

We believe that under the circumstances the customers of both institutions [6] will actually derive many advantages, privileges, and conveniences from this merger. [7]

If you have any questions regarding this merger, we will naturally be very glad to answer them. Sincerely [8] yours, [161]

436 Mrs. Banker: When I studied the plans and specifications for our new transportation building yesterday, [1] I was extremely annoyed. I discovered that some person had made several important modifications [2] in the specifications. These modifications were made without justification and without authority. [3]

Under no circumstances should any further modifications be made in the specifications without [4] my written approval or that of our general superintendent, Captain Max Smith.

Please acknowledge this [5] memorandum as soon as you receive it. Lydia Stern [111]

437 Dear Mrs. Billings: Today the scouting movement is stronger than ever. It is giving our children every [1] opportunity to grow up to be strong, upright citizens. It is still teaching the principles of self-reliance, [2] self-confidence, and good sportsmanship. We should continue to work for these ideals with

justification and [3] pride.

Under the circumstances, Mrs. Billings, shouldn't you give your unselfish support to this movement? You can [4] readily do so by making a substantial contribution to the Baldwin Scouting Council. A stamped, self-addressed [5] envelope is enclosed for your convenience in sending us your check. Sincerely yours, [117]

438 Dear Ms. Day: The following paragraph is taken from a letter we received from a person who took the Empire [1] Self-Improvement Course. It will, I am sure, be of interest to you. "While I was taking your self-improvement [2] course last year, I discovered that I had many valuable assets that I was not using. After I completed [3] the course, I found I could handle myself under the most trying circumstances. The course has been a source of [4] stimulation and gratification to me."

Our course will give you greater self-confidence, self-assurance, and [5] poise. When you are requested to speak before a group of people on any subject, you will be able to express [6] your ideas convincingly. The course will develop your sense of responsibility.

You will be making [7] no mistake, Ms. Day, by enrolling in our course. If you want more particulars, call us at 156-1171. [8] Sincerely yours, [166]

439 Gentlemen: I am enclosing a copy of the specifications we have drawn up for the construction of [1] our new factory in Westport. Circumstances beyond our control prevented us from completing the [2] specifications sooner.

Please have members of your staff study the specifications and suggest whatever changes [3] they think are desirable.

As I must present these specifications formally to the management committee [4] on January 6, I would appreciate it if I could have them back by Tuesday, January 4. [5]

This has been a long, tedious project, and I will be glad when I can turn it over to our building committee. [6] Sincerely yours, [124]

440 Mr. Banks: Our new self-improvement course will be in our shipping room on Friday, October 15. Please send a [1] notification to this effect to the sales staff. Ellen C. Baker [33]

441 Dear Mr. Nelson: If you are like the average junior business executive, the chances are that you [1] fervently wish that you had more self-confidence and self-assurance when you must address a gathering such as [2] a general meeting, a board of directors meeting, or just an informal meeting of your immediate [3] associates. You wish that you could overcome that frightening feeling of stage fright.

Our experience tells us [4] that there are two ways of accomplishing this. One way is to strive for self-improvement by yourself, but this is a [5] most difficult, discouraging way. The other is to enroll in the Weston public speaking course. In this course [6] you will work with others who are in the same circumstances that you are. Under the supervision of your [7] instructor and with the encouragement of your fellow students, you will develop self-expression and self-confidence. [8]

Return the enclosed card and we will send you complete information about our courses. Sincerely yours, [179]

442 Dear Mr. Morton: Many people are skeptical when a sales clerk tells them that they will have their furniture in [1] three weeks or less. In many stores they have reason to be skeptical. In those stores, clerks feel that if they want to make a [2] sale, they must make an early delivery promise.

At the Eastern Furniture Store you can be sure that when a [3] representative of ours gives you a delivery date, we will back up the promise. We can deliver most of our [4] furniture two weeks after the date of purchase.

We cannot, of course, be responsible for delays caused by strikes [5] which are beyond our control. But if a delay is necessary, we will call you immediately. If you [6] do not wish to wait, you can cancel at that time.

Come in and select your new furniture from our large stocks. Remember, [7] you can always count on our delivery promise. Yours very truly, [153]

LESSON 45

449 Dear Dr. Myers: You will recall that at the morning session of the Adult Education Association [1] on Wednesday, February 15, you told me that the World Publishing Company was interested in [2] computerizing its accounting operations next year. I forwarded this information to one of our [3] representatives in the Chicago area, and he immediately called on them.

The first result of his [4] call was a series of very satisfactory and rewarding meetings between the executives of the [5] company and our experienced consultants. The ultimate result was a new, highly profitable account [6] for our organization which will be worth in the neighborhood of $1 million to $2 million [7] in sales in the short period of five years.

Thank you, Dr. Myers, for this valuable lead. If I [8] can ever return your thoughtfulness, I will certainly take advantage of the opportunity. Sincerely [9] yours, [181]

450 Dear Parent: The time to start thinking about the physical fitness of your children is when they are in school.

A [1] regular system of physical education will result in rich rewards for every young boy or girl. When [2] they are physically fit, children are less prone to childhood illnesses, and there is less likelihood that they will [3] miss days at school.

Physical fitness can ultimately transform insecure, uncertain, and awkward children into [4] self-confident, successful performers. Furthermore, a regular system of exercise during boyhood [5] or girlhood will stand children in good stead when they reach adulthood.

Under the circumstances, we suggest that you [6] strongly support and encourage physical education in your neighborhood public schools. In our opinion, [7] it is just as important to train children's bodies as it is to train their minds. What do you think? [157]—*Physical Fitness Council*

451 Dear Mr. Dixon: I find myself in a particularly awkward, difficult position, Mr. Dixon. [1] As you know, on June 15 your district superintendent placed an order with us for 500 feet of lumber, [2] 300 pounds of cement, 1,000 feet of wire, and quantities of other miscellaneous items. [3] We filled the order promptly and billed you for $2,000. Your payment was due several months ago, but [4] we have not had a reply from you to any of the notifications we sent you requesting payment.

I [5] must tell you frankly that unless I receive a remittance soon, I will have to refer your account to our legal [6] division. I would appreciate your helping me with this awkward position by sending me your check now [7] for $2,000 in the enclosed stamped, self-addressed envelope. By doing so promptly, you will preserve the [8] good relationship that has existed between the Empire Processing Company and us for so many years. [9] Sincerely yours, [183]

452 Gentlemen: The January issue of *Family Magazine* will be devoted to children's fashions. As [1] a progressive, forward-looking dealer in children's clothing, you will wish to advertise in this issue because: [2]

1. Our publication has a circulation of more than 1,500,000 subscribers.
2. [3] These people have the ability to purchase the best of everything they want. Their income is 77 [4] percent higher than the national average and is continuing to rise annually.
3. A majority [5] of them spend $700 or more each year on children's clothing. Consequently, they are exceedingly [6] desirable prospects for your children's line.

If you are interested in obtaining advertising [7] rates for this special issue, return the card that is enclosed for your convenience. Sincerely yours, [158]

453 Ms. Faye: I am impressed with the draft of the circular you prepared for our new correspondence manual. I [1] notice that your manufacturing specifications call for the use of one photograph and three colors.

We [2] have never used three colors for the promotion of a professional work of this character, and ordinarily [3] I would object because of the expense. But I recognize the importance of getting this correspondence [4] manual off to a good start. Consequently, I am approving your specifications on this occasion. [5]

By the way, where do you plan to print the circular? A. R. Wilson [113]

LESSON 46

461 Mrs. Overmeyer: Yesterday afternoon about 4 p.m. I had a cablegram from Dr. Powers, [1] our electronics consultant. He said that his plane had a mishap during an electrical storm somewhere in [2] the area of Paris and that he would not be able to leave France for probably two or three days. Fortunately, [3] he was not harmed. This means, however, that it will be impossible for him to take part in the program [4] on electronics in business being sponsored by the Chamber of Commerce in the Municipal Government Building [5] on Friday, February 15.

Do you yourself know of some prominent person with general electronics [6] training who can substitute for Dr. Powers on the program and contribute some worthwhile ideas? [7] If you do, please call me at my State Street office between the hours of 9 a.m. and 2 p.m. We will, of course, [8] be glad to pay the speaker our usual fee of $500. Max H. Banks [174]

462 Dear Mr. Jennings: Within the next three or four days I will forward to you a diagram and some specifications [1] I am preparing for the placement of the furniture and equipment of the National Steamship Lines [2] in your new quarters in the Chemical Building. When you receive this material, please have someone study the [3] diagram and specifications carefully. I want to discuss with him or her some questions regarding the [4] permanent installation of electrical outlets for electronic calculators, electric typewriters, [5] and other electrical equipment that requires outlets.

The best time for me would be in the neighborhood [6] of 3 p.m. on Friday, August 18. Is that time convenient for you, Mr. Jennings? Sincerely [7] yours, [141]

463 Dear Mr. Singer: As you will see by the enclosed copy of our advertisement in this morning's newspaper, [1] the Superior Bookstore will open a new electronic calculator center in the Chamber of Commerce [2] Building.

We have endeavored to bring together the full line of electronic calculators of two [3] acknowledged leaders in the electronic calculator field. We have also stocked our shelves with modern computer [4] manuals, technical books, and periodicals on many business subjects.

We are, of course, primarily [5] a commercial bookstore. However, we are also a self-contained, responsible information facility [6] for every professional need.

Come to our grand opening on Monday, November 15, from 10 a.m. [7] to 6 p.m. We have planned an exceedingly interesting and enjoyable program throughout the day, and [8] each person who enters the store will receive a worthwhile souvenir. Very truly yours, [176]

464 Dear Mr. East: This morning I sent you the following telegram: "We have not yet received diagram for [1] installation of electronic computer you were going to transmit to us a week ago. Electricians [2] need diagram within next few days."

Unless we receive this diagram by 9 a.m. on Monday, the programming [3] of our organization's accounting operations could be seriously delayed. Under the circumstances, [4] you and your employees should give a particularly high priority to the completion of this [5] diagram. Yours very truly, [106]

465 Dear Mr. Billings: We have scheduled Monday, August 15, as the day on which our electricians will examine [1] and repair the electric wiring on your floor. This is part of our regular maintenance program for the [2] Chamber of Commerce Building. This will necessitate shutting off electric power on your floor from 11 [3] a.m. to 3 p.m.

We are sorry to have to deprive you of electric service for this period of [4] time. We are confident, however, that you will be well pleased with the more efficient electric service that will [5] result from the work of our electricians. Sincerely yours, [111]

466 To the Staff: On Friday, October 15, we

purchased a controlling interest in the National Electronics [1] Institute. This institute offers self-study programs in several branches of electronics.

The [2] institute enrolls more than 40,000 students each year, most of whom are adults between the ages of [3] 25 and 40. The institute is known for its pioneering efforts and leadership in the development [4] of technical education and training in this country.

We expect the institute, with its present [5] forward-looking and progressive management, to contribute significantly to the revenue that we derive [6] from continuing education. Ed Jones [129]

467 Dear Mr. Brown: Where can electrical contractors and engineers get help in testing complex electrical [1] equipment? The answer is at our electrical testing and troubleshooting seminar scheduled for Monday, [2] June 10, in our conference room.

The session will cover problems with transformers, motors, and insulators.

The [3] seminar will be under the direction of our technicians. If you wish to register, fill out and return [4] the enclosed form. Very truly yours, [87]

LESSON 47

471 Dear Mr. Cunningham: Many people think that the Lexington Men's Shop in Harrisburg is an expensive store. [1] This definitely is a fallacy. We invite price and value comparisons with any other quality [2] store in Harrisburg. As you will see by the enclosed circular, our prices for sport coats start at $60, [3] and our executive suits start at $100.

We have always operated on the old-fashioned [4] principle that whatever is best for you, our client, from the standpoint of price, value, and workmanship, is best for [5] the success and progress of the Lexington Men's Shop. Our courteous, efficient employees have dedicated [6] themselves to making your shopping experience with us as pleasant and rewarding as possible.

When you are [7] in our neighborhood, I wish you would stop in and discover what superior, unsurpassed buys we offer. We [8] are open every day except Sunday from 9 a.m. to 5 p.m. We are sure you will enjoy your visit, [9] Mr. Cunningham. Sincerely yours, [187]

472 Dear Ms. Buckingham: Thank you for your prompt reply to our telegram requesting your payment of $900 [1] for the quantity of electronic products you purchased for your Pittsburgh manufacturing plant last June. [2]

We are, quite naturally, sorry that you cannot send us your check immediately. However, your [3] justification of the delay is satisfactory. Under the circumstances, we willingly grant you an [4] extension of 30 days. We look forward to receiving your check for $900 on or before August [5] 1.

We hope, Ms. Buckingham, that business conditions in the Pittsburgh area improve very substantially [6] within the next year or two so that you will be able to take care of your debts on time. Sincerely yours, [138]

473 Dear Mr. Harrington: Some people never seem to be able to save. They have too many things on their minds. They [1] have to buy too many things they need.

These reasons are not good enough, however, if you save at the [2] Jacksonville National Bank. We have a helpful plan in which monthly deposits are automatically transferred from your [3] checking account to your savings account, where they draw a high rate of interest.

If you want to transfer funds from [4] another institution to the Jacksonville National Bank, just bring in your passbook. We will gladly handle [5] all the details, Mr. Harrington.

You will be making no mistake by banking with us. Sincerely yours, [118]

474 Mrs. Overman: The World Publishing Company in Evansville recently issued a book entitled [1] *Correspondence for the Executive.* In my opinion, it is an extraordinary publication. [2] It handles a difficult and important subject in a simple, objective manner.

I suggest that you place [3] an order for several copies and put them in our organization's library.

A. R. Brown [78]

475 Dear Ms. Cunningham: At the present time, you are probably a long way from actual retirement, but haven't [1] you already wondered what you would do if you had only your social security check to live on? We [2] are certain that you have.

As a result of new tax regulations that went into effect a few months ago, [3] you now have an opportunity to provide for an income very much larger than your social security [4] check. Simply open a retirement account with the Nashville Trust Company. You can easily set up [5] a retirement account with us. Just fill out, sign, and return the enclosed form to us with an initial [6] deposit of $5 or more. Then continue to make regular payments in stamped, self-addressed envelopes that [7] we provide for your convenience.

The sooner you own one of our accounts, Ms. Cunningham, the more you will have [8] when you retire. Sincerely yours, [167]

476 Dear Mr. Lexington: We have learned through our local newspaper, *The Daily Times*, that you have just moved to Bloomsburg, [1] and we want to be among the first to extend to you a warm welcome to our friendly city.

We also extend [2] to you a warm invitation, Mr. Lexington, to use the facilities of the Greenburg National [3] Bank, the city's largest, most progressive bank.

When you are settled in your new home, please stop in to see us. It will [4] be a pleasure to welcome you personally and to introduce you to the other officers of our bank. [5] Sincerely yours, [102]

LESSON 48

477 *Recall Chart*

1 Becomes, rushed, almost, childhood, reported, function.

2 Seriously, divided, encouragement, furniture, consumed, utilities.

3 Perplexing, dependable, compliance, kingdom, ultimate, emphatically.

4 Healthful, termination, circumstantial, disappoint, themselves, himself.

5 Transmission, conveniently, forwarded, yellow, yard, motor.

6 Self-contained, swing, authorities, verification, create, relationships.

7 Printings, entertainingly, self-impose, purchases, overpowered, faculties.

8 Wire, genuine, ahead, whale, quietly, brothers.

9 Thermometer, modern, congratulations, underinsured, however, February.

10 Friday, direction, misplaced, interested, tabulated, introduced.

11 Different, details, creditor, program, articles, defeat.

12 Efficiency, patient, unforeseen, dental, greetings, devotion.

13 Promptly, mend, turns, readily, exceedingly, months.

14 Require, telegraph, Birmingham, Harrisburg, Louisville, Washington.

15 Years ago, to be, I have not been able, to know, to me, to make.

16 To do, let us, at a loss, let me, if you want, of course.

17 $300,000; several hundred, a pound, 3 feet, 6 percent, p.m.

479 *Reading*

Think for a few moments what the character of your life would be like if you were unable to read. Certainly [1] reading has contributed much to your accomplishments and pleasures. If you were unable to read, you would not [2] have reached your present level of education, and you would not be able to get the additional education [3] you need to reach your business or professional goals. Without the ability to read, you would not [4] be able to drive a car or vote. You would not be able to read the sporting news in the newspapers or the [5] articles in national magazines. Reading can and does contribute to your wealth of information. Your reading [6] ability is even more important to you after you complete your formal education and you [7] enter adulthood.

Reading for Pleasure. Reading provides you with many hours of pleasure, whether you prefer to [8] read the latest best-seller, the daily newspaper, or your favorite magazine. However, reading makes other [9] important, worthwhile contributions to your personal life. Reading makes you a more effective citizen, [10] for it enables you to keep up to date on current public happenings reported in newspapers and [11] magazines.

Reading in School. As you well know, reading is an essential part of your school program. Students who have [12] difficulty with some phase of reading seldom make superior grades. If you go to college, you will have to do [13] much reading. It is estimated that a successful college student spends about a thousand hours a year with [14] books and that in four years of college, an average student reads about 30 million words.

Reading on the [15] Job. All successful people recognize the importance of reading. They read reports, letters, notifications, [16] and other miscellaneous types of communications. No matter what business position you hope [17] ultimately to hold, reading will play a useful part in your professional life.

A survey made by the National [18] Management Association, the largest association of its kind in the world, indicates that the [19] higher a person's position in the business world, the more that person reads. The survey showed, in addition, [20] that so-called "self-made" executives who did not have the advantage of very much formal schooling usually [21] had gained much of their knowledge through extensive reading.

Because of the importance of reading, one manufacturer [22] of electrical equipment in Pittsburgh offered a free program to help his executives speed up [23] their reading. When the executives completed this program, they were able to cut significantly the time [24] they needed to spend on essential reading. Under the circumstances, the manufacturer was richly [25] rewarded for his investment. It resulted in an annual saving of $40,000 in executive [26] time that could be devoted profitably to other duties. [533]

CHAPTER 9

LESSON 49

481 Mrs. Smith: Do you realize that you left your sweater in the back of my car last night? I have the sweater at [1] home.

If you need the sweater, please phone me. I will mail it to your Park Lane address. But if you do not need it, I [2] can leave it with Mr. Baker, who can give it to you at the May sales meeting. Cathy White [57]

482 Mr. West: As you know, Mr. Day, the head of our Akron store, had a big increase in sales in April. Mr. [1] Day admits that he did well, but he feels that he might have had an even greater increase if he had had three more [2] sales clerks. I agree with him. I am writing him to increase his staff to 14 as of the 15th of May.

Please [3] notify the payroll people of the course I am taking. Helen Bates [73]

483 To the Sales Staff: It is my sad duty to write you that Mr. Dean Ray is leaving our sales staff in May. He plans [1] to go back to selling cars in Memphis. We will miss him.

We are assigning Mrs. Helen Dale to Mr. Ray's [2] territory starting May 15. We know that Mrs. Dale will do well in that territory. Barry Smith [59]

484 Dear Harry: My head file clerk, Mr. Ned Davis, will visit your store in Moline the first week in April. Please let [1] Mr. Davis see your line of filing cabinets. We will buy 12 cabinets of the type that he feels will best [2] meet our needs.

I have asked Mr. Davis to telephone you the day he arrives in Moline. Fred Smith [58]

485 Mr. Taylor: Can you spare me an hour or so to help me plan our sales meeting in May? I know that you are busy, [1] but I need your advice in selecting the people to invite to the meeting.

Can you see me April 15 [2] or April 16? Henry Harper [47]

486 Dear Dad: I have a bit of news that I know will please you. I passed my history final with a grade of 95. [1] I did not do so well in chemistry, but I passed with a grade of 80.

As you may know, my last day of [2] school is May 28. I will fly home May 29. My plane will arrive in Gary at six in the evening.[3] Can you meet me? Mary [64]

487 Mrs. Day: As I wrote you in my letter of April 10, I will add three clerks to my staff in May. I need three [1] desks to take care of these clerks. Do you have three desks that you can move to the fifth floor in a day or so? If you do [2] not have three desks that you can spare, I will buy three new desks. Harry Meade [53]

488 Dear Abe: Since the heavy rainstorm we had in May, we have had a deep hole in the road leading to our barn. I wrote [1] three letters to Mr. Weeks advising him that the road needs care, but I have not had an answer to my letters. [2]

May I ask you, as mayor of Moline, to help in getting our road paved or at least in having the hole taken [3] care of. Ethel Smith [64]

489 Mrs. Drake: As you know, our sales are growing so fast that I will have to add a new clerk to my staff in April [1] or May.

I will need a desk to take care of the clerk. Can you spare a desk that I can move to my floor? Henry J. [2] Casey [41]

490 Dear Bill: I have a great favor to ask of you, Bill.

I plan to go to Dallas the week of April 15 to [1] help my dad sell his home. He is going to live with my niece in Erie.

If I fly to Dallas, I cannot meet [2] my history class at the Harper Evening School. Can you take the class while I am in Dallas?

If you can, please wire [3] me. I will then mail you my set of lesson plans.

I do hope you can help me. Henry [75]

491 Mr. Grace: Last evening I glanced through the paper you are going to read to the meeting of the Moline High School [1] typing instructors. It is fine. I know that the typing instructors of Moline will like it.

The title of [2] your paper, "Typing Tricks of the Trade," is appealing.

As I read through your paper, I marked two minor errors your [3] typist made.

Please remember me to Mrs. Bates, the principal of Moline High School. I know her well. Ellen Harper [4] [81]

492 Mr. Davis: You will remember that last week we made plans to meet with Mrs. Helen Levin, the head of our [1] sales staff, to take steps to increase our sales of school supplies.

I regret that we will have to cancel our plans. It seems [2] that we have had a big fire in our Dallas factory that will keep me in that city during most of April. [3]

Please tell Mrs. Levin why I had to cancel our meeting. Tell her that we will meet late in April or the first [4] week of May. Catherine Harper [85]

493 Dear Phil: My wife tells me that you will arrive in Mobile during the first week of April. Can you plan a little [1] visit with me during your stay? While you are here please plan to meet my niece Mary Grace who has lived in our [2] home since last May. Mary knows your wife well. Harry Smith [50]

LESSON 50

496 Dear Sir: Our records indicate that on March 15 our James Street office filled your prescription for a pair of dark [1] glasses. We sincerely hope that your glasses fit properly and that they have been giving you good service.

If you [2] should lose your glasses, all you need do is call our James Street office. We have your prescription on file and will be able [3] to prepare a duplicate pair for you in a matter of hours. Sincerely yours, [75]

497 Dear Jim: My secretary, Mrs. Jane Flint, and her sister plan to spend from June 15 to June 21 in [1] Dallas visiting their aunt, who is a patient in the hospital there. Their plane arrives in Dallas at 3 o'clock [2] on the afternoon of June 15.

Could you meet them when they arrive and drive them to the Baker Hotel, which [3] is on Third Street and Fifth Avenue? If you cannot meet them, would you please arrange to send a member of your staff. [4]

I know I can rely on you to take care of this matter for me. Sincerely, [95]

498 Dear Sir: I have a small favor to ask of you. Please pay your bill for $90 which should have been paid on or [1] before July 1. This bill is for the following goods that were bought from our store by your secretary on April [2] 15: 400 file folders, 1,000 leaflets, 2,000 clips.

Before you place this letter aside, please [3] write a check for $90 and mail it. Don't make it necessary for me to write you again. Yours very [4] truly, [81]

499 Dear Chester: I am sorry to have to write you that I will not be able to meet you on July 15 in [1] Atlanta as we had arranged on June 25. Because of the illness of my dad, I have been called home to [2] Memphis. I will leave by the end of the week.

I would still like to take the sales position you have open in the [3] East. I will call you when I get back to Atlanta with the hope that we can arrange a meeting on a day that [4] will suit both you and me. Sincerely, [87]

500 To the Staff: It is with a heavy heart that I write you of the death on March 12 of Mr. Charles Baird, chairman of [1] the board of our firm. Mr. Baird had been spending a week's vacation with his married daughter in Deerfield Park when [2] he had a fatal stroke. Mr. Baird would have been 50 on March 30.

Mr. Baird played a vital role in the [3] rapid growth of our firm. He inspired the entire staff. His pleasant smile and helping hand will be sorely missed. [4]

Our deepest sympathies go to Mrs. Baird and his daughter Janice. A. B. Mild [94]

501 Dear Sir: On June 15, you will recall, we wrote you a letter reminding you that you had not paid your bill of [1] $80 for the three pairs of shoes you bought from our West Street store in April. You wrote me in your letter of [2] June 18 that you could not pay the bill in June but that you would pay it in July. We agreed to wait till July [3] 5. Here it is July 21, but we have had no check from you nor have we heard from you.

Please tell me when [4] we may hope to be paid. We have been patient, but our patience is being sorely tried.

Don't make it necessary [5] for me to take legal action. Sincerely yours, [109]

502 Dear Madam: It is a pleasure to answer your letter of March 18 asking me if I know Mr. Henry [1] Small. I am happy that he is applying for a job with the Mild Food Stores.

When I had charge of the Akron Food [2] Mart, I hired Mr. Small as a cashier. After only six weeks he became head buyer. I had planned to promote [3] him again, but he left because of poor health. I would hire him back if I could, but we do not have an opening. [4]

I assure you that Mr. Small will do a fine job for you if you hire him. Sincerely yours, [97]

503 Dear Sir: On April 18 we had the pleasure of filling for you a prescription for a pair of reading glasses. [1]

Do the glasses fit properly and are you happy with them? If not, please stop by so that we can check them for [2] you. There will be no charge for this service.

If by chance you should lose your glasses or break the lenses, remember that [3] we have a record of your prescription in our files in our Third Street store. Therefore, all you need do is call [4] 116-1181, and we will have a new pair ready for you in a matter of hours. Sincerely yours, [98]

504 Dear Jeff: I am sorry but I will not be able to play golf with you on June 10. I bruised my left arm badly, and [1] I cannot even lift a driver.

I will call you when I can play again. Remember

me to Mary. Sincerely, [2] [41]

LESSON 51

507 Dear Dr. Cook: Perhaps you do not realize it, but six months have passed since you last visited the Doyle Men's Shop [1] or placed an order with us.

It has been our policy for many years to manufacture nothing but the finest [2] in men's fashions and to offer the best, most reliable service.

Have we failed you in any way, Dr. [3] Cook? If we have, please tell us about it. We value your business. It is important to our company. We [4] will be glad to correct any errors we may have made.

May we hear from you soon. Yours very truly, [98]

508 Dear Fred: Thank you for the chance you offered me yesterday to talk with you about your insurance needs. I was deeply [1] honored that you were willing to talk about your personal matters with me.

As I promised you, I will work [2] up a suitable plan for you on the basis of the facts you gave me. You should have it one day next week.

If you [3] would like to have more details about our services than I gave you at our meeting, I will be delighted to [4] supply them if you will call me at 116-1181 any morning between nine and twelve. Sincerely, [5] [100]

509 Dear Ed: Shortly after the first of the year I will move to Oakland, where I have been assigned by my company [1] for the next three years. We are launching a sales campaign in Oakland for our garden supplies, and it is of great [2] importance that the campaign get off to a good start. I have been appointed director of the campaign.

Could you assist [3] me in finding a six-room home in or near Oakland? We would like one with a large yard where the children can play [4] in safety.

Thank you for any help you can give me in getting located. Sincerely yours, [97]

510 Gentlemen: Today you can get sharp, clear copies of all kinds of papers for less than 3 cents a copy. The Mason [1] 116 copier produces easy-to-read copies from any original at the rate of ten [2] copies per minute.

What does a Mason 116 cost? You can purchase one for only $350. [3] Read all about this machine on the enclosed circular. We think you will be amazed at the number of things [4] it can do for you.

If you prefer, we will be glad to send our salesman, Mr. Best, to your office with a sample [5] machine. Simply tell us on the enclosed card when he may call. Sincerely yours, [114]

511 Gentlemen: Mr. Barry H. Green, the person you are thinking of hiring as the manager of the Troy branch [1] of the Dwight Manufacturing Company, was with our company for about eight years before he resigned last [2] month.

Mr. Green started as a purchasing agent, but after a number of promotions, he became our [3] treasurer.

He won many friends for our business, and we were sorry that he decided to leave. He left with the [4] goodwill of all of us.

I am sure that Mr. Green will do a fine job for you as manager of your Troy branch. [5]

If there is anything else I can tell you about Mr. Green and the work he did for us, please do not hesitate [6] to write me. Sincerely yours, [126]

512 Dear James: Thank you for the letter you wrote on my behalf to the Dwight Manufacturing Company. I received [1] a letter from the personnel director this morning telling me that the job as manager of their Oakland [2] branch was mine.

I am sure that the letter you wrote had a great deal of influence on the personnel director's [3] decision to offer me this important and desirable position.

I begin my new duties the first [4] of next month. The job is a real challenge, and I can't wait to get started.

Once again, James, thanks for writing so [5] persuasive a letter. Sincerely yours, [107]

513 Dear Dr. Price: Mr. Barry, our first selectman, has asked me to notify the members of the village board [1] that there will be an emergency meeting on

May 18 at 8 o'clock. The purpose of this meeting is to [2] appoint an acting treasurer to replace Helen H. Baker, who has resigned for reasons of health.

Because of the [3] importance of this meeting, please try to be with us. We should be able to finish our business by 9 o'clock [4] at the latest. Sincerely yours, [86]

514 Gentlemen: Are your valuable records protected against fire and theft? They will be well protected if you keep [1] them in a Harris safe.

We are enclosing a booklet that shows the 12 models we manufacture, one of which [2] surely meets your needs perfectly.

If you would like to have a Harris agent call to help you select the type of [3] safe that is best for your needs, simply sign and mail the enclosed card. It needs no postage. Sincerely yours, [78]

LESSON 52

518 Dear Ms. Overman: Many people have purchased a dictating machine only to find out suddenly that they [1] did not obtain the right one.

To make sure that this does not occur to you, we suggest that you get a General [2] dictating machine. We offer our customers many advantages. For one thing, we have several models [3] for you to choose from. For another thing, we let you keep your machine for two weeks' time to see whether you like it. [4] If you don't, you simply ship it back and we will immediately and without question send you another model [5] to try.

The enclosed booklet contains a complete listing of our models. Place an order for the unit that [6] appeals to you. Keep it for two weeks before deciding definitely whether to keep it.

You must acknowledge, [7] Ms. Overman, that this is a very fair offer. Take advantage of it now. Yours very truly, [158]

519 Dear Mr. Moses: Thank you for your application for a position in the personnel relations division [1] of our organization. At present we do not have an opening in that division, but in October [2] or November we will have a vacancy in our advertising department for a person who can create [3] effective advertising copy for the national media in which we advertise. This opening [4] represents a fine opportunity for the right person.

If you would like to know more about this opening, [5] stop in to see me on Friday, August 30, or Monday, September 2. Sincerely yours, [117]

520 Dear Mr. Brandon: Have you ever considered advertising your office equipment through the medium of [1] the magazine section of the *Daily Times,* which is issued every Sunday? Your advertisement in this issue [2] will reach the people who make purchasing decisions for many of our largest companies.

The cost of a one-page [3] advertisement in this section is reasonable—only $1,000. If you send your advertising [4] copy to me in the next ten days, we can insert it in the Sunday, December 15, issue. Your [5] advertising message will reach your potential customers at just the appropriate time when they are making [6] advertising plans for next year. Sincerely yours, [128]

521 Dear Mrs. Mild: As a property owner, you know that your trees are a very valuable asset. Healthy trees [1] provide beauty and shade. They increase the potential value of your property by thousands of dollars.

But trees [2] suffer from insects, storm damage, and other reasons. Whenever trees cannot fight back, they must rely on humans [3] to provide the care they need to remain healthy.

One definite thing you can do for your trees this fall is have them [4] thoroughly inspected before winter arrives.

If you would like to have your trees inspected by our competent [5] tree surgeon during October or November, just fill out, sign, and mail the enclosed card to me. Very truly [6] yours, [121]

522 Dear Ms. Newton: As you know, during the last two years we have been mailing you each month a copy of the *National* [1] *News Magazine.* We are confident that you have derived many hours of pleasure reading the news as it was [2] presented by our large and talented staff of writers and editors.

We find, though, that the February issue [3] will be the last one you will receive because you have not sent us your renewal.

It is easy to renew, Ms. [4] Newton. Simply fill out and mail the enclosed card which needs no postage. We will bill you later. Yours very truly, [5] [100]

523 Ladies and Gentlemen: May I tell you how delighted we are with our advertising in the *Daily Times.*

The [1] number of replies we have received from our advertising is most gratifying. I assure you that we will [2] include advertising in the *Daily Times* in our plans for next year. Sincerely yours, [55]

524 To the Staff: It gives me a great deal of pleasure to be able to announce that beginning Monday, November [1] 1, Mr. David J. Devine will be the new general manager of our financial division.

Mr. [2] Devine has a fine financial background, having been treasurer of the National Development Company [3] for 15 years.

Mr. Devine's first order of business will be to reorganize our accounting practices. [4] He will work with Mr. John C. Charles, vice president for corporate matters. Jane H. Smith [96]

LESSON 53

527 Dear Mr. Banker: Next Saturday I am to speak at the Newspaper Editors Association meeting [1] in Trenton. I have been assigned the subject "Recent Progress in Printing." As you are a recognized leader in [2] the printing field and have had many years of successful experience as a pressman, you probably have some [3] new ideas regarding printing processes that I can pass along to the members.

I will appreciate [4] any help you can give me with the preparation of my speech. If you wish, simply jot your ideas at the [5] bottom of this letter and mail it in the envelope that is enclosed. Sincerely yours, [116]

528 Dear Mr. Underwood: I am enclosing a special petition, signed by 120 residents living [1] in the Worth Street area, requesting that bus service on Worth Street be placed on a regular half-hour basis. [2] In addition, the petitioners would like to have the bus depot changed from Fifth Avenue to State Street to [3] bring it closer to the shopping area on Banks Street.

It is our opinion that these two changes would [4] encourage many people to use public buses rather than their private cars.

I hope that the City Council will [5] act on these ideas as soon as possible. Very truly yours, [113]

529 Dear Mr. Myers: Can you answer technical legal questions such as these:

1. Are you responsible for [1] unusual damage caused by your children to a neighbor's property?
2. What can you do to satisfy creditors [2] whose bills are unpaid?
3. How much should you ordinarily pay a lawyer for a particular job?
4. [3] When and how should you make a will?

You will find answers to these and hundreds of other difficult legal questions [4] in a new publication entitled *The Law and You,* issued by the World Publishing Company. This extremely [5] useful book contains 600 pages, carefully indexed, dealing with all phases of the law that affect [6] the average person. *The Law and You* should be on your library shelves. It sells for only $12. Place your [7] order for a copy today. An envelope is enclosed for your use. Sincerely yours, [156]

530 Dear Mr. Harding: Harry Wilson is a world-famous golfer. In his book, *The World of Golf,* he shares his life with [1] you. He tells you how he won more than 100 top golf events. He tells you how he keeps going in spite of many [2] physical difficulties. He tells you how he corrected his hook and how he handles pressure on the greens. [3]

In addition, he outlines the way he keeps physically fit the year round.

You will enjoy *The World of Golf.* Get [4] a copy from your local bookstore. It sells for $8. Sincerely yours, [94]

531 Dear Mr. Quinn: Beginning with next Monday's issue, the *Miami Sun* will carry a new department in its [1] main section. This department will be devoted to current news about the state civil service. It will bring our [2] readers a complete list of jobs that are available, public examinations that will be held, and appointments [3] that have been made in the civil service.

We are sure that as a regular reader of our newspaper, you [4] will find this practical service extremely helpful. If you have any suggestions or ideas on how we [5] can increase the usefulness of our newspaper even more, we hope you will let us have them. Very truly yours, [6] [120]

532 Gentlemen: Thank you for the notice you sent me regarding the expiration date of my travel insurance [1] policy.

While I was on the staff of the Public Service Commission of Philadelphia, I needed this [2] policy because of the extensive traveling that I had to do. I have, though, resigned from that position [3] and accepted one with the National Publications Company of Toledo. In this new position I [4] will probably do very little traveling. I have decided, therefore, to let my policy lapse.

If the [5] time should come when I will again have to travel, I will, of course, purchase another policy. Sincerely yours, [6] [120]

533 Dear Mr. Dexter: When Harold Smith founded the Smith Investment Company in 1885, his motto [1] was, "Invest a customer's money as carefully as you would invest your own, perhaps even more carefully." [2] Today that is still our motto. It may be the principal reason why so many of our customers have been [3] with us for 20 or more years. It may be the fundamental reason for our growth from a single office in [4] 1885 to a national organization of 90 offices today.

If you would like to [5] entrust your investments to a company that handles your money as carefully as it handles its own, open [6] an account with us. The addresses of our 90 offices are listed in the enclosed booklet. Sincerely [7] yours, [141]

534 Dear Bill: I have just learned that you are soon to be the vice president in charge of production at Wilson and [1] Company. After all your years of dedication to that company, you have certainly earned your promotion.

You [2] have my best wishes in your new and challenging job. Sincerely yours, [53]

LESSON 54

538 Dear Mr. Billings: A few weeks ago you mentioned to me at the national executive's banquet in Phoenix [1] that you were never happy in your government job as a correspondent and that you wanted to get into [2] a more interesting vocation eventually.

I wonder, Mr. Billings, whether you would be [3] interested in the opening for a sports writer described in the enclosed letter from my friend, James C. Stern, one [4] of the editors of the *Westport Times.* You have the experience, the knowledge, and the creative talent for [5] the job. I suggest you correspond directly with Mr. Stern if the job appeals to you. I am sure he will [6] be glad to give you further information about the job.

You may, of course, use my name as a character [7] reference. Sincerely yours, [144]

539 Mr. Best: Throughout the last five weeks I have had only one objective—to complete our annual furniture [1] catalog by November 15 so that we can have printed copies by Monday, December 5. I am happy [2] to say that despite many interruptions, I easily achieved my objective. I think, Mr. Best, that [3] we will actually have copies of the catalog in our district offices by December 3.

I will, [4] of course, send you a quantity as soon as I receive a supply. Alice Green [94]

540 Dear Mrs. James: This year, Mrs. James, do something novel and different for your vacation. Spend ten days in London [1] seeing historical sites, touring government buildings, shopping in some of the world's finest stores, and seeing [2] entertaining plays in our famous theaters.

Your trip will be carefully planned by International Airlines,[3] one of the world's most experienced airlines. We will pick you up at the airport when you arrive in London, take[4] you to a comfortable residential hotel, and also provide you with tickets to four great shows.

Enjoy[5] a ten-day vacation you will never forget. Fill out the enclosed form and return it to us. We will promptly[6] send you a folder containing complete information. Sincerely yours, [132]

541 Dear Mrs. Long: We think, Mrs. Long, that you will be interested in the experience of Mrs. Mary[1] Grace, of Westport, with a Nelson washing machine. In her letter she writes:

"Our first washer was an inexpensive[2] brand. We wanted to buy a Nelson, but we thought we could not afford it. It broke down after a few years, and we[3] decided to get a Nelson. That was ten years ago. With three children in the family, our Nelson has been[4] averaging 18 to 25 loads a week. But it still works like new."

We cannot guarantee that every[5] Nelson washing machine will equal that record. We can assure you, though, that no one builds a finer washer today[6] than we do.

Make your next washing machine a Nelson. You will never regret it. Sincerely yours, [138]

542 Dear Mr. Ford: I know you will be interested to hear of the excellent returns we received from the short[1] advertisement we inserted in the Monday, October 15, issue of the *Miami Tribune* featuring[2] our modern outdoor furniture. This ad brought us more orders and requests for information than any other[3] ad we have used since we have been in the outdoor furniture business.

I can assure you, Mr. Ford, that[4] we will schedule many more ads in the *Tribune* while I am advertising manager of the Hastings Outdoor[5] Furniture Company. Yours very truly, [108]

543 Dear Mr. Sterns: Thank you sincerely for your order of Monday, April 6, for a quantity of Interboro[1] sporting goods. Unfortunately, we cannot ship your order on open account because our credit information[2] on your company is incomplete.

As time is short, Mr. Sterns, may we suggest that you mail us your advance[3] check for $380. As soon as we receive it, we will ship your order. We will, of course, make[4] further credit investigations in the hope that we can offer you our regular terms on future orders.[5] Sincerely yours, [103]

544 Dear Mr. and Mrs. Blair: We have just learned from Mr. A. C. Smith, one of our leading real estate brokers, that[1] you will soon move to Plainfield. We are confident that you will enjoy the many recreational opportunities[2] it has to offer.

We at the Wilson Construction Company wish to extend to you a very special welcome[3] in two ways:

1. By giving you our newcomers' gift certificate that entitles you to $10 worth[4] of our merchandise. It is enclosed.

2. By inviting you to let us tell you about our home counseling service.[5]

We are ready to help you, whatever your household needs may be.

Stop in to see us when you arrive in Plainfield.[6] We are located at 115 West Street. Yours very truly, [133]

545 Dear Charles: Thank you for the copy of your executive's handbook. I will use it as a model for the executive's[1] handbook we are planning for our own people.

I will, of course, give your company credit whenever I[2] quote from your handbook.

I hope, Charles, that I may soon have an opportunity to reciprocate your kindness. Yours[3] very truly, [63]

LESSON 55

549 Dear Ms. Banks: If you like salesmanship and would like to improve yourself significantly by transferring to[1] another line of employment, why not consider the possibility of becoming a broker with the[2] Empire Securities Company. Your progress with us and your earnings will be limited only by your[3] aptitude, your ability, and your energy. We are one of the most respected brokerage houses in the [4] world.

If you are selected, you will receive training in every phase of the investment area for a [5] period of six months. You will receive a substantial salary while you are learning, Ms. Banks. You will find the work [6] enjoyable, stimulating, and exceedingly interesting.

If you want more information, fill out the [7] enclosed data sheet, attach your photograph, and mail both to us. Sincerely yours, [154]

550 Dear Mr. Quinn: The Smith calculator is small. Consequently, you can easily take it with you whenever [1] you travel.

On the Smith, you will be able to do rapid calculations on all types of statistical work. [2] It is exceedingly simple to operate. It requires no special aptitude to use it.

The Smith calculator [3] is a great technical achievement. We invite you to check it for quality, dependability, [4] and durability against substantially higher-priced calculators. When you purchase a Smith, it will pay [5] for itself in a short time.

For full information about the Smith calculator, fill out and return the enclosed [6] card. We will send it to you promptly. Sincerely yours, [130]

551 Dear Mr. Myers: As you know, ever since you inherited 100 shares of the stock of the Empire Steamship [1] Company two years ago, your dividend checks have been mailed to us. We, in turn, have been transmitting them to [2] you.

I think it would be easier, Mr. Myers, if you would give us authority to transfer title to [3] these securities to your name. The dividends would then be mailed direct to you by the Empire Steamship Company, [4] thus saving several days in transmittal time.

Stop in at your convenience and sign a simple form [5] consisting of two or three paragraphs. It will require only a few minutes to dispose of the whole transaction. [6] Sincerely yours, [123]

552 Dear Fred: You will recall that on your last visit to Memphis, I told you that there was an exceedingly strong [1] possibility that I would have to transfer to Westport to take over our securities department there. That [2] possibility is now a reality. Our manager in Westport submitted his resignation for [3] reasons that the president will undoubtedly explain to you himself when he visits Westport next week.

You will [4] also recall that you promised to help me find a house in the event I had to transfer to Westport.

Helen [5] and I will be house-hunting on June 18, 19, and 20. If you could line up some houses for us to look [6] at, you will have my gratitude. You know the type of house that would be ideal for us.

We will consider it [7] a privilege if you and Mary would have dinner with us on Friday, June 19. Sincerely yours, [158]

553 Dear Mr. Samuels: The wise thing to do when you are buying or selling a house is to see a competent [1] and reliable real estate broker. Real estate brokers can save you time, effort, and money. They know [2] the market. They know who the best prospects are. They know real estate procedure and can be helpful to you with [3] the perplexing details that enter into a real estate transaction. It is smart to have them on your side [4] when you buy or sell property.

To find a broker in your locality, check the listings contained in the [5] classified pages of the *Daily Times* every day. Real estate brokers run far more advertising in the *Daily* [6] *Times* than they do in any other newspaper in this area. Very truly yours, [137]

554 Dear Mr. Billings: We have not yet selected a speaker for your annual meeting. May I suggest that you [1] invite Dr. James Davis, our dean of faculty. He is a dynamic as well as interesting speaker. [2]

You can reach Dr. Davis at 415-1177 any weekday morning after 10 o'clock. [3] Sincerely yours, [63]

LESSON 56

558 Dear Mr. Wilmington: As you will no doubt

agree, washing dishes is a tedious, unrewarding chore. No[1] adult actually enjoys washing dishes. This chore can be disposed of quickly, however, if you have a[2] Superior electric dishwasher in your kitchen. The Superior electric dishwasher can be installed[3] easily because it is portable. It is 3 feet deep, 3 feet wide, 4 feet high, and it weighs only[4] 120 pounds.

How much does it cost? It costs from $200 to $500, depending on[5] the model you want.

See our various models. They are on display in our showrooms in the Transportation Building.[6] Sincerely yours, [124]

559 Dear Mr. Long: A few days ago I read in our local newspaper, the *Wilmington Times,* that you have been[1] promoted to the position of supervising editor of *Electronic News.* Your promotion was obviously[2] the result of the superb job you did as supervisor of circulation during the past six years.[3] The promotion should be a source of gratification and self-satisfaction to you. You have reason to be[4] proud of yourself. I am confident, Mr. Long, that you will do a superior job.

If my present plans work[5] out, I will be in Louisville on August 15, 16, and 17 to take part in a program on[6] neighborhood planning that will be held in the Chamber of Commerce Building. When I arrive in Louisville, I will call[7] you with the hope that it will be convenient for you to have lunch with me on one of those days.

I look forward[8] to the pleasure of seeing you again and of congratulating you in person. Sincerely yours, [178]

560 Dear Mr. Cunningham: I have completed my formal review of the manuscript for a self-teaching course in[1] electronics by Charles Sweet. He has produced an interesting, worthwhile program. It has great potential. Under[2] the circumstances, it is my recommendation that you publish it.

There are two chapters, however, that need[3] substantial clarification and one that contains misstatements that should ultimately be corrected. I have[4] made notes in the margins of those chapters suggesting how some of the sentences might be revised.

I am returning[5] the manuscript to you today, and you should have it soon.

Thank you for the opportunity to make this review.[6] I look forward to the possibility of making other reviews for you.

My bill for $500[7] is enclosed. Sincerely yours, [146]

561 Gentlemen: Our client, Frank H. Washington, does not deny that he was partly[1] responsible for the collision between his car and your client's taxi at 8 p.m. on Friday, January[2] 15, in the neighborhood of West Third and Albany Streets. However, the fact that your client was driving[3] without lights contributed to the result.

It is our firm belief that no jury would award your client[4] the $20,000 he is suing for. In view of the circumstances, we are willing to settle for[5] $300. Very truly yours, [107]

562 Dear Dr. Billings: This morning I read in the *Wilmington Times* that you were elected superintendent of[1] schools. That is indeed wonderful news for both the children and the adults of Wilmington.

Everyone is, of course,[2] familiar with the worthwhile self-improvement programs you started when you were assistant superintendent.[3] We all look forward to an extension of these exceedingly practical programs in the future under your[4] leadership.

I hope, Dr. Billings, that you will never hesitate to call on me when I can be of assistance[5] to you in my capacity as president of the Citizens Council. Sincerely yours, [117]

563 Dear Mr. Harrington: Your check for $500 to take care of your June, July, and August balances[1] arrived this morning. To say that I was delighted to receive it would be an understatement.

We appreciate[2] your cooperation in devising a payment program that met our requirements without ultimately[3] placing an impossible burden on your finances. May we offer you our congratulations, too, on[4] overcoming the trying circumstances that made things so difficult for you during the past six months.

We look forward [5] to serving you again when you need electrical appliances. Very truly yours, [117]

564 Dear Mr. Harrington: A few days ago we completed work on a new jet airplane engine that does not emit [1] any smoke. We invested $10 million in the creation of this engine as part of our effort [2] to reduce air pollution.

The engineers in our organization are using all their skills and [3] imagination to make air travel cleaner, quieter, and more efficient. It is a big job and a costly one. [4]

No doubt you are wondering where the money will come from to pay for all this. The answer depends on earnings. Yet [5] consider this fact: In only one year in the last ten have the major airlines earned what the government calls a [6] fair and reasonable return. In most years they have not even come close to that mark.

How can you help the airlines give you [7] the type of service you want? You can help by understanding the challenges and problems that they face.

For [8] facts about the airline industry, send for our booklet, *The Future of the Airlines.* We will be glad to send it [9] to you, Mr. Harrington, if you will fill out and mail the enclosed card. Cordially yours, [196]

565 Dear Fred: Helen and I would very much like to have you as a guest at our cottage at Sunshine Lake during the [1] weekend of July 18. If you are free at that time, you can take the 4 p.m. train out of Chicago on [2] Friday and arrive in Sunshine Lake at 6 p.m.

Mary and her father will also be on that train.

I hope [3] you can come, Fred. It will be good to see you again. Sincerely yours, [73]

CHAPTER 10

LESSON 57

568 Dear Mr. Short: If anything were to happen to your wife, could you take care of the children? Could you work throughout [1] the week and at the same time give them the ordinary attention they require? If something should ever happen [2] to you, do you think your family could go on living the way you wish them to live?

You can make sure that they are [3] satisfactorily provided for if you have a State General life policy, which is briefly described [4] on the enclosed circular. This policy is issued by one of the most successful, progressive insurance [5] organizations in the world.

We suggest that you invite one of our responsible, experienced [6] representatives to discuss your particular insurance needs with you. Simply tell us on the enclosed card what day [7] and what hour will be suitable. When you request an agent to call, his visit places you under no obligation. [8] Therefore, why not take this important step regarding your future soon, Mr. Short. Sincerely yours, [177]

569 Dear Ms. Underwood: For several years we have been sending our magazine, *Publishing Opportunities,* without [1] charge each month to executives in the book manufacturing and publishing businesses.

Because of the [2] very sizable increases in the price of paper, printing, and other regular publication costs, we [3] decided at this morning's meeting of our company's executives to charge for *Publishing Opportunities,* [4] effective immediately, in order to help defray a part of our costs. We will also accept [5] advertising for the first time.

We hope, Ms. Underwood, that you have been well served by our magazine over the years [6] and that you obtained many valuable and profitable ideas from it. We hope, too, that you will take [7] advantage of the enclosed order form and envelope to send us your subscription. Very truly yours, [158]

570 Dear Mrs. Yale: Income tax time is about a month away. If you feel you are going to have difficulty [1] paying your taxes to the government, come to the State National Bank on West Street, where you can get a special [2] loan. After we receive your application, we work quickly. That is our usual way of handling every [3] loan, and that is one of the reasons why we have won so many friends and have made more than twice as many loans as [4] any other bank in the city.

And while we are speaking on the subject of taxes, why not have yours done by [5] a recognized expert. There are six of them on our staff. They will answer your questions willingly and prepare your [6] return for a reasonable fee.

In my opinion, Mrs. Yale, you will find our services satisfying [7] and well worthwhile. Sincerely yours, [147]

571 Gentlemen: This letter acknowledges receipt of the quantity of business correspondence tests you mailed us. [1] They arrived Tuesday morning, August 11.

It was a matter of considerable importance to us [2] to have these objective tests this week because I must administer them next Friday to about ten candidates [3] who are applying for positions with our organization.

Thank you for such prompt service. Sincerely yours, [79]

572 Dear Mr. Green: New York State leads the country in the number of manufacturing plants, in the production of [1] manufactured goods, and in the number of people engaged in manufacturing.

Since 1850 the [2] National Bank and Trust Company has been an important part of this impressive picture. Today we reach more than [3] 200 cities and towns with our 300 offices. We are the country's twelfth largest banking system. We [4] know New York State. It follows then that we are also the bank that knows how to serve manufacturers.

If you do [5] business in New York State, take advantage of our long experience in the state.

Our executives are ready [6] to serve you. Sincerely yours, [125]

573 Dear Mrs. Underwood: Our general sales manager gave me some news this morning that I was unhappy to [1] hear. He informed me that you have not used your charge account with us for several months.

Have you been dissatisfied [2] with our goods, our services, or our prices? If you have, please give us an opportunity to regain your friendship. [3] We value it greatly.

A stamped, self-addressed envelope is enclosed for your convenience in telling us [4] why you have not used your account. Sincerely yours, [89]

574 Dear Ms. Harvey: Thank you for your order for six of our No. 18 tennis rackets. These rackets will be shipped [1] shortly from our Chicago warehouse.

We are enclosing a copy of our latest tennis catalog. We think [2] you will be pleased with the low prices of our tennis equipment. An order blank is enclosed with the catalog. [3] Yours very truly, [64]

575 Dear Dr. Smith: As you have probably read in yesterday's newspaper, Jim Grant was named public relations [1] director of the publications division of our organization. We never had a director before, [2] but we have long needed a person of Jim's character, forcefulness, and drive to look after our public relations. [3]

We are planning a little party for Jim on November 20 from 5 to 6 o'clock to which you are [4] invited.

I am taking Jim and his wife to dinner after the party. If it is possible for you to [5] join us, would you be good enough to fill out and return the enclosed card to our corresponding secretary [6] so that we will know how many people to plan for. Cordially yours, [133]

576 Mr. James: This is just a note to thank you for taking such good care of me on my visit to New York last week. [1] Thank you also for the delightful dinner at your beautiful home. I thoroughly enjoyed meeting your family [2] and spending a little time with them.

I thought the sales meeting was very much worthwhile. I was impressed with the [3] new people who joined our staff during the past year. Charles C. Brown [71]

577 Dear Mr. Grace: Many companies face an ecological problem today. They have to meet an increased demand [1] for goods and services with less energy and without polluting the environment. We are helping these [2] companies meet this problem.

Our pollution-control division has applied sound engineering principles to [3] all types of pollution and has come up with solutions that are in strict compliance with government regulations. [4] In some cases the pollution-control systems we have installed have actually enabled companies [5] to recover valuable by-products which more than paid for the installations.

Are you contemplating building [6] new plants or factories in the future?

If you are, give us an opportunity to work with you. Cordially [7] yours, [141]

LESSON 58

580 Dear Mr. Grace: The coming Christmas season should be one of the most profitable in years for retailers.

No [1] doubt you will soon be placing your orders for Christmas goods and, of course, we want to be in a position to fill [2] them promptly. We may not be able to do so, however, if your account is not up to date.

May I suggest [3] that you send us a check for $800 as soon as possible. As you know, that is the amount you owe [4] us for the goods you purchased three months ago. In that way we will be able to make delivery of your orders [5] without any credit complications.

Enclosed is a stamped, self-addressed envelope. I hope you will use it to [6] mail your check to us. Very truly yours, [127]

581 Dear Mrs. Wilson: Here is one of the most convenient methods yet devised for placing your orders for books [1] you want to read and own. When you decide you want to buy a book, call 115-1118. Your order will [2] be taken by one of our courteous clerks, and it will be shipped within two or three days. On each book you buy you [3] will be able to make a saving of more than 40 percent over the price you would have to pay in a [4] commercial bookstore.

If you wish, you can pay for your books by personal check or charge them on your credit card.

So the [5] next time you want a book in a hurry, let us serve you. Call us at any time of the day or night. Sincerely [6] yours, [121]

582 Dear Mr. Temple: If you have just moved into Fairfield County and don't know which bank to use, let us help you decide. [1]

If you want a bank that has an office near your home or job, the chances are that the State National Bank is [2] the one for you. We have more than 50 offices in the county.

If you want a bank whose policies and [3] services are geared to today and tomorrow, it can only be the State National.

If you would like to entrust [4] your banking affairs to a large, successful, and experienced bank, the State National, one of the world's largest, [5] is the bank for you.

Come in soon, Mr. Temple, and let me tell you all about us. Sincerely yours, [118]

583 Dear Mr. Jones: Thank you very much for your letter of several days ago asking about the facilities [1] of the Benson Hotel and expressing your interest in spending two or three weeks with us.

In a few days [2] we will receive from the printer a new brochure describing our facilities in detail. When I receive a [3] supply, I will send a copy to you.

I hope, Mr. Jones, that you will be able to spend some time with us in [4] the future. I know that we will be able to make your stay enjoyable, interesting, and refreshing. [5] Sincerely yours, [102]

584 Dear Mr. Phillips: The booklet you requested several days ago describing our kitchen equipment was [1] mailed to you a day or two ago. You have no doubt received and read it by this time. We hope that it answered many [2] of the questions you may have had about our equipment.

Early in February one of our representatives, [3] Ms. Alice Meade, will be in Chicago for a few days. She is in a position to help you plan your kitchen [4] and show you how to use our equipment to the best advantage.

As soon as Ms. Meade arrives in Chicago, [5] she will call you for an appointment.

If we can supply you with any other information before Ms. Meade[6] calls, please let us know. We want to serve you in any way we can. Sincerely yours, [134]

585 Dear Mr. Benson: Thank you very much for your order of December 22. We were especially happy[1] to have it because it is the first time that you have dealt with us.

It is our practice—and we are sure it is[2] yours as well—to ask a new customer for routine credit information. Will you please be good enough to fill[3] out and return the enclosed form. You may be sure that all information you give us will be kept in strict confidence.[4]

A stamped, self-addressed envelope is enclosed for your convenience in returning the form. Yours very truly,[5] [101]

586 Dear Mr. Lee: On Monday, January 12, we will issue a special National Boat Show booklet. The purpose[1] of this booklet is to help you and others in the boating business reach excellent prospects at a time when[2] their interest is at a high point. This is the time that they will be shopping for new models, boating equipment,[3] and new boating accessories.

This Boat Show booklet will reach more than 2 million readers.

Plan to reach these people[4] with your advertising in our Boat Show booklet. Cordially yours, [93]

LESSON 59

589 To Our Passengers: Many of you, unfortunately, were delayed on your trip home on Friday, July 23.[1] The delay was caused by a failure in our Albany power plant. One of our boilers broke down yesterday,[2] and despite the intensive efforts of our employees, it could not be repaired in time to handle the evening[3] rush hours. Power was not restored until 7 p.m.

Our improvement program is making substantial, encouraging[4] progress. If all goes well, we should be able to close our existing plant and purchase commercial power[5] on or before January 1. When this conversion is completed, we will be able to eliminate[6] completely all delays resulting from power failure.

We apologize for any personal inconvenience[7] you may have been caused on July 23. The Central Railroad [153]

590 Dear Ms. Brown: Recently I discovered a copy of the research report, *The Future of the Furniture Market,*[1] in our library. I understand that this report was prepared by your concern for the United Furniture[2] Manufacturers Association. I think it is excellent, and I thoroughly enjoyed reading it.[3]

I would like to have a copy of my own to share with some of my colleagues in the advertising department.[4] May I have one? I would be delighted to pay for it, Ms. Brown, if you will let me know the cost. Sincerely yours,[5] [100]

591 Dear Mr. Blair: We are delighted that you enjoyed reading our special research report, *The Future of the*[1] *Furniture Market.* Unfortunately, our initial supply has been completely exhausted. I will, however,[2] have a reproduction made from my personal copy, and I will mail it to you before the end of the week.[3] Please accept it with my compliments.

If we can be of assistance to you in formulating your own advertising,[4] promotion, or distribution plans, please do not hesitate to call on us. Sincerely yours, [98]

592 Dear Mr. Harper: We have received replies from all of the organizations to which you referred us for credit[1] information about your concern, and we are pleased to report that without exception they had nothing but[2] praise for your methods of conducting your business. Please accept our sincere congratulations on your impressive[3] credit rating. We have shipped your Order 1166 by Empire Express and you should receive the furniture[4] by Friday, December 12.

We are confident that you will enjoy doing business with us. We will certainly[5] do everything we can to deserve your business. Sincerely yours, [112]

593 Dear Mr. Dwight: I ran into Jim Smith yesterday on the Suburban subway, and he gave me the distressing [1] news that you had been involved in an accident in which you suffered some internal injuries. He assured me, [2] however, that you were improving rapidly and would leave the hospital in perhaps a week or ten days.

As [3] you know, I own a cabin on Lake George. After you are discharged, why not plan to spend a few days with me there. It [4] is an extremely delightful place to convalesce. We have a comfortable guest room, and I would enjoy your [5] company. How about it? Sincerely yours, [108]

594 Dear Mr. Minor: We were sorry to learn of the inconvenience you were caused on November 15 by [1] the late departure of Flight 116 from Washington to Albany. Unfortunately, the equipment on [2] Flight 116 had engine trouble, and it was necessary to replace it with a plane that had to be flown [3] in from New York. This, of course, resulted in a delay of about two hours.

We do our best to maintain our [4] equipment in perfect condition, but occasionally we encounter problems that are beyond our control. We [5] are exceedingly sorry that you incurred additional expense in the amount of $15 in order [6] to reach your destination. A check for $15 is enclosed.

We are confident, Mr. Minor, that [7] on your next flight with us you will enjoy our usual efficient service. Sincerely yours, [156]

595 Dear Customer: If you have been wondering what the heating oil prospects are for the coming winter, we have an [1] encouraging report for you. We expect to go into the winter season with full tanks of heating oil that [2] should enable us to meet our customers' needs this winter.

Here is what we are doing now to keep homes and [3] offices warm this winter:

1. We are making more heating oil. We have been making and storing heating oil all summer, [4] but now we are increasing our production.

2. We are importing heating oil. These imports provide about [5] 10 percent of our supplies through the winter.

You can depend on us to keep you warm this coming winter. Your Gas [6] Company [122]

LESSON 60

598 Dear Mr. Stern: After 75 years as one of the nation's most reputable tailors, we find ourselves [1] heavily in debt and in need of urgent financial assistance.

We had a meeting with our creditors last [2] week, and we made an arrangement with them that enables us to reduce our debts considerably. This arrangement [3] makes it possible for us to mark down our clothing for quick sale.

If you come to the Nashville Men's Shop between [4] December 10 and December 14, you will be able to obtain ready-made suits for $50 to [5] $75, sports coats for as little as $30, and leather jackets for only [6] $22.50.

Don't deny yourself this wonderful opportunity to replenish your wardrobe for the [7] future, Mr. Stern, and to make a considerable saving at the same time. Cordially yours, [157]

599 Dear Mrs. Baker: As you know, summer is just a few weeks away. If this coming summer is a repetition [1] of last summer, we can expect warm, humid, and uncomfortable days and nights. When you have an efficient, [2] dependable Johnson portable air conditioner in your house, that won't bother you, Mrs. Baker.

A [3] portable air-conditioning unit will maintain your house at an even temperature all day and all night. A [4] portable air conditioner is not expensive. Depending on the kind you choose, it will actually cost you [5] between $200 and $300.

Treat yourself and your family to a delightful summer. [6] Determine today to install a Johnson portable air-conditioning unit in your house. Sincerely yours, [7] [140]

600 Dear Mr. Swan: What do taxes and cars have in common? Just this, Mr. Swan: It is possible to pay for both [1] with low-cost, easy repayment loans from our credit union.

To pay your income taxes, you can readily obtain [2] a loan on your signature in 24 hours or less. In 48 hours or less you can obtain a [3] 36-month car loan.

Only through your credit union do you actually have painless repayment through payroll [4] deductions.

If you need a loan to take care of your taxes, to buy a car, or to purchase some other worthwhile, [5] useful item, avail yourself of our services. Yours very truly, [113]

601 Dear Mr. Day: I read in yesterday's *Jacksonville Times* that you and your brother will open an office [1] furniture and equipment store on Eastern Avenue.

We have heard, of course, of the enviable reputation your [2] organization enjoys in the furniture and office equipment industry. Consequently, it is [3] possible for us to offer you very favorable credit terms.

Whenever you need any of the leather [4] products we manufacture, please call on us. Your orders will be filled speedily, carefully, and efficiently. [5]

When you are actually settled in your new store, I will call on you and welcome you personally to our [6] delightful city. Sincerely yours, [127]

602 Dear Ms. Thomas: Thank you for your letter regarding the bank statement that reached you in an unsealed envelope. We [1] pride ourselves on taking every precaution to keep our depositors' financial affairs completely confidential. [2] We are grateful to you for calling this matter to our attention.

We are taking steps, Ms. Thomas, to [3] see that all your future statements arrive in a sealed envelope.

The next time you have business that necessitates [4] your personal visit to the Mutual Trust Company, please stop in to see me. My office is on the second [5] floor. Sincerely yours, [104]

603 Dear Ms. Samuels: Wouldn't you like to dispose of your Christmas shopping easily, quickly, and with a [1] minimum of bother? Then give your friends yearly subscriptions to *The National Sports Magazine,* one of the most [2] popular magazines on the market today. Take a few moments now, Ms. Samuels, to list on the enclosed form [3] the names of your friends to whom you wish to send subscriptions and mail the form in the envelope that is also enclosed. [4]

The January issue will contain a beautiful card telling your friend that he or she will receive *The* [5] *National Sports Magazine* with your compliments for a full year.

Do this today. Save yourself considerable [6] time and bother. Sincerely yours, [126]

604 Dear Mr. Davis: If you would like to stretch the purchasing power of your money, be sure to get a copy [1] of our new book, *Increasing Your Purchasing Power.* This book is full of money-saving recommendations. It [2] will tell you, for example, how to:

1. Save money on food.
2. Save on gas, oil, and automobile upkeep.
3. [3] Buy life insurance wisely.
4. Get the best possible buys in clothing for your family.
5. Obtain maximum [4] interest on your savings.

Increasing Your Purchasing Power sells for only $8. Get a copy [5] from your local bookstore. Or if you prefer, order a copy by filling out and mailing the enclosed order [6] form. You will be making an investment that may save you hundreds of dollars during the course of the year. Very [7] truly yours, [142]

605 To the Staff: Do you need money to take a vacation, to buy a new car, or to send a son or a daughter [1] to college? Then consult your friendly credit union. It stands ready to serve all members of our organization. [2]

The rates are good and the service is fast. For example, a $500 loan for 12 months will cost you [3] only $44.60 per month.

If you need financial help, call Miss Green on Extension 2415 [4] or drop in at the credit union office on the ninth floor. A. C. Bates [94]

LESSON 61

608 Dear Mr. Underwood: Our representative,

Ms. Overmeyer, wrote us recently that you have written a [1] self-improvement course for supervisory personnel and that you are interested in having us publish [2] it. We are always interested in reviewing new prospects in the area in which we publish.

If you [3] would care to send me a copy of your self-improvement course, I will transmit it to the supervisor of our [4] editorial department, Mrs. West. She will study it and decide whether we can publish it with profit [5] to you as the author and to us as publishers.

Thank you for giving us an opportunity to consider [6] your self-improvement course for supervisory personnel. Sincerely yours, [134]

609 To the Staff: On Friday, June 15, the management board of the National Electric Company adopted [1] a new moving policy.

When circumstances make it desirable in the best interests of company [2] efficiency to transfer a supervisor from one city to another, we will pay all costs involved in [3] packing, insuring, and transporting the supervisor's family and furniture and household effects.

As I [4] am sure we will all agree, no employee should suffer financial hardship as a result of a transfer that [5] is made in the best interests of our organization. A. H. Overman [114]

610 Dear Mrs. Washington: Intercontinental Airlines has just introduced a brand-new entertainment package [1] on our LC 14 flights.

In the first-class section we have added a lounge and a buffet. In the coach section [2] we have added new electronic games for your enjoyment. On our LC 14 you will like the convenience [3] and efficiency of overhead storage and our free stereo entertainment.

We would like you to have [4] a good look at all the services and features that we now offer on the LC 14. We have, therefore, prepared [5] the enclosed eight-page brochure that we know you will find interesting.

Please read it. Better still, fly on our [6] LC 14 the next time you have occasion to go to one of the cities that we serve. Cordially yours, [138]

611 Dear Mr. Overmeyer: We appreciate your telling us of the report you are making on the advantages [1] of electric typewriters over manual machines. As you know, since 1940 we have been [2] manufacturing the Interboro electric typewriter, the leading electric machine on the market. Under [3] the circumstances, we are interested in everything pertaining to the field of electric typewriting. [4]

You will find enclosed a booklet that describes the experiences of superior teachers who have used [5] our electric typewriter for teaching beginning typing and transcription.

We hope, Mr. Overmeyer, that [6] this booklet will provide you with all you need for your report. Sincerely yours, [134]

612 Dear Mr. Baker: Have you ever been passed up for a supervisory job even though you were better [1] qualified for it than the person who actually received it? Many people have had this frustrating experience [2] and often the reason for being passed up was an inability to get across their ideas [3] to their superiors.

This is where the Harris Self-Development Course can help. It teaches you how to organize [4] ideas and present them with self-confidence and self-assurance to your superiors or to groups of [5] people. What is more, it makes you a more interesting, more entertaining person.

If you will return the enclosed [6] card, we will send you an introductory lesson without charge. Return the card now. You have everything to [7] gain and nothing to lose. Yours very truly, [148]

613 Dear Mrs. West: One of my most distasteful duties is to transfer a customer's account to a collection [1] agency, but that is what I will have to do with your account unless I receive your check for $500 [2] by July 5. This will make us unhappy because we will probably lose your business. It will make you [3] unhappy because your credit standing will suffer.

Under the circumstances, Mrs. West, isn't it in your best [4] interest to send us your check for $500 without delay? You know that it is! Sincerely yours, [99]

614 Dear Mr. Overman: I was interested to learn that Miss Mary Underwood has asked for an interview [1] with you regarding a position with the National Electric Typewriter Company.

I do not know her [2] very well, but her supervisor tells me that she is a superior employee with a great deal of [3] self-assurance and self-confidence. However, she is not happy in her job because she is working in an [4] area in which she has no training—electronics. She majored in college in transportation, but we have no [5] openings in that area for her. Under the circumstances, she has decided to look elsewhere for a [6] position.

We will be sorry to lose her and wish her well. Sincerely yours, [134]

615 Dear Miss Underwood: Today I have sent you a print of our film, *The Power of Electricity.* This is a [1] 30-minute interesting and entertaining film prepared under the supervision of our public [2] relations department.

The purpose of this film is to make children aware of the importance of the role that [3] electricity plays in our everyday living.

I hope, Miss Underwood, that you will review *The Power of* [4] *Electricity* and let us have your reaction to it by filling out and returning the self-addressed card that [5] is enclosed with the film. Sincerely yours, [107]

616 Dear Mrs. Clay: As we reach the close of the year, I wish to take this opportunity to offer you my sincere [1] thanks and appreciation for the frequent use you have made of the services and facilities of [2] Intercontinental Airlines. As our New York area representative, I am proud to have you as a friend [3] of our airline.

On behalf of our entire organization, Mrs. Clay, may I wish you a delightful [4] holiday season. Sincerely yours, [86]

617 Dear Mrs. Brown: When the James Supermarket started out as a little dairy about 70 years ago, [1] butter was our specialty. We sold only the finest butter.

Though we have grown into a major food [2] store, we are still as fussy about the quality of our butter now as we were then.

We know you will enjoy our butter. [3] So get a supply the next time you visit the James Supermarket. Yours very truly, [77]

LESSON 62

620 Dear Miss Cunningham: For some time we have been having complaints from the employees in our circulation and [1] correspondence departments that the poor lighting in their offices is causing them discomfort and hardship. We have [2] had our neighborhood electrician, John Smith, make a study of our lighting facilities. His findings have confirmed [3] that the complaints are justified, and he has made several logical, practical recommendations to [4] eliminate a majority of them.

Accordingly, we would like to carry out his recommendations. [5] To avoid any misunderstandings, however, we would like your permission before we proceed with the work. [6]

We have been working on the plans and specifications for several days, and they're now ready, Miss Cunningham. [7] When you are ready to study them, I will be glad to forward them to you. Yours very truly, [157]

621 Dear Mr. Billings: Water is one of the things that made it possible for us to be on earth. We cannot exist [1] without it, nor can any animal or vegetable.

To say that it is exceedingly important [2] for us to clean up the waters of the earth is true enough, but the whole truth is that we have no choice if we want [3] to survive.

As you will learn by reading the enclosed booklet, making chemicals and specialized equipment for [4] water purification is our business. If you have a water purification problem in your plant, let [5] one of our engineers suggest a practical program to solve it. To arrange an appointment, simply indicate [6] on the enclosed card when one of our engineers may call.

Sincerely yours, [134]

622 Dear Ms. Washington: Do you feel that your present investment program is the best for you? If you do, don't bother [1] to read any further. But if you are not sure and would like to have an impartial, technically competent [2] member of our staff study your security holdings and give you an unbiased opinion of them, this [3] service is yours at no cost.

Come in any time between 9 a.m. and 4 p.m. from Monday through Friday. No [4] advance appointment is necessary. We will assign one of our experts to review your securities and [5] make whatever recommendations are appropriate. Sincerely yours, [113]

623 Dear Dr. Wellington: It is a genuine pleasure for me, Dr. Wellington, to congratulate you on [1] your appointment as dean of faculty in the School of Business of Billings University. You richly deserve [2] this appointment on the basis of your technical qualifications as well as your leadership in [3] developing forward-looking programs in the fields of data processing, accounting, and marketing.

I will be [4] in Washington on Friday, November 18. While I am there, I will offer you my sincere congratulations [5] in person. Yours very truly, [107]

624 Dear Mr. Billings: I wish with all sincerity to thank you and your staff for the outstanding job you did over [1] the past weekend in repairing the critical damage to our facilities that resulted from an [2] unexplained fire in our Buckingham plant. Your staff willingly worked around the clock and did not stop until the job was [3] completed.

This was typical of your organization's tradition of providing the finest service [4] possible.

Congratulations, Mr. Billings, on a job well done. Sincerely yours, [94]

625 Dear Mr. Wilmington: The two copies of the contract you forwarded to me covering your sponsorship of [1] a program on our television station on Friday, December 12, between 8 and 9 p.m. arrived in [2] this morning's mail.

I regret, Mr. Wilmington, that because of circumstances beyond our control, our facilities [3] will not be available during that hour.

We have just received notification that at 8 p.m. [4] on December 12 the President will address the nation on the present critical problems in the Near East. [5] We will, of course, carry his message.

Mrs. Jennings, our circulation manager, will be in your neighborhood on [6] December 18. I have asked her to call on you to discuss the possibility of your sponsorship of [7] another program in the near future. Sincerely yours, [150]

626 Dear Mr. Washington: Congratulations on your decision to open a savings account in the branch of [1] the Chemical Savings Bank in your neighborhood.

It has been our experience, Mr. Washington, that a [2] majority of the people who open savings accounts with Chemical are not aware of the other exceedingly [3] practical and useful services we offer our depositors. We have, therefore, prepared the enclosed [4] booklet that describes the classifications of services that you may wish to use some day.

We look forward to [5] many opportunities to serve your banking needs in the days ahead. Yours very truly, [117]

627 Dear Mr. Tarkington: May we ask a favor of you? We have prepared a 64-page booklet about [1] detergents. Naturally, we describe our own high-quality products in it, but in addition we have included [2] a great deal of information that will be of value to anyone who has the responsibility [3] of keeping a plant clean regardless of the detergents used.

Since the booklet is of value and interest [4] primarily to people with this responsibility, we want to be sure that the proper person gets our booklet. [5] Would you be good enough to supply us with the name of that person in your company? Simply jot it down [6] on the self-addressed card that is enclosed and mail it.

I assure you, Mr. Tarkington, that no sales representative [7] from our organization will call on that person. We sell all our products only through authorized dealers. [8]

Thank you for your cooperation. Cordially yours, [170]

LESSON 63

630 *Tons of Food*

A human being who lives to be 70 years old consumes a great amount of food. He eats 1,400 [1] times his body weight or over 200,000 pounds of material.

The amount of food that he will [2] eat includes 6,000 loaves of bread, 7 cows, 4 sheep, and 300 chickens. The amount of fish he will take [3] in includes 2,000 large fish and 3,000 sardines, flounders, and herring.

He will eat in the neighborhood of [4] about 9,000 pounds of potatoes, 12,000 pounds of other vegetables, and 14,000 pounds of [5] fruit.

He will drink 6,000 quarts of milk, 12,000 quarts of coffee, and 10,000 quarts of water.

In addition, [6] he will consume 1,000 pounds of salt, 5,000 eggs, 8,000 pounds of sugar, and about 2,000 [7] pounds of cheese. [144]—Your Health

631 Dear Harry: Yesterday, November 10, we processed your order for 15 typewriters. The machines should be in [1] your office in a few days.

I wonder whether you realize that November 10 marks the tenth anniversary [2] of the initial order you sent us. As I recall, you purchased two adding machines, and the order [3] amounted to $300 or $400. In that decade, you have placed orders with us amounting [4] to between $50,000 and $60,000.

I assure you, Harry, that it has been a pleasure [5] doing business with you. You may be sure that I will do all I can to see that our pleasant, profitable [6] relationship continues for many years to come. Thanks for everything. Sincerely yours, [136]

632 Dear Mr. Jacobs: I have some very good news for you and the others who have been working on the Fairfield County [1] United Fund Drive. The drive is an unquestioned success.

Our latest count indicates that on June 15 we [2] were already about 20 percent ahead of our goal of $200,000. The actual amount [3] that has been collected and pledged is $242,000. What is more, we can still count on another [4] $10,000 or $12,000 before we close our books.

When you consider the following two [5] circumstances, this is an unprecedented achievement:

1. Our budget was more than 10 percent higher than [6] last year's.
2. The economy has been depressed and uncertain.

Congratulations, Mr. Jacobs, on a job [7] well done. Sincerely yours, [144]

633 Dear Mr. Newton: If you like unusual statistics, here are some about credit cards that will amaze you. [1]

1. Over 120 million people have credit cards issued by retail stores.
2. Over 90 million [2] people have credit cards issued by oil companies.
3. Over 55 million people have bank credit [3] cards.
4. Over 2 million people have air-travel cards.

You can now charge just about everything with a credit [4] card.

We hope, Mr. Newton, that you will like the new charge card you will shortly receive from the Wilson Men's Shop. We [5] hope, too, that you will like the simplified monthly statement that we have devised. When you receive your card, be sure to [6] sign it. Cordially yours, [125]

634 Dear Mr. House: I wonder whether you would be kind enough to do me a favor. It won't take you long to grant [1] it.

For some time you have been using Temple file folders, and I have reason to believe that you are happy with [2] them. If that is the case, please answer the few questions about Temple file folders listed on the enclosed questionnaire. [3] Your answers will be helpful in planning a new line of folders that we hope to place on the market next year. [4]

I am confident, Mr. House, that I can count on your cooperation. Sincerely yours,

PS. An envelope [5] is enclosed for your convenience in returning the questionnaire. [113]

635 Dear Mrs. Trenton: Some months ago I wrote you expressing my concern over the fact that we had not received [1] any orders from you recently for our men's accessories, and I requested that you let me know why. Thus [2] far, however, I have not heard from you.

I realize, of course, that there are many reasons why a customer [3] stops buying from an organization. But losing an excellent customer like you is an important matter [4] to me, and I want to know the reason for it.

When you have a few minutes to spare, won't you please drop me a [5] note and tell me what has happened. Sincerely yours, [109]

636 Dear Mr. Lord: While all of us like to make new friends, the friends we appreciate most are old friends. That is the way [1] we feel about the old friends we have made since we started in business 40 years ago. When we do not hear from [2] an old friend for many months, we become concerned.

That is why I am writing you. We have not had an order from [3] you for almost 11 months, and we are concerned. Have we unintentionally done something you didn't like? [4] If we have, please tell us. We want to continue to number you among our old friends. Sincerely yours, [98]

637 Dear Mr. Mild: May I welcome you to our family of Wilson coffee dealers. We have welcomed thousands of [1] friends to our list of dealers, and we are delighted to add the name of the Continental Food Market to that [2] list. We have been serving the coffee needs of the country since 1890, and since that time we have learned many [3] things about roasting and blending processes.

If you should encounter any problem distributing our coffee, [4] please be sure to let us know. Sincerely yours, [88]

638 Dear Mrs. Fenton: This morning I received the good news that I have been promoted to the position of [1] national advertising manager of Baker and Company. As a result, I will be moving from Chicago [2] to Los Angeles in two or three weeks. This means that I will have to give up my post as treasurer for the [3] Girl Scouts, a post that I thoroughly enjoyed.

I will stop in to see you before I leave and turn over to you [4] all my records. Sincerely yours, [86]

LESSON 64

641 Dear Mr. Dunne: Have you given some serious thought to what you will do with your income tax refund? If you cannot [1] decide whether to save it or to spend it, the ideal solution is to do a little of each.

Spend some [2] of it to pay a few bills, make an addition to your house, or treat yourself to something special. Then deposit [3] the remainder in the Union Savings Bank, the city's largest savings institution.

If you don't have a [4] regular account with us, we will be glad to open one for you. Then the next time you want funds for something special, [5] you will have them available.

We have various types of accounts, Mr. Dunne. Select the one that meets your needs. [6] Our courteous, efficient staff is ready to serve you. Sincerely yours, [133]

642 Dear Mr. Hudson: There are various reasons why people like to shop at Wilson's Supermarket. We have an [1] enviable reputation for offering our customers the finest foods, meats, and dairy products available. [2] In addition, we help them stretch their food dollars with our special offerings.

But best of all, we have the [3] courteous, thoughtful people who make shopping at Wilson's a genuine pleasure. They care about you, our customer. [4] They want to help you in every way they can.

We are aware, of course, that we are not perfect, but we are [5] continually working for perfection. When you have any compliments or constructive suggestions regarding [6] our products or services, please get in touch with us. Sincerely yours, [133]

643 Dear Ms. Baker: As you know, I wrote you some time ago that the guest speaker at our November luncheon would be [1] Dr. Mary H. Cummings,

dean of the faculty of the Graduate School of Music at Harrisburg Municipal [2] University. I have just had a communication from Dr. Cummings saying that she will not [3] be able to be with us because she will have to spend a period of six or seven weeks in London on [4] personal business.

I have been fortunate, however, to get Professor Charles H. Green, a man who has a [5] reputation as a dynamic speaker. He accepted my invitation to speak on the subject of "The Law [6] of Business." You will enjoy his presentation.

I am looking forward to seeing you at our November luncheon. [7] Very truly yours, [144]

644 Dear Major Rush: Please consider this letter your invitation to be our weekend guest at Hudson Lake. If you [1] accept this invitation, you will stay at one of Maine's most popular motels. In addition, all your meals [2] will be paid for by us.

Hudson Lake is a novel idea in vacation communities. All home sites are [3] a minimum of one acre in size. In the immediate area are ideal amusement facilities [4] where you can ski, fish, and boat.

Why not accept this invitation to be our guest and see Hudson Lake in [5] the early stages of development and share in the excitement of its growth.

Return the enclosed card. When we [6] receive it, we will send you complete details. Sincerely yours, [131]

645 Dear Ms. Rush: About this time of the year, don't you get that tired, listless feeling? We have a suggestion for you. [1] Pack up your bags and come to the Victory Hotel in Miami. March and April are delightful months in [2] Miami.

Many doctors come to Miami for health and recreational reasons. We suggest that you follow [3] their example.

Here you can "recharge your batteries" after a cold winter. Have fun playing tennis or golfing [4] or swimming or just relaxing in the sun.

A card is enclosed for your convenience in making a reservation. [5] Fill it out and mail it. Then begin packing your bags! Sincerely yours, [114]

646 Dear Mr. Judge: When you receive the July 5 issue of *News Magazine*, it will be the final one you will [1] receive on your present subscription. Your subscription really expired on June 5, but we have continued sending [2] copies to you in the hope that your renewal would arrive shortly.

You may not realize it, but during [3] the past year our columns contained more than a thousand pages of national and foreign news. We know you will not [4] want to be without this news in the future. So please renew your subscription without delay. A convenient [5] renewal form is enclosed.

If you wish to give your friends gift subscriptions, there is room to include their names on the [6] renewal form. *News Magazine* makes an ideal Christmas present. Sincerely yours, [135]

647 Dear Mr. Dunn: One of my married clients, Mr. Henry C. Mason, is much happier today than he has [1] been for years, and he has every reason to be. Why? Well, for the first time he is genuinely comfortable [2] about his future. As a result of a new insurance program that I prepared for him, he now knows that if [3] anything serious happens to him, his wife and family will receive a lump sum payment of $50,000 [4] and $800 a month for a period of 20 years.

I am going to call you sometime [5] soon, Mr. Dunn, to ask you to invite me to tell you about the plan I worked out for Mr. Mason. I [6] will be glad to come to your home or office at any time that is convenient for you. Sincerely yours, [139]

648 Dear Mr. Masters: As you may know, Dunn and Company now has an office on the fifth floor of your building. This [1] will make it easy for you to take advantage of the many services that we offer to investors. These [2] services include a research department that will be glad to:

1. Give you a careful estimate of the value [3] of your present holdings.
2. Recommend securities that will help you meet your personal objectives.
3. [4] Recommend mutual funds for your long-term objectives.

Why not stop in on the fifth floor one day soon. I

will be [5] delighted to discuss our services with you personally. Sincerely yours, [114]

649 Dear Mary: I have two seats to the ball game on July 18 that I cannot use. Would you like to have them? If [1] you would, call me and I will mail them to you. Sincerely yours, [31]

LESSON 65

652 Dear Mr. Trenton: The United Bank is currently working hard to keep the country's energy sources from [1] running dry. For example, we are assisting in financing the development of oil fields in the Pacific [2] Ocean, in the Rocky Mountains, and in many other parts of the world. The intense search for new domestic [3] and foreign sources goes on month after month around the clock. We are involved in the financing of tankers and [4] refineries from the day they are planned to their ultimate construction.

If you wish to invest money in oil [5] or in any other energy field, remember us, Mr. Trenton. We are the bank that is constantly working [6] to keep these vital, urgently needed sources from running dry. Yours very truly, [136]

653 Dear Ms. Flint: As I am sure you will agree, this is a type of letter that merchants seldom receive. It is a [1] letter of commendation.

The television set we bought from you arrived on Monday, February 16. [2] Unfortunately, one of the legs was broken. We brought this damage to the attention of your local agent, and [3] he came to my rescue the next day. When he completed his examination, he called a carpenter who came [4] the same day to make the necessary repairs.

That is what I call excellent service, and that is why we have [5] dealt with you for so many years and will continue to deal with you in the future. Sincerely yours, [118]

654 Dear Mr. Temple: Would you be interested in a fire-prevention system which guards your residence [1] efficiently every minute of the day and which, in the event of a sudden fire, promptly and automatically [2] dials the fire department?

Would you be interested to know that such a system is manufactured [3] and sold by the Continental Development Company, a leader in the fire-prevention field? [4] Our system carries a special lifetime guarantee.

Let us tell you about our system, Mr. Temple. Call us [5] at 151-1161. Sincerely yours, [109]

655 Dear Mr. Drake: Do you think that your business is too small to own a computer? Our new Model 114 might [1] change your mind.

It is not expensive. It is easy to operate. In fact, it can be run by someone in your [2] office after only a few hours of training.

The Model 114 is just about the size of an ordinary [3] desk. Therefore, it is small enough to fit almost anywhere in your office.

Yet despite its low cost, easy [4] operation, and small size, the Model 114 is an efficient computer that can provide you with [5] many of the same benefits that big companies get from their big computers.

Since we brought out the Model [6] 114 in January, thousands of companies have bought it.

If you still think that only big companies can [7] benefit from a computer, find out more about our Model 114. We will send you complete information [8] if you will fill out and return the enclosed card. Very truly yours, [173]

656 Mr. Fenton: This morning I attended a meeting of the National Manufacturers Association [1] in the Hotel Trenton where I had the pleasure of listening to a talk by James Temple, president of [2] the Temple Management Company. Mr. Temple spoke on methods of improving employee relations. I [3] thoroughly enjoyed his talk.

He gave the audience a great deal of helpful information and at the same [4] time kept the people entertained by his dry wit and good humor. He is definitely one of the best speakers [5] I have heard in more than a decade.

As director of personnel, you might wish to consider inviting Mr. [6] Temple to our next management meeting. Frank Baker [130]

657 Dear Captain Temple: Our new magazine, *Money Management*, can help you save hundreds and even thousands of dollars [1] on home maintenance, taxes, and many other items. The ultimate objective of the magazine is [2] to assist you in managing your money so that you can get the best value when you buy, sell, or invest.

See [3] for yourself whether *Money Management* isn't everything we say it is. Order 12 issues at the special [4] rate of $7. If you do not feel that *Money Management* is for you after you have read the first issue, [5] simply write "Cancel" on your bill and return it.

A convenient order form is enclosed. Sincerely yours, [6] [120]

LESSON 66

660 To the Staff: At its meeting yesterday afternoon, the board elected Mrs. Mary Overmyer chief [1] executive officer of the World Manufacturing Company. This was done at my suggestion. Her promotion [2] is effective immediately, and it will be announced in the newspapers tomorrow morning.

At the [3] board's request, I will continue to serve on the executive committee. All operating divisions of [4] the organization will now regularly report to Mrs. Overmyer.

In my opinion, these [5] changes are important, logical steps in the orderly procedure of transferring responsibility [6] for the successful running of our business in anticipation of my retirement in the early part [7] of next year. A. A. Underwood [146]

661 Gentlemen: We are glad to acknowledge receipt of your order of August 15 for the printing of a [1] quantity of circulars advertising your new publication, *What Every Public Official Should Know.* Thank you [2] for it.

I wish we could proceed with the work at once, but we cannot do so until we receive a remittance [3] of $300 from you for the circulars we printed for you in April.

When anyone is more than [4] two months in arrears, it is our policy not to extend further credit. I am sure you can see the importance [5] and wisdom of this policy.

If you will send us a check for $300 in the enclosed envelope, [6] we will proceed with the work as soon as we receive it. Sincerely yours, [134]

662 To the Staff: As you probably know, the position of manager of our general testing division has [1] been open for some time. We have had several applicants for this position, but none of them have had the [2] particular qualities of character, experience, and talent necessary for the job.

I am very [3] glad to tell you, however, that we have finally found just the person for this position. He is Dr. James [4] C. Dwight of Evansville, and he will assume his new duties shortly after the first of the year.

Dr. Dwight has [5] had valuable experience in the testing area with the state government as well as with industry. [6] He is a recognized authority on the subject of objective testing, and he has contributed many [7] worthwhile ideas in articles he has written for several technical publications.

I know that [8] he will have your best wishes for his success in a difficult, challenging position. A. R. Bates [178]

663 Dear Ms. Gates: Frankly, I was somewhat surprised when you wrote me that Mr. James Green listed my name as a character [1] reference on his application for a position as correspondent with your organization. [2] Actually, Mr. Green was with us for only six months. During that time his performance in our advertising [3] department was never up to our usual requirements. In addition, his general attitude left [4] something to be desired. I had to speak to him several times about his lack of efficiency, but I [5] made no progress in straightening him out.

I am sorry to have to give you such an unsatisfactory report. [6] If I can answer any other questions for you, please send them to me at our West Street office. Sincerely [7] yours, [141]

664 Dear Mr. Underwood: Perhaps you have been in the position where you thought of and worked out

a new idea [1] that would increase your company's business, but you could not sell the idea to your superior. If you have [2] had this difficult experience, we have good news for you.

We have just published a book that will train you to present [3] your ideas convincingly—*Persuading People,* by Helen C. Short. Ms. Short is a former newspaper [4] reporter, a government official, and a very successful business executive. In her publication [5] she outlines the progressive methods that have worked so successfully for her.

The book sells for only $8, [6] and you can obtain a copy from your local bookstore. Yours very truly, [134]

665 Dear Mr. Overman: It is a pleasure for me to be able to give you a favorable report on [1] Mr. William H. Bennett, the young man who is applying for the position of correspondent with your [2] organization.

Mr. Bennett joined our company about five years ago as a junior clerk in our [3] accounting department. However, he quickly showed he had talent. In the short space of two years he received [4] several important promotions.

About two years ago he joined the Navy. When he was discharged, we offered him [5] his former position. He felt, however, that he would probably be happier in a larger organization [6] where opportunities for advancement were more abundant.

I have no doubt that Mr. Bennett will be [7] an asset to your organization regardless of the capacity in which you employ him. Sincerely [8] yours, [161]

666 Dear Mr. Bass: You will be glad to know that on or about August 1, the General Oil Company will open [1] a new service station at 14 State Street. This service station will be under the supervision of Mr. [2] Barry Newton and will be staffed by experienced personnel who will be able to take care of all your [3] car requirements.

We hope, Mr. Bass, that you will bring your car to us whenever it needs servicing. You will [4] receive a warm welcome. Sincerely yours, [87]

667 Gentlemen: Your advertisement for an experienced correspondent in yesterday morning's *Daily Times* [1] interests me very much.

As you will see by the enclosed data sheet, I have had several years of successful [2] experience with the Harris Publishing Company, one of the country's largest publishing houses.

I am [3] well satisfied with my present position, but for personal reasons that our general manager understands, [4] I must move to Chicago. He suggested that I use his name as a reference when I apply for a [5] position in Chicago.

May I have an opportunity to discuss my qualifications for the [6] position with someone in your personnel department when I visit Chicago on December 15?

An [7] envelope is enclosed for your convenience in replying. Sincerely yours, [157]

668 Dear Mr. Short: Dust can be a source of annoyance in a school workshop. It can affect the eyes, the nose, and the [1] lungs. Dust doesn't belong in a school workshop. You can get rid of it immediately with proper dust-collecting [2] equipment.

That is where we can help. We at the National Manufacturing Company have been making [3] reliable dust-collecting equipment for more than 30 years. Over 80,000 of our units have [4] been installed throughout the country.

We make a wide range of models that meet every workshop need. They are all self-contained, [5] economical, and easy to install.

We will be glad to tell you what type of equipment we think your [6] shop needs. Invite us to call by filling out and returning the enclosed card. It requires no postage. Sincerely [7] yours, [141]

669 Dear Mr. Doyle: We have just published a book that should be on the shelves of every homeowner. It is called *Fix It* [1] *Yourself.* It tells you in simple step-by-step instructions how to repair, maintain, and build things around the house with [2] nothing more elaborate than seven simple tools.

After you have read the introduction to the book, we think [3] you will be convinced that you should not be afraid to tackle simple jobs around the house.

Order a copy of [4] *Fix It Yourself* by returning the enclosed card. When the book arrives, keep it for ten days. If after that time you [5] decide that the book is everything we say it is, send us your check for $10. If you decide it isn't, [6] place the book back in the box and return it. That will be the end of the matter. Sincerely yours, [137]

LESSON 67

672 Dear Alice: All of us here at the office were very much disturbed when we learned of your bicycle accident [1] a week ago. We feel relieved, however, to know that the leg fracture is mending and that you will be able [2] to come home in a few days.

As you will see by the enclosed card, we are all thinking of you and wishing you a [3] speedy recovery.

If there is anything you would like us to do to make your convalescence more bearable, [4] please let us know. Sincerely yours, [87]

673 Dear Mrs. Dix: I cannot tell you how much we appreciate your order of Friday, December 15. It [1] was shipped two or three days ago, and you should have it soon.

We were very much afraid that we had done something to [2] lose your friendship. When we did not receive an order from you for more than three months, we thought that you had decided [3] to place your business elsewhere. We are, of course, glad that that was not the case.

I am enclosing one of our latest [4] catalogs. We hope, Mrs. Dix, that you will be impressed with many of the new items we have added. You will [5] be happy to know that we have been able to hold the line on prices. You will find that many of them are [6] substantially lower than last year's. Yours very truly, [130]

674 Dear Mr. Drake: My secretary reminded me a few minutes ago that Monday, September 15, will [1] be the first anniversary of the opening of our store at 16 Main Street. A first anniversary [2] is not, of course, one of the most important milestones, but we want to celebrate it with a party for those who [3] have made our first year so interesting, eventful, and successful.

You will remember that you were one of those [4] who were with us on our opening day, and I hope that you will be with us on our first anniversary.

So [5] that we may know how many people to plan for, won't you please take a few moments to let me know as soon as [6] possible on the enclosed card whether you can be with us. Very truly yours, [134]

675 Dear Mr. Wade: As you know, Christmas is not far away. May we at this time thank you for your orders in the past [1] year and for your understanding when we were not able to fill them as rapidly as we would have liked. Your patience [2] during those trying times was a source of comfort to us.

I assure you that we plan to do everything in [3] our power to take care of your future needs promptly at the lowest possible prices.

I hope, Mr. Wade, that [4] you and your family have the happiest of Christmas seasons and that the new year will be a happy, prosperous [5] one. Sincerely yours, [104]

676 Dear Mr. West: For the past three years I have been working in the statistics department of the company, and [1] I have enjoyed my work and the people I have been working with.

But as I told you some weeks ago, I wanted [2] very much to obtain a position in which I could take advantage of my stenographic training. This morning [3] I had offered to me a secretarial position with Smith Associates, one of the largest, most [4] successful law firms in the world. I accepted the position. I am, therefore, submitting my resignation [5] effective July 21.

Thank you very much for the many kindnesses you have shown me during the years [6] I have been with the company. Sincerely yours, [129]

677 Dear Mr. Barnes: Do you want people to give you their full attention when you speak? Do you want to sell large quantities [1] of your goods? Do you want to convince your employer to give you a raise in salary? Whatever it is [2] you want in life, you can obtain it if you will learn those things that persuade people to act the way you want them to[3] act.

For more than ten years Mr. Harry L. Myers, one of the most successful salesmen in the world, has been[4] convincing people to act as he wants them to act.

What has been the secret of his success? You can find out if you[5] will read his book, *The Art of Salesmanship.* His book, published less than three months ago, has already sold more than[6] 50,000 copies.

Let us send you a copy on approval. We will be glad to do so if you will sign and[7] return the enclosed form. Sincerely yours, [147]

678 Dear Mr. Lexington: It has been our policy ever since we opened our doors more than 30 years ago[1] to make banking at the Wilson Trust Company simple and easy. This policy has won us many friends. In[2] light of this policy, all of our seven branches will be open on Saturdays for two extra hours between[3] December 7 and January 11. Each branch will be open from 8:30 to 3 p.m.[4] This will make it even more convenient for you to take care of the financial problems that always seem[5] to crop up every year around Christmas. Beginning Saturday, January 18, we will revert to our[6] regular Saturday banking hours of 8:30 to 12 noon. Our entire staff wishes you a very merry[7] Christmas and a happy, prosperous New Year. The Wilson Trust Company [154]

LESSON 68

681 Dear Mr. Gates: Today, Mr. Gates, you can buy $30,000 of life insurance at the incredibly[1] low rate of only $8 a month. This is the sum you pay at age 30 for a $30,000[2] five-year term policy at the West Side Savings Bank.

Our five-year term policy is available in amounts[3] ranging from $5,000 to $30,000 to anyone who lives in New York State.

Join the[4] judicious lawyers, engineers, and accountants who are buying this quality life insurance protection at[5] the West Side Savings Bank.

If you would like complete information about the rates for your age, fill out, sign, and mail[6] the enclosed form. Yours very truly, [127]

682 Dear Mr. Gray: On Monday, January 15, the Westport Savings Bank reduced its rates on all new insurance[1] policies. Consequently, low-cost savings bank insurance becomes an even better, more economical[2] buy than before.

The low rates include special reductions on policies between $10,000 and[3] $20,000 and even greater reductions on policies between $20,000 and[4] $30,000.

We have been offering savings bank insurance for some time, and we have on our staff a group of[5] trained people who can help you work out your own life insurance needs.

Visit any of our 13 offices today.[6] If you prefer, mail the enclosed card to receive a copy of our leaflet, *Savings Bank Life Insurance.*[7] Sincerely yours, [142]

683 Dear Stockholder: As the year comes to a close, I am pleased to write you that your company is in fine shape. Both sales[1] and profits increased substantially. Earnings increased 24 percent over our performance of the previous[2] year. Our net income this past year was $32 million compared with $27 million[3] the previous year. Sales and other revenues were $840 million compared with[4] $702 million the previous year.

Complete financial information will be issued in our annual[5] report. When it comes off the press, you will receive a copy. Meanwhile, I thought you would like to have this summary[6] of our company's progress. Very truly yours, [130]

684 Dear Ms. Green: Thank you for your flattering letter regarding my contribution to your conference on consumer[1] affairs at Baker Institute. I am glad that the participants received my contribution so favorably.[2]

Thank you also for the check for $200. I would like to donate this money to the Baker[3] Institute Library Fund for the purpose of buying new materials dealing with consumer affairs. The [4] endorsed check is enclosed. Sincerely yours, [87]

685 Dear Mr. Wilson: Thank you for your letter informing us of your inability to pay your bill amounting [1] to $700 for some of the furniture you purchased from us on November 17. We [2] appreciate your frankness, Mr. Wilson. We are happy, therefore, to arrange for you to pay this sum in seven [3] monthly installments of $100 each.

If this arrangement is satisfactory, please sign and return [4] the enclosed form. Your first payment of $100 will be due on January 2. Yours very truly, [5] [101]

686 Gentlemen: At the Pittsburgh Manufacturing Company we have always considered the Wilson typewriter [1] a superior machine. We will soon be in the market for 15 new machines, and we are entertaining [2] the idea of buying electric machines.

Under the circumstances, we would like to have answers to the [3] following questions before we make a final decision:

1. Are there any studies that prove that the operator [4] of an electric machine can type at a greater speed than a manual operator?

2. How long [5] will it take to retrain an operator of a standard machine?

A self-addressed, postage-paid envelope is [6] enclosed for your convenience in answering these questions for us. Sincerely yours, [135]

687 Dear Mr. Bryant: Your franchise to sell National products exclusively in Ohio has been a profitable [1] one for you as well as for us. We want you to continue enjoying the benefits of this franchise [2] in the future, but you are making it difficult for us to leave it with you by not taking care of your past-due [3] balance of $800.

We have been considerate and patient, but we have received neither a payment [4] nor an answer to our letters.

Please send us your check for $800 without delay. An envelope [5] is enclosed for your convenience. Sincerely yours, [110]

688 Dear Friend: A few days ago a customer of ours wrote us a letter in which she said in part: "What justification [1] does the Lexington Electric Light and Power Company have for advertising? I can't buy my [2] electricity from anybody else, can I?"

That is true. Our customers can't buy their electricity from [3] another organization, but unless we advertised, they could not learn about the new appliances we [4] place on the market, the new services we make available to our customers, and the new facilities [5] we are building to be sure that we are able to meet the needs of our customers in the days ahead.

Whenever [6] you have any questions about our facilities or services, please write or call us. We are at your service. [7] Sincerely yours, [144]

689 Dear Mr. Drake: The Tiger 125 has a front-wheel drive. Therefore, it pulls itself uphill and out of ruts [1] and through snowbanks that might stop cars with a rear-wheel drive. It operates on the same principle that leads people to [2] put dogs in front of dogsleds.

Of course, any car can get stuck. But the front-wheel drive on the Tiger 125 [3] will get you through snow and mud where conventional cars will not.

Come in and let us demonstrate the Tiger 125 [4] for you. Drive it a few miles yourself. We are convinced that you will be so pleased with its performance that you [5] will make it your next car. Very truly yours, [108]

690 Dear Mrs. Martin: Welcome to our family of charge account customers. Your card is enclosed.

If you would like [1] to have a card for your husband, we will be glad to issue one to him upon request. Sincerely yours, [38]

LESSON 69

693 Dear Mr. Green: On making the customary room inspection after a guest's departure, our housekeeper [1] reported that two woolen blankets, replacement value $40 each, were missing from the room you occupied. [2] May we respectfully ask that should you discover these blankets on unpacking your luggage, you return them to [3] us.

Very often in their haste to catch a train, plane, or bus, guests unknowingly place such items in their bags. They [4] return them, of course, when they discover them in unpacking. Very sincerely yours, [95]

694 Dear Mr. Roy: I was desolated to learn after reading your tactful letter of Friday, September 4, [1] that you have guests at your hotel who are so careless as to check out and take such slight souvenirs as blankets when [2] packing their neckties. By the same token I presume that passengers on some of our leading railroads are apt to [3] carry off a locomotive or a few hundred feet of rails when getting off the train on reaching their destination. [4] Or a visitor to a big city zoo might conceivably take away an elephant or a [5] rhinoceros, concealing it in a sack of peanuts—after removing the peanuts, of course.

In this particular [6] case, however, I may be able to assist you in running down your blankets. As I had a lot of luggage, [7] I needed all the storage space you so thoughtfully provide in each room. The blankets in question occupied [8] the bottom drawer of the dresser. Because I wanted to place a few white shirts (replacement value [9] $8.50 each) in that drawer, I removed the said blankets and placed them on a chair. When the maid came in later, [10] I handed her the blankets (same blankets and same replacement value), telling her in nice gentlemanly language [11] to get them out of the room. If you count all the blankets in your establishment, I predict that you will find [12] that not a blanket is missing. Yours very truly,

PS. Have you counted your elevators lately? [258]

695 Dear Mr. Green: I wish to thank you for one of the most interesting, delightful letters it has been my pleasure [1] to read in my entire business career. My sincere congratulations.

Yes, it is essential that we [2] do a lot of counting around here. I've counted the elevators, and they are right where they should be and operating [3] —every one of them. What I want to count now is more important to me. I want to continue counting [4] you as a friend of this hotel.

Twenty-five thousand dollars' worth of our finest silverware is carried away [5] annually by our guests. A similar total is cherished annually by guests who like our linens as [6] a souvenir of their visit. So it goes. We are sorry indeed, Mr. Green, that you were bothered. Yours very [7] truly, [141]

696 Dear Ms. Baker: May I take this opportunity to express our appreciation of your purchase of a [1] new Tiger. Our local agency tells me that they delivered your car several days ago.

To get the best [2] performance from your car, Ms. Baker, may I make two suggestions:

1. Read your service policy carefully. It [3] was placed in the glove compartment of the car.
2. When your Tiger needs servicing, take it to the dealer from whom [4] you bought it. This is the person who can best keep your car in good operating condition.

After you have driven [5] your Tiger a week or two, we know you will agree with us that it is one of the finest cars ever built. [6] Sincerely yours, [124]

697 Dear Mr. West: Thank you for your letter of Monday, June 15, expressing interest in National insulating [1] products.

The enclosed booklet, *A Warm House,* explains what our insulating products can do for you, how easy [2] they are to install, and how much they will save you on heating costs.

Our representative in your area, [3] Ms. Jane C. Davis, will call you in a few days for an appointment to discuss National insulating products [4] with you. She will be glad to answer any questions you may have after you have had an opportunity [5] to read the enclosed booklet. Sincerely yours, [108]

LESSON 70

700 *The Telephone*

Much of today's business is transacted over the telephone. It is extremely important, therefore, that the [1] secretary know how to utilize this medium of communication effectively.

What you say and [2] the way you say it determine

the mental picture that the person you are speaking to gets of your company.[3] When you use the office telephone, you become the voice of that office.

You may not be born with a good telephone[4] voice, but you can develop one if you analyze your problem and then undertake a carefully designed[5] self-improvement program.

Fast or Slow? If people do not understand what you say, it may be that you speak too fast.[6] Or perhaps you speak so slowly that people lose interest. Under the circumstances, you should strive to speak at[7] a moderate speed, a speed of perhaps 120 to 150 words a minute.

Pitch. The pitch[8] of your voice is determined to some extent by the way you breathe. Consequently, a voice may be described as either[9] high or low according to its pitch. A woman's voice is usually pitched higher than a man's. Pitch tends to[10] rise when a person is under stress, and this causes the rate of breathing to increase. Always try to control the[11] pitch of your voice when you are on the phone so that it is neither too high nor too low.

Volume. The degree[12] of loudness of a voice is called its volume. Some people speak so softly that you must strain to hear them. Others speak[13] so loudly that the sound is offensive to the listener's ears.

Neither extreme is desirable. To achieve[14] good volume, learn to increase your volume for emphasis and then to decrease it. Never shout and never let your[15] voice trail off at the ends of sentences.

A Pleasant Voice. Telephone callers are more readily impressed with a[16] "voice with a smile." It is not so difficult to speak pleasantly and to feel pleasant if you cultivate an[17] attitude of genuine interest in others. A pleasant voice will make you more valuable to your employer.[18] It will, in addition, make you a nicer, more agreeable person to have around the office.

Telephone[19] Courtesy. Telephone courtesy simply means making a caller realize that the call is welcome. It[20] is an extension of the same kind of thoughtfulness that should be practiced in daily living. Every caller should[21] be greeted pleasantly. If your voice is friendly and generates sincerity, your telephone callers will be[22] attracted.

Try to use the caller's name. There is no sweeter music to a person than the sound of his or her[23] own name. Try to visualize the person to whom you are talking. Be attentive, listen politely, and do[24] not interrupt. If you say "thank you" to your telephone callers, they will recognize that courtesy is a[25] natural part of your company's business dealings.

Receiving Calls. When your telephone rings, get the conversation[26] off on the right track by answering promptly and pleasantly. When you answer promptly, you give the impression of[27] wanting to be of service. You also help build a reputation of efficiency for yourself and for your[28] company.

When the telephone rings, lay aside the task at hand so that you can be friendly and helpful to the[29] telephone caller. Avoid giving the impression that you have been interrupted.

Transferring Calls. If someone[30] else is more qualified to handle an incoming call, you should offer to transfer the call. As you know, transfers[31] can be disturbing to a caller, especially if the caller has already had to describe a problem[32] several times. To avoid irritating the person further, explain why the call should be handled by someone[33] else. Then be sure that the person to whom you transfer the call is actually on the line before you hang up.[34] [680]

701 *Appreciation*

All of us like to have others appreciate our efforts and tell us when we have done a good job. Showing[1] appreciation is not really difficult. Yet many people forget to recognize and praise the efforts[2] of others.

Commending others on a good job increases their desire to perform well. Failure to recognize[3] and acknowledge effort, on the other hand, often results in discouraging them.

So when you find people[4] doing a good job, pat them on the back. They may pat you on the back when they see you doing a good job! [98]

702 *Judgment*

Judgment is the rarest of qualities. It consists merely in deciding correctly. That sounds very simple,[1] but to judge a question correctly in business often requires sifting the most complex facts and considering [2] a large number of possibilities.

The beginning secretary is not ordinarily called upon [3] to exercise judgment on questions of great importance; nevertheless, the faculty of good judgment is one [4] that is invaluable to even the beginner in business.

Situations arise every day [5] in the business office that call for instant decisions. The secretary must be ready to meet these situations. [6] An analysis must be made of the known facts and circumstances. Each point must be weighed carefully.

Good [7] judgment comes from correct reasoning. It is not a matter of impulse or what is commonly called a "hunch." It [8] is almost an axiom in business that when one guesses, one guesses wrong.

Situations arise in which the [9] evidence is so evenly balanced that it is difficult to make a decision from the facts at hand, but [10] a decision is nevertheless necessary immediately. In such cases we can always fall back [11] on common sense. We cannot expect all our judgments to be correct, but our rating in the business office will [12] be the result of our average of successes. [250]

APPENDIX

RECALL DRILLS

Joined Word Endings

1 Treatment, alignment, supplement, amusement, compliment, experiment.
2 Nation, termination, station, operation, inflation, relation, caution, portion, section, promotion.
3 Credential, confidential, essential, commercial, socially.
4 Greatly, namely, nicely, mainly, nearly, highly, only, properly, surely, mostly.
5 Readily, speedily, easily, hastily, necessarily, family.
6 Careful, thoughtful, delightful, mindful, usefulness, awful, helpful, powerful, respectful, faithful.
7 Dependable, reliable, profitable, table, troubled.
8 Gather, gathered, together, rather, either, leather, bother, bothered, neither.
9 Actual, actually, gradual, schedule, annual, equally.
10 Furniture, picture, nature, stature, captured, miniature, failure, natural.
11 Yourself, myself, itself, himself, herself, themselves, ourselves, yourselves.
12 Port, sport, import, report, deportment.
13 Contain, retain, certain, container, contained.
14 Efficient, sufficient, deficient, efficiency, deficiency, proficiency.

Disjoined Word Endings

15 Childhood, motherhood, neighborhood, brotherhood.
16 Forward, backward, onward, afterward, rewarded.
17 Relationship, steamship, authorship, professorship, championship.
18 Radical, technical, political, article, chemically, periodically, logically.
19 Congratulate, regulate, stipulates, tabulated, congratulation, regulation, regulations, stipulations.
20 Willingly, exceedingly, knowingly, surprisingly, grudgingly.
21 Readings, mornings, sidings, dressings, savings, drawings, sayings, blessings, feelings.
22 Program, telegram, diagrams.
23 Notification, modification, specifications, classifications.
24 Personality, ability, reliability, facilities, utility, generalities.
25 Faculty, penalty, casualty.
26 Authority, sincerity, majority, minority, clarity, sorority, charity, seniority.

Joined Word Beginnings

27 Permit, perform, perfect, pertain, persist, purchase, pursue, pursued, purple, purse.
28 Employ, empower, embarrass, embody, empire, emphatic, embrace, emphasis.
29 Impress, impression, imply, impossible, impair,

impel, imbue, impact.

30 Increase, intend, income, inform, inconsistent, indeed, inference, inferior.

31 Enlarge, enforce, enlist, encourage, encounter, encircle, enrich, enrage.

32 Unkind, unwritten, unwilling, unsuccessful, undo, unpleasant, untie, unpopular.

33 Refer, resign, receive, reform, reorganize.

34 Beneath, believe, belong, before, became.

35 Delay, deliver, deserve, diligent.

36 Dismiss, disappoint, discover, discuss, despite.

37 Mistake, misquote, misspell, misstate, misunderstand, misapplied, mistrust.

38 Explain, excite, extend, excuse, express.

39 Comprise, comfort, comply, completed.

40 Condition, consult, continue, confident, convey, confess.

41 Submit, substantiate, subdivide, sublease, suburban.

42 Almost, also, already, although, alteration.

43 Forget, forceful, performed, forecast, foreman.

44 Furnish, furnished, furnishings, furniture, furnace, further.

45 Turn, turned, term, attorney, determine.

46 Ultimate, ulterior, adult, culture, result.

Disjoined Word Beginnings

47 Interested, internal, interview, intercept, introduce, introduction, enterprise, entrances, entertain, entered.

48 Electricity, electrician, electrical, electric wire, electric fan, electric light, electric motor.

49 Supervise, supervision, supervisor, superhuman, superb.

50 Circumstance, circumstances, circumstantial, circumvent, circumspect.

51 Selfish, self-made, self-defense, self-respect, self-conscious.

52 Transit, transfer, transact, transplant, translation.

53 Understand, undertake, undergo, underpaid, undermine, understate, underline, underscore, understood, undercover.

54 Overcome, overdue, overhead, overture, overpay, oversee, overdraw, overgrow, overlook, overnight, oversight.

Key to Chart on Page 447

Brief Forms of Gregg Shorthand in Order of Their Presentation

3 I, Mr., have, are-our-hour, will-well, a-an, am, it-at, in-not.

5 Is-his, the, that, can, you-your, Mrs., of, with, but.

8 For, would, there (their), this, good, they, which, them, be-by.

11 And, when, from, should, could, send, after, street, were.

13 Glad, work, yesterday, circular, order, soon, enclose, was, thank.

15 Value, than, one [won], what, about, thing-think, business, doctor, any.

17 Gentlemen, important-importance, morning, where, company, manufacture, next, short.

19 Present, part, advertise, Ms., immediate, opportunity.

21 Advantage, suggest, several, out, every-ever, very.

23 Time, acknowledge, general, question, organize, over.

25 Difficult, envelope, progress, success, satisfy-satisfactory, state, request, wish, under.

27 Particular, probable, regular, speak, idea, subject, regard, newspaper, opinion.

29 Responsible, worth, public, publish-publication, ordinary, experience, usual, world, recognize.

31 Never, quantity, executive, throughout, object, objected, character, characters, govern, government, correspond-correspondence, corresponded.

Index of Gregg Shorthand

In order to facilitate finding, this Index has been divided into six main sections—Alphabetic Characters, Brief Forms, General, Phrasing, Word Beginnings, Word Endings.

The first figure refers to the lesson; the second refers to the paragraph.

INDEX OF BRIEF FORMS

The first figure refers to the lesson; the second to the paragraph.

INDEX OF BUILDING TRANSCRIPTION SKILLS

The first figure refers to the lesson; the second to the paragraph.

Brief Forms of Gregg Shorthand

IN ORDER OF PRESENTATION

A	B	C	D	E	F	G
3						
		5				
				8		
						11
	13					
			15			
					17	
						19
					21	
				23		
			25			
					27	
29						
		31